FREELANCE AND BUSINESS AND STUFF

A GUIDE FOR CREATIVES

Second Edition, 2025

By Amy Hood and Jennifer Hood of Hoodzpah, Inc.
HoodzpahDesign.com

Quickened Publishing • Newport Beach, CA

Freelance and Business and Stuff: A Guide for Creatives

Second Edition, 2025

ISBN 978-0-9847363-5-5

Quickened Publishing

Printed in Orange County, CA, USA by MK Printing
a Minority Business Enterprise certified company.

Disclaimer:

This book is made up of our personal research and experience, and it should in no way be a replacement for personalized business, legal, or financial advice, as every person's individual circumstance is different.

Written by:
Amy Hood & Jennifer Hood
Co-founders/Creative Directors of Hoodzpah, a brand identity and type design studio based out of Southern California.

Layout by:
Amy Hood, Jennifer Hood, Bea Morgan, Natahsha Priya, and Jose Sojo

Illustrations by:
Amy Hood, Jennifer Hood, Bea Morgan, and our merry band of guest artists

Edited by:
Jenny Ely, Quill & Cauldron

Biggest Thanks to:
Our business mentor, The Bear

Thank you also to: Jason Staggs, for giving us our first chance at working as real designers; Liz Logsdon for dreaming big dreams with us when we were twelve; Grandma, for starting her own businesses when she was young, normalizing entrepreneurship in our mind, and encouraging us to penny-pinch; Austin, our cuz, for holding down the fort in Kentucky like a true warrior in baby blue scrubs; Dad, for bringing us to his construction job and including us in his fix-it projects—they made us industrious; Mom, for teaching us not to be afraid of hard work; Troy Puckett for unknowingly inspiring our first ever logo in 5th grade; Paul Hutchison for being a mentor without perhaps knowing it; Nick Slater for referring us to speak at Creative South, and Mike Jones for making it happen—this book grew out of that first conference talk prompt; Catharin Eure for giving us our first teaching opportunity at LCAD, which helped us fine tune this book; Bea Morgan for being the best Assistant to the Regional Manager; our amazing community of creatives in the FABAS Slack who have given us feedback and been a sounding board and provided endless laughs and support daily—you are the best co-workers; Jose Sojo and Arturo Jimenez for helping us hold down the Hoodzpah fort and put out amazing work; and all of you for reading this and supporting independent creatives.

www.hoodzpahdesign.com

@hoodzpahdesign

Hoodzpah® SHINE ON.

There was no AI used in the writing, illustration or design of this book.

How to start your creative business, grow your client base, and promote yourself without selling out or starving. This no faff, no fluff guide is peppered with actionable advice we learned running our business (Hoodzpah), unasked-for humor, and worksheets to help you just get started already. Because raw talent and good ideas aren't enough. And because you can do this. Really. →

Table *of* Contents

Pregame Huddle

Difficulty Meter

EASY → HARD

1	Breathing
2	Building an IKEA Shelf
3	Training a Dog
4	Running a Half Marathon
5	Modern Dating
6	Starting Your Own Business
7	The "Stairway to Heaven" guitar solo
8	Hiking the Pacific Northwest Trail
9	Winning Your Mother's Approval
10	Faking Your Own Death

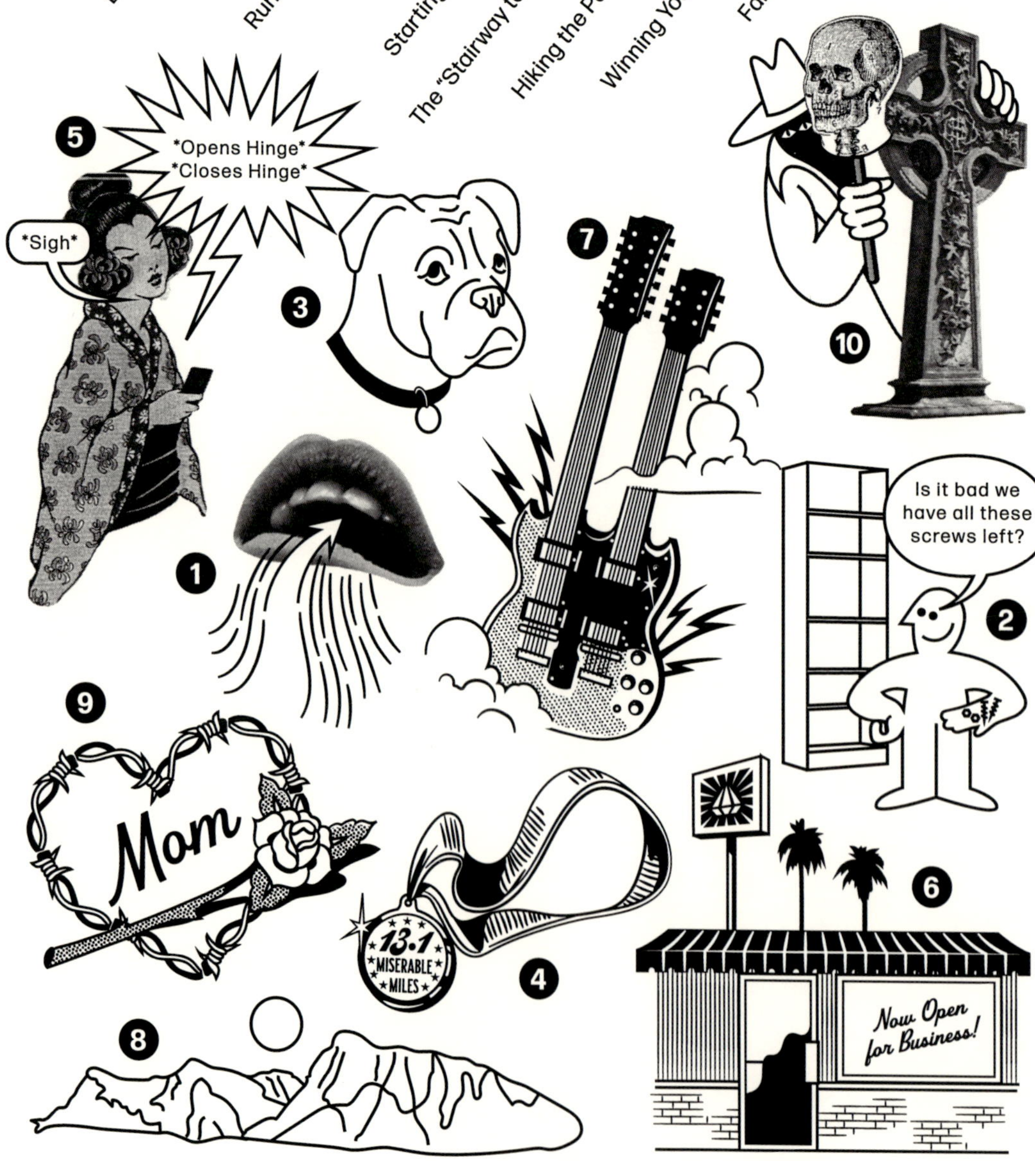

Will This Be Hard?

On a scale from one to ten (see graph), starting your own business lands somewhere between building an IKEA shelf and playing the "Stairway to Heaven" guitar solo. In other words: It's not easy, but it's not impossible.

Running your own business will take hard work, a marketable skill, a healthy hunger for knowledge, the ability to collaborate, good communication skills, and adaptability.

If you often find yourself starting new projects or you love DIY-ing, you're probably someone who likes figuring things out. Whether it's starting a band, learning a new language, or fixing something instead of hiring a professional repair person, you have that thing in you that says, "I could figure that out." If you're good at problem-solving via internet digging, reading, and YouTube rabbit-holing (that . . . came out weird), then you are likely a great candidate to run your own business. There will be a lot you don't know, but you'll be okay learning and pivoting along the way.

The Good News

You truly don't have to be a genius to start your own business, and you don't need thousands and thousands of dollars. You don't need a college degree. And you don't have to be the next Saul Bass or Annie Leibovitz.

Best of all, you don't need permission. But if you'd like someone to tell you "you can," let us be the first to say it. "You can!" There are no Muppets in the balcony seats waiting to heckle you. That said, it's always good to jump in with the right expectations and as much preparation as possible. That's where we hope to help.

Our Origin Story

Hi there, we're Amy Hood and Jen Hood, your author guides on this journey. We started our own studio called Hoodzpah in 2011. It wasn't glamorous or brave. It was mostly out of necessity. Cue the flashback sequence because this story starts back in 2008. We were both four years into a two-year degree at Saddleback Community College studying Fine Arts. AKA: Every parent's waking nightmare. We were working full-time and going to school part-time, which meant school was taking ... forever. Jen was working at a Capistrano Beach sandwich shop called the Kultured Kitchen, serving fat-free yogurt and healthy sandwiches to the local water polo moms, and Amy was a barista at Kaylani Coffee in San Clemente, serving sickeningly sweet flavored lattes to the construction workers and surfboard shapers. One of Amy's regulars was Jason Staggs, a larger-than-life man with the voice of a classic rock radio DJ. Jason was the art director at a local magazine and print house. Either he was blown away by Amy's work ethic and chalkboard menu art, or he took pity on this girl who was clearly lost on her career path, because one day, he offered her a job. Jason was looking for some designers to help him at the magazine and print house. Amy told him she had only taken Graphic Design 101 at college, but luckily, he wanted hard workers and was willing to teach whatever technical skills she lacked. For someone working minimum wage plus tips to pay for college and rent, this felt like Amy had found a cheat code. The magazine paid a couple of bucks more, and she got to learn a creative profession on the job. He asked if she knew anyone else who was creative and hardworking, so Jen was tagged in.

Pretty much from that point on, our creative careers have been linked. We stopped taking classes at college and started the job full-time. Now, "magazine" was a very generous term for this publication. It was mostly a coupon book with local interest stories peppered in. Almost 80 percent of the stories were advertorials. But we learned so much at this job. Jason taught us how to recreate logos with the Pen tool in Adobe Illustrator when the only logo file a client had was a grainy 150px-wide JPEG. He taught us how to do press checks on the magazine at the offset print house in Los Angeles. He taught us how to set up print files and manage clients. He introduced us to "The Joker" by Steve Miller Band. He showed us how to organize hundreds of clients and files and manage a job board to keep track of deadlines. He showed us how to work fast and scrappy.

We eventually gained more responsibility and began pitching ideas to make the job more creatively fulfilling. We wrote articles, did photoshoots, whatever needed to be done. Amy started a celebrity interview column, and due to the magazine's large circulation numbers, we were able to hoodwink a number of stars connected to the Orange County, California area to agree to interviews: Buzz Aldrin, Steve Martin, Merle Haggard, Lauren Conrad, Henry Winkler, Geoff Rowley, and even Matt Barnes and Metta World Peace (formerly Ron Artest) of the LA Lakers. But about three years into this job, the magazine industry as a whole began to take a dive. Magazines were folding left and right, and ours ended up being one of them.

We were unemployed, and on paper, we were unhireable. We were community college dropouts, and our design portfolio was predominantly ads laden with yellow starbursts and dotted cut lines for coupons. We couldn't get a call back for a job interview, let alone a full-time job. We knew we had all the skills to be a great hire if we could just get our foot in the door. After about a month of nearly fruitless job hunting, we realized we needed to beef up our portfolio and somehow pay the rent.

Ever since we were kids, we have always been very entrepreneurial, whether making T-shirts and selling them to friends or trying to hawk art at the local street festival. So we thought, "Why don't we start our own design business, make some work we're proud of for our portfolio, and make ends meet until we find another job?" We threw together a name and a website, and Hoodzpah was born! We weren't too precious or picky. We just went live and optimized as we went along.

The year that followed was peppered with mishaps and mistakes. "Quarterly taxes, whuh?" "Contracts, huh?" But that first year was also stacked and packed with great learning opportunities and growth. Jen luckily got a part-time job as an ad designer at another local magazine (thank you, Luke Hodsdon!), which supplemented income while we built up our client list and our studio found its footing. We did a lot of passion projects that helped reposition our portfolio to attract the kind of work we wanted to make. We did a lot of work for trade and offered severe discounts to friends who didn't have a ton of money. But it was exciting work, and those friends started referring us to their friends and employers. We started charging a little more, then more, and even more. We started building up our savings so we didn't have to live check to check.

By three years in, we had mentors, we had systems, we had interns, and a few employees. We had a full roster of clients, we had found our niche, and we were certain that Hoodzpah was in it for the long haul. We were doing rewarding work, and we were more than financially profitable. More than a decade later, our studio is still going strong. We've had the opportunity to work on bucket-list projects with dream clients, all while keeping the lights on and the bills paid. We still have our fair share of hiccups and issues, but we love working for ourselves.

A few years back, we wrote the first version of this creative business book based on a talk we gave at Creative South (thanks to Mike Jones for this speaking opportunity). We wanted to write something simple, actionable, geared toward creatives, and—dare we say—enjoyable to read. Which brings us to you.

Many Have Gone Before You

According to The Upwork Research Institute's 2023 Freelance Forward survey, in the United States alone, 38 percent of the workforce is freelancing. That's sixty-four million people. Remember this when fear starts silently creeping up behind you like a Prius. You aren't the first pioneer, and you're absolutely not alone in this. Our goal is to give you a clear roadmap with our best advice, so you know how to make this dream a reality.

More Freedom, More Responsibility

Working for yourself can truly enrich your life. And you don't have to do it full-time to reap the rewards. It can be a way to make side cash to supplement your income, test a new skill without ditching your steady day job, and work on projects that fulfill you (if you're feeling stifled or stagnant at your 9–5 job).

When you run your own business, you have more power to choose how you work (when and where), what you work on, who you work with, and how much you charge. You gain flexibility and control. The trade-off is more responsibility. You have to take on roles and tasks you likely never even considered. Don't worry; we'll share systems and workflows to make this less of a hassle. And if all else fails, you can always hire someone to help you.

Full-Time or Part-Time, Freelancing Has A Lot to Offer

Even if you don't end up freelancing or working for yourself full-time, the principles you'll learn in this book will be a huge asset to how you operate at your day job. You'll learn what goes on behind the scenes to keep a company running, how to communicate with collaborators and manage projects, how to calculate project rates and communicate value, and hopefully gain more confidence when negotiating salaries and landing higher positions.

Isn't Freelancing Risky and Unstable?

A lot of people talk about how uncertain and inconsistent freelancing feels compared to being employed by someone else. But here's how we see it: When you run your own company, you're directly involved in the decisions that impact your business's success. You have a hand in determining your future, rather than being at the mercy of your employer's decisions.

Personally, we find more security in having this control and knowing the full picture of our business. Our friend and fellow Laguna College of Art & Design adjunct professor, Jamie Stark, is a veteran freelancer who's worked with big-name ad agencies from New York to Los Angeles for over twenty-five years. While recently discussing the spike in tech-industry creative layoffs and the ups and downs of freelancing, he made an interesting point: "As a freelancer, you've automatically diversified your income streams by having multiple clients. If one of those clients falls on hard times and cancels their contract with you, you still have your other clients providing an income stream. Whereas, if you work full-time for one company, if that company goes under or has to lay you off, you've lost 100 percent of your income."

The truth is, nothing is 100 percent stable. The markets will go up and down, advancements in technology will start to take over tasks we used to be paid to do, industries will thrive, and sometimes they'll die. The only thing you can count on is change. The best way to find some stability in an ever-changing world is to learn to wisely manage your finances and build up your savings. A good cushion of savings makes the ebbs and flows of freelancing less scary. In upcoming chapters, we'll help you plan your income and expenses, encourage ongoing work with clients, and book out your schedule for financial stability.

Will You Tell Me The Secret to Success?

This book is a collection of lessons and advice we've learned over the years from a variety of resources.

- Friends
- Fellow entrepreneurs
- Mentors
- Books and resources from pros
- Countless deep-dive Google searches
- Good ol' trial and error

If there's anything we've learned from all these resources, it's that there is no secret. There are just tried-and-true business principles that, when coupled with a good product or service and a great customer experience, equal a business that people will hopefully use and refer to again and again. We'll cover these key principles, as well as some personal practices of our own. As you adopt and test these methods, you'll see what is foundational, what is optional, and what is just not right for you. And, of course, you'll discover your own angles and strategies along the way.

Big Names that Started Small

Ralph Lauren was an employee of Brooks Brothers when he had the idea to start a company to make bolder, more exciting neckties. The business did $500,000 USD in its first year, and now Ralph Lauren is a household fashion name.

YouTube was founded by three guys working at PayPal with the intention of giving people a place to upload—get this—video dating profiles. At an SXSW appearance, co-founder Steven Chen said the idea came from ". . . three guys on Valentine's Day that had nothing to do." No one signed up, so in a few days, they pivoted to a broader use case, and the site blew up.

IKEA was started in 1943 by a sparky seventeen-year-old named Ingvar Kamprad with money →

A Caveat

Many incredibly talented and smart people have started their own businesses, and things have not worked out as they hoped. For one reason or another, they ended up closing up shop and going back to working for a company instead of themselves. On the other hand, many less qualified and less talented people have built thriving businesses. All to say, despite the best advice, best skills, and best intentions in the world, there are many outside factors that can affect your business plans. If you've tried freelancing before and failed, you might be all too familiar with this. Don't be hard on yourself if, after your best efforts, freelancing and self-employment don't work out for you. There's a lot to be said about the right place, right time, and right set of circumstances. All you can do is put in your best effort and keep your eyes on your profitability. If it becomes clear that freelancing isn't working for you, there's no shame in going back to working for someone else. Try not to let things get financially bleak before making this kind of call. Hope for the best, but prepare for the worst, and always keep your finger on the pulse of your business.

Start Small

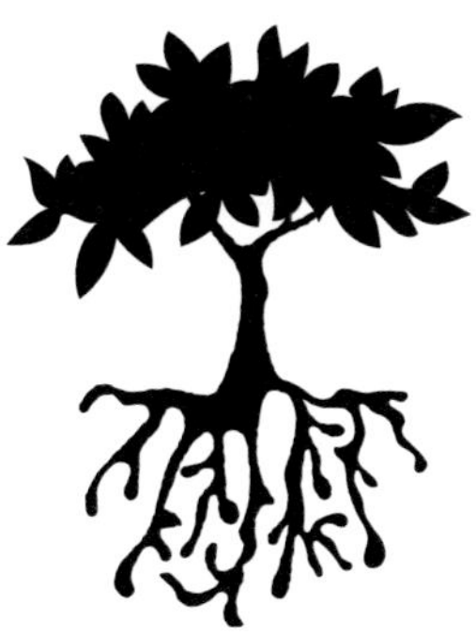

We recommended a low-risk and low-cost approach to starting a business. Best-case scenario: You have a steady job while trying out freelance on the side. Wade in, take your time, build your savings, and prove your concept before going full-time freelance.

As you gather input to get started, don't let the big picture daunt you. In some ways, we are so grateful for our naive confidence and the circumstance of necessity when we started our studio. If we had been too obsessed with the perfect end goal, or had all the time in the world to fuss and fret over it, we might never have started.

It's unrealistic to expect to know everything going in. Waiting till you know everything means you could be waiting forever.

So, if you've been curious about freelancing, wonder no more! Just start. Don't worry about starting with something perfect. Start a work-in-progress side gig that you can perfect along the way.

→ he earned from his parents for getting good grades in high school. Ingvar sold pens, pencils, postcards, and other small items by mail and fulfilled orders from a shed in his parents' backyard in Sweden.

Nike started as Blue Ribbon Sports, with founder Phil Knight selling Japanese Onitsuka Tiger shoes from the trunk of his car. Phil started the company with Bill Bowerton, his track coach from the University of Oregon. Bill was a DIY cobbler who worked on his own running shoes. Bill came up with the waffle sole, and the company was renamed Nike in the early '70s. The rest is history.Ingvar sold pens, pencils, postcards, and other small items by mail and fulfilled orders from a shed in his parents' backyard in Sweden.

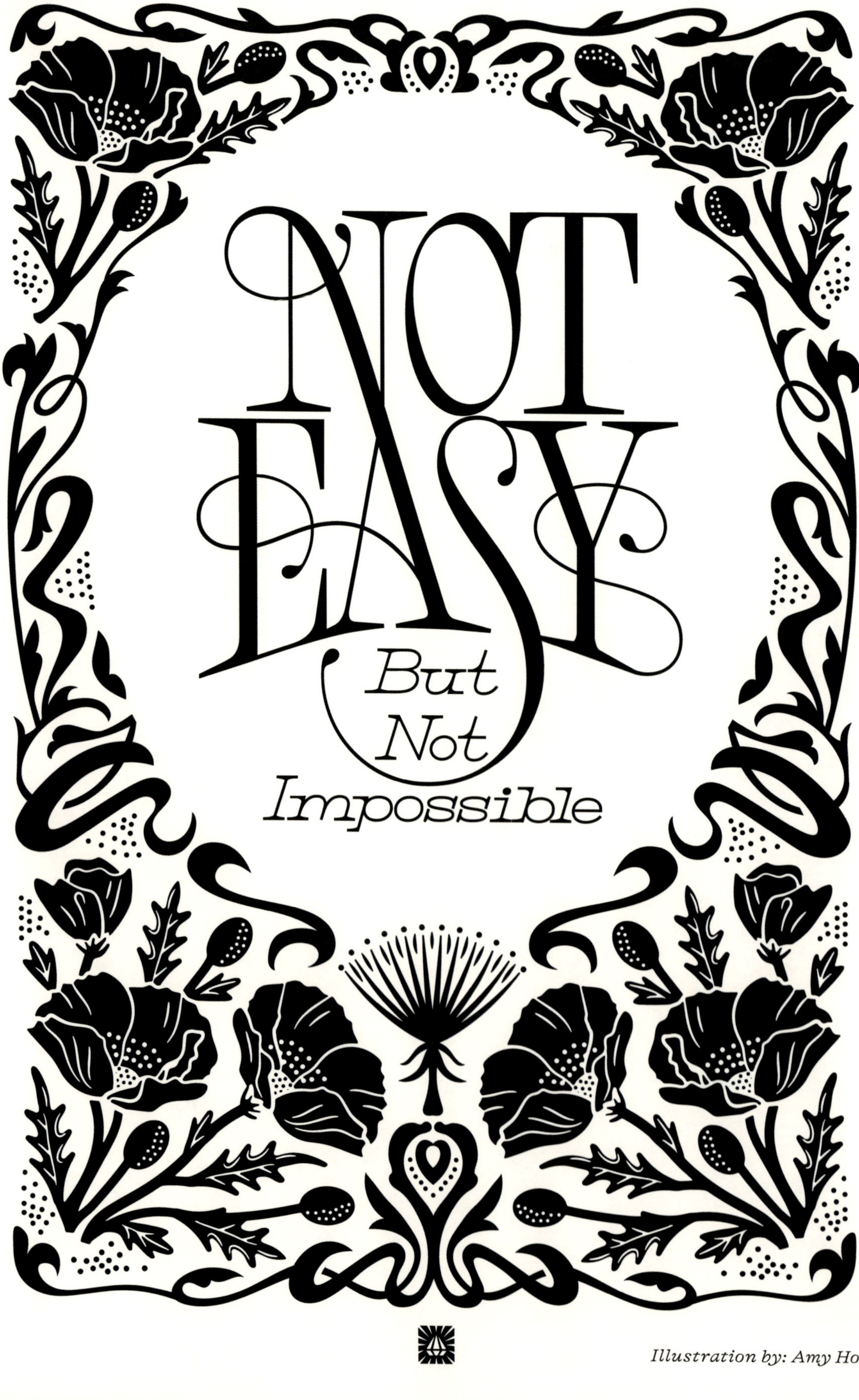

Illustration by: Amy Hood

1

Not Easy, But Not Impossible

Before you throw in the towel at your 9–5 job, let's assess what this adventure requires. Like Rocky Balboa, if you want to prove you're not "just another bum from the neighborhood," you have to consider your intellectual, emotional, social, financial, and creative strengths before you put on the gloves.

What it Takes, Personally Speaking

Adaptability

Starting your own business will be awkward and unfamiliar at first, like a baby deer on a trampoline. You're building new skills in an unfamiliar environment.

Fearing what you don't know or don't understand can only last as long as you let it. Don't beat yourself up when things don't go as planned or when a decision backfires. Don't let the inevitable missteps and mistakes shock or dishearten you. Expect them. As sure as the airport chase scene at the end of every romantic comedy. Adapt and be patient with yourself as you find your groove. There are enough haters out there. You shouldn't be your biggest.

It's important not to classify every hiccup as a bad omen. You have to put in the time to figure things out. Even after you've dialed in your systems and procedures, there are countless unforeseen wrenches headed your way. The sooner you get over your fear of failure and the idea of perfection, the sooner you can focus on big-picture problems. Plus, all those bumps in the road are exactly the kind of anecdotal fodder you'll need for your tell-all memoir.

Responsibility and a Good Work Ethic

Are you a self-starter who can meet deadlines (without a manager) and troubleshoot when things go wrong? When you're out on your own, there's no one to pass the buck to but yourself. If you get careless and make a mistake—or if something goes wrong despite your best planning—you have to take responsibility. It's going to happen. Even the most careful and detail-oriented people make mistakes or run into unforeseen outcomes.

As much as we all want a good work-life balance, in all honesty, the first few years of a new business don't have a lot of it. Even after becoming well-oiled, your business will often run into unexpected issues. As the owner and often sole employee, you'll have to deal with it. After fourteen-plus years running our own studio, the work-life balance is much better, but those early years were more of a marathon than a jaunt in the park.

You'll often have to transition from your creative role to a problem-solving, customer support role. Can you set aside your personal feelings (embarrassment, frustration, etc.) to do what's best for the business/client/fill in the blank? Pride is a tough pill to swallow, especially when the problem stems from a mistake. Taking responsibility for your work and your mistakes, and doing what it takes to make things right, is an invaluable skill.

As a freelancer or business owner, you need to learn how to be productive, get past creative blocks, and keep yourself, your team (if you have one), and your client on track even when you're tired and uninspired. If you consistently fail to deliver timely, well-executed work, you could lose your greatest asset: a trustworthy and professional reputation.

"Your reputation is your salesperson, and it costs nothing."

Much of your reputation is in the hands of your clients and peers. It's based on how they perceive you from their own experience or what they've seen and heard about you. But you can absolutely help frame that perspective by being responsible and ethical in how you do business.

A good reputation among your clients spreads into referrals and, hopefully, spurs repeat work. It is as important—if not more important—than talent. It's the best way to organically gain new clients and keep existing ones. Your reputation is your salesperson, and it costs nothing. Responsibility + work ethic + talent = reputation.

Patience

Being a freelancer requires patience with your client, yourself, and the world at large.

Your Client:
In *The Fog of War*, a documentary about the Vietnam War, former Secretary of Defense Robert McNamara is asked what he would have done differently looking back on it all. His number one lesson: "Empathize with your enemy." We're not saying that the client is your enemy, but some days it's sure going to feel that way. Some days you'll wonder what in the world your client is thinking and why in the world they're acting the way they are. In those times, remember that humans are just a person-shaped bag of emotions. They, like you, have their own burdens, biases, and points of reference. Try to get out of your own frame of reference to see things from their perspective. What is the source of their stress? What timelines and responsibilities are motivating their actions? Meet people where they are. Try to help them succeed and troubleshoot. No two clients are alike. In other words, approach each client uniquely, with lots of mercy and plenty of patience.

Yourself:
When you start working for yourself, you'll be tempted to overpromise on deadlines, deliverables, and measurable goals. You'll think you can do things faster than you actually can. You will expect to see your business grow faster than it will. Your best-laid plans will fall by the wayside when you realize the time and effort it actually requires to see them through. So be patient with yourself. Don't get frustrated when you miss personal deadlines or internal goals for your business. You'll get the hang of things and become more efficient after a few years of trial and error.

The World:
Patience with the world at large is the hardest of the three. You have no control over what markets will do, what vendors will do, how industries will change, how culture will shift. And there's not much you can do to foresee outside forces like these. The only thing we've found to be helpful is learning how to communicate clearly and honestly to clients when unforeseen things happen—i.e., natural disasters, a printer who doesn't deliver on time, a subcontractor who ghosts you, traffic jams, random injuries, pandemics, server crashes, computer problems, medical emergencies—all things that are out of your control, but still affect your work. Be

honest with your clients when these things happen, and let them know how you're working to lessen the impact or find an alternative solution. For the most part, we've found people to be very understanding. After all, this is life. It doesn't always go to plan. Work with a lawyer on your contracts to include clauses that account for unforeseen outside forces (force majeure clause, etc.) to try to lessen any liability you might incur as a result.

Organization

It's not the glamorous side of business, but it's definitely the framework of a successful one. You'll need to be able to take a project from seed to soup: getting the correct specs and goals from the client, creating and sending invoices, making contracts, logging your hours, making sure you remain on budget, meeting project benchmarks, and logging final job data for broader business review. You have to manage every aspect of your client's customer experience, your project time schedule, as well as your own personal and business responsibilities (like posting to social media, updating your portfolio, etc.). Organization and planning will be key.

The Gift of Research

New freelancers and small business owners are a lot like new parents: scared and unsure ("You're just going to let me take this home?!" said the new parents to the weary nurse). However, both seem to survive with the gift of research. You can't know everything, but you sure can look like you do if you know how to find the answers. You'll spend a lot of time troubleshooting business and project questions via Google, online forums, creative groups, mentors, and text threads with friends and family. So build your roster of expert panelists and ace resources. Remember to reward good advice with thank-you notes, gifts, six-packs (our personal favorite), and unbridled praise.

Delegation

If there's one true thing about business, it's this: Despite your best efforts and planning, there will be times when the business is really busy, and you have more work than you can handle, and there will be times when the business is really slow, and you don't have enough to do. The easiest way to flex to a swell in demand is to delegate to trusted subcontractors. By contracting someone for a specific project instead of hiring them as permanent employees, you keep your ongoing costs down and only pay out as you have the projects to justify the expense. Research the contractor laws in your state or country, as some areas are more restrictive about who and how you can contract.

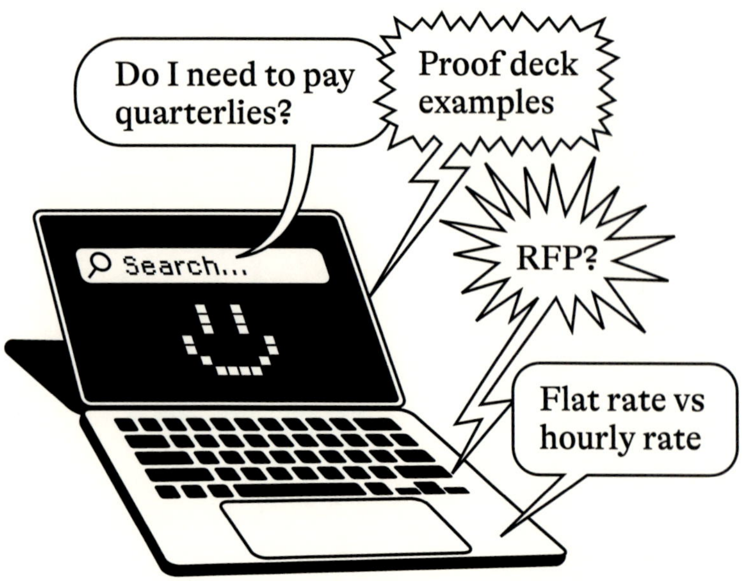

You can delegate tasks you don't have the skills to do or things you just keep putting off. When you're thinking of outsourcing, consider the following:

- Does outsourcing leave me more time to do something more profitable?
- Can someone else do this task better or more efficiently than I can?
- Do I have the funds to justify the cost? Early on, we did a lot of tasks someone else could have done better, purely because we didn't have the money to outsource. As long as we weren't making a hatchet job of things, we did those tasks until we could afford to have someone else do them.

Once you delegate, you have to learn to be a good project manager. Delegating is pointless if you micromanage and redo the work. But also, as you train a great subcontractor, there will be some hand-holding as they learn your preferences and methods. You'll be tempted to say, "I can do it faster myself." That's probably true. But investing the time to teach someone to do what you do will save you more time in the long run.

Can you vet contractors, give them adequate project information, communicate clear design direction and feedback, and keep them on track to meet your goal? Finding people who fit your style of work can be a hurdle in itself. Try to test subcontractors on smaller, low-risk jobs to see if you work well together. Vet them before you need them. If, after a decent trial period, the results don't justify the cost, reassess. Try new players until you find the right fit.

Humility and Ego

These are equally important attributes when working alone or spearheading your own business. They serve as a great check-and-balance for not going full wallflower or full megalomaniac. You need ego to take on a project with confidence. Ego keeps you competitive and sharp, and it drives you to prove to your clients and peers that you are capable (or is that our parental validation issues?). It makes for great work; just don't let it keep you from constructive criticism.

Trusting yourself is one thing, but being deaf and blind to outside input is just plain stupid. After you've used your ego to land clients and create initial proofs, it's time to tap into humility. Listen and learn; it'll make your work and your work systems better. You don't have to act on all the advice you get. But if you can't find a good reason to bypass the input, consider whether your stubbornness is actually for the benefit of the project or just wounded pride. Freelancing is football, not golf. You're not on a solo mission; you're part of a team working collectively to push a football-shaped idea down a field. A healthy, competitive ego should actually encourage you to take the advice and input you need to improve and succeed.

What it Takes, Technically

Know-How

Are your creative skills ready to handle the projects that you're seeking? Stay on top of advancements in technology and software. Grow your skills to match ever-improving tools. Are you laying out books in Adobe Illustrator (oof) and designing logos in Photoshop (ooooof)? If so, you may want to work on your program knowledge. Owning power drills doesn't mean you know how to build a house. One great thing about the Internet Age is that you don't have to go to school for four years to learn these skills—though that is certainly one way to do it. You can learn almost anything through a Google or YouTube search. You can learn from books, mentorship, apprenticeship, and internship. Online courses, skill-specific workshops, and trade schools can teach you what you need to know for a fraction of the cost and time of a four-year degree.

Even once you've learned your craft, new technology can come along and change everything. There's a documentary called *Light & Magic* about the history of Industrial Light & Magic, the groundbreaking visual effects company George Lucas started in 1975 to work on *Star Wars*. The documentary shows how, at one time, all the visual effects in movies were practical: puppets and matte paintings and machinery and film. But soon the computer came along and changed everything. With the invention of Photoshop and other computer graphics software, effects began to go digital. By *Jurassic Park*, artists were creating fully-formed digital creatures. Eventually, the practical effects artists had to make the decision to either retrain and transition to computer graphics or move on. These major industry shifts happen all the time. It's never too late to learn how to harness a new tool in your creative practice.

Experience

You need to know how to guide your client toward making the educated decisions they may not be able to get to on their own. If you are intuitively gifted at interacting with people, that's excellent news. If you're unsure or timid, consider working at an agency or any business where you can learn a few more of these soft skills before going full-time freelance on your own. Established businesses usually have systems and procedures set up for client onboarding and project management, and you can learn valuable lessons about what to do—and what not to do.

What it Takes, Logistically

Financials

In your first year, you will have quite a few expenses, even if you are working from home. Before you start out,create a budget outlining the costs you'll need to cover (don't worry, we'll be doing this in an upcoming chapter). Once you know the expenses you have in store, here comes the hard question: Do you have the money? If not, what's your plan to save the money you'll need? How can you minimize costs? Do you have a financial buffer of savings in case you have some lean months? Have you figured out your project rates (we'll cover this in an upcoming chapter)? How many projects will you need to land at those rates to be profitable (we'll also work on this together)? These are some of the questions you need to explore. If you don't have the money ready, perhaps you keep your day job while you test out your freelance on the side. Or maybe you get a part-time job to supplement your freelance. That job doesn't even have to be creative-related. Maybe you work a service-industry job like bartending while you do your freelance. There's nothing wrong with doing freelance part-time until you can justify the full-time leap financially.

Tools and Venue

Do you have a computer, the necessary programs and software, the equipment (looking at you, photographers and film friends), a desk, and an ergonomic chair that won't wreck your butt and break your back after a day's work? In your business plan, you need to account for all these things, whether you have them, need them, or can do without them, until you start making more money. Can you work from home, or will you need to rent space? The little things add up: pens, accounting software, word-processing software, domain hosting, and website-builder tools. Let us not forget the giant tubs of Red Vines from Staples. It does take some money to make money in the sense of your baseline tools of the trade. And good news: In upcoming chapters, we'll show you how to cut costs in your first few years.

Demand

Do you have a skill set and style that will succeed as a solo act? Are enough people seeking the kind of work you do? Is there a specific gap in the market that your skills fill? If not, then be ready to widen your offering. When you start out on your own, you might have to be more of a generalist, doing work that is outside of your personal aesthetic or your preferred project type. Our friend Patric Yandoc always used to say, "One for the reel and one for the meal." Sometimes you work to keep the lights on and to fund the work you're passionate about.

"One for the reel and one for the meal."

If you aren't booked up, say yes to as many kinds of projects as your bandwidth and skills allow. You never know what it could lead to down the line. Branching out of your comfort zone can lead to lots of lessons and plenty of new possibilities. You may find a new creative skill or revenue stream. You'll also discover what you don't want to do, and that's just as crucial. As the demand for your work grows, you can be more selective.

Client Base

Do you have existing freelance clients? Do people you know show interest in your talents? Before making the leap into working for yourself full-time, post your work on a portfolio website and share it with your friends and followers. Do they respond well? Are people reaching out about projects? If yes, awesome! This is the network you'll probably get your first clients from. Ideally, you'll start freelancing part-time on the side and build up a roster of clients until the demand for your work is too much to handle as a side job. That's when you can make a safe transition to full-time freelancing.

Meet the Many Hats

As a freelancer and small business owner, you'll wear many hats. One of the harshest realizations we had when starting Hoodzpah was that the creative work was only a fraction of our day. Making proposals, scheduling social media posts and marketing, responding to inquiry emails, talking with potential clients, onboarding new clients, convincing existing clients to choose a direction, making case studies, navigating website problems, scheduling quarterly taxes, keeping the bookkeeping up to date—these are all time-consuming elements of a freelance work week. For us, the management-to-creative work ratio can sway between 40/60 and 60/40. But it's around half and half. For some of these tasks, you might hire a

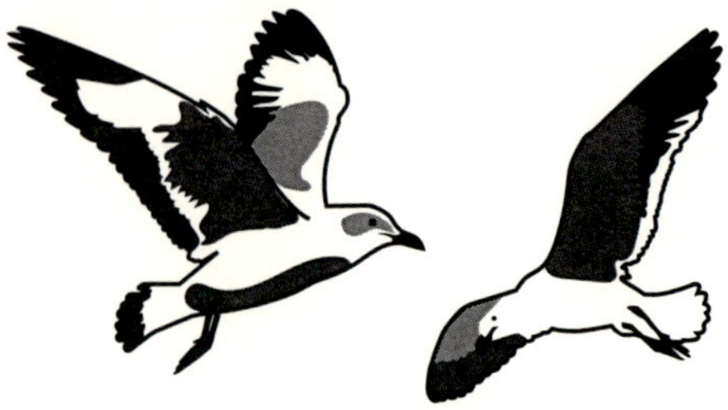

subcontractor. But for us, we managed as many of these things as we could as we built up our revenue and proved our business model. We wanted to keep our expenses as low as possible.

You will be responsible for wearing some or all of the following hats:

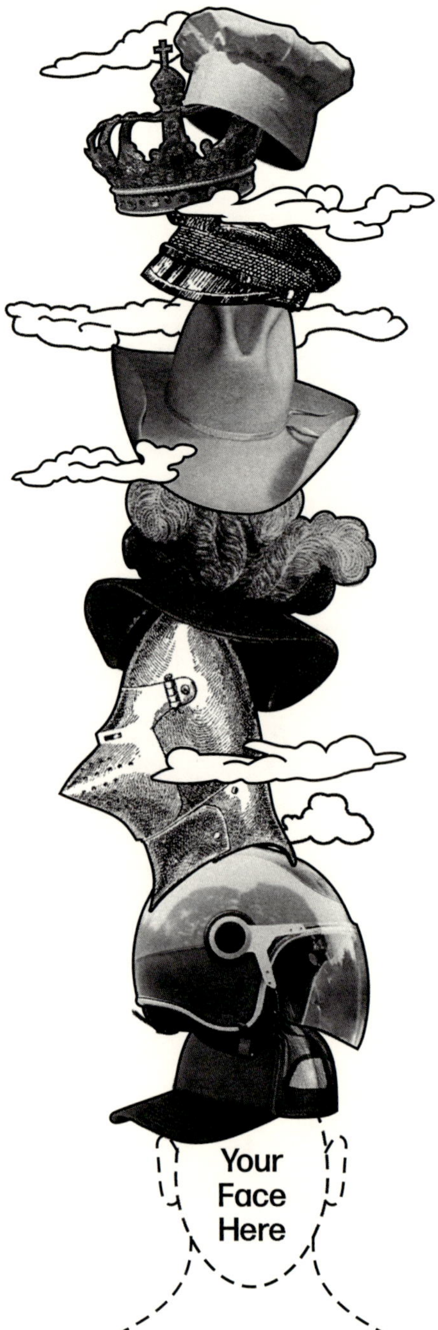

Chief Executive Officer (CEO)

You will decide the direction of your company. You'll look around and ahead to try to anticipate changes in the market, pivoting your approach to hedge your bets for success. You'll keep up with your industry and even the industries of your clients, devising new ways to stay competitive. You'll evaluate your successes and failures to better steer your company's actions in the future.

Chief Financial Officer (CFO)

You will oversee your company's cash flow and finances. You'll keep your books up to date (or oversee the person you hire to do it), gathering all the needed info and receipts for your accountant when taxes are due. You'll keep an eye on your cash flow and make sure you've got plenty of money coming in to cover salaries, expenses, and savings. You'll keep an eye on the acceptance versus rejection rate of your proposals and quotes. You'll decide when to raise or lower your rates.

Creative

This is the fun part. This is what we're all here for. You know this bit.

Marketing Manager

You will promote your company and services—hopefully, in unique and effective ways. You'll manage your social media accounts, make and update your online portfolio (be it a website, Behance, Dribbble, or otherwise), place ads, create campaigns to increase awareness or drive sales, find your target market, increase your brand presence through online and offline events, and so much more.

Sales Manager

You will look for clients, send cold emails, write awkward intro messages on LinkedIn, warm up leads via X and Instagram, and attend events to grow your network. You'll do introduction meetings and calls, create quotes and proposals, and eventually send agreements. You will learn to speak about yourself confidently (even in real time, in real life!) and learn to make a case for why people should choose you over the next person.

Accounts Receivable

You'll make and send invoices, and then send them again when they go unpaid. And then call and email until it gets paid.

HR Manager

If you subcontract or hire employees, you'll be responsible for their growth, engagement, and making sure everyone—including you—is treated fairly and respectfully.

Administrator

You will deal with all the emails, scheduling, organization, and file management that keep your projects and company running smoothly. You might get an assistant for the more mundane facets of admin, but it's unlikely you'll be able to pass it off entirely.

Despite all this, running your own studio can be so rewarding.

Don't let these lists scare you. It's important to know what you're in for. But once you land your first project, wrap up your first case study, get that first glowing testimonial—it's so worth it. You'll see. Many of our friends who run their own gigs can't imagine going back to working for anyone else. Or maybe you'll try freelancing for a while and realize it's not for you. There's nothing wrong with that! At least you'll never have to say, "What if?"

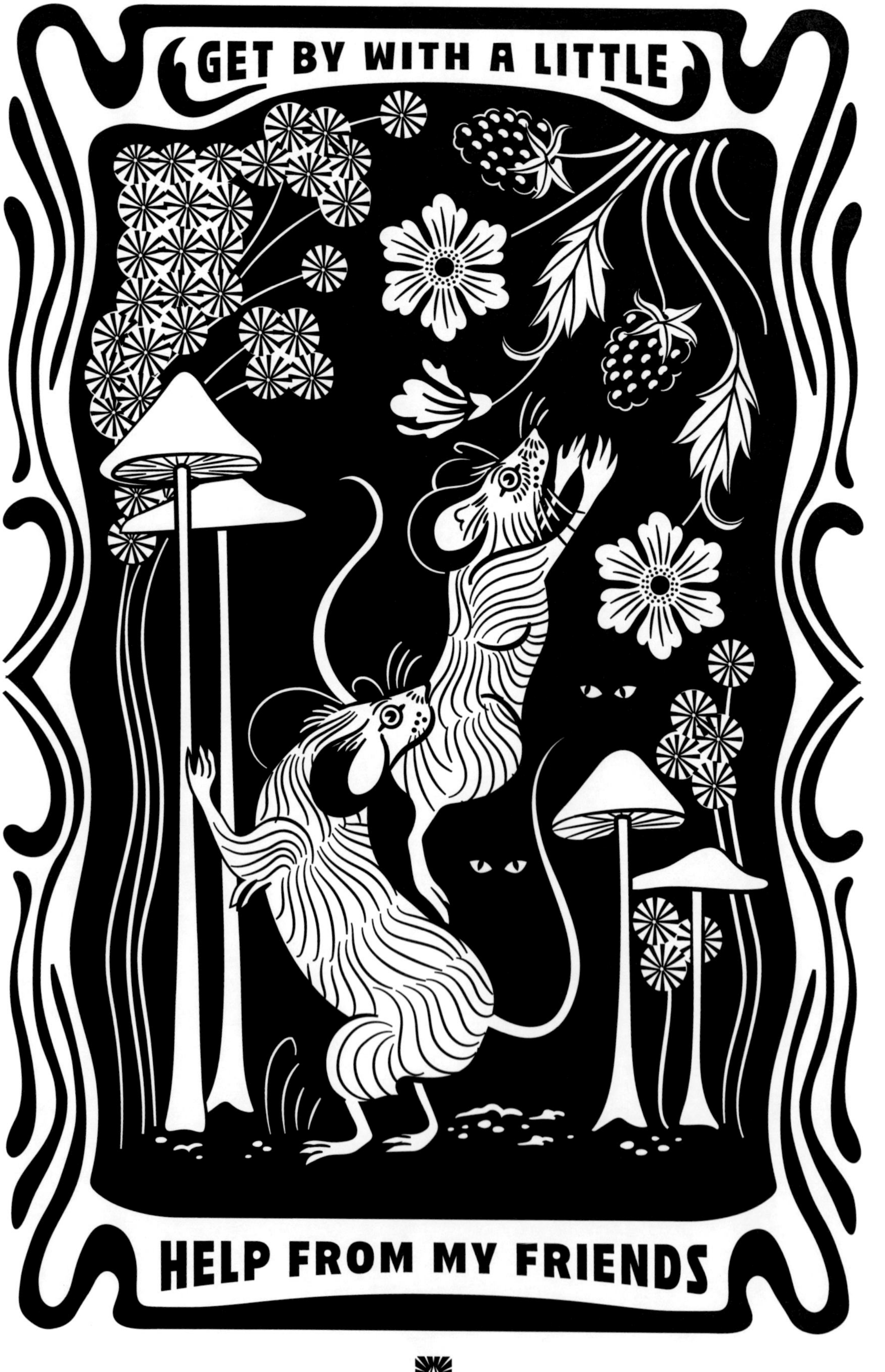

Illustration by: Amy Hood

2

Get by With a Little Help

Assemble Your A-Team

No one is an island. We're a lot more like Hobo Stew: the joint effort of all the people who offered knowledge and insight to us over the years. "Standing on the shoulders of giants" and all that.

In business, ignorance is not bliss. Get used to advice and constructive criticism from people within as well as outside of your industry. The ability to consider differing opinions and advice is crucial. It keeps you aware and adaptable. You don't have to take every note you're given, but considering things from other perspectives will stress test your concept in a way you couldn't do alone. It almost always results in a better product, process, or service.

Recognize areas where you're weak, and gather people around you who can fill those gaps. Frodo would never have made it to Mordor without his crew (Gollum included).

Whether you're starting a creative studio on your own or you've got a crew of partners in your business endeavor, you're going to need help from some (or all) of the people and organizations below.

Bank

Find a bank and set up a business bank account separate from your personal account. Especially if you have business partners who will need access to the account. When choosing the bank, consider their savings account interest rates, services offered, and their reliability. Having a separate account for your business isn't required by law. But it makes bookkeeping and general accounting a lot easier. Like, A LOT. If you have to comb through one shared account every month to separate personal and business income and expenses, you're self-inflicting unnecessary pain. And you are more likely to make a mistake. Spare your sanity and save your time by keeping them separate.

New business checking accounts are often free to open as long as you keep the minimum required balance. The documents needed to open an account vary depending on your business structure (we'll get into this later), but have a conversation with your banker to know what information to provide when setting up the account.

If possible, choose a bank account that is insured. In the USA, the FDIC (Federal Deposit Insurance Corporation) is a government corporation that supplies deposit insurance to depositors in American commercial banks and savings banks. So if your bank account is FDIC-insured and your bank fails (not unheard of; just consider Silicon Valley Bank), the FDIC will cover up to a certain amount of the funds you deposited (usually $250,000 at FDIC-insured banks). It's meant to instill trust in the American banking system. Other countries and regions have similar bank insurers—for example, the Deposit Insurance Corporation of Japan, the Canada Deposit Insurance Corporation, and deposit guarantee schemes in the EU. You can search it on the internet to find if there's a similar deposit insurer in your country. FDIC insurance doesn't apply to financial products like stocks, bonds, money market mutual funds, other types of securities, commodities, or crypto assets. Just something to keep in mind.

Traditional brick and mortar banks aren't your only option. There are virtual banks with no physical branch locations. Instead, everything is handled online. Some of these offer insured accounts and better interest rates. But virtual banks can also be harder to deposit physical cash into, and you might have to pay fees when using their ATM network. With the use of physical cash being less and less, this may not be an issue for you.

If you'll be accepting payments through services like PayPal or Venmo, avoid keeping large amounts of money in these types of accounts. Why? These services are not FDIC-insured (as of writing this). Transfer the money to your insured business bank account regularly.)

A Business Mentor

This is someone you know (whether personally or by reputation) and trust who can offer you guidance. Usually, this person is already in your life, and they're already taking an interest in you. If you find yourself asking a person for their help again and again, they're already your mentor.

A good mentor can be one of the most important people in your business life. Take advantage of the fact that they've walked this road—or a similar road—before you and are willing to let you learn from the blood, sweat, and tears they've shed. You'll more than likely have a few different mentors throughout the course of your business life. As your understanding evolves, you'll find different people who can help you grow.

If you don't have such a person in your life, you can seek one out more officially. Some creative groups like AIGA (American Institute of Graphic Arts) offer mentorship opportunities. Some creative professionals also offer mentorship via courses, one-on-one sessions, and paid workshops. This might not be an ongoing relationship, but it can still be valuable to get input from someone you admire.

You can get great business advice from people who aren't in your industry. Do you know someone who is generally business-savvy? Ask to take them to coffee or lunch. Reach out via email and see if they'd have time to go over some business hurdles you're up against. Good business is good business, regardless of the industry.

The most important thing about mentors? They are precious; do not take them for granted! If you need more than a quick opinion, tell them you'd like to pay them for an hour or two of consultation. If your mentor is unpaid and informal, go the extra mile to make them feel appreciated for everything they do. If they refer you to clients, you could send them a referral fee (percentage of the project landed). Buy them lunch, send a handwritten note (never goes out of style), or a personalized gift. It's not about the price tag of the gift; it's about the sentiment.

You never want these business guardian angels to feel taken for granted. They don't owe you anything, and yet they are putting time and effort into you. You never want to take advantage. It's one thing to ask for advice; it's another to ask for your mentor's play-by-play game plan of how they run their own business. The saying "I didn't take you to raise" comes to mind. Be sensitive and respectful of boundaries and of their proprietary information. They may only be allowed to tell you so much, or they may not want to share all of their own trade secrets. The last thing you want is to become a leech or a burden.

Are You My Mentor?

*
A quick quiz to test who in your circle might make a good mentor.

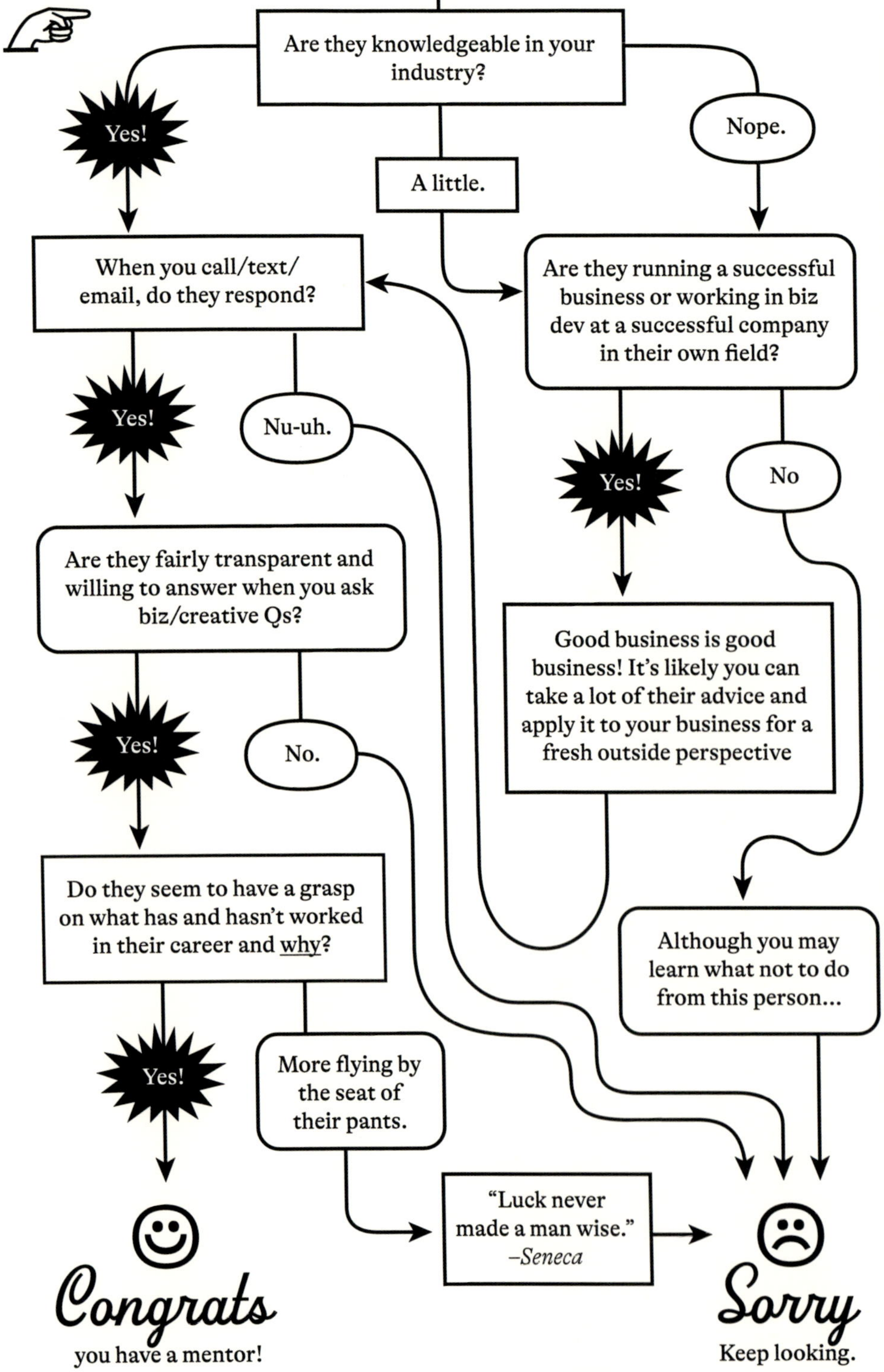

❶ Van Gogh & Gaugin

Vincent Van Gogh and Charles Gaugin had a friendship so off the wall it could be an A24 movie. Van Gogh's brother Theo was Gaugin's art dealer in Paris. Theo was worried about Vincent and paid a short-on-funds Gaugin to live with Vincent in Arles (in the famous yellow house). Vincent wanted to start an artist commune and thought Gaugin could be a mentor that drew other artists. A wild friendship/sometimes-mentorship ensued between the two. Van Gogh (33) was disorganized while Gaugin (40) was methodical. Van Gogh loved Arles while Gaugin called it "the dirtiest hole in the South." They had mutual respect for one another but also an unstated rivalry, often painting the same subjects. Things began to crumble quickly. According to Gaugin's journal, he would find van Gogh standing over him as he slept. Vincent also spent their shared funds on absinthe and women. Gaugin declared he was leaving, prompting van Gogh to chase him through the streets with a razor blade before finally returning home and cutting his ear off.

Famous Peer/Mentor Relationships

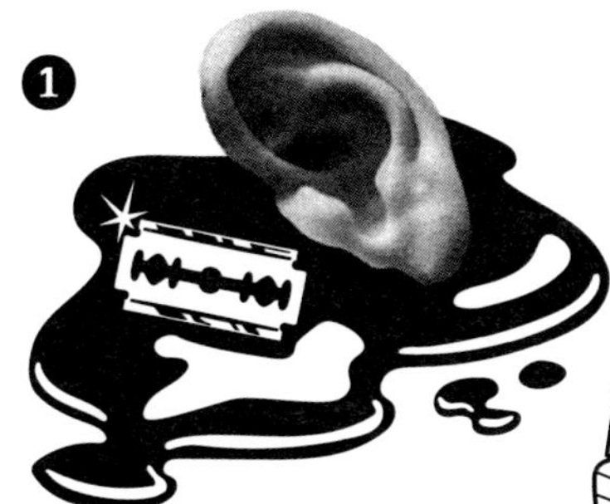

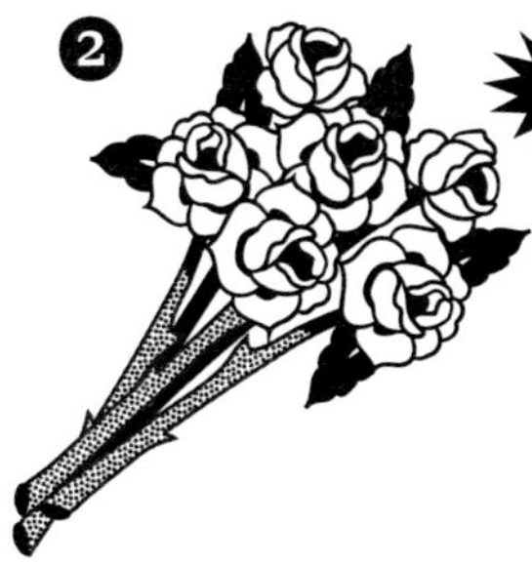

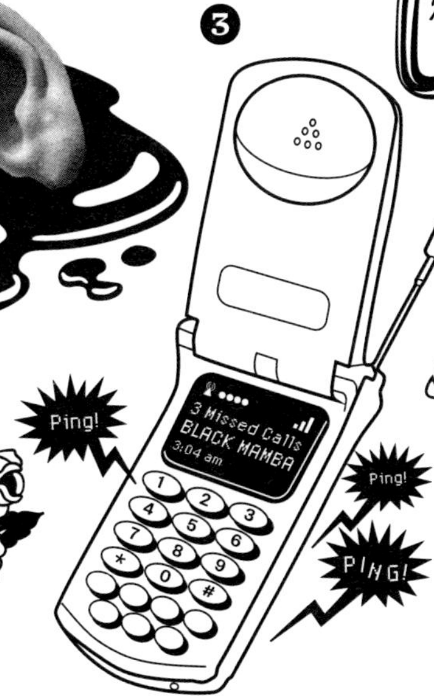

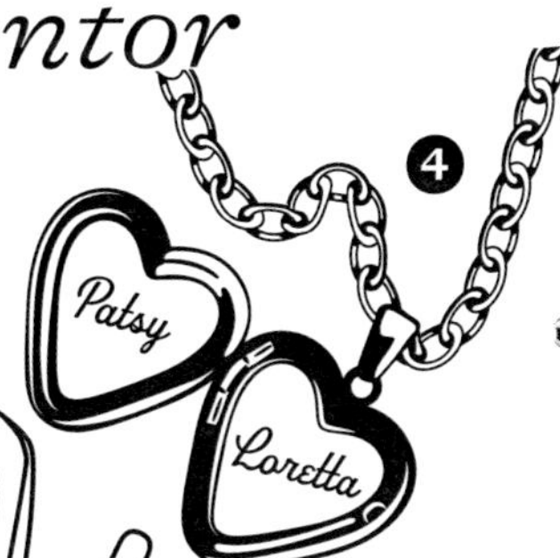

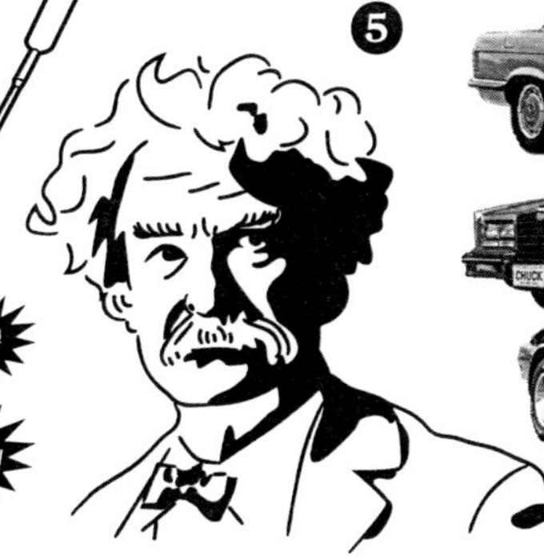

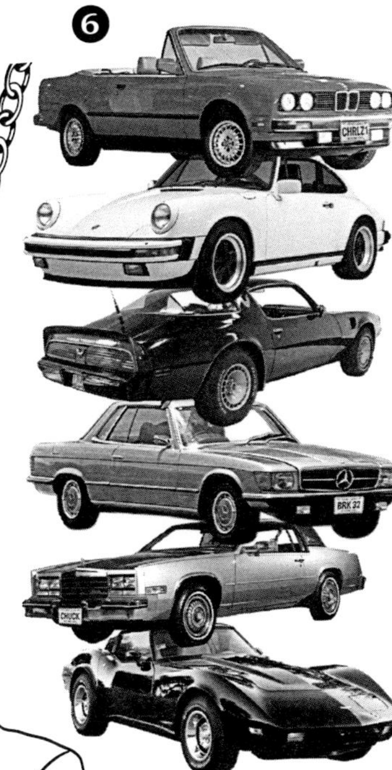

❷ Lucille Ball & Carole Burnett

Carole Burnett and Lucille Ball were great friends following their first meeting backstage after Ball saw Burnette in the musical Once Upon a Mattress in 1959. As told by Burnette at the 2016 SAG Awards, Ball visited Carole backstage telling her, "Kid if you ever need me for anything, give me a call." A year later Carole asked Ball to be a featured guest in a CBS special she was filming, and before Carole could finish asking Lucille said, "when do you want me?" Ball hosted Burnett's baby shower and sent her flowers every year for her birthday.

❸ Michael Jordan & Kobe Bryant

MJ said on The Ringer's "Icons Club" podcast that he told Kobe to call him if he ever needed advice. The Lakers star more than took him up on the offer, apparently calling him all hours of the night. The two had a great relationship over the years affectionately calling eachother "big brother" and "little brother."

❹ Patsy Cline & Loretta Lynn

Although Patsy Cline and Loretta Lynn were the same age, Cline was a well established star when Lynn was just becoming known in the country music world. Lynn covered one of Cline's songs at the Grand Ole Opry and dedicated it to her. Cline was touched and arranged a meeting. After that Patsy and Loretta became great friends with Patsy taking Loretta on tour with her, giving her hair and style tips, and even helping with money and groceries for Loretta and her 4 kids. Every time Loretta visited, Patsy would cook her dinner and load her up with clothes from her own closet. Now that's a true BFF.

❺ Mark Twain & Nikola Tesla

Twain and Tesla were big fans of one another's work. Twain was a big tech enthusiast, and when Tesla was recovering from a near fatal illness he said Mark's books got him through. Tesla used to host salons where friends would come and hang at his laboratory in New York City. Twain was often in attendance, even taking part in many experiments, a favorite of which was taking x-rays of his own skull with Tesla's x-ray gun.

❻ Dr J. & Charles Barkley

When Charles Barkley was a rookie on the 76ers, Julius Erving used to give him all sorts of career advice, telling him to ditch his signature track suits for a *suit* suit, and to be smarter with his money. Barkley shared on an episode of All The Smoke podcast, "One day, [Julius] says, 'Charles, how many cars do you have?' I said, 'I got like six.' Then he said, 'Well, how many of them can you drive at the same time?... Why do you have six cars?... Charles, everybody knows who the fuck you are. You ain't got to impress these people.'"

References: (Biography.com article "Inside Patsy Cline and Loretta Lynn's Instantaneous and Unbreakable Bond"; ESPN.com article: "Inside Kobe Bryant and Michael Jordan's private friendship"; Biography.com article "How Vincent van Gogh's Tumultuous Friendship with Paul Gauguin Drove Him to Cut Off His Ear"; Studio 360 podcast episode "Tesla and Twain."

The Movie Brats

Steven Spielberg, Brian De Palma, Francis Ford Coppola, George Lucas, and Martin Scorcese (sometimes referred to as the Movie Brats) used to often help each other out with one another's films. Lucas created the character of Indiana Jones but gave the movie to Spielberg to direct, thinking he'd be better suited. Spielberg helped De Palma direct the shootout scene in *Scarface*. Lucas directed the second unit shoot for Coppola's *The Godfather*. And the list goes on. So whether you do it officially with a regular meetup or unofficially, just find your crew.

Tact is especially important if your mentor is in the same field of work as you. Regardless of how close you are, you're still their competition. The rule of thumb with mentors is to ask questions about how to run your business, not to ask them about how they run their business. The great thing about this approach is that usually, if you're transparent, others feel comfortable sharing in kind. Let them offer information about themselves willingly rather than being invasive. Remember: They're a resource; they aren't here to do the work for you. Do your own research to come up with your own plan, then ask for their input. This shows initiative and that you value their time.

Industry Peers and Friends

Even if you don't have a mentor at the moment, you probably have made friends in your industry. They do what you do, they know the struggles, they know the frustrations. Get together with peers like this to compare notes and think tank problems. You might have heard this called a "mastermind group." The term mastermind group was coined by Napoleon Hill to define a group of peers who offer one another advice and input to solve problems. We were invited to join one by a friend, and it was hugely beneficial. We had a standing meeting every two weeks.

Industry peers are people you can gather referrals from and send creative proofs to when you're feeling stuck. We have a few text threads with other designers where we mostly roast each other and talk about TV and music. But there are a few super helpful moments of "Which of these logos is better?" or "Do you know any great copywriters?" If you're having issues with a client, these are the folks you can turn to.

In our online course, *Freelance and Business and Stuff*, the part that students love most is the Slack community. It's a place where freelancers (including us!) can jump in, ask questions, get feedback, give moral support, celebrate wins, and more. It's so nice to have a quick sounding board, especially if you work alone.

Don't have industry friends yet? Start attending in-person meetups or events, take a course or class with a community component, or get more active in starting conversations with people you admire via social media platforms. Don't wait for someone to talk to you; go out of your way to start a dialogue about anything, not just creativity.

An Accountant or CPA (Certified Public Accountant)

Your accountant or CPA (a special designation that guarantees a high level of training) can help with things like bookkeeping (the recordkeeping of your income and expenses used to file your taxes), tax compliance, and financial planning. While some business owners manage their own day-to-day bookkeeping with software like QuickBooks or Xero, we recommend hiring an accountant or CPA for taxes to make sure everything is properly filed.

Here are some important traits to look for in your accountant or CPA: patience in spades, doesn't mind taking the time to explain things to you, will help you weigh the pros and cons of your financial decisions, and can speak plainly when it comes to taxes, planning and the like.

When you first start your business, don't wait till tax season to talk to a CPA or accountant. Unlike personal taxes, some businesses have to pay quarterly estimated tax (this may vary depending on the country you live in). So contact your CPA or accountant to help you set up your tax payment schedule. Getting this wrong could result in missed payments and late fees.

A Lawyer

Consult with a lawyer, preferably one who specializes in Small Business Law. Show them your business plan and get their advice, because chances are, they've seen a lot of people do what you're about to attempt, and they may save you some grief. Two things to get their input on are your contracts and the structure of your business (will you be a sole proprietor, a partnership, corporation, LLC., etc.).

If you don't have the money for a lawyer, look to friends or family who are lawyers. Maybe they'll do you a favor and give you some pro bono advice in exchange for a coffee or lunch. If they're not close friends/family, you could offer a trade: your creative skills for their legal expertise. Be direct, respectful, and clear about the parameters and scope of the trade. And be OK if they say no.

You don't have to keep a lawyer on retainer—but it's great to have their input on your business structure and legal-document templates for clients and subcontractors. You can also buy pre-vetted legal templates from lawyers who offer this as a product. Our small business lawyer, Keren, offers this through her company, Not Your Father's Lawyer.

An Insurer

Even if you work from home, there are insurance options to consider for you and your business. Larger clients often require you to carry certain insurance in their contracts. Some states and regions require certain types of insurance as well. So, research your area and ask your lawyer or CPA. The following are some insurance options to research:

Personal Health Insurance. Many people get their health insurance through their employers. If you are now your sole employer, it falls to you to provide this.

Disability Insurance. If you get hurt or become seriously ill and cannot work, this kind of coverage can generally replace around 60 percent of your income.

Indemnity or Professional Liability Insurance. Sometimes referred to as Errors and Omissions Insurance, Professional Liability Insurance protects you from being sued by clients who claim your negligence caused an error or omission in the product you made for them. Whether you're right or wrong in the incident, legal fees associated with fighting a lawsuit could be crippling to your business. When you work with larger businesses on larger contracts, this insurance is often required in the contract.

Business Insurance. The breadth of this insurance depends on your situation. It could include property insurance (homeowner's insurance doesn't always include business property and equipment), business interruption insurance, and general liability insurance.

Workers' Compensation Insurance. Broadly, this covers medical expenses, lost wages, etc., for workers who are injured on the job. This is often required, so research according to your location.

Remember that you aren't required to have every kind of insurance. You will be solicited to buy every kind of insurance out there, so be smart and get what's necessary for you. As your company grows and your liability grows, you'll need to adjust your insurance coverage to suit. The bigger the project and payout, the bigger the liability and the more you have to lose. Weigh the pros and costs and pick wisely.

Also, remember that you're human, and honest mistakes can happen despite your best efforts. These accidents or unintentional situations (like unintentionally making a design that looks really similar to someone else's) can still lead to lawsuits from unhappy or harmed clients. So it's good to be protected.

Subcontractors

Subcontractors who offer complementary services to yours can allow you to quote larger projects you couldn't accomplish on your own, where you act as the creative director, keeping the overall vision in line. For example, at Hoodzpah, we do brand identity design, but clients often come to us wanting not only the rebrand but also a new website to match, and they prefer working with one partner rather than managing multiple partners. So in that case, we've subcontracted developers to implement our designs. Same thing with motion design, messaging, or photography.

Subcontractors who offer the same service as you can allow you to take on more work than you could alone—without the permanent cost of hiring an employee. In some states, like here in California, you're not allowed to subcontract another California resident for a service you are capable of performing in-house. So double-check the rules in your area.

As a small studio or a studio of one, the difference between needing more work and being maxed out could be one project, depending on the scope. Even a few delays in your existing project workload could mean that everyone needs everything all at once. These are times when having trusted subcontractors can be really handy, especially ones you've already vetted and collaborated with. We have a standing agreement with a couple of subcontractors that has the general terms for our working arrangement. As projects come up, all we need to do is agree to a specific scope of work, and the terms of the standing agreement still apply.

Test working with people on low-stakes projects so you know who you work well with when a last-minute need arises. Attend in-person or virtual portfolio reviews at colleges and universities where you could meet your next great intern or future subcontractor. We've subcontracted around five or six people we met this way. Creative meetups and communities are another great place to meet potential subcontractors. We've easily subcontracted thirty people we've met through our course community, and a handful of others we've met organically offline at events.

There are, of course, risks to any business relationship. Always have an agreement with your subcontractor that is very clear about the project expectations, scope, deliverables, timeline, and intellectual property. The project fee and payment terms with your subcontractor should correspond to the terms you have with the client. So if you're getting paid a flat rate on a project, it's ideal to pay your sub at a flat rate so you have a controlled cost. If your client is paying hourly, pay your sub hourly. In your subcontractor agreement, schedule your subcontractor payments to go out after you get paid by the client to keep on top of your cash flow. So if your client pays an invoice after round one, arrange to pay your subcontractor after round two so you're using your client's money, not advancing your own. If, for some reason, your client ghosts you and stops paying, at least you're ahead of what you owe your subcontractor.

For more than fourteen years, we have flexed our team to meet an ever-changing client demand by using a strong network of subcontractors. Some people call this an "elastic" agency model. We get the benefit of hand-picked talent per project without the risk of scaling our studio's staff permanently. We love being a small and agile team, so the elastic model works great for us.

Chapter Checklist:

① Get a business bank account.

② Gather your A-Team of advisers, professional consultants, and peers.

③ Look into optional and required insurance for your business.

④ Start a log of potential subcontractors so you have a directory when you need them.

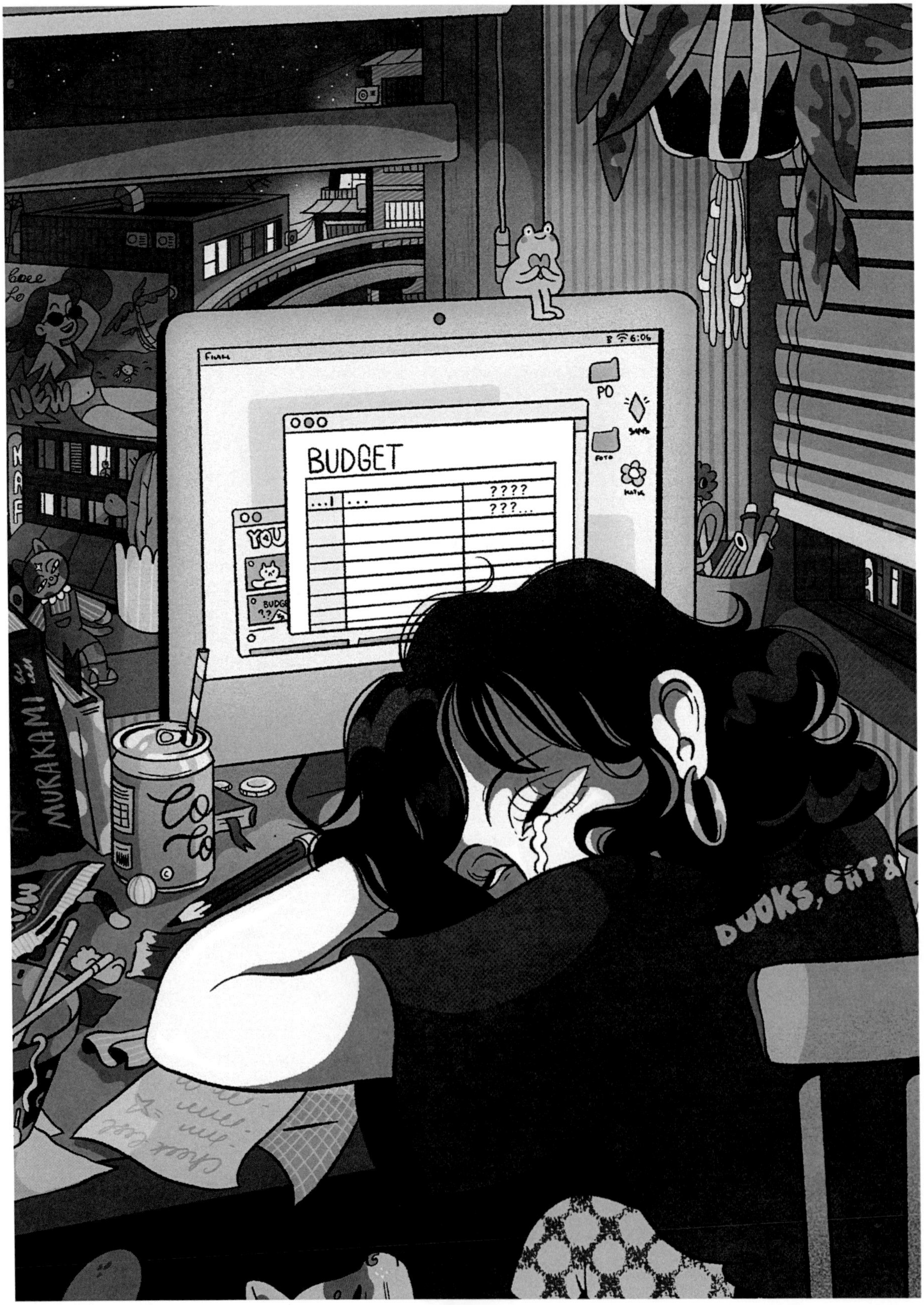

Illustration by: Polina Alexeenko

3

Budgeting and Income Planning

Defining Our Terms

Budget:
An estimate of the money you plan to make, spend, and save for a set period of time.

Expense:
Money spent.

Personal Income:
What you personally earn from your wages and any other investments or ventures.

Profit or Net Profit:
Your total business revenue minus expenses (taxes, supplies, payroll, equipment, etc.)

Profit/Loss Statement (PNL):
A financial statement that totals the money coming into your business (revenue) versus money going out (expenses) for a specific period of time.

Revenue:
Money you or your business earns from your services, products, and investments.

Let's start this chapter with a vow to have fun with it. Why? Because for the most part, money is fun and awesome. It pays for your everyday needs, your food, your shelter. Maybe it supports your family's needs and goes to initiatives you're passionate about. It funds your thrifting habit, your coffee habit, and your Jordans habit. It's your gateway to fun experiences like Lakers games, weekend getaways, and parking at the state beach. Money puts overpriced phones in your hand and ensures that your Netflix addiction proceeds without interruption.

For all these reasons and more, making more money rather than less of it is great, right? More money means you can pay off your student loans faster, save up for a vacation, plus lay away for "what-ifs" and your retirement in Palm Springs (can you see the 65+ community populated by seniors with Cary-Grant-level tans?). Let's start making plans for all this.

Important Disclaimer: This chapter is based on our own personal experience and does not constitute professional legal or financial advice. Review this plan with your CPA or financial adviser to make sure it's a good fit for you.

The Almighty B Word: Budgeting

Congress gives budgeting a bad reputation. Making a budget is easy when you don't have to get the approval of 535 people to pass it. In this case, it's just you and your business partners. A budget is a great reference point to set your income goals, salary, and pricing. Knowing your budget means knowing how much you can spend and how much you need to make to reach your financial goals.

In this chapter, we'll start by making your personal budget. This sheds light on what you need personally to survive and thrive (including expenses for anyone who relies on your financial support). Then we'll make a business budget. This paints a picture of what your company needs to make in revenue to cover your wages, the cost of doing business, and any savings/reinvestment plan you set up.

Think of your budget like a financial food pyramid. You aim for certain quantities of certain food groups to stay healthy. Our financial food pyramid is made up of three groups: needs, wants, and savings.

In the next few pages you'll find the Personal Budget worksheet, which uses a simple equation created by Elizabeth Warren and Amelia Warren Tyagi in their book, *All Your Worth: The Ultimate Lifetime Money Plan*. They call it the 50-30-20 Budget. You take your personal after-tax income and plan to use 50 percent of it for your needs, 30 percent for your wants, and 20 percent for savings. It's a very user-friendly system that can hardly be called austere. This budget will put you on track to pay off debts and build savings without suffering in joyless scrimping (blow-up mattress + Cup Noodles every meal = sad face). This breakdown might not always be feasible during tough economic times. But it's a good goal to aim for when starting out.

For your Business Budget Worksheet, we'll follow a more tailored formula. We'll calculate your overall expenses to run your business (including estimated taxes and wages/salaries for you and any business partners or staff), add in some savings and reinvestment goals, and then figure out how much you need to earn in business revenue to cover that goal. To give you a reference, at Hoodzpah, our goal for business savings in the very beginning was to get two months' worth of operating expenses stowed away in the bank (meaning, we could run our business as usual and pay our wages without any new work coming in for two months). Ideally, we would have saved this before we started our business, but necessity prompted our business rather than choice, so we saved it after the fact. The more you can save, the better.

Now, get your pencils and pens ready. We're going to dive into the budget worksheets!

Make a Personal Budget

Step One: Calculate your Monthly "Needs"

We're going to start your personal budget by calculating your needs per month below. If you have people who depend on your financial income, be sure to include their expense needs too. Exclude savings. Exclude wants (meaning, leave out anything non-essential, like vacations, motorcycles, anything from Erewhon, etc.). It'll be hard to separate some needs and wants, but just do your best. Exclude business expenses. This is only for personal needs. Fill in the blanks next to each item in the sections below. And feel free to add any expenses that are unique to you, which we might not have made a specific section for. Add section totals together for the monthly "needs" subtotal. Multiply the subtotal by twelve to get your yearly needs total.

[Fig. 1] →

Loans/Debt	per/mo.	**Home/Utilities**	per/mo.
Min. Credit Card Payment		Mortgage/Rent	
Min. Student Loan Payment		Gas	
Other Loan Min. Payment		Electric	
Personal Care		Water & Sewer	
Clothes		Maintenance	
Groceries		Phone	
Personal Hygiene (hair, etc.)		Cable/Internet	
Out of pocket medical		Security	
Insurance		**Transportation**	
Health		Car Loan/Lease	
Auto		Maintenance/Etc.	
Home		Public Transit	
Life		Gas	
Dependents		**Other**	
Child/Elderly Care			
Pet Care			
Subtotal Monthly Needs: *(add all costs up)* →			
x 12 = Yearly Needs →			

From here, we're going to work backward to get our total budget amount. Remember the 50-30-20 Budget breakdown: 50 percent is for needs, 30 percent for wants, and 20 percent for savings. So use the equations below to finish your budget. The total yearly budget will be what you're aiming to make after taxes are taken out, so we'll adjust for taxes at the end.

Step Two: Calculate your Yearly Total Budget

Use the following formula to determine the amount you need to take home after taxes:

Yearly needs × 2 = yearly total budget

Example: According to the 50-30-20 Budget model, if your yearly needs total $50,000, your yearly total budget is $100,000 ($50,000 × 2).

Step Three: Total Yearly Budget × 0.3 = Yearly Wants Budget

Step Four: Total Yearly Budget × 0.2 = Yearly Savings

Example:

According to the 50-30-20 Budget model, if your yearly needs total $50,000, your yearly total budget is $100,000 ($50,000 x 2).

50%: $50,000 for yearly needs ($100,000 × 0.5)

30%: $30,000 for yearly wants ($100,000 × 0.3)

20%: $20,000 for yearly savings ($100,000 × 0.2).

Step Five: Roughly Adjust for Taxes

Your final yearly income goal needs to have extra padding to account for the taxes that the government will take. Ask your accountant what your tax rate would be based on your personal yearly budget and your federal and local tax laws. Or you can do an Internet search to find this info via your federal or local taxing entity's website. Example search query: "Tax bracket percentage for $x/year income in the USA."

When you know your tax rate(s), you can calculate what your estimated taxes will be per year. Example: If your take-home income goal is $100,000/year and your tax rate is 22 percent, then $100,000 × .22 = $22,000 in taxes per year*. Add that on top of your $100,000 take-home income goal to get your total yearly income goal of $122,000.

Example:

Example: If your take-home income goal is $100,000/year and your tax rate is 22 percent, then $100,000 × .22 = $22,000 in taxes per year*. Add that on top of your $100,000 take-home income goal to get your total yearly income goal of $122,000. ** This equation isn't an exact method since 22 percent of your income before taxes won't be the same as 22 percent of* *your income after taxes (it's a bit brain-frying). But this simple equation is good for a rough approximation. To factor in your deductions and get an exact number for your yearly taxes, try an online tax calculator like www.smartasset.com/taxes/income-taxes. Thanks to Ethan Young Unzicker, a reader who sent in thoughts and suggestions regarding this topic.*

Now we know what your personal yearly income goal is! This is your ideal estimate. But in order to justify it, you'll have to bring in the work at the right price to support it.

The 50-30-20 Budget is not for everyone. Maybe you want to be more specific about your savings and wants budgets. If so, that's fine. Just add your needs, wants, and savings together to get your own personal yearly income goal total.

Check your Calculations Against Real Industry Averages

[Fig. 2] →

Total Yearly Needs *(Number from Step 2.)*	
+ **Estimated Income Tax Owed for Federal**	
+ **Estimated Income Tax Owed for State**	
= **✻ Personal Yearly Income Goal ✻**	

See how your personal yearly income goal stacks up against employed creatives across the United States. Check out The Creative Group's yearly resource called the "Salary Forecast" (at the time of writing, you can get this forecast free if you subscribe to their parent company newsletter at www.RobertHalf.com). In it, they list average salary ranges for the most common creative positions. The list shows variation depending on experience level and location in the United States. Websites like Payscale also provide this info, and AIGA (American Institute of Graphic Arts) does a yearly census that's also worth looking at. By comparing your personal yearly income goal with the industry average for people working at agencies or in-house (meaning directly employed by a brand or organization), you can see if you're competitive, shooting high or below the average. You don't have to adjust your number to match the average. If your work is highly sought after, or your skillset is rare or expert, you can charge more. There are tons of factors that go into what your salary can be, but it's always interesting to get a sense of where your number sits in the industry landscape.

Now that we've worked out what you need to make personally in take-home pay, we're going to calculate your business budget.

Make a Business Budget

Step One: Calculate Monthly Business Expenses

Step Two: Add in Savings, Profit Goals, and Estimated

← [Fig. 3]

Office	per/mo.	**Team & Subs**	per/mo.
Rent/Lease/Mortgage		My Salary	
Postage/Shipping		(before taxes)	
Supplies		Employee Salaries	
Maintenance		Subcontractors	
Phone, Internet, Utilities		Lawyer	
Software/Hardware		Accountant/CPA/	
Subscriptions		Bookkeeper	
Furniture			
Marketing/Networking		**Bus. Loans/Debt**	
Advertising		Credit Card	
Website		Business Loan	
Promotional Collateral (business cards, printed marketing materials, promo zines, swag, etc.)		**Etc. Business** Licenses & Permits	
Travel (for Conferences, trade shows, business trips, etc.)		Liability Insurance Other	
Client Gifts etc.			
Subtotal Monthly Expenses: *(add all costs up)* →			
x 12 = Yearly Business Expenses →			

Taxes

Take your total from Fig. 3 and add your savings goal (per year), plus estimated business taxes (If you are a sole proprieter, S-corp, or partnership, your have a pass thru business and you already reported your taxes in your personal taxes, so you can ignore this part.

[Fig. 4] →

Yearly Business Expenses *(Number from bottom of Fig. 3 chart)*	
+ Savings Goal (per year)	
+ Estimated Business Tax (per year) *if applicable*	
+ Profit Goal (per year)	
= ✻ Business Revenue Goal✻	

Otherwise speak to your accountant about this), plus desired profit to get your business revenue goal (Fig. 4)

Congrats, you business-savvy numbers wizard! You've figured out your business expenses and business revenue goal. Now, your aim is to bring in enough work to meet this budget goal.

Budgeting is something you should do regularly. We update our personal and business budgets yearly, sometimes more often if our situation changes.

In our pricing chapter, we'll help you plan out your income sources with your income goals in mind. As you do business, it will be important to look at your company's profit/loss statement each month to see if you're on track with the amount of needed income to support your budget. Monthly fluctuation is normal, but beware of longer downward trends. If you have a few slow months in a row, you need to rethink your strategy. You may need to pivot how you market yourself, what services you offer, or what you charge. Consistently spending more than you make leads to financial and emotional heartache. Once you build up savings, the very normal ebb and flow of work becomes less stressful. Your backup cash will cover your months of famine until the months of feast come back.

If you start to realize you won't be able to meet the business revenue goal, find ways to trim down your expenses. How? Glad you asked. Here are some ways to drastically reduce your cost of doing business.

Expense Hacks

Avoid Getting an Office Space

Avoiding the costs of renting or buying office space is one of the best and biggest cost-cutting choices you can make early on. The COVID-19 pandemic forced many people to work from home. So you might already be used to this. Companies and clients today won't think it's weird to work from home, whereas in the early 2010s, it was less normalized in work culture.

Your first few years of freelancing will be stressful enough as you try to gain new clients and bring in consistent work. So keep your overhead costs as low as possible to lessen your financial burden while ironing out the kinks in your process and income streams. There's less risk, and working from home is more convenient. Can you imagine signing a two-year lease on an office and then losing your main client two months later? Quelle nightmare!

Working from home has its perks. You work when you need to and take breaks when you want to. If you had an office open to the public, you'd have to keep regular office hours and deal with unexpected walk-in clients. You'd have to deal with traffic like the rest of the rat race. Working from home means no commute and fewer car expenses as a result. Plus, you won't have to cover as much insurance as you would for an office space. Hoodzpah is a fully dispersed, remote office. We choose to work from our respective home offices and favorite coffee shops to this day because we prefer the convenience and flexibility.

If you decide to work from home, set boundaries with partners, roommates, and family members so they respect your work area. Sadly, pets do not recognize boundaries, but that's why we love them.

Routine and structure will be key to staying on task and getting work done in such a familiar place (especially when the TV and kitchen are so close at hand). Try to find a daily routine that works best for you. Winging it and waiting till you feel "inspired" every day won't cut it. Freelance freedom is easily abused and can spiral into a demotivated nightmare. Some days, you'll battle the boredom. You'll need creative feedback. You'll crave social interaction from someone besides your cat. That's why it's hugely important to stay plugged into the creative community, online and offline. We have a Slack channel for our online course based on this book *(Freelance and Business and Stuff: The Course)*, and it has become our virtual office. Don't like Slack? Start a text or email thread with some creative pals who don't mind you sending them progress shots of your work or client horror stories throughout the week. Most of them have probably been craving a creative confidant just as much as you.

Most of all, when working from home, remember that your home isn't an office 24/7. Try to create physical boundaries between your "workspace" and your living space in your home. Even a curtain you can pull closed to hide your desk at the end of the day can help put work out of your mind. Make a pact to ignore your computer during off-hours. Once work is over, your personal time is for friends, family, and just plain loafing around. Your business may be in your home, but you can't let it dictate your life all the time. Be thoughtful of segmenting the two. It will preserve your sanity.

There will be days when you just need to escape your home office and see something new. Find fun places to work from that inspire you, but also are affordable. Grab your laptop and head to a place with free Wi-Fi—the library, a coffee shop, a restaurant, and even a bar can all be your office-away-from-home for a few hours. Bring headphones if you need more quiet. If you don't have all your programs on your laptop, use this remote work time to do logo sketches, prepare quotes and proposals, or write up a blog post on a recent project. You'll remain productive while stimulating your senses and curing your cabin fever. Who knows, maybe you'll meet your next client while out and about. You could also reach out to friends who have office spaces for their own businesses. They may have an extra desk you could crash for the day.

Co-working

If you need an office space, consider a co-working space or sharing a space with a friend. Co-working spaces are popping up everywhere, offering reasonable rates for shared spaces with like-minded folk. You can rent an office for a day (if you have a big meeting), or get a desk for a few days a week. It's cheaper than paying for your own office, and it gives you the community/work/life balance you need.

Curb the Itch to Upgrade Until Necessary

When you land that big project or get that first big freelance check, it's going to be tempting to spend it. But here's the thing, if you spend more money as you make more money, you're not really making more money. The biggest trap of new wealth is to live to—or beyond—your means rather than living to your needs. We see it with new actors and athletes all the time. They get drafted, or they get the big part, and they start spending like they'll always be making that kind of money. Then a lull happens in their career or an injury strikes, and they wind up bankrupt. They weren't saving, and they let their expenses grow to match their income. As your income grows, try to keep your expenses low. You can treat yourself, of course, but don't let your expenses grow to match your income. You'll never save money this way.

When money comes in, you'll be tempted to upgrade your car, your closet, your equipment, and your office. Unless you have good cash flow and savings to justify it, put these upgrades off and make do with less to start. If you have an old car, and you're worried big clients won't take you seriously if they see you drive up in it, then take a car service to your meeting. A few Lyft rides are better than the burden of a new car loan. If you have an older iPhone, you don't have to upgrade just because everyone else is. A slightly older computer or laptop won't kill you so long as it can handle the programs and processes you need it for. If you have a good shared rent situation with someone, you don't have to move out into your own place yet. Just because you're an entrepreneur doesn't mean you have to 2.0 your life. Keep things as they are for the first year of freelancing if you can. Then, look at your year, the trends, and what you've saved, and see where you can reinvest (new equipment, etc.) or treat yourself.

There can be a lot of pressure in creative industries to look a certain part and have certain toys. But you know what's cooler? Not having to stress about making a car payment when you're starting a new business. Not having to take crap jobs just to make rent. Not getting ulcers from stress about work. Make a habit of curbing your spending impulses. This talent will serve you well in economic downturns and tougher years. The economy won't always be awesome. Bad stretches will happen, and you won't get a heads-up on when they'll hit. Low expenses and fat savings will make these dips in the market easier to survive.

Rent Expensive Equipment Rather than Buying

For some creative skills, the equipment can be varied and expensive. Our dear photographer and videographer friends know this well. If you're strapped for cash, try renting equipment instead of purchasing. Many camera stores offer this option.

Saving for Freedom and Flexibility

For both your business and personal budgets, your goal is to make more than you spend. Eliminate your credit and loan debts as soon as possible, and start your "F*** You Fund." Michael Korda wrote an article for The New Yorker profiling Irving Lazar, a famous talent agent who represented the likes of Humphrey Bogart, Truman Capote, Faye Dunaway, and more. Lazar tells Korda, "The first million bucks you make—put it away! You don't ever touch that, you hear me? That's your 'F*** you' money. That way, anybody ever tries to make you do something you don't want to do, you can tell 'em, 'F*** you.'" Some iteration of this proverb is echoed across books and memoirs by all kinds of authors. Your number might not be the million Lazar recommends (we can't all be Bogart). But the point is, it's easier to choose your path when you have the financial freedom to say "no." Building up savings gives you the confidence to be more selective in who you work with, what you work on, and how.

But saving isn't just about freedom of choice. Having business savings could mean the difference between your business surviving economic downturns when work is slow or going bankrupt. When it comes to personal savings, this cushion of funds will help you navigate the many curveballs life can throw: an unexpected car repair, an unforeseen medical expense (are they ever foreseen?), a surprise expense for a dependent, etc. As much as possible, avoid debt, be smart about interest rates, and seek financial stability by making a plan for how you can save, save, save. Reminder: investing is not saving. Investing some of your savings can be lucrative, but it is also a risk, and there is no guarantee of a return. There's a reason it used to be called "speculation," so tread carefully, be informed before you invest, and maybe rewatch *Boiler Room* and *Wolf of Wall Street* for a healthy dash of skepticism.

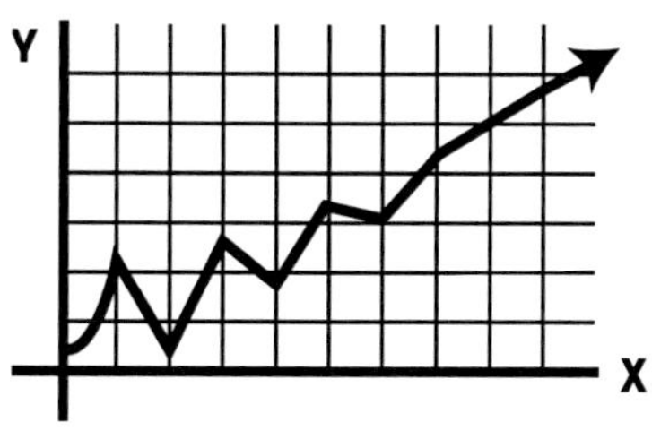

For the self-employed, retirement is something you also have to plan for. You won't be able to work forever. Just another reason to set aside as much as possible now.

Chapter Checklist:

① Make a personal budget.

② Calculate your personal yearly income goal.

③ Make a business budget.

④ Calculate your yearly business income goal.

→ Extra Credit: Set monthly or quarterly calendar notifications to check your profit/loss statements and acceptance vs. rejection rate of the proposals you've sent out.

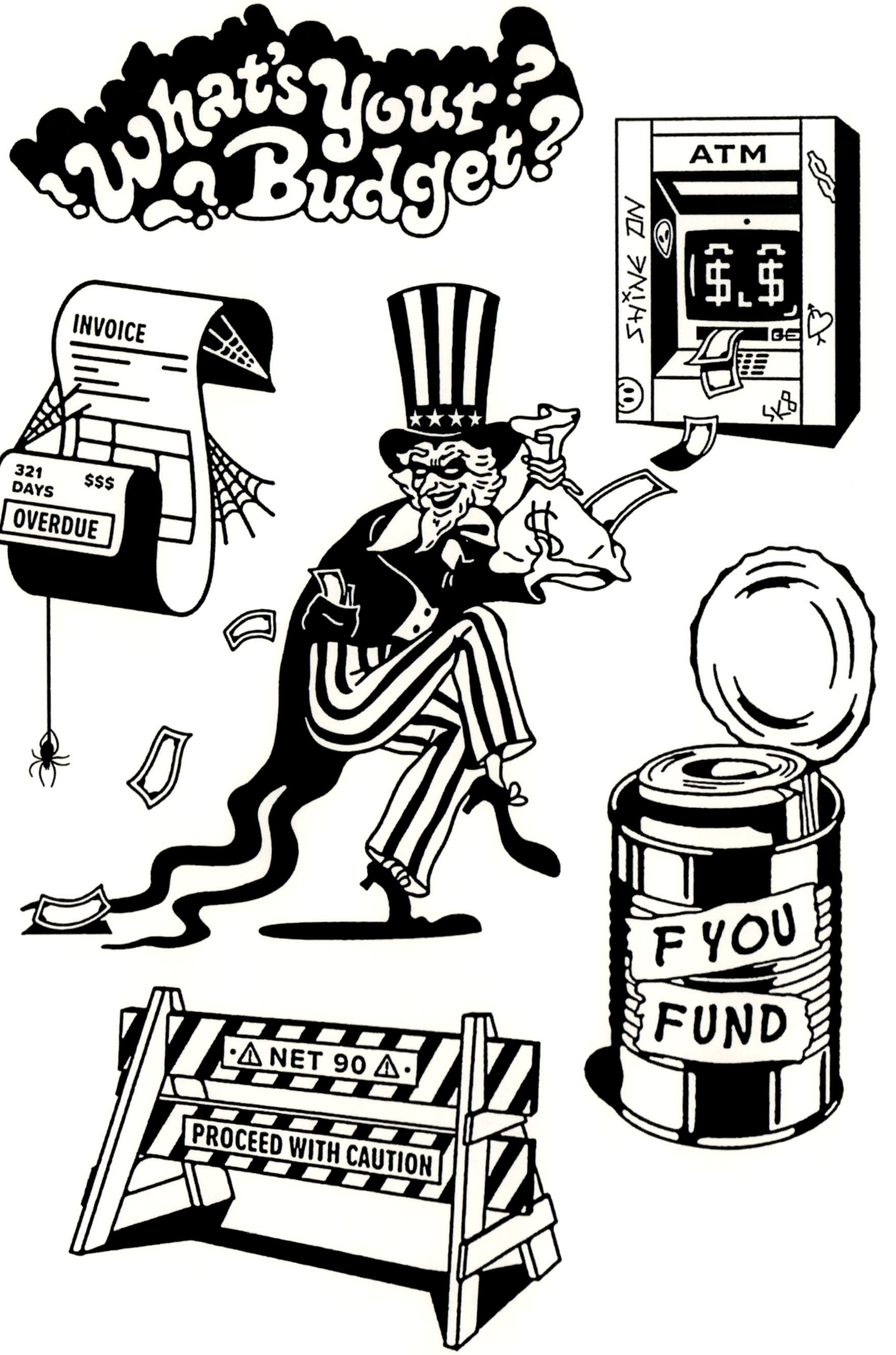

Illustration by: Lauren Griffin

4
Pricing

What to charge: That's the big question! Maybe it's the only reason you bought this book. There are an infinite number of right answers to this question, and it's not just down to the cost of your time and tools.

Your pricing should reflect the following:

- Your experience.
- The demand for your work.
- The level of skill required for your work
- The value of the project in relation to the client's business goals. Is the project a small initiative that will only be used internally for a short period of time, or something that will publicly represent the company long term?
- The rights and deliverables the client will get. Is the client licensing the work non-exclusively for a short term, or do they need a full buyout, exclusively, in perpetuity? Will the client get all working files, or only one final asset?
- The timeline. If it's a rushed deadline, that costs extra.
- And at the very least, the cost of your time and any tools or materials you'll need to perform the work.

Perceived Value vs. Cost

As much as you can, your goal should be to set your prices based on the value of your work, not just the cost of your time and tools. This is value-based pricing, and most creative studios and agencies take this tack for their banner services like web design, branding, marketing campaigns, photoshoots, and anything where the value of the end product or deliverable is greater than the cost to create it.

"Value isn't inherent, it's proven."

Of course, the value of your work is subjective. Especially based on who you ask. What you think your service is worth versus what a stranger thinks it's worth will be very different. Be careful not to define the worth of your services in the vacuum of your own opinion. If the majority of your potential clients are turning down your quotes, your price does not match their perceived value of what you do, right or wrong. So you have three choices: Lower your price to support your clientele's budget, better communicate the value of what you do, or look for clients that can support your prices.

When pricing, imagine yourself in your potential customer's shoes. What motivates them?

- Why do they need your service? What problem will it solve for them?
- What benefit will it bring them in terms of their own business's success?
- How will this service make their life easier and less stressful?
- What frustrations have they likely experienced without your service?
- Why should they trust you?
- How do they know they'll get a great end result for their money?
- How do they know you can meet their deadline?

These are the questions you want to preemptively answer in your brand messaging, via conversations and emails, and in client proposals before you reveal your price. Why? Because these assurances and answers set a potential client's mind at ease. It gets them thinking about the benefits gained from this service rather than the money spent.

Besides communicating the value of the project to your client, you want to show how you are uniquely suited to perform this service. Your goal is to present yourself as a valuable asset with invaluable skills and experience. How do you know what your worthy attributes are? Listen to your potential and existing clients.

- When new people connect with you, why do they reach out?
- Were they referred by another client who thoroughly enjoyed their experience with you?
- Do they want your specific style?
- Do they need your specific skill?
- Did they see a project you launched that was critically well-received, and they want a similar outcome?
- Do they want to work with someone with your caliber of clientele?

Start listening to compliments and feedback to refine your list of "pick me" qualities.

Promoting yourself and your value can be one of the hardest things to get comfortable with as a creative in business. It's not icky or gross to present yourself in the best possible way to win a project. Unless you're grossly misrepresenting the facts, of course. In all the years we've been in this industry, we've found most creatives tend to undersell their skills to their own detriment. However, with practice, you can become braver and more confident when talking about your services and qualifications. Instead of thinking about this from your own perspective, think about it from your potential client's. They want to know why you fit the bill for what they need. So frame your qualifications in relation to how you can help them reach their own goals. This will feel less "me, me, look at me" and more "this is why and how I can help you."

Without learning to communicate the benefits and value of what you do in relation to your audience's goals, you're left trying to capture clients with bargain-basement prices. When we started Hoodzpah, we were definitely not picky about work. We didn't have the demand or reputation that allowed us to be picky. We worked at cheap rates to build our portfolio and gain experience. But it's no way to live long term. Winning projects on cheap prices alone leaves you with a mercurial clientele who will drop you the minute they find a better deal. So we focused on visually and verbally communicating value, leveled up our website and proposals, practiced talking about ourselves, and slowly started reaching an audience that better valued our services.

Value-based pricing is not one-size-fits-all. If you were to give the same package pricing to two potential clients, one client might be unable to support the cost based on their income, while the other client may think the price is more than fair. For our most common services, we have set pricing tiers as starting points for small, medium, and large-sized businesses. Then, we customize further per client as needed.

Every person you talk to won't be a right fit for your pricing. You'll probably find pretty early on

A case for time tracking

Hear us out... it takes a long time to get comfortable with pricing, and a big part of that is just generally knowing how long different tasks will take. It's the most basic way to start formulating a quote (before adding for value, what-ifs, experience, etc.). So we dare you to track your time for your first year in biz. It's a great way to really have a grasp on your process for timelines and quoting but it's also amazing for calculating your profitability per project. You can postmortem your projects and figure out your actual hourly rate and further refine your quoting. It's also helpful when you are hiring subcontractors and want to offer a fair rate.

that the kind of clients you're excited about working with just don't have the budgets to support your pricing. A classic example is the music industry. We all want to work with bands on merch and album artwork. But the truth is, unless they're the top one percent of artists, they likely don't have a big budget set aside for merch. Same thing with non-franchised restaurants and bars. They often have very slim profit margins. Be careful about niching yourself into an audience that can't support your ideal rates. Cast a wide enough net to meet your income goals. Sometimes, you take on projects that aren't the most groundbreaking, but they come with a great budget. The income from these allows you to pursue lower-budget projects that you're more passionate about.

Value-based pricing works best with a flat-rate approach. Meaning there's a set fee for a set scope of work and deliverables. But flat-rate pricing isn't the right fit for every project. Let's jump into your pricing options.

Hourly Pricing

Hourly pricing is charging a client for the exact hours you take to complete a project, based on an agreed-upon hourly rate. Neither you nor the client knows the exact total hours required to complete the project. But if the client knows your hourly rate, you can give them an estimate of how many hours you *think* the project will take (emphasis on think). This helps clients get an idea of what they might owe so they're not shocked when the final bill comes. Many studios (including us) have two hourly rates, one for production work and a higher one for creative work where we are setting the art direction and creating something new. We rarely bill hourly for creative work (we almost always use a flat-rate quote based on value). But on the off chance we do, we use a higher creative hourly rate that accounts for the value inherent in making something completely new, as opposed to production-style work. This creative hourly rate can also be a great starting point for estimating flat rates. When working on a project at an hourly rate, remember to bill the client regularly—weekly, every two weeks, or monthly.

When to Charge Hourly

- **Creative projects with a scope you are unfamiliar with.** If you're truly not sure how long something will take, suggest doing a small portion of the project at an hourly rate to get a sense for the time it takes. This will help you put together a more informed flat rate quote for the rest of the project.
- **Production work with a vague scope.** Production work is not hugely creative. It's work that follows a defined style guide or template. You just need to carry out that style across more assets or make edits to existing work.

"Clients should never be shocked by their invoices. Send regular updates if you're charging hourly."

Pros of Hourly Rate

You get paid for every hour of work you do. There's no going over budget here. It's accurate and nixes the need to write up detailed scope-of-work documents and proposals (like in flat-rate quoting). You invoice based on 20/20 hindsight. We usually tell clients that we invoice in fifteen-minute increments (rounding up to the nearest fifteen minutes as we track time). Another thing to consider is implementing a minimum invoice fee. This is the minimum hours that must be billed on an invoice. Let's say your minimum billable invoice fee is one hour. If someone comes to you with a small job that only takes fifteen minutes, you'll still bill them for a minimum of one hour.

Cons of Hourly Rate

Your client may be shocked when they get the final invoice. This is why giving your client regular updates on time spent throughout the project is important. Try to avoid hourly work invoices turning into bad surprises. You can even give your client a loose estimate of how long you expect a project to take (a ballpark is fine—i.e., "about six to seven hours"). You don't have to itemize and explain the invoice like a flat rate quote. Let the client know that the estimate of hours is just that, an estimate, and that it is likely to fluctuate, but you will keep them updated. When giving an estimate, we always estimate on the higher end to account for any what-ifs. Updating the client on hours spent also encourages them to be more decisive with changes and edits because they can see the invoice growing. So set your invoicing terms up front (weekly, every two weeks, or monthly), and stick to it.

Your client may try to rush you. If the client knows they have to pay you for every hour worked, they may try to rush the project to get a smaller invoice. This doesn't help the creative process and will annoy you in general. Remind them that fast work doesn't equate to good work.

You may miss out on additional cash. If you charge hourly for work with a lot of value to the client beyond the hours you spend, you're missing out on some well-earned money you could have gotten with a flat rate for the project.

You might have to chase payments. With flat-rate projects, we always require a percentage up front, which keeps the payment ahead of our work. With hourly-rate projects, the work comes ahead of the payment. This is another reason we prefer flat-rate projects. We've had instances where clients just disappear and leave an invoice unpaid. It can be a pain in the butt to follow up on these unpaid invoices until they're resolved.

Flat Rate Pricing

Flat-rate pricing is a fixed price for a fixed scope of deliverables, regardless of the time it takes to complete the project. The second part (fixed scope) is key to a flat-rate project not turning into a runaway train full of burning money. With flat rates, the client knows exactly what price they'll pay and what they'll get for it. There's no question mark about what they'll end up spending by the end of the project.

When to Charge a Flat Rate

1. **The scope and deliverables of the project are clearly defined.**
2. You can accurately estimate the cost of time and materials it will take to complete the project. Usually, this is a service you perform regularly so you know the average amount of time that goes into it.
3. You want to charge a client for not only time and services but for value. For example, the logo is a core visual representation of a company. It is how the company will be recognized for years to come. Value and equity accrue every year that the logo is used

within a positive brand experience. Its value is often hard to measure. McDonald's golden arches, Coca-Cola's iconic script, Nike's famous swoosh—they're worth so much more than just the hours spent designing them. Why? Because they are intended to become the core reference point of a brand or company (at least this is our hope for any logo we work on). So you'd bill it at a flat rate, not hourly.

Here are some examples of services we charge a flat rate for (providing there is a clear scope of process, deliverables, and intellectual rights):

- **Logos and branding projects**
- **Illustration**
- **Photography**
- **A Research or Discovery Phase.** If a project is too big to be quoted without extensive research, charge a flat rate for a discovery phase. At the end of this phase, you have a game plan and a proposed quote for the next phase or the full project. This is good for projects where clients need help figuring out their goals and deliverables, but where the work is not appropriate to bill hourly.
- **Production work with clear parameters and deliverables.** For example, if you are laying out yet another pitch deck or catalog and you know roughly how long it takes to design per page, it may be worth creating a set price. It also gives your client the comfort of knowing exactly what the final invoice will be.

Pros of Flat Rate

Everyone knows the price tag. The client knows exactly what they'll pay for a specific outcome, and you know exactly how much you'll earn to perform and deliver that outcome.

You don't have to worry about tracking hours. With a flat rate, you don't have to invoice and update the client regularly on your time consumption. However, we still track time internally at Hoodzpah so we can make sure we're profitable with our set budget.

The price reflects the value. You can price the rate to reflect the impact and importance of the project to the client, not just your time and tools used to complete the project.

Cons of Flat Rate

Undefined scope cuts into your profit. If you haven't clearly defined the project scope, the client may use up more of your time than you expected, cutting into the profit of your fixed price.

You earn the fixed price, even if you underestimate your hours. If the project takes you longer to complete than you estimated, you still have to deliver what you agreed to for the fixed price. You might end up making less than you would have by charging hourly.

Clients might get sticker shock. A client may not perceive the value of the flat-rate price. A large lump sum can sometimes be shocking to clients who aren't familiar with your industry and don't know what to expect with pricing.

Retainer Pricing

Retainer pricing means charging a client up front to reserve a specified number of your working hours per month, usually over a long time period. Most retainers are at least four to six months long and are based on a certain amount of allocated hours per month (for example, twenty hours per month for six months). The price is usually based on your hourly rate and the total number of hours reserved. But you may offer the client a discounted hourly rate because they are paying in advance for guaranteed work, and as an incentive to book a longer term.

The retainer typically covers a range of pre-approved services, which clients can request to use the monthly hours toward. We typically only do retainers for production work, not creative. On most retainers, the monthly allotted hours do not roll over or accrue even if the client doesn't use all their hours in a month. If the client needs more hours in a month beyond the retainer cap, they have to pay our normal production hourly rate for any work exceeding the cap, and that's providing we have time in your schedule. The benefit to clients using a retainer is knowing you will be available for the specified hours and knowing they will get a certain level of priority in your schedule. Clients typically know they have an ongoing threshold of work they need you for, so they're willing to pay in advance to reserve your time, even if they don't always use that time each month. Without this, they might have to wait to get on your schedule.

Pros of Retainers

You get paid in advance. Self-explanatory benefits on this one.

The client knows what they're paying and what they're getting. Clients know up front what they will spend per month, per quarter, etc., and they know they will get a certain amount of your time and priority in your schedule. Plus, the client usually gets a slight discount on your hourly production rate for booking in bulk, in advance.

Guaranteed income. You know you have work coming in for the duration of the project. This takes away some of the stress about how you will bring in money during those months.

Less admin work. You don't have to make custom quotes, proposals, and agreements for every project. Instead, you have an ongoing agreement that covers a specific type of project or service.

You establish a rapport with the client. When you work continually with a client, you build trust and a common shorthand in how you work. You get to know them well enough to anticipate what they like, what motivates them, and what they need. This makes doing appropriate work for them easier. Working with a client you know is usually easier than working with a new client you don't have a dynamic with yet.

Cons of Retainers

You could miss out on new or more lucrative projects. The reliability of a retainer can also be a liability if a larger project request comes in and you don't have time in your schedule. It's a gamble to leave room in your schedule for a one-off project that could pay more for value versus filling your schedule with reliable retainer work that is nevertheless still hourly work. For this reason, as a branding studio, we keep a fair amount of room in our schedule open for new clients. However, we have an amazing designer on staff (Hey Arturo!) who mostly takes care of the retainer clients, so we don't leave that reliable income on the table. After we work with a client on branding, we often build such a great partnership that they want ongoing work (be it project by project or retainer). Having an on-staff designer makes this possible while leaving our time open as brand designers to work with new clients.

Retainer work tends to be less glamorous. This could take time away from projects that help move your portfolio forward so you can continue to grow your studio and attract new clients.

Unused hours can frustrate clients. If clients don't use as many retainer hours as they thought they would, it can be frustrating since the hours don't roll over, and they have to pay for them regardless of whether they used them or not. This is why we like to start clients on a non-retainer hourly agreement for a month to see how much work they generally need, then formulate a retainer agreement based on that test month.

Clients may get frustrated at how much time certain tasks take. What they think is an easy fix could take three or four hours. So they get frustrated when they don't see as much progress as they anticipated. Or they might have unrealistic expectations about how soon you can turn things around, even when they are getting priority on your schedule. We still charge retainer clients a rush fee against the retainer (so for every hour spent, we deduct one and a half hours from the retainer) if they need tasks returned in an expedited time frame. So if they email us at three in the afternoon and need a new ad turned around by the end of the day, we'll charge rush. Why? While we do give retainer clients guaranteed hours and priority in our schedule, we still have other clients and work to do. So rush projects have to be compensated as such. This encourages clients to still plan ahead as much as possible.

Familiarity breeds contempt. It's easy to take retainer clients for granted and for them to take you for granted. A long-term partnership thrives with respect and patience. But if a client is rude, has unrealistic expectations, or you start slacking because you're getting bored, things could turn ugly. Treat a reliable ongoing client with the utmost respect and encourage positive communication habits. These are your steadies.

Retainer Considerations

- Hours per month
- Percentage discount for pre-booking (if any)
- Types of work and projects covered in this retainer
- Turnaround time
- Does unused time rollover?
- Terms for hours over the retainer cap
- Terms for rush work
- Retainer length
- Payment plan
- Terms for termination

Retainer Equation

← Retainer Equation

Hours per month

× Production hourly rate

× Number of months

× Discount percentage

= **Retainer fee**

Sample Retainer

← Example

- **Hours per month and duration.** Twenty-four hours per month. Six months to be paid up front.
- **Rate.** Your retainer will be calculated based on our hourly production rate of $90, with a 10 percent discount for pre-booking.
- **Type of work covered.** Retainer hours can be used toward production work where the design request is based on pre-existing templates or current brand guidelines. This retainer does not include strategic creative work, foundational brand identity work, or original campaign creative developed from scratch.
- **Turnaround time.** Requested retainer tasks will be returned to the client within one to two days for most simple items. Turnaround may vary depending on the volume or complexity of the requested work. We will be sure to respond to any work requests within one business day to provide an estimate of the turnaround time.
- **Unused time.** Any unused hours at the end of the month will not accrue or roll over into the next month.
- **Added hourly work.** Hours above the retainer limit will be billed on top of your retainer fee at our hourly rate (non-discounted). We cannot guarantee we'll be able to take on all requested extra work beyond the retainer hours, but we'll do our best to accommodate.
- **Rush tasks.** Any tasks that must be turned around the same day will be charged against the retainer at time and a half. Example: One hour of rush work will count as one and a half hours against the retainer.
- **Termination.** Since we are turning away work to reserve time for you, termination will require a three-month notice. Once you give notice, you will have three months of your retainer left to use. Unused retainer months beyond the three-month notice will be refunded from the initial payment advance. Example: If you give notice of cancellation after one month of the six-month retainer, you will still have three months left to use. We will refund you for the two unused months.

24 hours per month × $90 (hourly production rate) = $2,160 per month

\+ $2,160 × 6 months = $12,960

\+ $12,960 × .90 (10 percent discount)

= **$11,664 retainer fee**

Subscription Pricing

Subscription pricing is charging a client a monthly rate to reserve a specified number of hours to use toward specific services and deliverables. The client continues to be automatically billed until they cancel the subscription. The price is based on either your hourly rate and the number of hours the client is reserving per month, or your fee to do certain services per month. Some subscriptions offer unlimited hours in exchange for a flat rate, which we wouldn't personally recommend. All you need is one zealous client requesting a ton of work, and you would be overloaded and unable to take on other clients.

Some people use the words "subscription" and "retainer" interchangeably. In our experience, a subscription is paid monthly with an ongoing contract that continues until a client chooses to cancel, while a retainer is usually paid in advance for a long but specific amount of time (it is not ongoing). Also, subscriptions can be easily canceled anytime. Retainers are much more structured, and there are monetary fees for canceling early. Usually, subscriptions are offered as a predefined offering that a client can purchase via a studio's website without ever talking to the studio runners. A retainer is tailored to a client's unique needs.

Pros of Subscriptions

The pros are very similar to the retainer benefits.

Cons of Subscriptions

Cons are also very similar to the retainer drawbacks.

- **Less reliability.** Plus, with subscriptions being easier to cancel, there's less reliability of the ongoing income.
- **More serious clients might question the quality of work.** Subscription pricing for high-value work, like building new websites, new apps, brand identity work, etc., could deter more serious clients from considering you as an option. It may sound weird, but when you can get something really cheap from one person that everyone else charges more for, you often question the quality of work. This could make you look small time.
- **Potential to be maxed out.** If you overpromise deliverables or time (like unlimited hours for a flat fee), you could max out your time for very little return.

Mixing and Matching Pricing Styles

Sometimes a project requires both a flat rate and an hourly rate. For example, at Hoodzpah, we charge a flat rate for visual identity packages. If we reach the end of the scope agreed upon in our contract, but the client needs some extra changes, we'll offer to continue revisions at our hourly rate and invoice separately. We even have it baked into all our contracts, so we don't need to draw up a new contract for the additional hourly revisions. We've already accounted for the value of the project in the original scope, so we don't mind handling small add-on revisions at a creative hourly rate.

Knowing when to bill a project as a flat rate versus hourly and how to accurately quote flat-rate jobs becomes easier as you gain experience. Tracking hours (even when doing flat-rate projects) will help you build and refine your flat-rate pricing by staying on top of how long it actually takes you to do things on average.

How to Calculate Your Hourly Rate

Step One: Estimate your Billable Hours Per Year.

"Billable hours" are hours worked that you can bill your clients for (creative time and project management time). "Non-billable hours" are hours spent managing your own business and taking care of your own thankless duties like bookkeeping, updating your website, putting together proposals, and so on (not to mention the occasional TikTok mental vacation or Instagram binge).

Estimate your billable hours for a week (if you're not sure what this is, start tracking your time and take the average of two to four weeks, or use a goal number for now). If you're freelancing full-time, your billable hours for a forty-hour week might only be thirty hours—thirty hours spent on work that you can bill a client for and ten hours spent on building and managing your own company. For part-time freelancers, it's best to tackle the following equations by thinking about what you would need to survive as a full-time freelancer. So use the thirty billable hours for the purposes of this equation. There are fifty-two weeks in a year, but you shouldn't be working all of them. You're not a robot (yet), just flesh and blood. Let's be European and account for at least four weeks off per year (for vacations, holidays, personal days, sick days, and other what-ifs). That leaves forty-eight work weeks in a year. Use the formula below to calculate your billable hours per year.

Weekly billable hours × 48 work weeks per year
= Billable hours per year (BHY)

Example: 30 weekly billable hours × 48 work weeks per year = 1440 billable hours per year

Step Two: Calculate your Baseline Hourly Rate

Refer to the Business Budget and Income worksheet in the previous pages for your business yearly income goal, and complete the equation below.

Business yearly income goal ÷ Billable hours per year
= Baseline hourly rate

← Hourly Rate Equation

Example: If your goal is to make $90,000 a year from freelance, then $90,000 divided by 1,440 BHY = $62.50 per hour

← Example

We call this your baseline hourly rate (BHR) because this is a starting point. This is probably a good starting rate for your hourly production work (low-creative work like updating templates, revising existing assets, etc.). You might need to raise or lower it depending on your experience, the demand for your work, and your skills. Adjust your BHR to what best suits you as well as what your audience can support/afford. It's all good and well knowing what you're worth, but if your target audience or the economy can't support it, you need to adapt and change course. Test your rates regularly, especially if you're really busy (raise them) or if no one is accepting them. If you can't land work at your desired rate, you might need to better educate your potential clients on why you're worth the investment Or you might need to lower your rate until you build up your portfolio/contacts. Or maybe the niche service or audience you thought you wanted to work with just cannot support the rates you need. We see so many new creatives desiring to work exclusively in the non-profit space. They niche all their marketing just for that type of client. But in reality, those clients barely make the income they need to do their own work and often have hardly any left over for creative services. Consider working pro bono for initiatives you care about, and use clients in other industries to bring in the money needed to support that work.

Also, consider that your calculated hourly rate assumes you're working every billable hour you have available. That might not be the case if you have slow months. It also doesn't account for flat-rate projects where you'll be making a lot more profit above the hours you spend.

Step 3: Calculate your creative hourly rate (optional)

Now that you know your average hourly rate, consider a higher hourly rate for creative work that requires more skill and has more value than production work. Like we said, we don't typically charge clients hourly for creative work, but it's great to have a general creative hourly rate in mind as a baseline for your flat-rate quotes. Then you can adjust for value.

How to Calculate a Flat-Rate Quote

You'll likely be unsure about flat-rating quoting as you start freelancing, but with time and experience, you'll get more comfortable. As we said before, we tracked all our time early on and still do, so we generally know how long projects take. This helps us fine-tune our flat-rate pricing and know how profitable we are on projects—based on actual hours worked.

Before you calculate your flat-rate quote, you need to have a clear picture of the project scope and goal so you can estimate the time and value. This usually requires some back and forth with the potential client.

Investigate and Ask Questions

If the project you're quoting is simple and straightforward, there may not be many questions to ask to come up with a flat-rate quote. But if the project is large or for a more established company, it's worth getting on the phone with the person inquiring to have a casual conversation. We like a phone call or video call for this initial inquiry because we can break the ice and start to build trust. The potential client can see our friendly faces and our excitement to learn about their project, and we can start to build a good rapport. Sure, they mainly want to know if we can do the work they need at the price they can afford, but never underestimate the human element. If we can make someone feel comfortable and understood on a call, that sets a great tone for our proposal. But if we come off as cold and uninterested, it could cast a bad light on any proposal I send. Clients want to work with people they feel they can trust and collaborate with.

The great thing about a live casual conversation as opposed to an email is that you can usually get more unguarded answers to questions about budget. Asking "What's your budget?" in an email is really easy for a potential client to avoid. But asking the same question after showing genuine interest in their company and project is harder to dodge. It's a less guarded situation where you are more likely to get good clues about the value this client puts on this project.

Here are some of the questions we like to ask potential clients prior to putting together a flat-rate quote (provided they haven't already told us in an intro email).

Tell me about your project and how it came about. The reason for a project is a great clue to the problem the client is trying to solve. Knowing their problem and desired outcome will help you communicate the value you're delivering in your proposal.

Tell me about your company. We like to go into meetings or calls with knowledge of the company. We look them up online so we can talk knowledgeably about their product or service. Then during our call, we'll say something like, "We saw you do *x* and *y*, and that you recently launched *z* to great success. We'd love to hear more about that." This is an easy and powerful way to create rapport and trust. If you know about them before they tell you, you show that you did your homework. You invested time to look into them. It shows you care and you're interested. People generally mirror back what you give them. If you are interested in the client and show excitement, it encourages them to be excited about you in return.

What's the desired outcome of this project? Usually, the goal reveals a lot about the project's value to the client and who their target audience is.

When are you hoping to start and finish this project?

Who will be involved in the decision-making? Surprisingly, this also impacts your price. If you have to present to and get approvals from fifteen different people in three different time zones, you know it will take a lot more work to gather feedback and get a consensus—not to mention the added time it takes to involve that many people via meetings.

What's your budget for this project?

We like to focus the beginning of the inquiry call on the potential client and what they have to say. It's so important that they feel like they are heard and understood. You wouldn't like going to the doctor only to be "talked at," with no room to explain how you're feeling or what you're experiencing. Getting a diagnosis without being able to explain your situation feels frustrating and hardly instills trust. Likewise, a client usually has a lot they want to communicate. They have high hopes for the project, and usually, there's some level of fear at the risk of choosing a creative partner. So listen first.

Once the potential client answers your questions, explain to them how you work, how your process usually goes, and about your experience. It can feel awkward, but the potential client is looking for cues that instill trust. Use their situation as an example as you explain how you would approach the project. Tell them how excited you are that they are considering you to help them on the project. End the call by telling them you'll send a proposal in a day or two. Now that you have your notes, you can formulate your flat-rate quote.

Flat Rate → Equation

Here's how we calculate our flat-rate quotes:

Estimated hours to perform the creative scope of work at your creative hourly rate

\+ Estimated hours to manage the project at your production hourly rate

+/- Size of the business

+/- Value of the project to the client

+/- Extent of use (licensing)

+/- Demand for your work

+/- Timeline (if it's a rushed timeline, you'll charge more)

+/- Buffer (because shit happens—this can mean adding 10–15 percent on top)

= Your flat rate

Let's go into each of these a little deeper.

How many hours do you need to execute/create the project? This includes sketching, strategy work, and prep time, plus execution of the creative deliverables and any rounds of revisions. Don't forget the time to export final deliverables.

How many hours will you need for project management? Depending on the project, management can take up to 50 percent of the total time, especially if there are a lot of people involved in making decisions. This includes meetings, phone calls (yuck), video calls (ack), making contracts, sending invoices, preparing proofs, presenting proofs, sending status updates, reviewing changes, clarifying client feedback, etc.

How big is the client that you are quoting, and what is the value of the project to the client? Value-based pricing usually scales based on the size of the company, the size of their audience, and the potential for your client to gain or grow from your creative work. The bigger the company, the larger the audience, usually the more potential to earn income or gain market traction from the work you create. When flat-rate quoting, consider whether the potential client is a large company with a huge market and audience, a medium-sized company, or a mom-and-pop shop with only a regional clientele. Their reach impacts their own income potential, which will impact what they can afford to pay you, which impacts your price. Try to learn about the client, their revenue streams, the goals of the project, and the target demographic. This will shed light on how valuable the project is to a client.

Also, consider that every project for a big client is not a high-value project. An internal flyer for Coca-Cola's employee softball team is much different than an external advertising campaign for the holiday season. The softball flyer reaches a very limited demographic and doesn't generate revenue for the company. The holiday campaign reaches a vast audience of Coca-Cola buyers and results in huge sales. Despite both being projects for a worldwide brand, one will have a low budget allocated to it, and one will have a large budget allocated to it.

Value-based pricing also scales higher for larger companies based on higher risk and the added attention and involvement a top-tier client requires. The amount of strategy and research that goes into a project for a large corporation is exponentially more involved than for a small mom-and-pop shop. The competitive analysis, the legal checks (if needed), the audience testing, and the presentations all require a high attention to detail. There are more people with approval power to convince. More checks and balances to go through to get projects shipped. And there is just more at stake. Big projects with bigger clients mean bigger risks, but they also mean bigger rewards.

To what extent will the client use your work? Just online? Just for a seasonal campaign? Or across all aspects of the brand going forward? The more use it gets, the more value it has and the more it should cost.

Is it a full buyout of your work (meaning they own the work in full and can use it to any extent, perpetually and exclusively), or is the client just licensing the work from you for limited use? If the client wants a full copyright buyout, this is much more than a limited license. More on licensing in a few pages.

Is your work in high demand? If so, you can justifiably raise your rates. Your time and talents are a limited commodity.

Do you have time, and does the client want the project done fast? If you already have a booked schedule and someone asks you for a quote, this can be an opportunity to ask for a higher rate than you normally would. You don't need the job. Maybe you don't even want it. And in order to do it with a full schedule, you'd have to work extra hours. So make the flat-rate quote a number that justifies the late nights and added stress. Use it as an opportunity to test higher pricing. Likewise, if a client wants a job done quicker than usual, then charge a rush fee. Same if someone wants work done over a weekend. Our rush fee is usually time and a half (your rate x 1.5).

Scaling Flat Rate Pricing for Small, Medium, and Large Clients

If you're unsure how to scale your pricing for small, medium, and large companies, here's a cheat code to get you started. First, calculate the baseline price you'll charge a small business for your service. That number will be x in the following equations. These are general ballpark figures to get you started, but be sure to consider nuance per client.

Small company price	=	x
Medium company	=	$3x - 4x$
Large company	=	$6x - 8x$

← Flat Rate Scaling Equation

Example →

As an example, let's say we're doing a spot illustration.

The scope for this illustration is

- Moodboard
- Two rough concept sketches
- Clean vector or raster proof of favorite concept
- One round of minor revisions
- Delivery of final files for print and web
- Full copyright transfer of the work to the client upon payment.

For a small business, like a restaurant with one location, we might charge them $500 for this scope. So $500 is our baseline "x" value.

Using our equation, we can find the medium and large-sized pricing for that same project scope.

Medium-sized-company rate: $500 x (3–4) = $1,500–$2,000

Large-sized-company-rate: $500 x (6–8) = $3,000–$4,000

Your Turn! Create a Flat-Rate Quote

Choose three services you do regularly (or plan to do), and scope them out. Write down the clear parameters of what the rate includes: strategy, how many initial concepts, how many revision rounds, the final deliverables, and the extent of use (full buyout or licensed). Then, calculate a baseline price using the flat-rate formula from the previous pages. After, you can calculate a tiered price for small, medium, and large companies.

Service #1

Service #2

The Graphic Artists Guild Handbook: Pricing & Ethical Guidelines is a resource that's updated almost yearly, with guidelines on pricing. Goodtype and AIGA also have pricing resources. There are also some studios sharing pricing rates and info on TikTok, YouTube, and Substack (Dan Mall, Amber Asay of Nice People, and Molly Jacques, to name a few).

Service #3

Example →

Standard Logo Package

Discovery

We'll work with you (the client) to zero in on and perhaps update some core principles about who you are as a brand.

The deck will outline our findings about the following:

- Target demographic
- Brand traits
- Core values
- Positioning among competitors
- Aesthetic moodboard to align on style

Logo

We'll present three unique initial concepts. From there, you'll choose one favorite concept and have up to two rounds of revisions to finalize.

Final Deliverables

Once you've chosen your final logo set, we'll save them in all the file types you'll need for print and web (CMYK, RGB, and Pantone). You'll be given full copyrights to this final logo design.

Typography and Color Proof

We will present you with two unique concepts, showing a sample layout with hierarchy of type, headlines, body copy, and color. You'll get two rounds of revisions of one chosen concept to refine and enhance. You will be responsible for licensing the final brand fonts for your own company's use.

Brand Guidelines

We'll summarize the foundational elements of your brand identity in a deck so you can have clear guidance on how to use your brand identity consistently and powerfully. This deck will include guidance on how to use your logo, typography, colors, design language, and any other deliverables we create for you during our scope.

Small company: $8,000

Medium company: $24,000 - $32,000

Large company: $48,000 - $64,000

Caveats and Adjustments to This Math

This method is not definitive. Each flat-rate-quote scenario truly is unique. But this method is a helpful way to make something nebulous more clear. Use it the next time you quote, then adjust the results to fit your specific client, project, and gut instinct.

Sometimes, even if the client is a big company, they still won't be willing to pay very well for work that could bring it great value. We've encountered a lot of very recognizable brands that leverage their name or popularity to try and get work for cheaper than you'd expect. They think, "Everyone wants to work with us, so we can find someone to do great work for cheap." We've been shocked at some of the budgets we've been presented by mammoth companies. On the other hand, you may be surprised at how much large companies with much less cultural relevance and brand recognition (like large real estate firms, industrial goods companies, or medical tech companies) are willing to spend on creative deliverables.

Consider what your audience is willing to spend for your creative service. Some services can support and justify larger prices than others, depending on the perceived value and how much long-term benefit they bring to your client. Traditionally, UI and UX work can garner much higher rates than, say, social media work. Brand Identity can support higher rates than illustration. Packaging can support higher rates than apparel designs. The longer you work in your industry and the more you learn from peers and mentors, the better understanding you'll have around these nuances.

Pricing Tricks

We started Hoodzpah back in 2011, so we've had a good chunk of time to test thousands of proposals and pricing scenarios. During that time we've garnered some favorite tricks to encourage people to approve a quote or approve a bigger scope. Really these are tactics, not tricks because they're used every day by plenty of industries. As with most things in business, it comes down to how you present it and how you brand it.

Pricing Tiers and Upsell Packages

Early on at Hoodzpah, we worked mainly with small companies and individuals. Most of our new business inquiries asked for "just a logo" rather than "a brand identity." This led to a portfolio full of, you guessed it, just logos. But in reality, our clients needed a brand identity. And we wanted to sell them on that larger package. But our portfolio didn't prove we could do it.

To get out of this catch-22 cycle, when someone asked us to quote them for "just a logo," we started offering three packages at different price tiers.

The baseline tier was just for the logo like they asked. And we called this something underwhelming like the "Bare Bones Package." The middle tier included a logo plus typography, color, and very basic brand guidelines. This middle tier was called something slightly more exciting, like "Branding Essentials." And we priced it only minimally more than the Bare Bones Package. In fact, it was such a minimal jump in price that a client would feel foolish not to chose this upsell. We made the Branding Essentials Package a deal that was impossible to pass up by comparison.

Then we added a third tier called something really exciting, like the "Pro Branding Package." This would include everything in the middle tier, plus two or three critical design assets. For example, if the client had a physical product, the added asset would be for packaging and point of sale display. If the client were a restaurant, the added assets would be menu designs, takeout packaging, and social media templates. Essentially, we would figure out the key touchpoints between the client and their audience and include those assets in the package to make it a high-impact return on their investment.

We were able to land the middle-tier Branding Essentials package more often than not, and we'd even book the top-tier package two or three times out of ten. This allowed us to show work with a broader scope in our portfolio, which got us out of the dreaded "just a logo" rut. If someone has three options—cheapest, most expensive, and somewhere in the middle—they'll almost always go for the middle option, especially if the price difference is slight.

As we grew our studio and reputation and started attracting larger projects, we didn't need to use this pricing method as much. Sometimes a prospective client asks you to quote such a large scope that it becomes difficult to offer tiered pricing. At this point, they usually have a decent budget, and this tiered method is no longer as applicable. In this case, we have another trick we like to use—we call it "the gimme."

Give the Client a "Gimme" or "Book-it-All Discount"

On proposals for large projects, we like to include one item as a gift or freebie. We'll usually line item the value, then put a strike through it with a note, "Our gift to you." This provides an incentive for them to book the whole package, rather than picking and choosing line items. And hopefully, it differentiates us from the other proposals they receive.

You can also use this tactic if a potential client seems unsure about the scope and you want to ensure they book you for more work rather than less. Example: A client tells you, "We need a visual identity rebrand, and we also may want to outsource the redesign of our website." The website is up in the air. They may opt to save money and do it in-house. So how do you sweeten the deal and persuade them to book you for the website and the rebrand? Offer a gimme line item for booking the larger scope. This isn't to say you give them the whole website design for free. But a small portion of the website. Or a certain percentage off the whole fee. It's like those late-night infomercials: "Buy our set of steak knives in the next twenty-four hours and receive a free knife sharpener!"

The gimme is usually a smaller line item. But it should have enough value to be a motivating factor. Something like a logo animation or a short logo reveal video. This is not only a great asset for our clients to share their new logo with their audience, it's something that will add value to our own case study. It's a win-win. To really sell the gimme, we'll include a link to some amazing examples of this item we've created for other clients. It's hard not to get hyped on the creative potential at this point!

Another less late-night infomercial way we approach this is by offering a "book-it-all discount" on large proposals. Perhaps we include an item in the quote that we really think the client needs, but which they did not directly ask us to quote. We know it will be very beneficial to the client, and we really want them to say "yes." So we'll include a line in the proposal like, "Book the entire scope for 8 percent off the total price." That might not sound like a lot. But when you're quoting things in the six digits, it makes an impact.

Licensing Your Work

A lot of people get overwhelmed by the idea of licensing their work rather than selling someone the full rights. Think of licensing as renting your work to someone. When licensing your work to a client, you give them the right to use it for a limited amount of time and/or to a limited extent, but you remain the owner. In fact, you can rent the same work to more than one person if you want to. In exchange for the limited use, the licensee/client pays a flat fee, a subscription, royalties, or whatever fee structure you agree to.

For example, when you see a *Star Wars* character on a Stance sock the image of that character is being licensed to Stance for that product. Lucasfilm Ltd. remains the owner of the copyrights. Otherwise, they couldn't license those characters to other companies for other products.

The key with licensing is to clearly define the limits of your license, which is where we get the term Limited License.

A license can be limited to

- a specific number of units (e.g., 50,000 T-shirts)
- a specific number of users (this parameter is often used for software, stock photos, font licenses, and music downloads)
- a specific type of product (e.g., only t-shirts)
- a specific geographic region
- a specific amount of time
- a specific medium (e.g., only online, not in print. Or only for LA store locations, not globally)
- a certain period of exclusivity (e.g., if Target licenses an illustration from you, do they want exclusivity too? Meaning no other brand can also license the work during the scope of their license.)

Creative services that are often licensed:

Photography. Let's say you do a self-directed photo shoot, then upload those photos to a stock photo site and sell licenses to other creatives to use them. Or you could get hired by a brand to do a photo shoot for them, and to make the price more accessible, you could license the photos to them under specific terms (for one year across all online use cases) If they want to continue using the photos ongoing or in broader use cases, you can charge them more.

Illustration and art. If you're a creative who is sought out for work that is your own unique style, you could license your popular work for things like notebook covers, posters, wrapping paper, puzzles, apparel graphics, pillows and bedspreads, etc.

Website themes. You could build a custom Webflow or Squarespace theme that multiple people can license to use for their websites.

More Resources on Licensing:

For more on this topic, Jessica Hische has an amazing book called *The Dark Art of Pricing* with a lot more nitty gritty on this topic. Goodtype shares so much free information on this topic on their site (good-type.us) and TikTok. They also have a course dedicated to a deeper dive called "Goodtype Art Licensing." The Graphic Artists Guild also has a great article called "License It" on their website.

Fonts. Most fonts you're familiar with are licensed products. I mean, how many of us have purchased Alkaline by Fort Foundry, or Degular by Oh no Type Co? Tons! We all bought a license to use it to a certain extent. But we as licensors don't own the copyright to these fonts.

Many creatives will create a dedicated portfolio for their licensing work. The great thing about creating this general work that anyone can license from you is that multiple brands can license the same work at the same time, which means you earn more income on the same creative asset.

While non-custom work made for a broad audience seems a more obvious choice for licensing, you can also license custom work for a specific client. Say Nike wants to hire you to create graphics for an upcoming marathon event in Los Angeles. If they don't have the budget for your full copyright buyout rate, you could specify a license that gives Nike an exclusive license to the work (so it can only be used by Nike), with that use limited to only the Los Angeles area (they can't promote or sell the work outside LA), for a period of one full calendar year. If the graphics are a hit and Nike ends up wanting to use the work for all their marathons in other cities in the future, you can negotiate a full buyout rate. It's a way for you to offer a lower price without losing the ability to make a future profit for expanded use. In this example, you can't license this creative work you made for Nike to their competitors (hence the "exclusive" license), but you are limiting Nike's ability to use the creative work by region and time period. If they want to broaden their license to use it longer or in more locations, they will have to pay you more for those expanded licensing rights.

Typeface designers too use limited licensing as a way to find a middle ground between a client's budget and their earning potential on a typeface. If a client wants a custom typeface developed but can't afford the full buyout, a type designer might offer a limited three-year exclusive license, which is a more affordable option. After three years, the client can either renegotiate a license for more use, buy out the full rights to the font if they really love it, or simply not renew their exclusive license. If the client doesn't renew, the type designer is free to license the font to the public or other clients.

Certain creative services don't suit licensing. Logos are a great example of a project where the client needs to own exclusive and full rights to the final output in perpetuity (legal speak for forever). A custom app or website design you make for a client like Nike would be a full buyout, not a license. Because they want to own that design exclusively and on an ongoing basis, without any limits. However, if you develop a website platform, you could license that platform to Nike, as well as other clients. For example WordPress and Squarespace are platforms many different users can pay to have licenses to use and build off of. The users don't own that code or platform, but they probably exclusively own the design they implement on top of it.

To Free or Not to Free

Some creatives are adamantly against doing free work. However, in very rare circumstances (emphasis on very), it can be okay and even exciting. Just be cautious about how you give these freebies away and who you give them to. It should be someone/something you want to invest in. Perhaps it's a good cause close to your heart or the opportunity to test and execute a skill no one thinks you can do. Or maybe it's a collaboration with a friend for a passion project where you're both investing your talents pro bono.

The Case for Doing Free Work

1. You get to stipulate that the work is your gift and, therefore, subject to your style and whims (client feedback is not allowed or very minimal). You get to play creative director and are in complete control of the end product. Of course, you shouldn't use the freedom against the client's best interests. The freedom should still result in something that works for the brand. And ideally, the client should like the end product enough to use it and give a good testimonial. After all, we're commercial artists, not fine artists.
2. You get to potentially help out a friend, charity, or family member with a job. This is either fulfilling, racks up valuable IOUs for the future, or both!
3. You get to work on a project you're passionate about (hopefully).

If you offer someone free work, stipulate in the deal that they promote you in return. For example, you create a logo for them, and in return, they give you a designer credit in the footnote of their website with a link to your portfolio site, they promote you three times on their various social media platforms, and once in their weekly newsletter. This could result in new business leads for you from their audience. It's a great way to make a one-sided deal into a win-win for everyone.

The Case Against Free Work

1. If you don't get something out of the free work, you will most likely find yourself feeling resentful and used. This could impact relationships.
2. You risk miseducating the person on the value of your work. Be sure that if you do free work for someone, you first explain the value of it and what you would normally charge. The key here is making them feel the value of your service.
3. You don't want someone telling everyone they know that you're the dummy who works for free. The person you donate work to should know how you prefer them to talk about your working arrangement to others. Either have them phrase it as a charitable donation or be sure they know the actual price you charge so they can relay that to inquiring parties.

The Case for Bartering

Unless it's a straight-up gift or donation, almost everyone has something they can barter for your services. This is why we love to barter rather than do things completely for free. It gets the other person to have some skin in the game. This ties your work to something of value to them, making the exchange more equally balanced. It also gives your bartering partner an idea of the price of your services in case they ever refer you to a friend or colleague. Bartering can be a great tactic with restaurants or coffee shops you frequent. Sometimes we would use this as a negotiating tactic for a portion of the project price. If a client couldn't afford our full rate, we would take 20 percent in trade.

Feast & Famine

The only thing that is constant is change. The economy is not immune from this. There are highs and lows, and you likely won't see the lows coming. There are times when certain services surge in popularity (remember the mural craze? It's doubtful there are many blank walls left out there with the amount of murals we've been laying down). There will be times when the getting is good and you'll have more work than you can handle. And then there will be times when your steady moneymaker suddenly dries up.

Depending on the state of the economy, a change in your industry, or just an unpredictably slow month, you could take on work at a lower rate than usual. If it's a slow season and people are declining your normal rates, but you want money coming in, counteroffer a reduced rate for a revised project scope. This compromise could win back the job for you without cheapening your value or services. It's nothing to be ashamed of. This is adapting.

The alternative? You can stick to the value of your services regardless. If you have built up a nest egg, you can ride out a few slower months. But be on guard. If you go through a few consistent months when no one accepts your proposals, reconsider your pricing, your services, or how you're communicating value. If you're not careful, sticking to your guns might stick you out of business.

If you pass on lower-paying jobs while waiting for work at your target rate, use your downtime wisely. Update your marketing tools (website and social being key ones). Send cold emails and reach-out messages. Work on your passive income streams and products. Freelancers often get addicted to being busy. But sometimes, downtime can be just what you need to jump-start your personal projects, create your own products, or learn a new skill. Maybe you'll realize business is slow because some of your services are becoming obsolete. What's an in-demand skill you want to learn but haven't had the time? Or maybe you want to create your own course, or font, or book, but haven't had a spare minute. If you have the savings, take this time to work on you! We'll talk more about passive income and products in a future chapter.

Talking about Pricing Before You Quote

The Pre-Quote Pricing Conversation

Talking about pricing with potential clients can feel awkward. Remember the nervous feeling of asking someone out? It's that same energy. And the same advice applies to both.

- The more natural the conversation, the better.
- The more you do it, the better you get at it.
- You don't want to be aggressive or desperate. Try to convey calm confidence even though it may be far from what you feel.
- Come prepared. It's as simple as a bulleted list of questions you need answered to provide an accurate quote. Be prepared with how you'll respond if they ask about your pricing, timeline, or process and how you'll handle any negative or hesitant feedback. Hints on this to follow.

If you're too freaked out to talk in person or over a call, start out using email. But the ultimate goal is to learn to talk about pricing in real time, either in person, over video call, by phone, or by whatever hologram tech brought 2Pac to Coachella. You may be thinking to yourself,

"What were computers created for if not to shield me from the pressures of being social and charming off the cuff?!" We feel you. We see you. We too fear the sound of a phone ringing without warning. But there are some real benefits to the live pricing conversation before you prepare a quote for someone.

People are never what they seem on paper, and neither are projects. This premise has kept the MTV show *Catfish* running for twelve years and counting. Written text will give you a mere fraction of what you can learn by talking with someone live. On a phone call or video call, you'll hear their tone of voice and learn their personality. You'll get a sense of the potential client's desired outcomes and their attitude toward you, your work, and the project. When talking with someone live, they'll often overshare and be more transparent about budgets and expectations than they would in writing.

Real-time conversations about pricing allow you to start building rapport with the potential client. Hopefully, your personality and professionalism shine through, easing their fears and planting the seed that you could be a good collaborator. Potential clients are just like you. They want this project to go well. They want to impress their higher-ups, and they want to keep their job. You are a part of that equation. What you reveal on your call can ease their mind and create a positive rapport before you send your proposal.

In just ten to fifteen minutes on a phone call, you can also understand if you're a good fit for the project and gather clues to help you prepare a quote. Here are a few things this quick intro call could save you from:

- Spending two to three hours making a proposal for a project that isn't even a good fit for your studio.
- Underbidding or overbidding because you misunderstood the proposal request or didn't know the context of the project.
- Sending a quote with no personal connection. If the potential client has never spoken to you or seen your face, your proposal doesn't have the benefit of the human connection that can do a lot of heavy lifting. When a client is comparing proposals of similar price and value, it often comes down to preference, impressions, and gut instinct. Those are human factors you can sway by making a connection with someone from the beginning.

Pricing Conversation: Mindset and Methods

Here's some good mindset prep before you talk to a lead about a project.

If you're feeling panicked or worried, remember this: The potential client asked you for the quote. The basics of commerce are supply and demand. You know you can supply the service, and now someone is demanding a price. This means they already think you are a good candidate; otherwise, why would they reach out? There's no need to wonder, "Am I good enough?" The lead has told you that you are good enough by their standards because they're willing to explore paying you for your service.

Remind yourself of the value you're providing. You can do something that others need, which they don't have the time or skills to do themselves. You do not have to be the best, the cheapest, or the most popular to make a case for why your skill can benefit a potential client. Try not to fall into the dark spiral of self-doubt. Think about all the ways your service could benefit your lead before you talk to them on the phone. The person you're going to talk to also knows your value to some extent. That's why they're reaching out. They already anticipate that the work you do could provide a positive return. And they're willing to pay some price for it. So try to understand their perspective of what they hope to get out of working with you, which will hint at the value they place on the project.

Remember, how you behave and interact with the lead is as important as what you say. This conversation is as much about your lead sussing you out as it is about you vetting them. They will also be picking up context clues and reading between the lines of what you say. So try to approach them warmly, and with a positive interest in their project.

Now for the more tactical methods of your call. In the Proposal chapter, we give you a list of questions to ask leads in order to prepare a quote and proposal. Refer to that list before your call. Here are some broader things to consider for your pricing conversation.

Budget questions. You should always, always ask this question by the end of the call: "What is your budget for this project?" It's a coin toss as to whether the potential client will honestly tell you, but nevertheless, you must try. Whatever they say can be helpful, even if it's not a hard number. Try to ask this at the end of the conversation rather than the beginning. Even though it's a perfectly valid question for a business conversation, it can come off as abrupt or invasive if it's unleashed too early. Try to establish a comfortable conversation first.

Research and prepare. Five to ten minutes of research on a lead can be all it takes to protect yourself from making stupid errors and separating yourself from the pack. Learn what the potential client's company does. Look up their website. Look up news articles about them. Look at their social media, and dig like you're investigating your best friend's new crush. This recon will help you speak knowledgeably to the potential client about them in your pricing conversation. It will show you took the time to learn about them before they paid you a cent. That will go a long way in establishing trust. People want to work with someone who is interested in them and values what they do. It's a simple, human truth. We have sometimes skipped this step and accidentally called a person the wrong name or misidentified their industry, and it is a bad look that is hard to recover from. A simple misstep can really ruin the mood.

Have a price range in mind. You don't have to tell a potential client your price on the first call, but you should have a range in mind. Based on how the pricing conversation goes, you might share this range. If you feel that the client is expecting a much lower price than you would likely quote, you can give them a range of what they can expect to pay. If they say, "That is much more than I was expecting to spend," you can either make a case for the value of the project or you can refer them to a more junior creative who could work within their budget. If a potential client won't share their budget and we are unfamiliar with their industry or some of their deliverables, we will usually hold off on sharing pricing info until we've had more time to research. We let the lead know we'll go through our notes and prepare a proposal to send in the next few days. This is fine and normal.

Prepare to talk about your process. Get used to clearly explaining what goes into your process, why you're qualified, and what people can expect from the experience. Don't think of yourself as a puffed-up blowhard. Think of it as honestly explaining what you do, and how you differ from other options out there. People are honestly looking for this kind of reassurance.

- **Your scope:** Sometimes, a price can be justified simply by the work involved. Potential clients may not have any clue what goes into your services. Explaining the process can reveal the value in relation to the price.
- **Your specialties:** These are skills or capabilities that are not industry standard: At Hoodzpah, a specialty we often tout is our ability to do custom type in our branding work. Our custom type skills mean we make wordmarks unique to each client—exactly what they want, not just what's available. This has been a huge selling point for us and a way to prove the value of a price.
- **Your experience:** Explain your expertise in relation to the competition. A lead might never have worked with someone in your field before. They don't know the industry rates or if your prices are competitive. So don't be afraid to tell them. One of the best phrases we ever uttered (and then continued to utter on almost every pricing call afterward) was, "We're not as cheap as a young freelancer, but we're more competitive than the big agencies, and we deliver work that is just as good as those big agencies." That one sentence told our client they could go cheaper for a less experienced freelancer and also poised us as a value option compared to the big-name agencies. Suddenly, a price out of context seems like a good, middle-of-the-road option.

If a client asks you a question you are unprepared for or don't know off the cuff, it's OK to say, "I'll look into that and follow up via email." Other alternatives: "Let me talk to my business partner and get back to you," or "I'll look into it once I'm back at my office and get you an answer as soon as I can."

You're allowed to tell someone you are not the right fit for the project. Many pricing conversations may lead to this conclusion. Save yourself and your lead time by just being honest about it. You could say something like, "In learning more about your project, I don't think we'd be the right fit, but I'd love to refer you to some people who may be." We've had people be so grateful for referrals like this. If they ask why you're not a good fit, you can respond with things like:

"Our packages are more involved than what you are looking for." This is a common response we give to people whose projects are a little too small for us.

"After learning more, I don't think we have the bandwidth or team to give you what you need on this project."

Negotiating

If a prospective client doesn't give the green light on your pricing, don't worry, it's not the first time and it won't be the last. It happens to everyone. The lead may say, "We can't afford this," or "Is there any way to bring this price down?" This is where negotiation can come into play.

Trim Cost by Trimming Scope

If your price was miles and miles away from what the lead expected or could afford, there may be too great a divide to bridge through negotiation. But usually you can get your price down a little by slimming the scope. And this is important: Negotiation involves compromise on both sides; otherwise, it's just surrender.

If you lower your price without any change in your scope or deliverables, the client will think the price was arbitrary—made up. They'll no longer see the price tied to definitive deliverables with a set value. You'll go from a skilled expert to a cheap hireling in their eyes. Now the conversation is no longer framed by value and expertise and is instead a game of "How low can you go?"

Trim the cost by proportionately trimming the scope or deliverables. Remove a round of revisions. Remove the least important items from the scope, and propose saving them for a second engagement at a later date. Suggest a change to licensing terms if that fits the project type. Scope adjustment has won back more jobs for us than we can tell you. In fact, we like to pad in an extra round of revisions in most of our packages, so we have an easy point of negotiation if needed.

Focus on Process, Benefits, and Risk

When negotiating, highlight the value and long-term benefits your work could bring to the potential client. Sometimes negotiation is just helping a client understand how involved a project is and what results they can expect in the end. Contrast the risks that come with hiring a cheaper, less experienced service provider. Here are some examples:

- "Sure, you could find a cheaper price, but in our experience, the cheaper rates are a patch job instead of a proper job. That means you'll be redoing this again in three years instead of getting something of quality that lasts." This is somewhat specific to branding, but you can see the thinking and adapt to your service.
- "Our rates are what they are because we are tried and true, and we have the portfolio to prove it. We really go above and beyond to ensure our customers get great work that suits their brief. That's why we've been able to work with companies like *x*, *y*, and *z*."
- "We're not the most expensive, but we're not cheap either. You won't pay a bloated agency price with us, but you will get agency-level work."
- "If you use a big-name agency, you often end up getting junior designer work pitched by a creative director. Creative directors at these places focus on their big fish clients and pass off smaller work like yours to the junior designers. At our studio, you are our big fish and will get the highest quality work from us, the principal creatives."

A harrowing anecdote can also work wonders. Every industry has its tragic lore. Here's an example: Tropicana launched a huge rebrand in 2009 with all-new modern packaging. They dropped the friendly arched wordmark and big juicy orange with the straw for a sterile, almost medicinal new look. Sales dropped by 20 percent. They had completely missed the mark, and before you could say "fresh squeezed oranges," they had reverted back to the original branding.

All that time and expense only to have to can it all. Referencing stories like this can show your client why choosing the right partner with the right expertise is so important.

Contextualize the Price

A lot of times, a potential client balks at a price for creative work simply because they have no experience or context for what it should cost. Meanwhile, they would happily pay much more for things like office space and equipment. So try to communicate the price in terms they can relate to.

For example, we once quoted a photographer on a logo design. When we sent the proposal and quote, the photographer seemed shocked at the price, saying it was "way more than I thought it would be." But we knew they charged similar rates for their photography sessions. We responded with, "The brand identity package will define how people perceive your company for the next ten-plus years of your business, and you'll likely be able to recoup the cost by booking one or two wedding shoots."

Another example: We quoted a brewery restaurant on a new brand identity package that included a logo, messaging, website, packaging, and more. The cost seemed high to them as an arbitrary number out of context. We explained that their brand identity presence would be the touchpoint between them and their customers for a decade or more, both online and offline. Just like their physical restaurant space, the identity needs to set the right mood and appeal to the right audience. We encouraged them to think of their identity in the same way they think of their physical location. The identity probably costs the equivalent of six months' rent in their location, but it would last them years and years more and help determine how many customers they get in the door. They could likely pay off the expense by one good month of business. This helped them consider the value in a new light.

Don't be afraid to walk away from a client if you really think your price is fair. Sometimes, potential clients may ask you to lower your rate just to see what happens. And this bluntness probably often works for them, like haggling at a garage sale. We have pushed back on a few quotes we knew we couldn't go lower on, and the potential client ended up moving ahead with us anyway. We didn't realize it, but we had called their bluff. We showed ourselves as confident in our offering and price, and people want to work with confident and capable collaborators. It also set a great tone for our project, because they knew we would stick to our convictions. It gave them a healthy level of respect for our input throughout the process.

Raising your Rates

At the beginning of your creative career, your rates will likely be lower than you want. You are just trying to win new clients, build a portfolio, and gain experience. But it won't last forever. Regularly test the boundaries of your rates, growing them in step with your experience, client roster, and talent. Don't stay in the same pricing model purely out of fear. A gallon of milk doesn't cost the same as it did five years ago, and your rates are no different.

Signs That You Should Raise Your Prices (Flat Rate or Hourly)

1. **The inquiring client is a larger name or company than you usually work with** For the reasons mentioned in the previous sections about value, you would charge them more than you would a smaller client.
2. **The inquiring client wants you to "do you."** If you start getting quote requests because of a unique style you are becoming known for, you're being looked at as an artist versus just a service provider. You likely have your own audience and reputation that clients want to leverage. There is a huge amount of value here. They're not bargain shopping for the cheapest option. They want you because you are uniquely qualified.
3. **You're getting more work than you can handle.** If so many people are saying "yes" to your quotes that you have to live off of three hours of sleep and work nights and weekends, then raise your prices. If you're booked out two to three months in advance, raise your prices. If landing work is too easy, try raising your rates. Adjust rates for your limited resources (time, creativity, and sanity) and the growing demand for your work.

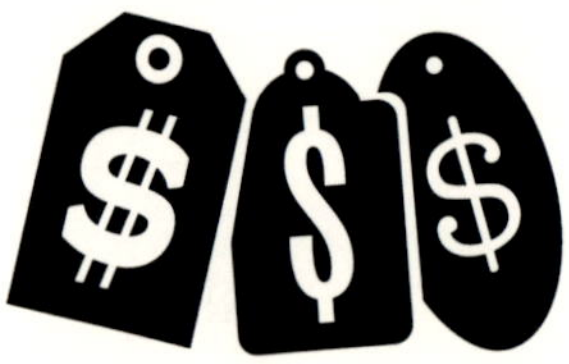

If you test a higher flat rate with a few new potential clients, the worst that can happen is you get a few "nos." You can try to negotiate the price down or potentially lose the client. This is why we like testing out higher prices when we don't need the work or don't want the project that badly. If it's a "meh" project or you're fairly busy, try upping your rate by 30 percent and just see what happens. If you land it, it will be worth it at least.

When you tell existing clients about a raise in your rates, explain things honestly and simply. Usually, it will be something like the following:

"You may notice the rate I quoted you is different from what we have done previously. I have recently raised my rates for the first time in *x* years to better match my experience, the quality of work, and our costs of doing business."

You don't have to apologize or overexplain.

When you raise your prices, you will likely lose some clients. You don't have to leave them high and dry. You can refer them to a trusted creative peer who's maybe a few years behind you in their creative journey and offering lower rates. You help your client and do a solid for your friend/colleague. It's a no-brainer.

But why are we looking at this purely from the negative? The best-case scenario is that they say, "Yes!" At this moment you'll wonder, "Why didn't I do this sooner?" or even, "Shoot, could I have gotten more?" You grubby little devil, you. You can test your limits again next time. Once you've quoted and the client has approved, don't get caught in the FOMO trap of begrudging the client that you didn't get more when you got what you asked for.

By raising your rates, you'll likely lose some clients, which makes room for new clients with bigger budgets. That's growing your business! This is not taking advantage but leveraging your skills and demand for the best return. We don't say Lebron James is taking advantage when he signs a two-year $100 million contract with the Lakers. That contract is earned through hard work and league-leading performance. We say, "Get that money! Keep racking up those triple-doubles! Get you another championship ring!" Cheer yourself on the way you'd cheer your favorite player on.

Chapter Checklist: To Do

① Calculate your hourly rate.

② Scope out and flat rate your three most common services.

③ Consider if any of your clients would benefit from a retainer for ongoing hourly production work. Scope a retainer proposal to review with them.

④ Consider what creative work you could license.

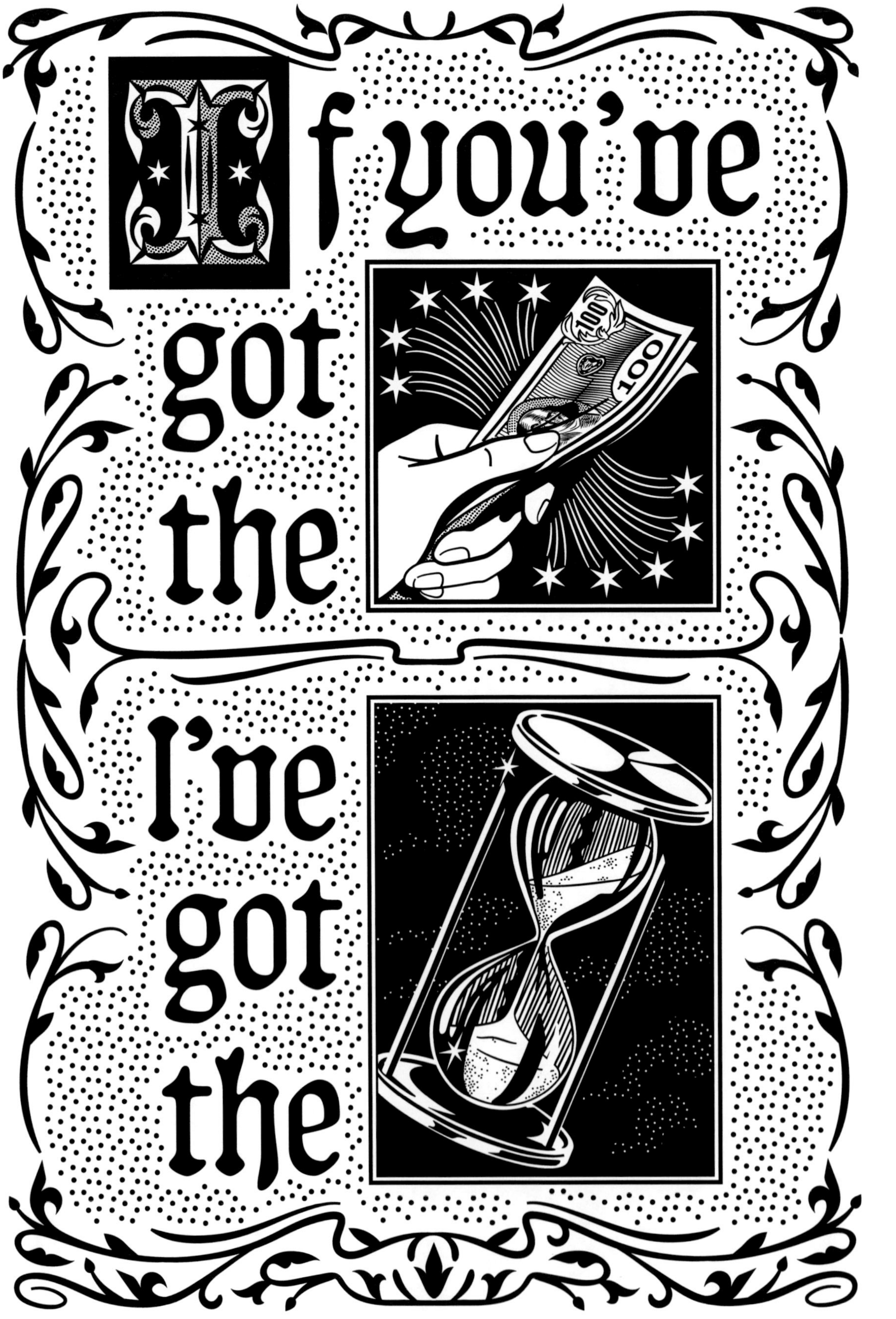

Illustration by: Amy Hood

5

Proposals: More Than a Quote

A huge part of proving the value of your pricing is your proposal. A quote presents the cost and scope, but a proposal contextualizes the value and process behind the quote. This is where you prove why you're the right fit for the client and how you can help solve their unique problem.

Quoting people is hard. Knowing what number to quote someone is subjective, and changes depending on who the client is, what the work is, how long the work will be used, whether it's licensed work or a full buyout, how many rounds of revisions, and so on. Ack, blah, blargh. But even when you feel your quote is right, the work is not done. Now you need to present it to the client. You can just send an email with the project scope and price typed out or as an attached doc or PDF. We used to do this when we first started our business. Understandably, we weren't booking much work. And the work we could book was really small, with people already familiar with us. We quickly realized that this quick-and-dirty method of presenting pricing was leaving a lot of room for misunderstanding between us and the client.

Why?

- It looked like we put little to no effort into the proposal.
- The price and scope had no context that proved why the price was worth it to the client, and would give them a beneficial return.
- We weren't proving that we were invested in their unique situation and project.
- We weren't proving that our unique skills were perfect for their project.

If you truly feel your work is good and your rates are fair, but you're not landing projects, it's probably down to one of these reasons:

- The client doesn't think they can afford you. (You need to prove the value of the project/ service to them in terms of their outcomes.)
- The client truly can't afford you. (You need to consider a broader or different target audience.)
- The client doesn't think you're worth the price, or your skills aren't up to the task. (You need to prove the value of your experience, service, and skills.)
- The client doesn't think you understand their unique needs. (You need to show you understand their project goal and what they need.)
- The client doesn't think you can deliver at the scale of a larger studio. (You need to frame your "small" studio or freelance position as a strength rather than a weakness).

We started using a proposal presentation deck to bridge these gaps, answer questions, and overcome doubts. A good project proposal includes the following:

- A simple and clear outline of the client's problem.
- A synopsis of the project audience and goals.
- Your general process.

- A little about you or your studio: testimonials, awards, media features, and experience.
- Portfolio examples of relevant work with markers of success. Choose work of a similar style or scope to the client's request or from a similar industry.
- An estimated timeline.
- A detailed scope and price.
- Any notes on important terms and conditions (payment milestones, deposit requirements, callouts on things your quote does not include, etc.).

Our transition to using this kind of well-paced, compelling presentation deck has been met with amazing feedback from potential clients. Many have said our deck was far and away the best one they received in response to their RFP (Request for Proposal). That's when we knew we did something right. We started landing more work and bigger projects. We confidently tested higher rates, knowing our presentation backed up our price.

Here's why a great proposal works so hard for you: It proves you're investing in knowing and serving a client before they even hire you. It shows care, diligence, and understanding. Also, many times the person you talk to about a project is not the final person who decides whether or not you land the project. A producer, project manager, or art director may reach out to you for a quote, but they have to review it with their team, their bosses, or even investors to get final approval. You can't control how your contact at the company portrays you to their team and boss. But you can control how you present yourself in your proposal deck. If you give your contact a great asset to use when presenting you to their team, they'll likely use it.

Your proposal controls the pace of how you tell your story, so much better than a quick cover letter and a price outline on a piece of paper. It forces the person reviewing it to build up to the price. They learn about you, see what you can do, learn the value of what you do, and then they see your price. It's a controlled presentation, no matter who it gets handed to and what information they have about you. Before we go deeper into this format, let's talk about how to vet potential clients and gather the information you need to make a great proposal.

Everyone Doesn't Get a Proposal: You're Not Oprah

Insert the Oprah "You get a car, and you get a car" meme here. Even when you have a proposal template, making the needed customizations for a client takes a decent chunk of time. It's an incredibly necessary step to land bigger projects, but it can easily suck up a lot of your time. Don't feel like you have to make one for every quote request that comes in. We work for ourselves because we love the creative work, not the admin work.

You'll likely know which projects definitely deserve a nice custom proposal: the big names, the big scopes, and the serious emails with a clear brief or an attached RFP.

We typically only send proposals for value-based projects, meaning projects where we have to prove value beyond the time and materials to accomplish the work (see pricing chapter for more on this). We wouldn't cook up a huge proposal just to get an hourly gig revisions on a

Pricing Tips from Some Pros

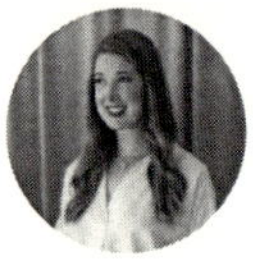

Amber Asay
Founder / Creative Director, Nice People

nicepeople.com

→ It took a good three or four years into working for myself full-time before I got confident in my pricing. **Now I charge five to eight times what I did at the beginning.**

→ We always provide three tiers as pricing options, placing their budget in the bottom or middle tier depending on the size. This ends up becoming a good upsell strategy because after they've filled out their ideal pricing on an intake questionnaire, and after I've shifted their mindset of how much their project would cost on a call, the tiers become one last way to stretch their budget to the Deluxe tier. In the past I've managed to turn initial $20K budgets into $80K projects.

→ **My goal is to add at least ten percent more to the project along the way.** We usually point out we can add x,y, or z to their project when we're further in. Especially if those are deliverables they decided to forego at the beginning. At this point in the project we've gained their trust, are either half-way or near the end, and they usually say yes.

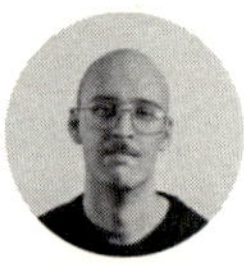

Soren Iverson
Founder at Iverson

iverson.inc

→ If you're just starting out, billing at more competitive rates allows you to build your book of business faster. Once you have high demand, you can increment prices up. This will likely involve dealing with some tough clients at the beginning of your career, but you learn a lot through this early work.

→ As a freelancer it's easy to mix personal feelings and your identity with work because people are approaching you for a service. Once I built the agency, it became more professional and less personal when a prospect didn't have budget.

→ **Generally, we try to align ourselves as client partners rather than an inflexible vendor** so we can have open and honest conversations about pricing. In a digital-first world it's easy to read into things that aren't actually there in an email. **I'm a big proponent of just picking up the phone and calling people, which makes conversations around price easier.**

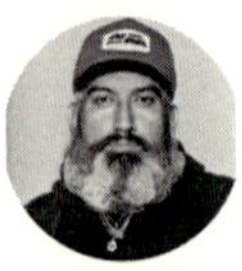

Francisco Reyes Jr. AKA Never Made

nevermade.com

→ **I often bundle design work to create more value for both the client and myself.** Instead of selling a single design, I'll package multiple concepts together as a set. This way, the client gets a stronger variety of options to work with, and I'm able to increase the overall scope. Bundling also helps build longer-term relationships, because clients see the added value and are more likely to return for future projects knowing they'll get both quality and flexibility.

→ **Your portfolio is proof of your value**, and it's important to remind yourself of that. The more you trust your own track record, the easier it becomes to stand by your rates.

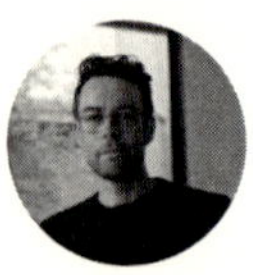

Kevin Twohy
Founder and Principal, Twohy Design Works

twohydesign.works

→ **Make it easy for the client to say yes, and continue to say yes as trust is built.** My projects are long-term and have no fixed cost or end-date; the client is free to end the engagement any time. They never do.

→ I looked back recently at the total billing for a long-term project, and the number shocked me. Even though the work was well worth the cost, if I had presented that figure to the client up front, it would be an incredibly difficult sale.

→ The best advice I have for building confidence around talking about money is to work to **build a "margin of safety" such that it's never painful for you to walk away.** This gives you confidence and leverage – clients can sense it.

We asked a handful of talented creatives their best advice around pricing. Their answers echoed common themes. Many agreed that tiered pricing and price anchoring are effective. Confidence is also key, which comes with practice and context.

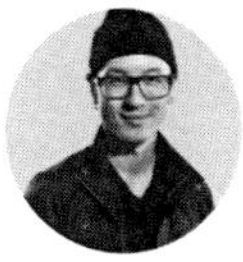

Chris Do

Founder and CEO, The Futur

thefutur.com

→ We have a few things that are in place prior to the pricing conversation. First is positioning. The prospects see the clients we've worked with, domain authority, testimonials, and social proof (followers, awards and press). Second, **before hopping on a call, discussion of ballpark budgets have already been brought up. The fit check happens early.** No need to hop on a call if we aren't in the ballpark budget, timeline and general expectations. Once we go through all that, if they decide they don't have the budget, we ask, "what is the budget that you have?" If we think it's worth getting creative to solve the budget gap, we will invest more time. If we're too far apart, we thank them and move on. No pressure to sell.

→ **As far as pricing approaches, price bracketing and price anchors usually do the trick.** We refrain from justifying price or explaining process. We prefer not to pursue but to be pursued. We adopt the "with or without you" energy.

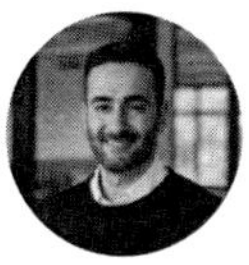

Todd Torabi

Founder of Wolf & Whale

wolfwhale.com

→ The market shifts constantly, so I try to be adaptable. Standing firm on value is important, but so is knowing when to adjust to stay competitive.

→ **I usually put three pricing options on the table.** The first is a leaner version where it technically works, but it leaves out some of the things they asked for. It's a useful way to show what they'd be missing if they try to cut back too much. The second option is the sweet spot. Exactly what they asked for, priced in that range of "fair" to "slightly above my budget," which gives us both room to negotiate...The third option is where I'll layer in bigger, more innovative ideas. Things they have not considered yet. It's not always that much more than option two, but it makes them think harder about the value they'd get by going bigger. **That anchor effect works well for us, and it gives the client options, versus just a "yes" or "no".**

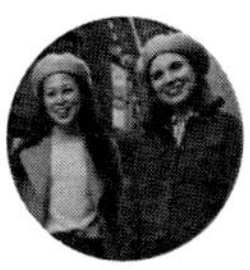

Jess Levitz and Do-Hee Kim

Co-Founders, Shoppe Theory

shoppetheory.com

→ Over the years we've become much more skilled at accurately estimating time and effort across different project scopes. We've also grown more confident in both our process and results, which has made us feel more comfortable pricing our work at a level that reflects its value.

→ **We typically present our estimates in three tiers:** a lower-cost option with a smaller scope, through to a higher-cost option with a more robust scope that often includes additional items we believe would benefit their business. We've been pleasantly surprised by the number of times a client chooses a higher-cost package! **To present proposals, we record and send a walkthrough video** rather than hosting a live meeting. This allows clients to review at their own pace while still getting clear answers to common questions and a better sense of who we are as a studio.

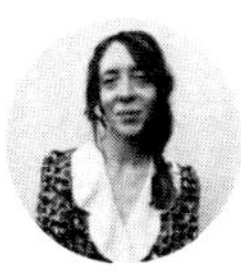

Rebecca Ramirez

PM & Design Strategist, Verynice

verynice.co

→ We're a small company (three to five), and we're always ready to negotiate with our clients, as they are helping us keep the lights on! Most of our clients are non-profits, start-ups, arts, or education organizations, all notorious for limited budgets. We having a pro-bono, **sliding scale system that we often employ**, and generally if the clients' budget is extremely small, we adjust the scope to cover the basics, ensuring our iterations are limited in number. It's tough, though–you want the client to be happy with the work, and you want the social impact brands to have fantastic designs. It all requires a lot of flexibility. If their budget simply doesn't work, we'll try to find a qualified designer in our network.

catalog that is already designed. That's more cut-and-dry and requires less fanfare.

If you work with a customer often and they know and trust your work and process, they likely won't need the big song and dance of a proposal. A simple quote with scope and price in an email is usually fine in that situation.

The same goes for smaller projects with smaller price tags. There's not as much value in selling to the client, so no need for an in-depth proposal.

Here are some more clues and red flags to help you gauge whether a lead is promising enough to send a tailored proposal:

The quote request is a hasty, non-informative email or DM. If the potential client hasn't taken the time to give you at least a simple sentence about themselves and their project, this is a red flag. An example of this kind of non-informational email could be something like, "Call me, I have a job for you," or "How much for a (insert your service here)?" No "hi," no "how are you?" Not even a full name in the signature, just an abrupt email. It usually means one of two things: They're overcommitted (either from a lack of delegation or funds) or they think their time is more valuable than yours. We are service providers, and we, of course, want to help, but we also don't want to turn into someone's personal assistant.

The way you start a relationship is likely how it will continue. So if a potential client sends half-baked emails to start the project, you'll likely be chasing them down for details and context till the end. It can also signify someone who acts on whims with little strategy or reasoning behind their decisions. The thing about whims is they're always changing. There's no solid foundation for decision-making and progress, and that's a problem. These projects usually end up as shifty as a McDonald's ball pit. The caveat here is that 5 percent of these short-request folks are worth it and just really trust their subcontractors. We have one such client. They make all requests by text, respond quickly, and usually have light changes. But these are the exceptions, not the rule.

The request email or message mentions previously working with multiple creatives on this project, with no success. These people usually imply that no one understands their vision. But if you look at the statistics, they're the common denominator in the series of bad relationships with creatives. They're likely not good at communicating goals or feedback, or just don't have a clear vision of what they need.

The project has a completely unrealistic deadline. If the potential client emails you about a full rebrand (new logo, type, color, messaging, website, etc.), and wants everything to roll out in two weeks, they have likely never done a rebrand before. They have no clue about the value or time that goes into this kind of project. Of course, we always try to educate our clients because the whole reason they reached out is because they don't do our job. We do. They don't have to know every facet of our process. However, this size of a learning gap can often be hard to bridge. If they thought it could be done in a month, and you know it likely will take six months to a year, the gap might be too hard to bridge to help them adjust their expectation.

No name or a shady email/profile name. Any email that comes in without a full name in their signature that we can use to vet the sender is an immediate no for us. The email address will tell you a lot. Is it attached to a business domain you can double check? Or is it just a random email address like 09ahxx0938@gmail.com? If they reached out via social media, take a look at their profile. Are the photos suspicious? Do they follow a ton of people but have no followers? If you do a Google search on their company name, does anything legit come up? There are so many scams out there these days, so you've got to stay vigilant. The surefire way to find out if they're a real, breathing human and not a bot is to get them on the phone. If they won't do this, trust your gut and ignore them.

You can tell from their email that they likely won't be a good fit for you. Sometimes you just know the kind of industries and clients you're not a good fit for, and you choose not to quote those projects. There's nothing wrong with simply choosing not to quote someone and telling them you are not a good fit or are not taking on new clients at this time.

Quote/Proposal Request Responses

Having a couple of template emails ready for responding to quote/proposal requests will save you so much time. They should cover the gamut from "no thanks" to "I need more info" to "heck yes." Here are some of the templates we use as a starting point:

"Thanks for your interest! Can we schedule a phone call? I'd love to hear more about this project."

This response is for promising inquiries that you want to take the time to investigate before quoting them with a custom proposal. Perhaps they gave you a quick overview, but you want to ask more about their company, project scope, project outcome goals, and budget. Or you may just want to get on a call to establish some friendly rapport and start getting to know the potential client.

"We're honored you considered us for your creative needs! However, we're not currently taking on new clients. But here are some referrals that could be a great fit . . ."

"Thanks for thinking of me for your project. Based on your description, I think I may know someone more suited for your needs . . ."

If you don't think the person can afford you, you don't offer the requested service, or you don't think their project or style aligns with yours, try to refer them to a colleague or friend. We have all kinds of freelance friends at different levels and with different aesthetics. Each one has a nice niche. We know that it can be hard to find work, and from the client's perspective, it can be hard to find good creatives. If you can connect people, it will often come back in spades, even if not right away. Plus, that creative peer will most likely do the same for you when the opportunity arises. You can even set up a referral fee with your peer since you're feeding them work.

"Thanks for telling me about your project. Based on your information, I prepared a proposal for you, which you'll find attached. Is there a good day this week that we can set up a call to review?"

If the person inquiring has given you enough info to quote on, and it seems like a business-as-usual type of project, then go ahead and send the proposal.

Hoodzpah RFPs & Proposals by The Numbers*:

300-400: average number of project inquiries we get per year.

~85%: average number of inquiries we politely decline and refer to other creatives. This is usually because the timing isn't right (the client needs the work fast, and we're already booked), the potential client can't afford our rates, or the project is just not a good fit for our studio (the request is for services we don't provide, services we prefer not to do, or for an industry we prefer not to work in, etc.). →

"Can you send me more details on your project, your company, and your budget?"

Maybe you're not sold on the company, and you don't need the work, but it could be interesting if you just knew more. You don't have the bandwidth to get on a call, and you're already leaning toward not taking it. But you want more info to be sure you're not missing out on a cool project. This email also works if you plan to refer them elsewhere, but need to know a little more, so you can connect them with the right person.

Gathering Intel for Your Proposal

In order to put together a compelling proposal, you'll need great insights into your potential client, their business, their project, and their goals.

Some creatives will try to make clients do the work of detailing this information as part of a detailed contact form attached to their studio website. We don't take this approach for a few reasons:

- A lot of serious clients are nevertheless busy and don't have time to fill out a detailed intake form to contact you. And they may not have answers to all your questions off the bat. Forcing them to give really detailed information with required fields like "budget" and "timeline" could dissuade them from reaching out at all. Clients usually have a general idea of what they need, and they want to be able to test the waters more casually via a simple email. Requiring a lot of info up front before they've even said hello could turn them off and make things feel transactional. Of course, as a business, we are transactional. But the truth is, people still want to feel excited about the team they're working with. They want to know they'll work well with you and get along with you.
- Larger companies reaching out for proposals will often already have a brief or RFP (Request for Proposal), which outlines all their scope, timeline, expectations, and budget. They don't want to have to copy and paste it into form fields just to contact you. They'd rather copy and paste a prewritten email and attach their RFP.
- Smaller clients may get overwhelmed by the questions or worry about not having the right answers and won't complete the form.

In UX design, the goal is to help users accomplish the desired action with as little friction or hindrance as possible. This is why we make our contact page on our website dead simple. It's a link to our info@ email address. Then we do the legwork via emails, phone calls, and video meetings to get to know potential clients and learn about their projects.

Some potential clients might even ask to meet in person before getting a proposal. Before scheduling an in-person meeting, we like to learn a little about the project via phone or video call to suss out how serious or promising the lead is. Plus, you can meet in person once they accept the proposal to kick off the project.

Once you get that email or DM from a promising lead requesting a quote, schedule a video or phone call. Fifteen minutes is plenty. We touch on this in the pricing chapter. The benefit of a call where people can see your face or hear your voice is that people can start dealing with you as a person, not just a faceless company. Hopefully, your client will see that you are excited about their project and knowledgeable about their company (do as much research as you can before the meeting), which establishes trust. Plus, people tend to be much more transparent in a casual, real-time conversation than they'd ever be in writing, where they can plan every response. You also have the added benefit of the element of surprise. Most people will dodge the portion of your email asking what they're budget is. But ask them on the spot on the phone, and they'll likely give you their answer or at least some great clues as to the answer.

Talking about budgets can feel like a staring contest; each party wants to be the last to blink. Sometimes people will beat around the bush and try to throw the question back on you. If they are hesitant, you can reassure them you know they have a marketing budget, and you want to tailor a scope to fit to make their dollar go as far as possible. You don't want to waste their time or yours if you're way out of their budget. It's truly not a trap. If they are still unsure, don't press the matter too much; just move on and try to gather clues elsewhere.

Some seasoned professionals will be comfortable talking honestly about budgets. But some people prefer to keep their cards close to see if you might give them a lower rate than they would have requested. Usually, smaller companies are the ones who get a little antsy about talking prices. Regardless of how shy they are about revealing their budget, you can usually get good clues by asking about the size and history of their business (how many employees, locations, years in business) and the type of product or service they offer (how many units do they generally sell, and what do those units cost?).

You probably won't outright ask, "What was your revenue last year?" but it wouldn't be weird at all to ask, "What's your best-selling product?" People love to brag about their business. They're proud of what they've accomplished and usually eager to share how much customers love it. We've had people tell us real numbers when it comes to bragging about how many investors they have, how much they did in sales last year, or how successful their latest launch was. This will give you context clues for what kind of budgets they might be able to support.

Here's a list of some questions you can ask while on the initial call (we went over a similar set of questions in the pricing section). Try to bring these questions up naturally and casually, rather than robotically going down a list. The goal is to get the person on the other end of the call feeling comfortable and conversational. The more relaxed they are, the less guarded they'll be. This shouldn't feel like a test or interrogation.

Pre-Proposal Questions to Ask Potential Clients

- Tell me about your company.
- Tell me about this project and how it came about. What is the goal you hope to accomplish?
- What are your company's main products/services, and how will this project relate to them? How do you expect this project to affect or generate growth/sales if at all?
- Is this part of any larger company initiatives?
- Is this the first time you've done a project like this?
- In your opinion, what would be the best result of this project?

→Cont.

~15%: average number of inquiries that we'll set up a vetting call for. These are projects that look promising, and we want to collect info to prepare a quote. About 30 percent of the time the call ends in us referring the client to a designer or studio who is a better fit for their needs.

~7%: average number of proposals we prepare per year. In addition, we send out about 20 casual quotes via emails to existing customers. These have almost a 100 percent success rate because the client already knows and trusts us.

*(*based on data from 2020-2024)*

- What would failure look like?
- Who is the target audience for this project?
- If the project is re-creating or updating something that exists, why is the old solution no longer working? (Knowing what doesn't work will inform what changes need to be made.)
- Who at your company will be involved with this project? (It's good to know how many cooks will be in the kitchen. Who has final approval? How many levels of sign offs are needed to launch, etc.?)
- Do you have a clear sense of what you want the aesthetic to be?
- What is your timeline for this project?
- What is your budget for this project?
- How did you hear about us? (It's always good to know how someone learned about you, so you can thank anyone who referred you and see which marketing channels are working best. Plus, bringing the conversation around to you will usually lead the client to explain why they thought you would be a good fit for them. Knowing this angle will help you present yourself as a uniquely qualified partner in your proposal based on what hooked their attention.)

You get the idea. These kinds of questions will help you better identify how serious your client is, to what scale they're doing business, and how realistic their hopes are for the outcome of your work.

Sometimes, as you are asking these questions, you start to realize this client and their project aren't as promising as you initially thought. Maybe it's clear that the budget is much smaller than you had anticipated, or the timeline is just not doable based on your existing workload. Or maybe the work isn't even in your wheelhouse (oftentimes, clients are confused about what kind of design they need). In these instances, if you feel confident it's not a good fit, address it on the phone to save yourself time. We often turn a vetting call into a referral call. We explain why we aren't a good fit, then give them some referrals. Clients are usually really grateful for the honesty and the help guiding them in the right direction. Sometimes these people have gone on to refer us to their friends or peers, even though we didn't work with them. Why? Because we were still a resource for them, and that built trust and respect.

But if the call makes the project more promising, you now have what you need to create a great proposal.

The Anatomy of a Great Proposal

This is our winning formula, which has led to amazing results.

Proposal cover page.

The cover page could be text only, or it could include a cover image that relates to the client (you can use nice photography on their site, or a stock photo relating to their industry). As long as their company name and their project name is clearly presented, the client will immediately know this deck was made especially for them. Your company logo and contact info should also be present, so they can easily remember who you are and how to reach you. They'll likely be getting a few proposals from different studios; this will help them find yours in the pack. We also include an expiration date or a note that the proposal is only valid for thirty days from the date of reception. Why? It creates a sense of urgency and saves you from having to honor old pricing if the client waits too long to accept it.

Hello page.

Here we say, "Hi, [client name], We're so honored you considered us as a partner for your [project description]." This starts things off with a warm and excited tone while letting them know we understand the high-level project needs.

A project description and goal summary.

This might be the most important step. If a client is going to trust you—someone they likely don't know very well— with their project, you have to show them you understand who they are and what they want. Customize the presentation to speak in terms of their unique goals, company, audience, and product/service. For us, this is usually across one to three pages. It doesn't need to spell out a solution. Use active rather than passive language: "We will help you achieve [project goal]" rather than "We understand you want [project goal]." This doesn't need to be three paragraphs. In fact, short and sweet is best. We like to think of these decks like slide presentations. In a great slide deck, you should only include maybe three to four sentences, max, per slide, or the text becomes too small for an audience to read on a screen. Same goes for our deck. We don't want people to get overwhelmed and bored at the sight of a cover letter with paragraphs of content. Explaining it simply shows the client we heard everything they said and were able to synthesize all the various pieces down into a focused statement. Now they have higher hopes that we can do the same for them creatively: hone all their needs and hopes into a focused creative solution. You'll be surprised how far these pages go in instilling confidence with your potential client.

A quick intro to your studio.

Now that you've put the client's needs first, you can give them two to three sentences that really highlight your unique qualifications and background. This is your elevator pitch, reminding them who you are, and helping them see your advantage over other studios or creatives they may be considering. Here, you can include information like how long you've been in business (if that number will instill confidence), how long you've been in the industry, and any awards or press you've received for your work. You could also speak to any highly unique skills you have. We like to tell people how we're type designers, not just branding designers, so they know we can do custom wordmarks. This is a selling point for us. Imagery accompanying this text could be of you and your team working on a project together (behind the scenes, not headshots), or a collage of some of your best work.

Two to three incredible testimonials from past clients.

These are priceless in instilling confidence!

Past or current client logos.

Capabilities Deck

A capabilities deck is a document that shows off your—well—capabilities. It includes information on your services, your team, your accolades, case studies, process breakdown, FAQs, etc. It's basically a proposal without the specific scope of work and price tag. You can send it to prospective clients to get them excited about using you as a vendor. Once you have your proposal deck dialed in, just make a copy, delete anything that is project specific, and "voila!" You have a Capabilities Deck. This is such a handy tool for business development and a great asset to attach to cold emails.

Even if the person looking at the proposal doesn't recognize the company names or logos, they'll still see a grid of people who have trusted you. It's another great way to say, "See? All the cool kids are doing it." It shows them you are not an untested entity.

Process overview.

This is a simple page that reveals the culture behind how you work, or any specific process points that might be insightful to the client. It doesn't have to give away your trade secrets to be informative. A simple statement like this would be enough to explain the discovery phase: "We start with a discovery session, meeting with your team and interviewing stakeholders to understand your perspective and goals. Then we research and recap these findings in a discovery deck, which will guide our design decisions." Or, you could highlight your approach to work rather than the specific steps. We highlight that we lean heavily on the discovery and research phase to lead creative, so we can all make informed decisions. Then, we talk about our collaborative mindset and how we value our customers' input. Clients usually like to see this. They want to be sure you aren't stubborn or inflexible and know how to gather consensus and harmonize opinions.

Team roster.

We show happy faces of the people they'll work with, and reveal some fun, personal details that could help humanize us or make a connection: what we're watching on TV, what we're listening to, or our hobbies. This isn't a memoir, but those two to three sentences turn us into people, not just a company.

Proof of experience through relevant case work.

Show case studies with similar scopes or industries similar to your potential client. This helps them see that you have conquered a similar task before. Beautiful portfolio photos with a short description of the project goal, markers of a successful outcome, and a bulleted scope is plenty. You may be thinking, "They already saw my website because that's how they got a hold of me. Why do I need to show this again?" Oftentimes the person requesting the quote isn't necessarily the only person making the final decision on who will be hired for the job. If they pass this proposal up the chain and present it to involved stakeholders, you want everything to be easily at hand. Even if you don't have any work in the potential client's industry or of a similar scope, just show your best work. The goal of this segment is to put the potential client's mind at ease by showing them you've worked with real companies (maybe even ones they've heard of!) and that you can do quality work. Three to four case studies is plenty. We used to put a collage of client work with a blurb all crammed onto one page. But then we realized digital PDF pages are free! So we gave each case study the due space to really show off the work with a blurb and a featured image on one page, two more images on the next page, then a final page of images.

Estimated timeline.

We show ours as a Gantt chart (see example). We include a blurb that shows the client our estimated timeline (operative word being "estimated") is based on client feedback being returned within three business days. If feedback takes longer, the project timeline could adjust proportionately. As best you can, lay out a reasonable timeline for each stage of the project. We tend to be hyper-optimistic about timelines, and then reality hits. So we overcompensate by making our timelines longer than our initial expectation. This gives us some buffer. You don't want this timeline coming back to haunt you like grocery store sushi.

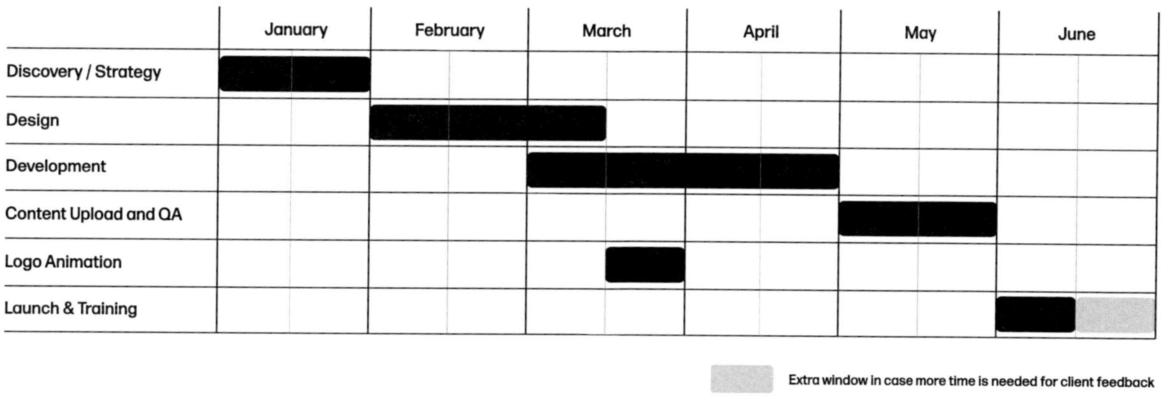

Scope and quote.

Now that you've set the scene, you can break down the actual cost. There's a reason why the realtors on those house-hunting shows do the grand tour first and save the asking price for last. You want to get the potential buyer invested. You want them to be convinced this is their dream house and already picking paint swatches and planning fixture upgrades in their head. You want to build up to the price, so by the time you share it, they're already talking themselves into the purchase. By setting up your deck this way your price is now justified, not startling.

You could include how many strategy meetings, initial concepts, and rounds of revisions for each phase; what deliverables they'll get for each phase; and a brief overview of licensing or intellectual property rights terms.

When we list our prices, we don't line item each deliverable granularly. If it's a large project with multiple phases and objectives, we bundle things that belong together into sections, showing the value of each section. Then, we add those section subtotals into a project total at the end. If the project has a limited scope, we list one price for the whole scope to show a holistic value. This way, the client can't look at each piece as a line-item price they can pick and choose from. We want them to see it all as a bundled value.

Your pricing page is where you can also test tiered pricing options and upsells (see the pricing chapter for more on this). The idea is to show the client a package with the exact scope they asked for and then give them one or two upsell packages with great extras they could benefit from for a fractionally higher price. Make the difference in price and value a no-brainer, encouraging them to book the bigger, higher-priced packages. The more they book, the more they save.

In each phase or package, we like to add one item that is an easy negotiation point for the future. We might include an extra round of revisions, a business card template, or something that's easy for us to do, but has a decent amount of perceived value. This way, if a client can't afford our price, we can easily negotiate the price down by removing this item from the scope. We never want to lower the price without consequence; otherwise, we're saying to the client that our services don't have definite value attached to them and that our original price was arbitrary. The value of your work loses credibility when you're willing to lower your price for nothing. Removing one round of revisions is an easy swap for a lowered price, and both sides win.

Real proof examples.

After we've shown the price, we have a page featuring three thumbnail images from past projects. These have a title under them that says something like "[Past Client] Round 1 Logo Proof". On this page we link to real past proofs, discovery decks, brand guidelines, etc., so the potential client can see the level of quality we deliver at each phase. We like including this at the end as a last exciting moment after the price page. It again contextualizes the value.

Terms, notes, and next steps.

The left side of our terms page shows a list of what the quote doesn't include, any payment terms, and other caveats or notes. The right side of the page shows the next steps they can expect. Something like, "If you're ready to move forward, email me at [email], and we'll send over the agreement and an invoice for down payment."

Back cover page with contact info. This usually just says "Thank you" prominently and shows our contact info so the client can easily follow up with us.

Get the Proposal Deck we Use at Hoodzpah

If you don't have the time or bandwidth to make your own deck, we sell the template that we use everyday at Hoodzpah in our online shop. Over the past 2 years it's been rated 5 stars by over 50 customers, so don't just take our word for it. Visit hoodzpahdesign.com/shop

★★★★★

100% Recommended!
— Julia D.

No-Brainer Purchase.
— Kevin S.

Everything I was expecting and more!... 12/10
— Christie T.

Just received a "Let's do it!" response to the largest quote I've ever pitched!
— Carla Carter

[Fig. 5] →

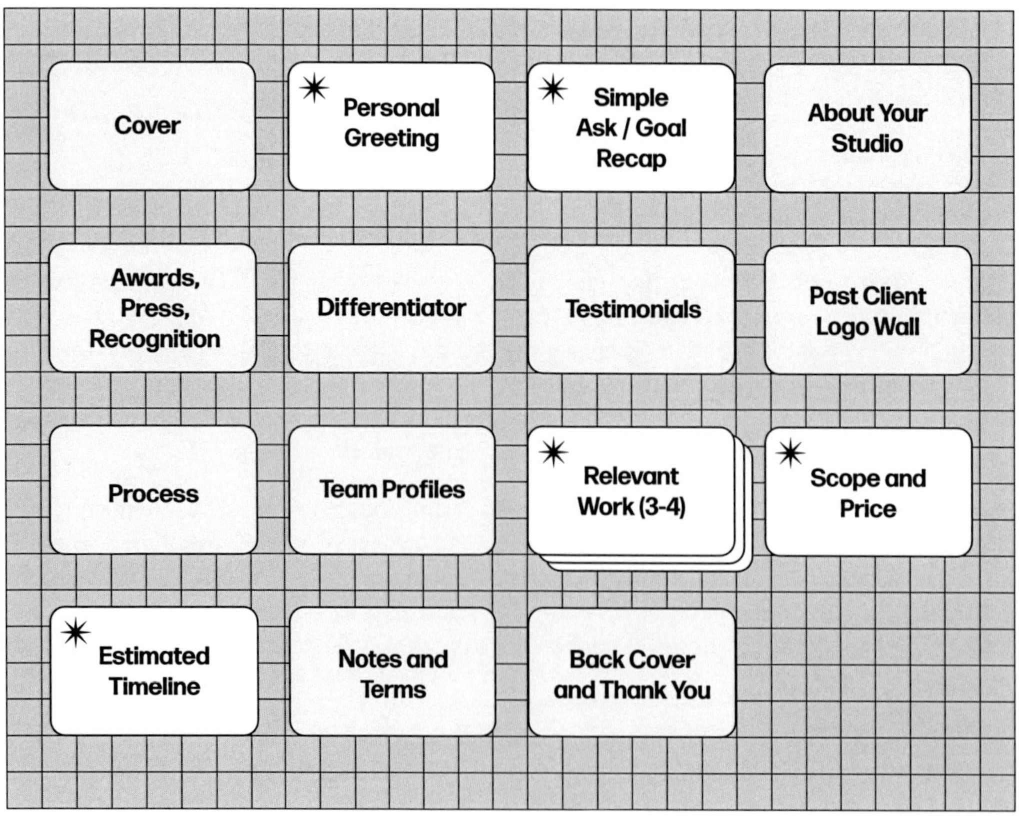

Proposal Templates

Always look for ways to make your non-creative tasks more efficient. Why start from scratch each time you make a proposal? At Hoodzpah, we have a template proposal ready to roll for our most commonly requested services, with applicable case studies already input and the process for that service outlined. Now, when someone writes in to request a quote, we just go into the template for that service, customize the few points that change per client, export the PDF, and send.

We've gotten so many comments about how our proposal deck was a huge reason why the client chose us over other studios. If you take the time and care to brand yourself and present yourself clearly, prospective clients can already see the care you'll take for them. 75% of the content stays the same on each proposal [see Fig. 5]. The five asterisked pages are all you need to customize. Still, it can take one to four hours to customize depending on complexity.

Sending Proposals and Following Up

We usually send the Proposal PDF by email attachment, or use a Dropbox link if the file is large and we don't want to bog down their inbox or risk the email being bounced. We don't walk the client through the proposal in real time (call/meeting) since we've already talked with them in the initial meeting. In certain instances we might record a quick Loom video highlighting some things or adding context. Loom is an amazing app that lets you screen record while you talk through something. The recording can be shared via a link; you can set viewing permissions if you want, and the app will even notify you when people watch it (a great way to know when a client has seen your proposal).

When we send the email, we might say something like, "Would you all like to get a meeting on the books to review this proposal sometime in the next few days?" This gives them time to digest it, but keeps the momentum rolling. During that follow-up meeting, we can answer any questions. Companies with lots of stakeholders generally take us up on this offer, while smaller companies often don't need it. But it's nice to show the client we are making ourselves available to them.

If we aren't able to book an initial pre-proposal call with the client to introduce ourselves and talk about their project, then we might walk the client through a proposal on a live video call. Why? To establish a good rapport, show excitement for the project, and answer any questions. This added human element can be so important when it comes to closing a deal. It changes the context from a faceless company to a real team of friendly, passionate people. After we present the proposal on the call, we'll follow up with an email and a link to a PDF.

Once you've sent the proposal, you might not hear back immediately. We like to follow up within a week to check in. A simple, "Hi [name], hope you're well! Checking in to see if you had any questions on the proposal." If we still don't hear back, we'll send a second email the following week. Our friend and talented musician Johnny Knittle (who made the custom music for our *Freelance and Business and Stuff* course) had good advice on this:

"Sending an email is free. If the client was always going to say 'no', the worst you'll hear back is 'no'. But even better, some will end up responding back with, 'I'm so glad you reminded me,' or 'Thanks for checking back, we're ready to get started.' Whether they finally respond now, or after four check-ins, it's free to remind them, and money you otherwise wouldn't have booked."

Johnny uses a system of checking back one week after sending the proposal, then one week after that, then a month later, then a year later. Then, he does yearly check-ins just to see how they are and if they need any new projects. You would think this would be a lot, but he swears he gets a lot of work from it. Not always for the original project, but sometimes for new projects that have come along since the original proposal.

Chapter Checklist:

① Create a proposal template or buy one.

② Create a couple of iterations customized for your most common service packages.

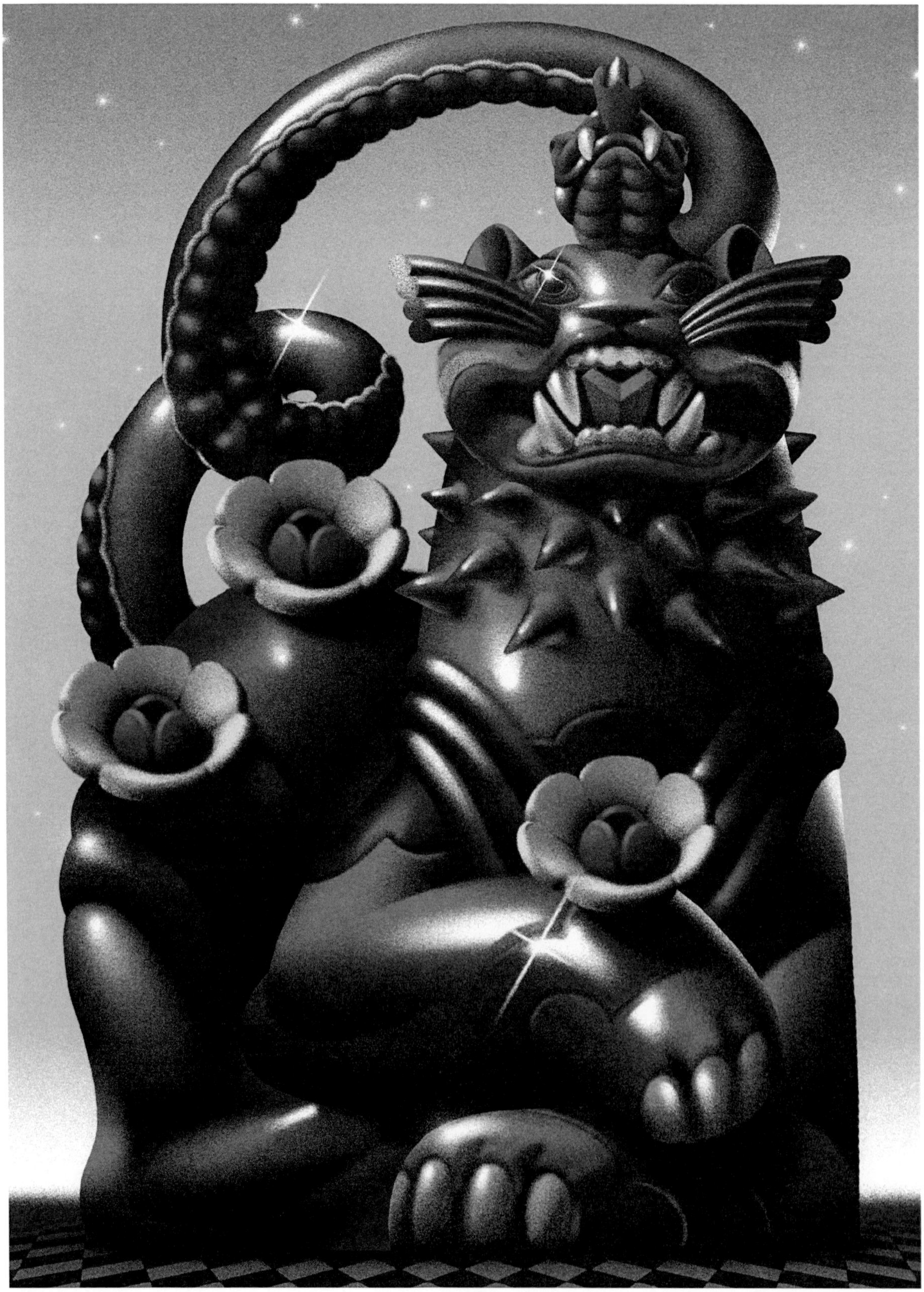

Illustration by: Cesar Canseco

6

Discovery and Positioning

Don't think of it as a business plan; think of it as the research and strategy phase before you start a creative project.

You've made it through a good chunk of this book and haven't given up yet. You've got gusto and dedication—that's clear! To make sure you're not operating on pure blind confidence, let's jump into some research and discovery. Don't get us wrong, there's something to be said for blind confidence. Joe Strummer, lead singer of The Clash, ran the 1983 London Marathon on a whim with absolutely zero training or preparation. When asked about his training, he said, "Drink ten pints of beer the night before the race . . . and don't run a single step at least four weeks before the race." Sometimes, that kind of naive spontaneity can spur us to try things we normally wouldn't.

But let's be honest, for every one person running a marathon drunk and unprepared, there are thousands of well-prepared runners who, nevertheless get winded and barely make the finish (but still put that "26.2" oval decal on their car to rub it in all of our faces—we get it, you ran more than two dozen miles while the rest of us were wedging a butt imprint into a sofa).

We're much more likely to thrive and achieve our goals with a plan. Almost anyone can start a business on a whim, but making it profitable, enduring, and fulfilling is another matter entirely. People hear the phrase "business plan" and immediately start to doze off. If it helps, think of it as the discovery session you would do with a client before diving into the creative work.

In a client discovery phase, you work to establish a clear goal to guide the creative work. You research the target audience and do a competitor analysis to uncover advantages and weaknesses. Then, create a plan or strategy for a design solution that meets your goals. That's exactly what we're going to do in this chapter. By the end of it, you'll have accidentally made a business plan. It's like crushing up your meds and putting them in a milkshake.

A business plan is not a crystal ball. And as sad as we are about it, you're not Miss Cleo. Or are you? Miss Cleo, if you're reading this book from beyond the grave, please email us a testimonial for the dust jacket of the hard copy. The rest of us are just normal people who don't know the future. That's okay. A business plan is not written in stone. It's sketched in pencil. You'll update and revise your business plan as you go along. Just like your budget, it's meant to be revisited as you learn and grow. This is why it's referred to as a "living document."

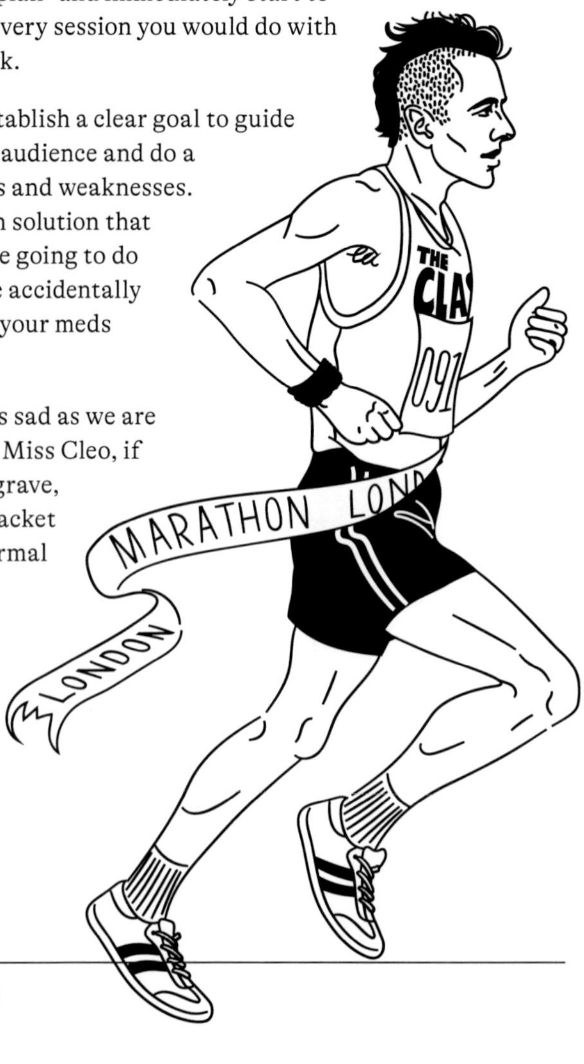

A business plan can establish short-term goals (one year) or long-term goals (three to five years) for your business. When we started Hoodzpah, we started small. We made a one-year plan. With so many uncertainties, it was all we could wrap our heads around. But even short-term planning was enough to give us a good North Star to help guide our next steps.

In the following pages, we'll ask you some questions to help get you started on this discovery and planning session. If something doesn't apply to you, skip it. If you get stuck on a point, just move on and come back to it later. If a question keeps hanging you up, reach out to a business mentor or a trusted friend. Sometimes, the very act of explaining a problem out loud is enough to help you find an answer.

Don't stress over this phase or avoid it. Just use your critical thinking to determine the best answer you can for right now. As with creativity, there's more than one right answer. And so much of this will become clearer once you get your feet wet and actually start to do business. But that doesn't negate the importance of making the plan, so at least you have a clear path forward. Planning is potential. Doing is realization.

Open up a blank Word doc or notebook page, and write your answers as you read through the following sections. Great news: we already figured out some of this stuff in previous chapters!

1. Describe your business and its purpose. What's the elevator pitch?

This seems like an easy question, but it also seems like a trick question to many people. Don't overthink it. Think about the reason you started your business. What kind of work did you dream of making? What kind of clients did you dream of working with? What was it about your old jobs that made you think, "I can do things better or differently?" These things usually guide what kind of business you want to run. And as far as your purpose goes, it doesn't have to be a wondrous oath for the uplifting of all humankind. Ours is: "Creating brand identities that people root for and helping legacy brands shine on." Our purpose speaks to what we do (branding), who we do it for (clients, new and old), and why it matters (helping them stand out and connect with their audiences).

Being able to introduce your business and relay your selling points confidently and quickly is a small but very meaningful talent. We co-founded and ran a creative meetup called Connecting Things for about five years. It was a free event for creatives and entrepreneurs, with a fifteen-minute talk from someone in the community, plus free pizza and beer from amazing sponsors. We were always meeting new people, and every conversation inevitably hit upon the question, "What do you do?" At one event, Amy saw a new face and introduced herself. "What do you do?" she asked. "Oh gosh, where to start," he said as he sighed heavily. "It's kind of complicated." This began a five-minute oratory, during which Amy was slowly backing away like Homer into the bushes. After he was done, she summed up, "So you're an Art Director who also does landscaping on the side?" No shade at all to this guy. To him, his life had become very complicated. But being able to present what we do confidently and concisely is a superpower not to be underestimated. So, that said . . . what do you do? Why does that matter (to you and your audience)?

2. Give a quick overview of you as the founder, and any partners or team members.

Introduce yourself and any partners in your new creative business. What is your professional history? What are your individual skills and qualifications? What is your experience in this field? What have former employers/teachers/colleagues/clients told you that you're great at? Talking about yourself like this doesn't make you a blowhard when you're framing your skills to show how they will help your clients. Include anything that highlights your professional strengths and personality.

3. What is your professional support system?

Do you have advisers and outside help? If so, what are their roles and to what extent? What are their qualifications? A credible adviser can lend experience to a new business. This will comfort investors and bankers. Refer back to the A-team we assembled in Chapter 2. If you make a physical product, who is your manufacturing outfit? If you make a digital product, who is your development team? If you require a staff, what type of individuals will you hire, and what qualifications will they have? And so on.

4. What are your services?

List at least three core services. Include a few backup services you can also do if need be. Early on, you might read some business books that say, "You must specialize!" And so you'll narrow in on one service that you offer to one very specific demographic. But this can actually shoot you in the foot if you do it too early. Offering limited services to a limited audience does just what the name implies—it limits who can hire you. If you don't have an audience or client roster built up yet, try to go broader on your services rather than hyper-specialized. That way you can cast a wider net to catch more clients until you get the demand to specialize. Once you list your services, describe what, if anything, makes your services unique and competitive. For example, if you have a sought-out or unique style, this could be a competitive edge. Don't be overly concerned if you don't have a unique competitive advantage. To be honest, doing good design work goes a long way.

5. What products, if any, will you offer?

Dare to think outside of services! With client services like logo design and videography, your earning power is limited by the number of hours you can work for services rendered. However, with products, there's the potential to make money from many clients for the same deliverable. It's the difference between doing a custom lettering project for one client for their exclusive use, versus creating a typeface you can license as a font and sell to unlimited clients. That being said, it takes time and trial and error to find the right products for your audience.

Products and services each have their unique advantages. Using the typeface example again, you'd have to sell many more font licenses to make the same amount of money you could from doing one custom lettering project. But that licensing income is on autopilot, whereas the custom lettering project is very hands on.

Finding Your Product

Products are a great way to diversify your income. Products can be physical or digital, helpful or delightful (ideally even both). Here are a few ideas plotted. Brainstorm your own.

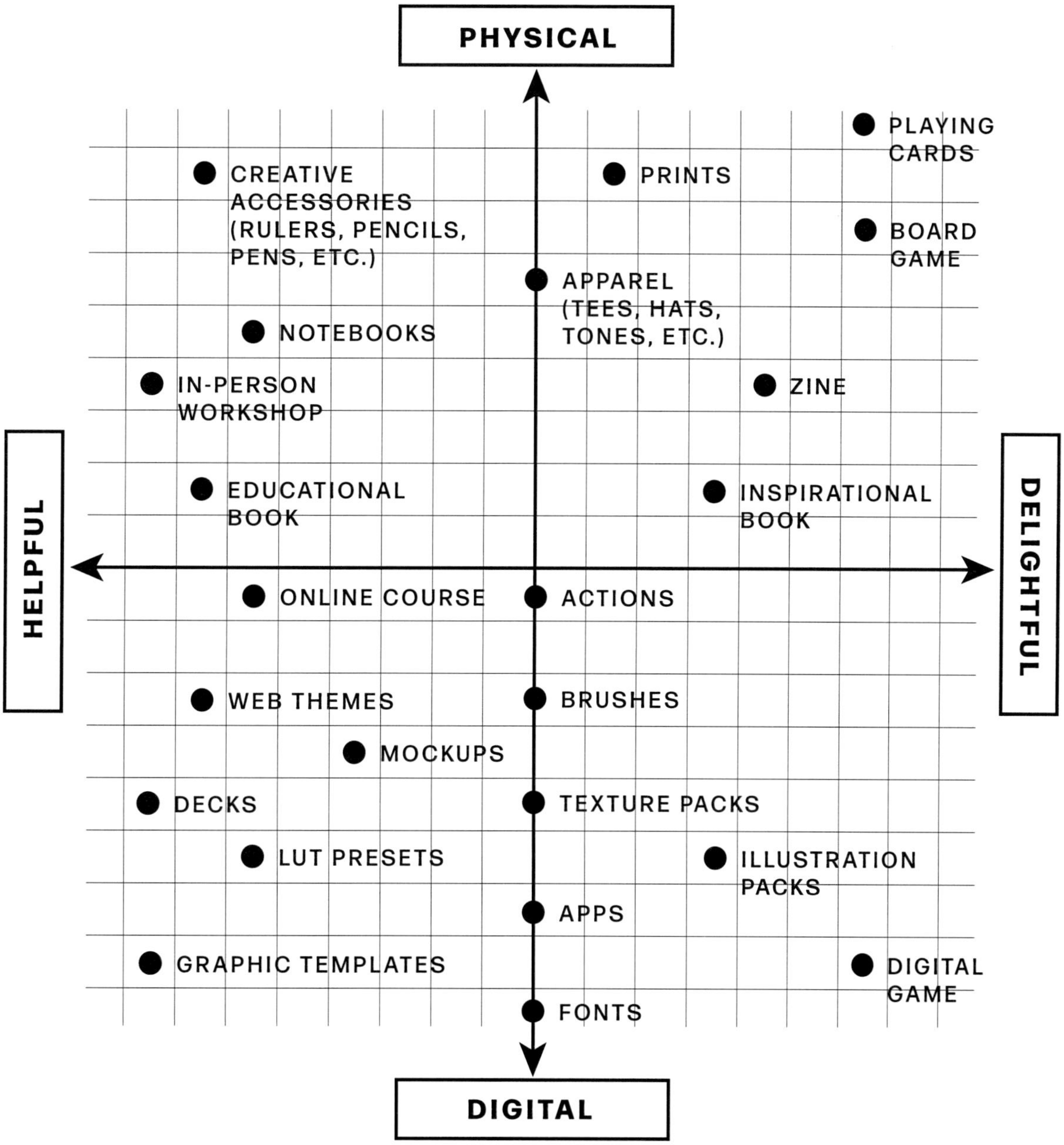

Digital products are an ideal place to start. Why? A digital product doesn't require as much cost in making prototypes, ordering and housing the stock, and fulfilling the shipping. It just takes your time investment to develop the product and any fees associated with selling the product online. You can sell your product on your own site or on a marketplace. Once the digital product is launched, your work is generally done (except for customer service and eventual updates to the product). Other digital products to consider: a pre-recorded, on-demand course, an eBook, a digital template, a software brush pack, a texture pack, an action or effect preset, and so on.

Physical products take more up-front planning and investment. You'll need to consider how to manufacture the good, what size breakdowns to order (if it's apparel), where to store it, how to ship it, and what to do if the product is defective or arrives to your customer broken. With physical products, the risk is greater if people don't respond well to them. You'll be left with a lot of goods you've bought up front.

If you're just starting out with physical goods, try low-cost one-size-fits-all options to make your life easier until you learn about your audience and what they want. Or you can test apparel through on-demand print partners. On-demand printers offer a variety of apparel, drinkware, bags, towels, notebooks, and other goods you can customize to sell. They allow single, one-off orders, which means you only pay for placed orders (rather than paying for a bulk of up-front stock from a screen printing or apparel company, and then hoping people buy it).

Many on-demand printers will even fulfill the order for you, drop-shipping to your customers on your behalf. But these on-demand print options for one-offs are expensive. You will barely make a markup on your costs. And the quality will probably be less than stellar. On-demand printers usually use direct-to-garment print techniques. This allows for full-color printing, but the quality is not great, the ink can look dull, and the printed areas tend to crack and peel more easily than screen printing or embroidery. Screen-printed apparel is usually of better quality, but it doesn't allow for one-offs. Minimums are usually at least twenty pieces for screen-printed items. Still, you could beta test products through an on-demand merch vendor until you can prove your concept. Once you know what sells with your audience, you can order them properly screen printed on better quality blanks at a fraction of the cost per unit and make a good upsell.

When it comes to how to sell your product, you have a few options: You can sell on your website and through your own payment gateway, sell wholesale to a retailer, or sell through a marketplace.

Selling through your site or through a Gumroad or PayPal link is great because you retain almost all the profits from the sale (minus a transaction fee for payment processing). You don't owe a fee to a marketplace. However, you're also solely responsible for driving traffic to your products for purchases.

Online marketplaces include outfits like Creative Market, You Work for Them, MyFonts (if you sell fonts), or Stocksy (for stock media). These marketplaces tend to take a hefty cut of your sales. As of printing, Creative Market and You Work for Them take 50 percent of every sale made on their platform. Gumroad marketplace takes 30 percent. Between 30–50 percent is fairly standard. Why do they take so much? Because they're providing you with an audience. Your products are being marketed with many other products to a targeted audience. You'll be discovered by people who would never have known to even look for your goods. But you're also competing for attention with other products that could be similar to yours. And you might get undercut by cheaper options from competitors.

If you make physical products, you can sell wholesale to a retailer. The goal with wholesale products is to price them to be at least double what you paid to make them. Optimally more. Then retailers who buy your items at a wholesale rate will mark up the cost by double again for the final price to their own customers. So if it costs you $6 to make a hat, you can set the wholesale price at $12–$15, and then a wholesale buyer will retail the hat to a final end-customer for $24–$30. Connecting with retailers augments your audience to the retailer's audience. They are bringing in customers. And your placement in the context of their shop can lend credibility and associate your brand with other brands carried at the store.

Be smart about how you productize your talents. Your products should never undercut the value of your services. For example, if you sell a licensable logo pack on a site like Creative Market for twenty dollars, why would a client want to pay you thousands of dollars for a custom logo? Optimally, your product will complement your services, not cannibalize them. If you have a great idea for a product, but it will negatively impact your service work, start a side brand where you can specialize in things that don't fit your service business.

Your product audience may be different from your service audience. At Hoodzpah, our audience is usually a brand or company. They're hiring us for a professional, strategic, custom engagement. Whereas our product audience is our peers. Individual fellow designers who like our aesthetic or relate to our plight.

If you're having trouble thinking about what product you could make, start paying attention in your workday. Look for tools and resources you need but cannot find. That might be your cue that there's a hole in the market you could fill. Don't limit yourself to things. Even your knowledge can become a product! You can turn your experience into a book, a report, a course, or a workshop.

At Hoodzpah, we mostly think about products as a way to make things we're interested in while promoting ourselves in a unique way. Probably 60 percent of our products are not high earners. But we learned something new by making each one. We had fun. We tried a new style. We learned how to coordinate production on a new item. Our most popular sellers have been our book, our deck templates, and our fonts. The tees, hats, prints, and mugs make a little money, but not a ton. In our mind, selling even a few hats and T-shirts to fans, and giving away the rest to friends and people we admire, is a great way to remind them we exist. We're maintaining our brand awareness every time a friend wears our shirt around their office.

While we never expected it, our shop and on-demand course have wound up making us a decent hunk of cash each year. It didn't happen overnight, and it might go away tomorrow, but as of now, we have built up a steady audience of people who look to us for design resources through a branding lens, and display fonts begging to be used in logos. This is our shop's strength.

It's so rewarding to make the thing you want, just as you want it. No revisions. No design by committee. If people buy it, the feeling is unmatched. If you make some money, that is a win. If you break even, at least you made something cool. If you don't make any money, you learned how to produce something that could come in handy for a future client project. Our past merch for our own store has led to us doing merch for brands and artists we admire (Jack's Surfboards, FREAK STORE in Japan, Noah Kahan, ILM, and even Nike). You can never guess what product will hit and what won't with your audience. Don't get down if the first one is a dud. You're lucky if even one in five is a hit.

Here are some questions to help you find your product:

- Is there a handy product you use often but feel could be optimized? Do you have the ability or connections to build a better option?
- Is there a product you use often, but it's lacking style? Could you make a more stylish option?
- Is there a resource you wish existed that you could make?
- Is there a question you get asked a lot about your process or creative practice? Could this be turned into a template, book, course, or workshop?
- Is there a phase of your creative process you could turn into a digital download? For photographers and videographers, this could be a LUT preset; for designers it could be a brush pack; for lettering artists it could be a font, etc.
- Is there a part of your workflow you dread? Is there a way to templatize it? For example, a plugin to save out final logo files, or a proof template to streamline making proofs, etc.
- What is a cool piece of merchandise you could make to promote your studio? Maybe a calendar, a game, a shop tee, or fridge magnets?
- What is a product your target audience would love? Custom bottle openers? Custom press-on nail sets? Custom necklace or charm keychains? Make something that will delight your ideal audience, and give it away to impress them if no one offers to buy it.

6. Who is your audience (both current and ideal)?

Think locally, regionally, nationally, and worldwide. Who could you work with among your friend group, family members, and acquaintances? List businesses in your area that could use your services. For this section, include specific businesses, brands, and general industries. Yes, think of brands you love. But also think of less glamorous brands you see in shops, on your drive to the grocery store, or in the grocery store. Potential clients are everywhere. And don't forget other agencies as potential clients. Large agencies usually have a stable of subcontractors they like to tag as they need help. Look up agencies in your area and broader locations.

Same as with your services, don't specialize in a specific industry or audience demographic before you have the demand to support that move. Saying you want to work with clients in the sports industry is a great goal, and you should definitely work to make that happen. But, if you don't have any clients at all yet, consider courting non-sports clients, so you can pay the bills while you work on bringing in sports-related work. Keep your options wide so you can attract more customers until you have the option to specialize.

Think about the following when doing your research:

- What does my potential client want in a service provider? Are they choosing based on style, reputation, or affordable rates?
- What kind of work would appeal to your potential client? Do you have work in the same industry or a popular style for their industry?
- What services would each ideal or potential client likely hire you for? If you want to work with restaurants or bars, you should probably have that kind of work in your portfolio. If you want to work in the consumer packaged goods space, you likely need to show you can do packaging and marketing work (social, ads, email marketing, etc.).

7. Does your portfolio appeal to your target audience?

Do you actually have the kind of work they desire or need? If not, can you create a passion project or donate work to a non-profit to fill those gaps in your portfolio?

8. What is the market demand for your services?

Can you tell that there is a need for your skills and services? Are the brands, companies, and industries you listed already working with creative teams to put out the kind of work you do? If so, you know they already value that work and hire for that service.

9. Who are your competitors and role models (both currently and aspirationally)?

What is the competitive landscape like in your industry/field? Think of creative studios in your region and also globally.

Don't just think of competitors, but also list out your company role models. These are other creative studios or agencies running their business in a way you admire and look up to. Look at their websites and social media. Try to find interviews with them. See if you can gain insight into how they present themselves, how they are attracting work, and why you think it's successful. Why did they originally appeal to you?

While researching your role models, try not to just use them as a template. You'll be able to glean a ton of great information from them, but remember, you need to carve your own path, not just copy someone else's. Just as with your creative work, there is an art to researching, but still creating your own unique solutions.

During your research, think about the following:

- Is there a consistent look or aesthetic of the agencies and studios that appeal to you? Does that shine light on a way you could do things differently?
- How do they describe their services? Could this help me understand common industry terms I could use to describe my services?
- What is their pricing? Most agencies don't have public pricing, but you might luck out with smaller studios that sometimes show package rates up front.

- What is their personality, and what are their brand traits? What do I want my brand traits to be?
- What is the tone or content of their messaging? Does it successfully speak to their audience?
- How do they prove their expertise? How do they instill visual and verbal trust on their websites, social media, and other marketing materials?
- How do they speak about themselves on their "about" page? Are they casual? Professional? Persuasive?
- What takeaways can you apply to your own business, or what weakness can you identify that you want to avoid?

10. How are you going to reach your audience and build your client base (marketing plan)?

A website and social media accounts are obvious musts, in our opinion. But what about cold emails? Or sending promotional materials or capabilities books with work samples to potential clients and agencies? Include a list of the ways you plan to get the word out. Here are some marketing avenues to consider when drafting this section:

Social media. The platforms will change, but the goal will stay the same—genuinely connecting with others. Resist the urge to rate your social success based on followers. Instead, look to have good conversations and build rapport with people. A small but invested following is much better than a big but indifferent one.

Networking events and trade shows. This is the original marketing—meeting people and talking! We can't tell you how many opportunities we have gotten purely by building relationships in our community. And we don't mean just telling your friends and family that you have a business. That is a great first step, but don't limit your audience to people you already know. Get yourself out there and meet new people. Broaden your circle. As twins, we have a built-in wingman, which is amazing. We highly recommend bringing a friend to a networking or creative event, and then walking up to strangers and starting a convo. When you start that convo, you don't have to only ask "Hi, what do you do?" Try to have genuine conversations people will remember. Ask them what they're watching on TV or what podcasts they're listening to. Offer up a funny story that happened to you that day. Tell them something new and memorable. People won't be expecting it and will often be dying for a breath of fresh air amidst awkward conversations.

Online and print advertising.

Referral programs. Reward friends and clients who send you work. The reward could be money, credit toward a future service, gift cards, etc. You can even reach out to friends with tangential skills to yours and set up a referral circle. You refer work to them, and they refer work to you. Referral fees could be 5–20 percent, depending on the project circumstances. Our referral fee is 7 percent.

Cross-promoting with friends, peers, and other brands. We often share things for our friends to support them, and they do the same for us. It helps us both grow our visibility.

Remember that creative meetup Connecting Things we were talking about? Connecting Things promoted brands that sponsored the event. In return, they promoted the event. Those business friends also became supporters of Hoodzpah and vice versa because we all got to know each other and wanted to help each other out. We ended up sharing about each other's companies even beyond the event. We were allies for one another. When you meet other entrepreneurs who you admire, give them a shout-out and share about them. They might notice, check out your company, and be moved to do the same.

Creating content in your field of expertise. Whether you create or write for an official media outlet or opt for a more casual blog/TikTok/YouTube/Medium/LinkedIn format, sharing your knowledge can help people find you when they need your services. It will also lead people to perceive you as an expert or leader in your field. We subscribe to a ton of newsletters. Getting great content from people we like, admire, or just want to stay in touch with reminds us to refer them clients or subcontract them. Regularly communicating what you think and know is also a great way to get on the radar for speaking events and podcast appearances. People are interested in hearing from those who have a unique or informative point of view.

Creating a passion project. This can garner press and appeal to your target audience. This is more of a long game, but it's a solid strategy we've seen work time and time again. Figure out who your dream client/industry is, make a passion project around that client/industry, and share throughout the project. Then, send the work to creative publications for press consideration. For example, Ty Mattson, an amazing designer and creative, used to create retro movie posters for his favorite shows. He did them in his signature minimal-modern flair. He made one for *Lost*, *Dexter*... the list goes on. He shared the work as he made it. His followers loved it and shared it with their followers. He made prints and sold them. The media company behind one of the shows sent a cease and desist letter from their legal team. Then, the same media company's creative team reached out to him to collaborate on a real poster for paid work. Results may vary in a venture like this, but we have heard so many of our favorite independent creatives tell this same story in some form.

Cold reach outs. These don't have to just be by email. You could message someone on a social platform. These feel awkward, but they work. It's a numbers game. We have had more than a few creatives reach out to us about working with Hoodzpah. And while we rarely subcontract, we are able to refer those people to other great clients, because we keep a Trello board full of referrals.

11. What resources will you need to execute your marketing strategy?

Keep in mind that you don't have to have a huge cash budget for initial marketing. There's so much that can be done to promote yourself on social media or in person for $$Free$$! You just have to be willing to put in the time. Organic growth of your audience can be slow going at first, but it will generally gather forward momentum if you're consistent and genuinely connect with people.

12. What are your financial goals and plans?

Luckily, we answered many of these questions together in the pricing and budgeting chapters. Refer back to get those numbers.

- What is your planned take-home income or salary? Not for the whole business, but just for you?
- What are your total estimated business expenses for the year?
- What is your annual revenue goal for your business?
    - → How do you plan to bring in that revenue?
    - → In the pricing chapter, you flat-rate quoted three of your most common services. Use those rates to estimate how many of those services you need to book to meet your revenue goal. If you also earn income for the business through products, retainers, or other means, include those in this plan.
    - → How much do you need to make per month to meet your yearly goal?
    - → How much work can you rely on from returning clients?
- Are there ways you can diversify your income so you're not just relying on one service or one big client to make your goals? You don't want to rely solely on one cash-cow client for 80 percent of your work. Why? If you lose them, you could be at risk of losing your whole business. Keep a happy balance of new and repeat customers. If you can, set up retainer agreements with the steady clients you do ongoing work for. You should also think of ways you can make additional passive income through products. As creatives, our revenue is mainly based on services rendered, meaning we only make money for the time we're working. If you can make a product once and sell it many times over with minimal maintenance, you are making money without having to work for every penny. A great example is selling a digital product that can be directly downloaded by your customer. You spent the time to create something once that you can charge multiple customers to download (unlike hard goods), with very minimal personal customer interaction, if any.

At Hoodzpah, our income breakdown can be seen in the chart at left. These percentages are based on trends and data we track in our accounting software. Tracking where our income comes from helps us plan and estimate our future income If we are going to release a product, font, or course, we know we can take on less client work. We have a few retainer clients we can rely on for steady production work (they book three to six months in advance). Then, we try to land one to two big branding projects a year, and two to three small to medium-sized projects per month.

13. What is your Value Proposition Statement?

This is where you distill your company's purpose and service into one statement. It should include what your product/service is and something that makes your business unique. You could speak to the value you bring, your approach, a niche audience you serve, or your style.

Hoodzpah Income Breakdown

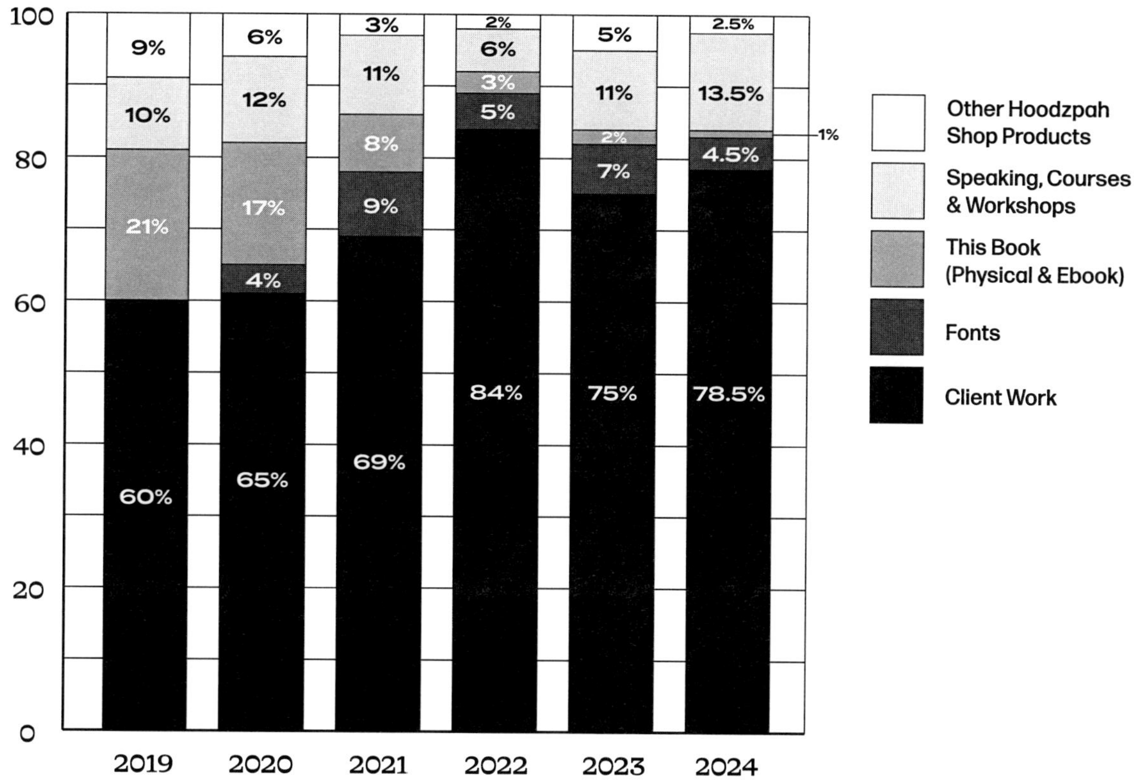

Hoodzpah Services Breakdown

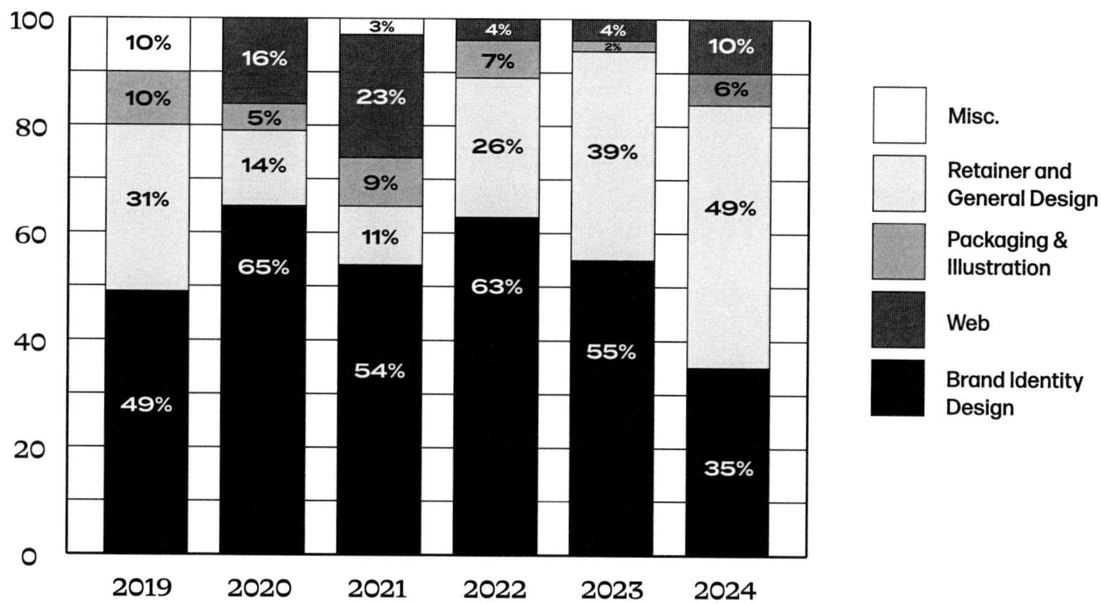

You did it! You made a plan. A real business plan. Sure, things might change, and you might have to pivot or adapt, but at least you generally have an idea of how to move forward. Save your answers to these questions somewhere safe, and refer back to them regularly to check on your progress or make updates as you learn more.

Chapter Checklist:

① Fill in your answers to the questions in this chapter to gather insights on how to move forward.

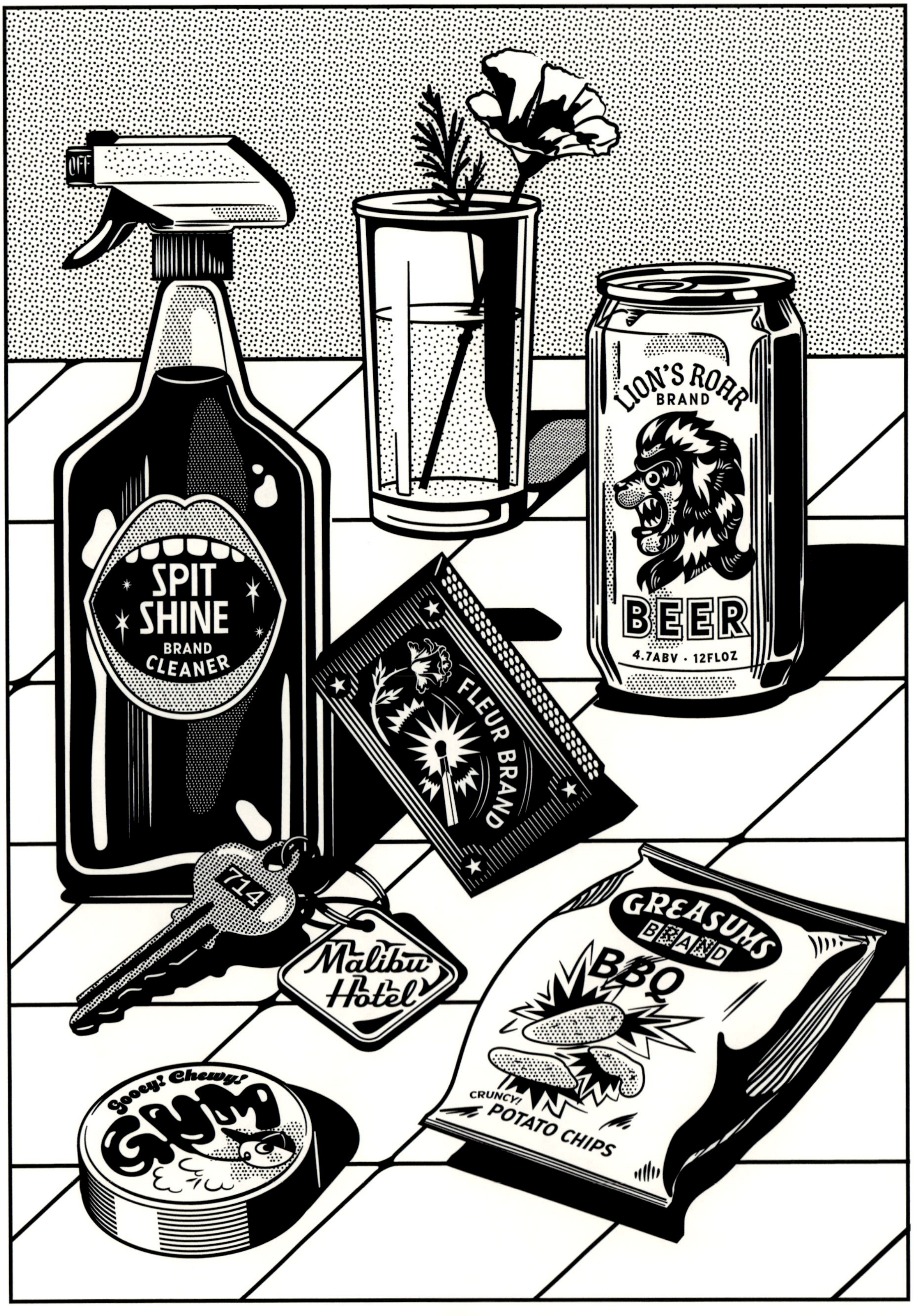

Illustration by: Amy Hood

7

Branding Your Business

Branding is ubiquitous these days. Thanks to the Kardashians, *Mad Men*, and social media, most of us know what brand is to some extent. But just in case you've been blissfully living off-grid, let's define our terms.

A brand *(noun)*: While your company offers a good or service, your brand is the personality, perception, distinct identifiers, and promise associated with your company's good or service.

Branding *(verb)*: This is the action you take to control and shape those perceptions and identifiers. When you're branding, you're trying to set expectations about your company. Branding might include creating a design system with a logo, type, and color that represents your company. Branding can also include creating messaging, developing a website, and filming a marketing campaign. The goal of branding is to communicate your brand's promise (what value you bring your customers) in a memorable and *consistent* way.

Brand identity *(noun)*: This is a collection of visual, verbal, and experiential identifiers of a brand. People often informally call this "the branding" (noun, not verb). The brand identity includes some or all of the following:

- Logo
- Brand traits
- Market positioning (Steinway is positioned as the premier piano brand, while Casio is positioned as the budget-friendly option.)
- Typefaces (Burger King's chunky, rounded serif)
- Brand colors (John Deere's green and yellow)
- Tone of voice (Honda's helpful and friendly tone)
- Tagline (Nike's "Just Do It")
- Product design (The design of a Mini Cooper or Volkswagen Beetle makes them instantly identifiable on the road without even seeing the logo.)
- Environmental and experience design (Think Apple's minimal stores or product onboarding)
- Packaging (The iconic teal Tiffany & Co. box, which is trademarked along with the color "Tiffany Blue")
- Sonic logo (Netflix's "ta-dum")

You get the gist. These outputs are the result of branding (verb). This isn't a complete list because the list can include almost anything and is ever-expanding as technology advances. Motion graphics, 3D, AR, VR, delivery and service vehicles, uniforms. Goodyear has a branded blimp!

Visual identity *(noun)*: The visual assets within the brand identity. Logo, type, color patterns, etc.

Logo *(noun)*: A graphic and/or typographic mark that distinctly identifies a company.

Without branding, your business is just a commodity. You're just another person selling products or services for cash. But with the right positioning, your brand identity makes you a specific choice for a specific kind of client, who is looking for a specific kind of outcome.

Coca-Cola and Sprite are both sodas. But Coca-Cola trades on classic nostalgia, happiness, and Christmas cheer (what other brand owns a holiday?), while Sprite embraces what's current with a bolder, edgier persona.

Now think of the known brand names in the creative services world. Studios and agencies like Gander, Jon Contino, Young Jerks, Louise Fili, Smith & Diction, Center, Hey, Fisk, Koto, Jessica Hische, Ragged Edge, Aaron Draplin, and Oh No Type Co. all have both a strong brand promise and a distinct brand identity. You could describe most of these studios' brand aesthetic and tone from memory. These studios are sought out for a specific style and aesthetic. So it makes sense for them to show that off front and center to attract like-minded clients. Young Jerks is well known for their clever copy and more-is-more approach to design. And their own brand identity reflects that without being overly imposing. Hey is known for a very bright, experimental, and irreverent style of work. Their own brand identity expresses that loud and clear.

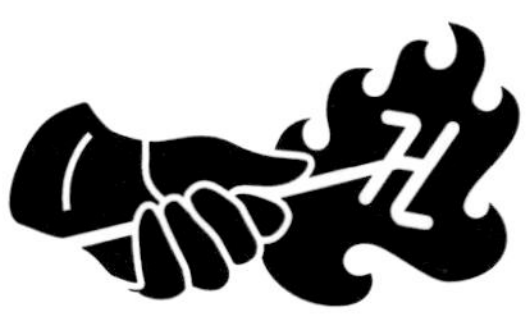

Now look at studios and agencies like Mouthwash, Jones Knowles Ritchie, Moniker, Manual, Order, Collins, and Porto Rocha. These are equally revered brand names in the creative space, but they have a more restrained approach to their own brand identity. Some of these have a logo and a brand typeface. Hardly any have a brand color. Some don't even have a custom logo. They just typeset their brand name in a sans serif typeface on their website. And yet, these are iconic brand names. Why? Because their brand promise and brand reputation are distinct through the creative work they put out and their approach to the work. For these studios, their visual identity is less about distinction and more about setting the right tone to reflect their brand traits and appeal to their target audience. They don't want their own studio's brand identity to eclipse or impose on their work. This approach is great for studios with a really strong portfolio and reputation.

Distinction in brand identity is very important. But if you take the goal of distinction too far, your brand identity can start to feel like a themed restaurant chain leaning too far into the bit. Every piece of your visual identity doesn't have to be wholly original and groundbreaking for your brand to be distinct. As you develop your studio branding, try grouping your brand identity assets into three buckets: distinct, vibey, and functional.

For the distinct bucket, you really only need to pick two things to get great results. For example, you could have a distinct logo and a distinct typeface (Dunkin' Donuts's rounded sans), a distinct logo and a distinct color (Land Rover green), or a distinct logo and a distinct messaging tone (Jack in the Box with Jack the mascot and his casual, deadpan comedic tone).

For the vibey bucket, think about assets that aren't necessarily distinct, but set the right tone and mood for your brand personality and audience. Typefaces, layout styles, motion, and messaging tone of voice might go in this category.

Lastly, the functional bucket. Not much to explain here. Sometimes things just need to be clear and straightforward, and that's fine.

The Brand of Santa

Did you know the version of Santa Claus we know today was created in part by Coca-Cola? In 1931, Coca-Cola commissioned artist Haddon Sundblom to paint Santa Claus for upcoming holiday advertisements. Up to that point, there were a plethora of depictions of Santa Claus from gaunt to portly, elvish to human, friendly to stern, dressed in everything from robes to animal furs. Haddon made Coca-Cola's Santa human, jolly, and rosy-cheeked, based on the description from the poem known as "'Twas the Night Before Christmas." Haddon drew Santa for Coca-Cola advertisements from 1931-1964. The longevity of these charming holiday campaigns has made Coca-Cola forever intertwined with nostalgic Christmas cheer.

More Than a Shoe

Consider Jordans. Are Nike Jordans leaps and bounds above any other sneaker technically speaking? Can they make you jump 10% higher or run 10% faster? Probably not. But they are some of the most popular shoes on the market because of the championship personality and broader culture they represent.

The shoe was released before Michael Jordan was a champion, but everyone saw his swagger. The shoes launched with a unique colorway (initially unsanctioned by the NBA—Nike paid Jordan's fines for wearing the shoes). New designs and colorways followed as Jordan's career exploded and the shoe became a cultural movement all its own, well past the end of Michael's basketball career (both times). →

If you find that leaning into a specific style for your brand identity comes naturally because it reflects the style of your creative service, go that route. If you are leaning toward more restrained, minimal branding because you want your work to be the defining element, follow that instinct. Your brand identity should reflect your genuine style, tone, and approach. Faking it will only result in a pastiche identity that attracts customers under false pretenses.

Your Brand, the Living Thing

A brand isn't something you can completely control—it is a negotiated reality. Your brand is a combination of the story you tell and the story others tell about you. When you start your business, you will attempt to target a certain audience through a specific aesthetic, tone, and offering (product/service). Ideally, the look of your logo, your website content, and the tone of your social media will attract your target audience. Then, it's up to you to deliver on your brand promises and the expectations you've set.

A beautiful brand identity with a poor product or bad service leads to customers feeling misled, disappointed, and frustrated. On the other hand, a great product with misaligned positioning or poorly executed brand identity could underperform or fail to attract the target demographic.

If the experience they have with your company matches the expectation you set through your brand identity, their feedback will be positive—even better if you exceed their expectations. But if your brand identity sets unrealistic expectations or promises something that your company fails to deliver, the customer feedback will be negative. And that feedback will likely spread fast and far.

Brands evolve. They go through stages. The highs, the lows, the occasional midlife crisis. They are pseudo-living things that need regular tending to reap the best fruit.

This all might sound terrifying—you little control freak, you. But you do have control over a few things in this equation.

1. Be Clear. Use your brand identity to embody what your company is good at and appeal to your true target customer. Set honest expectations for what you can do for your clients.
2. Deliver. Consistently provide an experience that positively aligns with your brand story and identity.

If you can do these two things, your clients will respond with positive emotions, praise, repeat business, and referrals. If you don't deliver, your clients will respond with complaints, bad reviews, refund requests, and maybe a public shaming via social media.

As an example, Wells Fargo has generally had a very consistent logo and brand identity system for decades. The classic serif typeface and the stagecoach logo. The red, yellow, and gold color palette. When you think of their brand identity, you can see they are trying to communicate that they are a legacy company you can trust. The look is traditional and solid.

Even though the brand identity has not changed much, Wells Fargo's brand reputation changed in a big way when it was reported that the company opened millions of unauthorized or fake accounts in 2016. The perception of their brand shifted from positive to negative, and it had nothing to do with the brand identity. Their reputation was now negatively impacting the brand identity, associating their logo with fraud and untrustworthiness.

In an opposite example, Kia entered the American market in the mid-'90s as a cheap, foreign car. Kias were not perceived as distinct, cool, or exceptional in any way. Kia was the budget brand. But in 2010, Kia hired Peter Schreyer, a former Audi and Volkswagen designer, and started a branding effort to strategically change the brand perception by focusing on quality and style.

The car designs became sleeker and more personality-driven. Kias actually looked cool, the features were better, and the marketing and messaging became distinctive and funny. The Kia Soul campaign with the giant hamsters took TV by storm in 2009—a weird and unexpected campaign for an equally weird and unexpected car model. Kia began to sponsor the NBA and became associated with the style-savvy culture of NBA stars. Blake Griffin soared over a Kia Optima to win the NBA dunk contest in 2011. The overall perception around Kia became more and more associated with style and relevance, not just value.

Through intentional branding and (more importantly) big improvements to the product and experience, Kia became a recognizable and sought-out brand, not just a nondescript carmaker. They embraced the shift in their latest brand identity redesign in 2021, which feels innovative, bold, and slightly defiant. Now the brand promise, brand experience, and the brand identity match. This brand is on the up and up (at least as of this writing).

People use certain brands as a reflection of who they are. Someone might buy Nike because they see themselves as someone who values performance and style, and they align with the competitive mentality of the brand. While someone else might wear Vans because they relate to the counterculture lifestyle associated with the brand. These choices we make about the shoes we wear, the cars we drive, the place we buy groceries, or the phone we buy are all tiny signals about how we want to be perceived by others. Our customers are no different. They choose to work with companies that reflect values or styles that resonate with how they want people to perceive their own company.

With this in mind, consider what ideals, expectations, and traits you want people to associate with your brand. Then, think about how you can visually and verbally communicate those things. This is the difference between a generic company and a distinct brand your ideal customer can relate to and identify with.

If you want to become an iconic, or at the very least, recognizable brand, the key is consistency. Everyone references Coca-Cola as the key example of brand consistency. They've had some variation of their script and that "Coca-Cola red" for more than a century. People recognize it instantly because the company has been consistent in its identity.

Just like your individual personality, your brand has unique features and mannerisms that unfold across your website, social media, tone of messaging and copy, logo, and so on. The goal is to find your unique and memorable elements and consistently lean into them. As people experience your brand more and more in a consistent way, you build brand recognition. It's hard to be recognized if you don't start with something memorable. But with the right brand identity pieces, consistently delivering on your brand promise, and enough exposure to your

→ Celebrities, rock stars, professional athletes from every sport, your cousin Scott, and even presidents have worn Jordans because they, like Ray-Bans or Levi's jeans, have become a symbol of timeless "cool." And that has very little to do with the insole or tech specs. It's about the cultural connotations associated with Jordans: being a champion, being the best, standing out, and flying high. How can you and your brand move past being just another commodity or service? How can you think of your brand outside of just services rendered and deliverables?

target audience, you can turn brand awareness (someone knowing about you) into brand salience (being a top-of-mind choice in a category).

If you're constantly putting on disguises and playing other parts, no one will remember you and what you stand for. Over time, brands that stick to their identity become more and more iconic. Barbie's ever-present pink. The minimal aesthetic of Apple's stores and products. Adidas's iconic three stripes on literally everything. Green slime is a classic identifier for Nickelodeon. Though the context around these core brand elements might change decade to decade, the elements themselves remain consistent, making them synonymous with the brands they represent. The Barbie product line today looks vastly different than it did forty years ago, but the pink remains as a core identifier.

Get in Line

In donut terms—let's look at Cafe Du Monde in New Orleans. They only sell three things: beignets, coffee, and milk. Yet, on any given day, there is a line full of people waiting to get in, snaking down Decatur Street. People don't complain about the lack of options. Instead, the cafe has become world famous for making the most delicious beignets since 1862. They claim to do one thing and one thing well. And they deliver on that promise.

Branding Discovery

What's the age-old adage? "Do unto yourself as you would do unto clients?" When creating your own logo and brand, treat yourself like a client. As with clients, good creative output needs to be tied to specific research and goals, or it will turn into a nightmare of conflicting ideas changing with every whim that comes along. Answer the prompts below to uncover what makes your brand unique and how your brand should be positioned in the market of options.

Positioning Exercise

Who am I trying to attract through my brand identity (Target audience)?

Think about your ideal audience's motivations, values, challenges, and budget.

How is my service/product unique from other options in the market? (Competitor analysis)

A competitor analysis is a great way to get cues about what resonates with you and what you could do differently with your brand identity. Look up studios similar in size in your area and abroad. Look up your brand heroes. Take notes on their target audience, their brand traits, logos, messaging, website, work niche, and more. Think about their strengths, weaknesses, and missed opportunities.

What are the traits I want associated with my brand? (Brand traits)

Choose three brand traits that encapsulate how and why you do business. Some traits might feel trite (creative, clever, approachable, etc.), but that's okay as long as they're true to you. We, as creatives, often feel that these words need to be wholly original or out-of-the-box in order to be effective. But brand traits are just like personality traits. There are only so many ways to describe people. Even personality tests like the Meyers-Briggs Type Indicator or the Enneagram test only have so many permutations for the many-faceted people on this very diverse earth. So don't worry if the words sound cliché. Bold, creative, trustworthy, elevated—the words are trite but can also be true. There's nothing new under the sun, really. It's all in how you put your own spin on it. Just answer honestly.

Once you have your traits, you will use your visuals, messaging, and customer experience to reflect those traits. We do branding for clients every day at Hoodzpah. We always agree to brand traits with clients before we start creative work, and we always gauge our work against how well it reflects those brand traits. We often refer back to the brand traits when client feedback veers off course from the agreed-upon goals, or if stakeholders are having trouble making a creative decision. They serve as a great gut check for staying on strategy.

"I am the *(adjective)* *(creative service)* for *(client type)*." (Positioning)

Now, try to sum up your unique positioning (based on your previous answers) by using this fill-in-the-blank phrase. You might be, "the rebellious creative agency for DTC brands that want to stand out." (Don't they all). Or "the elegant photographer for high-end hospitality brands." "The scrappy, Swiss-Army designer for Southern California small businesses." "The clever copywriter for companies wanting funny ad campaigns that convert." This isn't public-facing messaging by any means, but it's helpful to start with the simplest summation of who your brand is and what you do. Then, you can finesse and add personality from there.

Branding Personality Quiz

Here are some more questions to get your mind thinking about your brand and visual identity from a new perspective.

1. If your company had a celebrity spokesperson, who would it be? Why do they represent your brand traits and values?
2. If your company had a theme song, what would it be (or at least what genre of music)? Why?
3. If your brand could be summed up in an animal, plant, or object, what would it be? Why?
4. What is odd or interesting about you? Any hidden talents, wild experiences, or relatable interests? Our past experiences shape who we are and can often make a difference in how we perceive and interpret the world. These might even lead to ideas for imagery or messaging regarding you and your company.
5. Who are your brand heroes? What brands appeal to you, both in the creative space and beyond your industry? Why?

Time to Create Your Own Brand Identity

Enough talk. Let's develop some key assets for your brand identity.

Company Name

Here are some things to consider when choosing your business name.

Availability

Check that your choice of business name hasn't already been used by someone else. A quick internet search of the name could yield some high-level results. Then, search your name plus "design studio," or "photography," or whatever your field of specialty is. If someone is already using the name in your field, they might have inherent rights even if they haven't filed a trademark.

Here's a list of some brand traits to get your mind running.

Friendly
Serious
Playful
Casual
Professional
Intelligent
Curious
Rebellious
Creative
Clever
Nostalgic
Charming
Timeless
Kind
Helpful
Innovative Fore-running
Thoughtful
Relevant
Ethereal
Simple
No Nonsense
Quirky
Snarky
Funny
Warm
Inviting
Relatable
Exclusive
Elegant
Luxurious
Accessible
Reliable Sophisticated
Self-deprecating
Sarcastic
Whimsical
Energetic
Passionate
Trendy
Credible
Youthful
Trusted
Ambitious
Experienced
Determined

Naming Resources

Onym is a studio that specializes in naming. They have an incredible online guide of naming resources.

Check it out at guide.onym.co

Online tools like TMview's trademark database and World Intellectual Property Organization's Brand Database can show results for pending, filed, and inactive trademarks across the world. Do some research in your region to find out which trademark categories your business falls within. You can only trademark your name and logo for your business category. This is why some brands share the same name but offer different products, and they don't infringe on each other's rights. For example, Delta is the name of a faucet company and an airline. They can both legally use their trademarked names because the trademark office deemed there would be no potential for confusion among consumers since the services and products are so different. Even still, be cautious of using names already synonymous with popular companies. Trying to compete with a very well-known brand of the same name as you could be a tough road when it comes to being found online.

Also check if the name is available on social media and for domain purchase. If the word on its own is taken, get creative with hyphens and added words to find available handles and domains. Example: Hoodzpah was taken when we started, so we added "Design" and were able to lock down the assets.

Originality

Try and find a name that is unique, but not too complex to remember, say, or spell. Depending on how you look at it, we either failed or aced this test with our company name: Hoodzpah. We spent about five years of our childhood in upstate New York where Yiddish was part of the common vernacular. "Chutzpah" was something we heard and said often. It means bold, unapologetic, and brazen. Oh how clever we thought ourselves when we realized our last name, Hood, somewhat slots into the word chutzpah. Unfortunately, a good portion of the rest of the country (and world) is not familiar with the Yiddish term. Not only that, but it's a hard word to pronounce and a harder word to spell since, technically, it's a remix of the original word. At this stage in our career, it's served as much as a talking point as it has a hindrance, and we're glad to have it. It proves a hassle to spell over the phone to tech support and new clients, but finding us online is dead simple, even if you spell it wrong. No one has a name even close to ours.

Another great option to consider is the non-sequitur name, which seems like it has nothing to do with your product or service. For example: Avocado Green Mattress. A food and a place to sleep? Why? And yet, it feels right because avocados are smooth and good for you, and Avocado Green Mattresses are soft and tout green practices. Sometimes, if the vibe is right for a name, that's enough.

Meaning

Does the name tell a story? Does it have meaning that can help explain the "why" behind your unique business approach and skill set? For example, legend has it that Steve Jobs chose the name Apple because he wanted people to start seeing computers as something universal, elementary, and approachable, not something that only niche tech hobbyists could enjoy. Few things are as disarming and simple as an apple. Even if that story is more apocryphal than true, it's a lovely myth and paints a perfect example.

Feeling

A made-up business name might be meaningless without context, but it should at least evoke a feeling that will align with your business as a brand. For example, "doinkus" is a fun made-up word to say, but the sound of it infers putzi-ness and ridiculousness. Choose a made-up word that feels in line with your services and brand personality. Need inspiration? Try www.Wordoid.com. This website will help you mishmash new words together based on your favorite letters and preferred length.

Mouthfeel should also not be overlooked. How does it feel when you say the name out loud?

Aesthetics

Consider if the letter forms in the name appeal to you from a logo design perspective. A capital Q is a blessing in a logo. While a capital I can be hard to add personality to, even with the most creative of typefaces. Sometimes, a group of letters just isn't visually pleasing. For a rough test, try quickly typing your potential name in a few different type styles (sans serif, serif, script, slab, uppercase, title case, lowercase, etc.). Choosing a name that has meaning and visual appeal is quite a triumph.

Logo

Oh the logo. Even if the rest of your brand identity materials are fairly restrained, a well-designed logo can provide so much panache and personality. But don't let the importance of this piece stress you out.

Emotional Journey of Branding Your Business

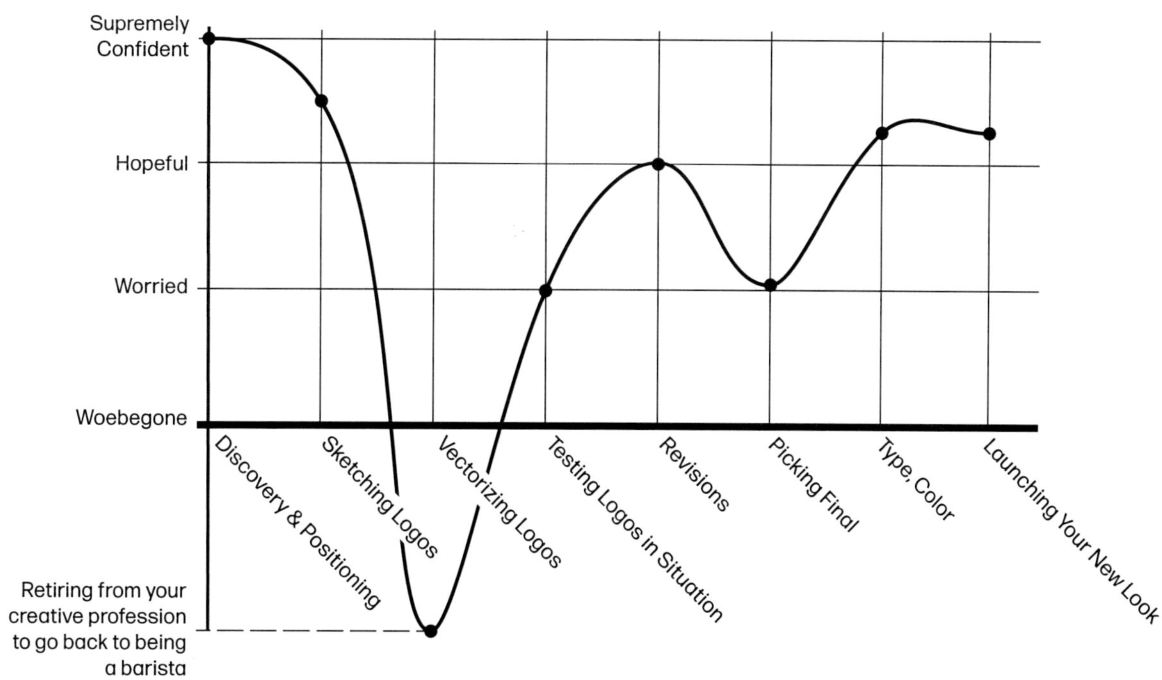

Yes, your logo should allude to your business's personality and values, but in no way will it tell the whole story. Don't be too precious about it, or you'll seriously delay getting your business started. Aim for a good solution, not a perfect one; otherwise, you'll never be done. It's perfectly fine to find something that works for now (even if you don't love it), then change it up in a year when you've learned more about your business and brand ethos.

The best you can do is treat this job as if it were a client's project. Consider your unique brand positioning, sketch concepts to get a lot of rough ideas out, then jump into your design program of choice and start rapidly iterating. Get as many ideas down as possible. Now, walk away from it. Come back with fresh eyes in an hour, in a day, in a week. Recheck the work against the target audience and brand traits you're trying to communicate. Don't worry too much about color. Just focus on the forms and letters in black and white to start. Seek critique and feedback from mentors and trusted peers. If more than one person gives you the same piece of critique, listen.

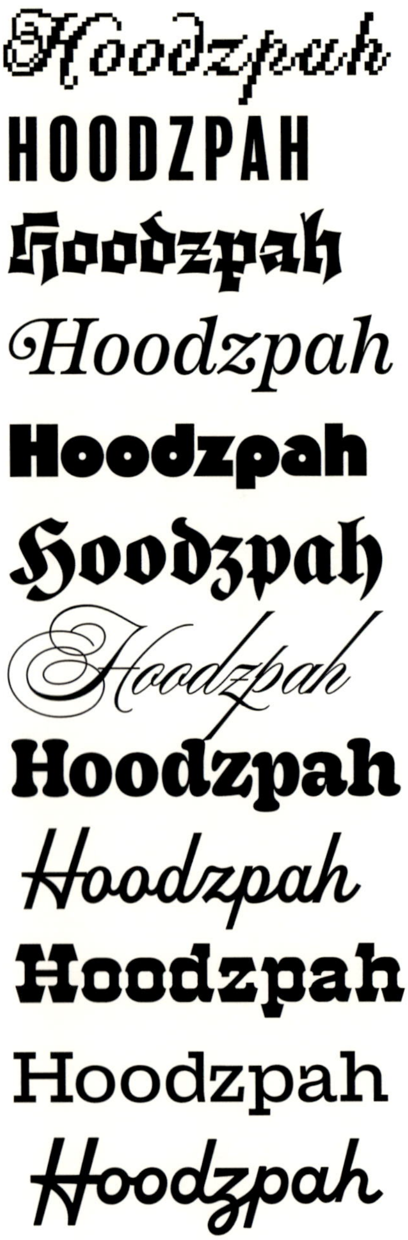

If you're really getting stuck on your logo, don't underestimate the power of a good typeface to bail you out. Typeset your company name in a quality typeface that reflects your company's personality and style. Sometimes less is more.

It can be easy to jump on the latest, greatest design trend when branding your business and designing your logo. And sure, you can totally do that. But consider that popular trends have already reached a max saturation of exposure. The more prevalent the trend, the less unique and ownable the look is, and the more likely it is that your design will feel dated in a few years.

Remember that your brand's supporting visuals (illustration, photography, graphics) that change more often can be relevant to current trends, while your logo should be evergreen so you can build equity in it across years and decades.

If you're working on a glyph or icon as part of your logo, think of the connotations of any imagery before making a final decision on your design. Research cultural perceptions of the icon to ensure you're not accidentally associating your brand with things you didn't intend to.

Practically speaking, the logo should easily scale down or up. Consider how it will adapt from its smallest state (a favicon in someone's web browser), to its largest state (building signage or on a big screen at a conference). If your main logo is more detailed, you might create an optically adjusted version for your smallest use cases. Create variations for the different applications you might encounter down the road: a version with the icon only, a version with the wordmark only, etc. Have all of these variations saved and ready for print and digital.

Once you've come up with a concept, do your due diligence to check that there aren't any similar marks already in use within your industry and region. Do a reverse image search on Google and through the WIPO Brand Database we mentioned earlier. Ask your lawyer to help you research and avoid any conflicting marks if you plan to trademark. If there are no conflicts and you want to protect your creation, have your lawyer file a trademark! You can also apply for a trademark through sites like LegalZoom.

Typography, Color, and Design Themes

Once you're happy with your logo, develop a system of typefaces, colors, and design themes that can support it. Making these design decisions at the beginning means you won't have to invent a new design style every time you have to make brand assets.

Choose one or two core brand colors to use the most prominently. Clients will associate those colors with your brand as you consistently use them. Then, if you want more room to play, you can build a supporting color palette for broader applications like illustrations/layouts, etc.

Brand typefaces are a great way to inject personality into your decks, social media, website, etc. Consider choosing one personality typeface with more character, and a more restrained workhorse typeface for things like client presentation decks, where the focus is on the client, not your studio.

"At the end of the day, you can't please everyone. You're not the Cheesecake Factory."

Why stop there? If you want more, think of design themes like photography treatments, patterns, illustrations, custom icons, and layout styles (collage, Swiss grid, brutalist, maximalist). There are so many creative ways to create a distinct look and feel for your brand identity.

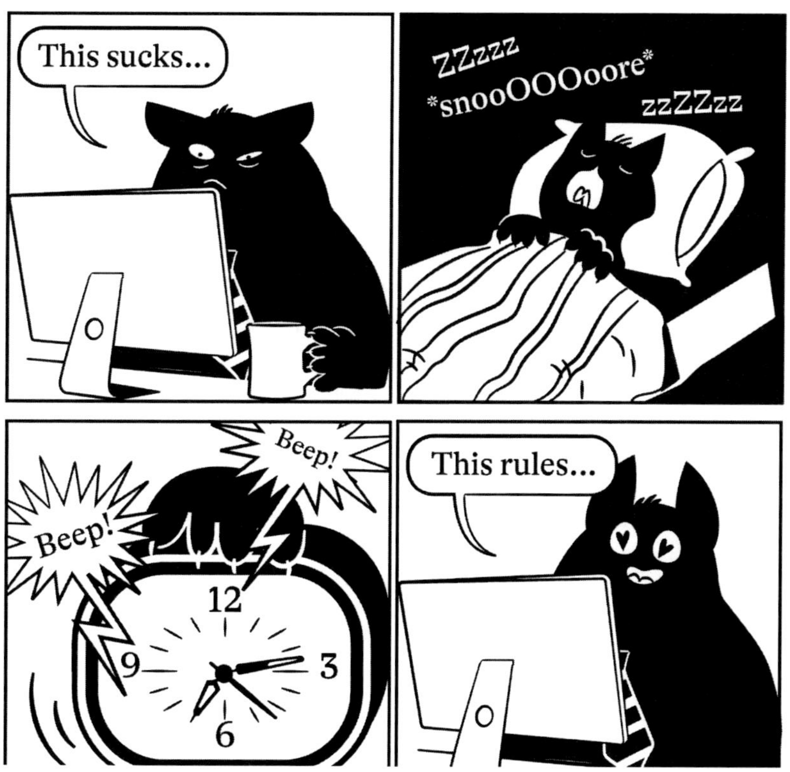

At the end of the day, you can't please everyone. You're not the Cheesecake Factory. Some people won't like your style, and that's okay. You're trying to attract folks who will. Just take a moment to consider the potential subtext or signals that your font, color, symbol, and design themes may infer about your business.

Messaging and Voice

Writing is a four-letter word to many creatives (well, except writers . . . obviously) and it shouldn't be. As a freelancer, business owner, and the promoter of your brand, you have to know how to write at least a little. And it's not impossible. We don't know who's perpetuating this persona about writing, like it's some mystic skill that only the chosen few can harness. It's not a level of nirvana. As scary as you think writing is, it's really not that far from what you do every day. When you talk to your friends, when you persuade your partner to watch *Love is Blind*, when you try for the millionth time to explain to your mother "what exactly you're doing with your life" as a creative—every time you use words to persuade a client, explain a proof, or connect with someone, you are exercising the chops it takes to be a great writer.

"What makes an epic writer is not grammar, sentence structure, or even spelling (there are color-coded squiggly lines in every word-processing program to help you correct those). What makes a great writer is being able to communicate to your audience in a way that they can understand and relate to."

What makes an epic writer is not grammar, sentence structure, or even spelling (there are color-coded squiggly lines in every word-processing program to help you correct those). What makes a great writer is being able to communicate to your audience in a way that they can understand and relate to. Stop thinking of writing as that five-paragraph essay you were trained to spew out for high school history class. Start thinking about it as a way to record a conversation for a future listener.

If you can learn to cope with and even enjoy writing, you'll be rewarded over and over again. Writing proposals and emails will get simpler and less daunting. You'll be able to better explain your proofs with annotations. You'll be able to better win over clients. You'll be able to connect with potential clients online through articles, social media, and portfolio blurbs. Your overall efficiency will go up, too. Here are some tips on how to tackle writing about yourself and your brand:

Start with a goal and succeed with a process. Have you ever started writing something only to find yourself completely lost on five different tangents two hours later? That's because you went into the project without a clear goal to check your progress against. When you start, have a concise purpose.

What's the main reason you're writing? To explain the value you can bring to your target audience, and relate to their motivations and needs, so they feel compelled to reach out to you. Now, make a quick list of the facts you want to include to support this goal. Don't worry about full sentences, just write your notes. Now you have an outline to guide your writing and keep you on track. Organize your notes into common themes, then turn them into sentences. To begin, focus on clarity. Then, you can get clever and add personality. Get a first draft out quickly. Then, step away and return with fresh eyes and edit. Run a spell checker. This writing process will serve you well no matter what you're writing.

Be genuine. Why are you trying to talk like Batman's butler? Why are you writing like an instructional manual reads? Unnecessary technical language or flowery words can just muddy the waters. Be you. Speak about what you know using terms you and your target audience are familiar with. Explain why you care. Being genuinely passionate about what you do and why you do it will come through in your writing.

Use a brand voice that reflects your brand traits. Just like a person, every brand has a unique tone and voice. When you talk about your brand on your website, what kind of language will you use? If you're naturally funny and feel your humor reflects your brand's values and message, that might be a great voice to channel. If you aren't naturally funny, don't try to be. If you are looking to convey a professional, reliable personality, you might avoid internet slang or cuss words. If you want to be perceived as a casual, laid-back brand, loosen up with your language (just tread carefully). Consider words you want to associate with your brand, and words you want to avoid. Develop a voice that naturally flows for you and works for your audience.

Have ready-made content. Once you've worked out what you want to say about your company, how you want to say it, and to whom, gather the following pieces in a folder that's easy to grab from later.

Your Company Bio. One or two paragraphs is fine.

Your Value Proposition Statement. A succinct synopsis (one to two sentences) about who you are and why customers should choose you over the next bloke. This is the thirty-second pitch for when you see Mark Cuban or Barbara Corcoran on the moving walkway at DFW airport. You've got to pitch yourself fast.

Your Service List. Name your services, and give a brief explanation of what they are and why they are valuable to clients.

Keep these assets in a master document. Having these things thoughtfully written out in your desired voice and tone, spell-checked, and ready for action will save you time and effort when you get ready to build your website and social media profiles. Winging it every time you create a new account is exhausting and often leads to an inconsistent brand presence riddled with differing info. Plus, interviewers, podcasts, conferences, and awards shows will likely ask for these things.

For those of you still not sold on writing or who can't find the time to do it well, hire a freelancer or a clever friend to help you out with these messaging assets. Give the writer the bullet points on what you want to say, explain the desired tone, and let them do their magic.

Brand Guidelines

A brand guidelines document summarizes your brand identifiers for future collaborators. Brand guidelines can include:

- **Logo system and usage guidelines.** Include your logo and any alternate variations. If certain logo variations are made for certain use cases, note that.
- **Core brand fonts.** Establish your display header fonts and which fonts will be used for body copy, etc.
- **Brand colors.** Define the RGB, CMYK, hex code, and Pantone color (if needed) for each swatch in your brand color palette.
- **Rules, dos and don'ts.** This is an especially helpful section if you have a team or plan to outsource your brand work/marketing to others. If you never want your logo at a 45-degree angle, specify that! If the logo should never be used on a photo background, specify that. If the logo has requirements for the amount of clear space or padding that surrounds it, specify that.

- **Brand traits.** A quick summary at the beginning is valuable.
- **Ready-made messaging.**
- **Misc.** Any other design themes you want to define and codify?

Collateral

Doing business comes with the usual trappings: deck templates, business cards (are we still doing these?), social media templates, hats and tees, branded frisbees, and so on. Create a unified set of collateral that will help position your company as a capable, exciting, and professional outfit to prospective clients. Tees and hats are great swag because they turn friends and colleagues into walking billboards. Find unique ways to show off your brand and delight your clients and peers.

Consider each piece as part of the whole so everything looks intentional and consistent. These are your subtle commercials to clients, showing them what you could do for their brand.

Website

Your website is one of the most powerful marketing assets in your tool chest. We talk about this more in future chapters, but the long and short of it is: You need a professional, branded website where people can check out your work, learn about the value you offer through your services, and submit inquiries for projects. Your website is as much about your brand story as it is about capturing and informing your future clients. When creating your site, consider things from their perspective. What do they need and want? What are their fears and motivations? How can you speak to the value you can bring them?

Invest in a legitimate domain name—www.JohnDoe.freesite.com doesn't cut it. You don't have to know how to code to get a great site on a budget. WordPress, Squarespace, Webflow, Cargo, and others offer themes and templates for creatives who might not have the time, patience, or coding knowledge to create something custom. Most themes come with demo content that can be installed with one click. Then it's up to you to customize the information, graphics, and images to suit your needs. Look for themes that have good user ratings, a high number of purchases, recent bug fixes and updates, and that are responsive or mobile-friendly.

Install Google Analytics or a similar app to keep tabs on your web traffic so you can see what content performs well and where you can improve. Connect a newsletter subscription form (through Mailchimp, HubSpot, Klayvio, or a similar service) so you can collect emails from people interested enough to subscribe (these are fans in the making). Many themes allow for an e-commerce store, too. Remember that plugins and customizing code can cause incompatibility issues, so be ready to invest time and money in upkeep. This is a part of business. A website isn't a one-time investment. It will need to evolve with you and with technology. Set aside a fund for fixes and renovations. Think of it as your online office. Even after buying the office space, you'll need to clean it and spruce it up here and there. This is true no matter what web solution you choose.

If you are determined to create a completely custom site but don't know how to code, trade with a web developer. Make a deal, sell a kidney, do whatever it takes to get a website that fits your branding, meets your online goals, and presents you as a professional. At the very least, you should have an up-to-date Dribbble or Behance profile as you build your income and client roster. These sites can fill a gap and help you get discovered—but a branded website is a testament to your studio's professionalism and dedication.

Your Brand Asset Folder

Collect your logo files, fonts, design templates, brand guidelines, collateral files, and any other commonly used assets into a well-organized folder. Do it. Seriously. Right now. We'll wait.

This is not an exhaustive list of all the things you could create for your brand identity. So take liberties and add to this list as it makes sense for your brand.

Chapter Checklist:

① Do the positioning and discovery exercises to determine your brand traits and brand positioning.

② Pick your business name and check for conflicts. Consider trademarking.

③ Create your logo. Check for conflicts. Consider trademarking. Save final files.

④ Create a simple brand guidelines book, and save a brand assets folder.

⑤ Create the collateral pieces you need to get started—business cards, proposal and proof decks, social media avatars and templates, etc.

⑥ Get your website up, or at least post a portfolio profile on a site like Behance.

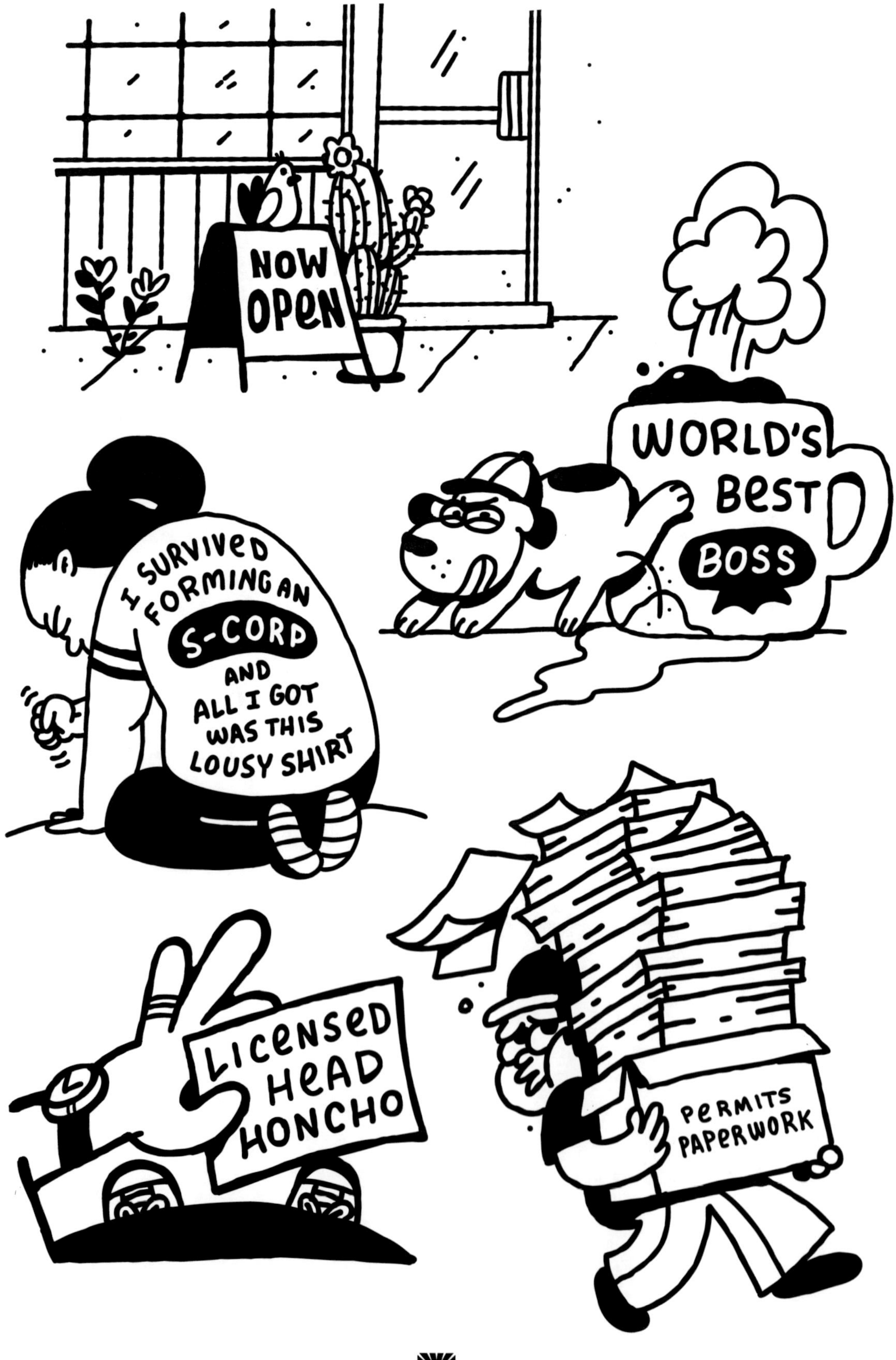

Illustration by: Joonbug

8
Making It Official

In order to start and maintain a business in good standing with your local, state, and national government, you'll need to register your business and potentially obtain some licenses and permits.

Why? Because your government wants its cut (taxes) and wants to peek over your shoulder to make sure you're complying with its rules and regulations. Plus, the business structure you choose could help offset your legal and financial risk.

It'll be tempting to treat your business like your high school babysitting gig (sweet, sweet cash under the table— completely untraceable by Big Brother). But truly, you don't want the mess, headache, and risk of trying to skirt taxes and laws. It could seriously come back to bite you. Go through the proper channels at the beginning to set your company up legitimately. And if you aren't paying your taxes yet, get that in order too, (just ask Wesley Snipes). Your clients will request forms confirming your business tax ID for their tax purposes. So you'll need to figure this out sooner rather than later.

When you register your business locally or nationally, you'll need to know what type of business structure or entity type your business will be. Your business entity options depend on your situation and location. Each option has its own perks and purpose when it comes to requirements you have to meet, taxes or fees you have to pay, and liability you want to offset.

If you plan to hire an accountant or lawyer to help you decide your business entity type and register your business, skip to the next chapter. If the thought of reading this chapter gives you stress sweats, maybe it's worth hiring a professional instead of doing it on your own. The process of legally setting up your business can be a little tedious and sometimes confusing. You might be thinking, "I don't want to shell out for a pricey accountant or attorney." We were you. We understand. But sometimes it's worth investing the money to make sure it's done right. Part of running your own business is knowing what you're good at and when to delegate.

If you have a close friend or family member who has already started their own business and gone through this process, reach out to them for advice after reading this chapter and gathering your best notes. Their input might give you all the guidance you need.

Since we're based in the United States, we'll be covering the business entity options for the USA. If you live elsewhere, you can do an internet search on "business entity options in [your country/state/city]" or see if your government gives guidance via their website. Many countries offer online filing for business entity status, and their websites will also likely explain the requirements for each. Remember, you might need to register or obtain licenses at local, state, and national levels depending on your location. Check each level, starting with the national.

Choosing the Right Business Structure

In the United States, the main types of for-profit business entities are: sole proprietorship, partnership, corporation, and Limited Liability Company (LLC). Within each entity, there are further entity options. You'll be glad to learn that one entity type doesn't even require any forms or registration to start!

Following, we go through each one, listing the pros and cons. Review the options, and ask your accountant, lawyer, or business mentor for advice before filing paperwork. You'll need to know your business entity type before you can obtain a Tax Identification Number (TIN) or Employer Identification Number (EIN), file for licenses and permits, set up a bank account, do your taxes, or even file for a DBA (Doing Business As). As your business grows, you can change your business structure to suit your changing needs.

The US Small Business Administration (SBA) is a government agency that offers guidance on which forms and steps are required to register each business entity type. The particulars can vary per state, and the SBA website will help you know what's needed for your location.

If you need help filing the paperwork, your accountant or lawyer can help you prepare and file. Or you could use a service like LegalZoom. For the simpler structures, you can often handle the paperwork on your own and save some cash. Once you choose your structure and file your forms, you've officially established a company!

How small is small?

The SBA considers you a small business if you have fewer than 500 employees, and/or your yearly revenue is under a certain amount. For graphic design that amount is $9M, but this number varies per industry classification. Refer to the US Small Business Administration's table of small business size standards if you're interested in learning more.

Sole Proprietorship

"A sole proprietorship is the simplest and most common structure chosen to start a business. It is an unincorporated business owned and run by one individual with no distinction between the business and you, the owner. You are entitled to all profits and are responsible for all your business's debts, losses and liabilities." - Small Business Association (www.SBA.gov)

The great thing about being a sole proprietor is that you don't have to file any forms to officially be one. However, you might need a license or permit to operate. Skip ahead to the "Obtain Licenses and Permits" section in this chapter to find out more.

Pros/Yay! It's the easiest and cheapest business structure to establish.

As a sole proprietor, in the eyes of the government, you as an individual and your business are one entity (when it comes to taxes, income, legal burdens, etc.). And because you are your business, any business income is counted as your income. You only file your personal income tax return using your Social Security number. No separate corporate income tax return is required because all the income passes through to you (which is why this is sometimes called a "pass-through entity"). You also don't file official paperwork to start, maintain, or close your business. You just have to make sure you're covered on permits and licenses for things like a DBA (Doing Business As filing allows you to use a business name other than your legal birth name) or a seller's permit (if you're selling goods/merchandise other than just services).

Cons/Bummer. You're liable, and you have to pay the self-employment tax.

Because you are your business, you are personally accountable for any debts owed by your business. Be aware that your personal property (car, house, personal savings) can be seized to pay your business debts. You also have to pay the self-employment tax. This covers Social Security and Medicare. When you worked for someone else, you saw this as the FICA tax on your pay stub. Now, you are your own employer, so you have to pay that yourself.

Choosing Your Business Type

Business Type	Ownership	Liabilities	Benefits	Taxes & Etc.
Sole Proprietor (SP)	Single owner	You are fully liable (sad trombone)	• Single tax return • No paperwork to form, maintain, or dissolve.	• Self-employment tax • Personal income tax
General Partnership (GP)	2 or more owners	You and your partners are fully liable (sad trombone)	• Single tax return • Shared responsibility • Extra contribution of skills and capital	• Self-employment tax • Personal income tax
Limited Partnership (LP)	At least 1 general partner and 1 limited partner	General partners are fully liable, and limited partners are liable up to their investment	• Single tax return • General partners gain investment without giving up management authority • Limited partners have limited personal liability	• Self-employment tax • Personal income tax
Limited Liability Partnership (LLP)	2 or more limited partners	Partners are only liable for their own actions and debts (not their partner's)	• Single tax return • Limited liability • Safe way to test business partners before forming an LLC or Corporation	• Self-employment tax • Personal income tax • Depending on state, flat annual tax (e.g., $800/yr in CA)
Limited Liability Corporation (LLC)	1 or more members	Members have limited liability	• Single tax return • Limited personal liability	• Self-employment tax • Personal income tax • Depending on state, flat annual tax • Requires EIN
C Corp (Corporation)	1 or more members	Members have limited liability	• Limited personal liability • Less ownership restrictions	• Corporate income tax • Owners must also pay Personal income tax • Filing fee to start • Depending on state, flat annual tax • Requires EIN
S Corp (Corporation)	1 or more shareholders, but no more than 100. All must be U.S. citizens	Members have limited liability	• Single tax return • Limited personal liability • Allows stock options	• Self-employment tax • Personal income tax • Filing fee to start • Depending on state, flat annual tax • Requires EIN

Partnership or General Partnership (GP)

This simple business structure caters to businesses with more than one owner.

"A partnership is the relationship between two or more people to do trade or business. Each person contributes money, property, labor or skill, and shares in the profits and losses of the business." - IRS (www.IRS.gov)

The most important part of forming a partnership is coming up with your partnership agreement. Let's pause for dramatic effect, because it can't be emphasized enough how important this document is. This document outlines boundaries, ownership percentages, and partner roles (this is especially helpful at the beginning). This might seem formal and even awkward for those of you starting your business with a friend or family member—but it's even more important for you because you have valuable relationships at stake. You don't want to blow up a relationship over a failed business. Things can get hairy when money comes into play. People's social personalities can be very different from their work personalities. Someone you love hanging out with might be a nightmare to work with. Get the details ironed out from the jump. It's a great initial stress test for your business relationship. If you can't see eye to eye on the basic pillars of an agreement, then you should reconsider the partnership or choice of partner.

You can find customizable partnership agreement templates online. Start with the template outline and then go through line by line, tailoring to your needs. Using a template initially helps save money, but it's highly recommended to get your final draft reviewed by a lawyer. You want to be certain everyone is protected and that you haven't missed any glaring loopholes.

A partnership agreement should include the following:

- **Ownership percentages.** Are you going in 50/50? Or perhaps one person is putting in more effort or money, so it's more like 65/35.
- **Profit and loss allocation.** Unless you clarify otherwise, this is usually divided equally among partners.
- **Salaries.**
- **Decision-making procedures and any hierarchy.**
- **Exit strategies.**
- **Roles and responsibilities.**

Partnerships are registered at the state level.

Pros/Yay! It's easy and cheap to set up, plus you have someone else contributing to the business with you.

The cost totals the fees associated with your licenses and permits.

Depending on your allocation of responsibility, you have someone to share in the financial commitments and growth of the business. Wisely chosen partners mean more good ideas, more marketable skills, and a larger existing network to draw upon for new clients.

Cons/Bummer. You're liable and you don't have full control.

With more than one person in charge, there's always the potential for conflicting opinions. Oh, and you have to share the revenue.

Like a sole proprietorship, a general partnership holds you personally liable for any debts owed by your business. This applies to any of your partner's actions as much as your own. Remember, they're taking a risk on you, too. Your personal property can be seized to cover debts.

With partners, you might disagree about how you want to run the show or grow your business. Maybe they're more of a quiet-night-at-home-playing-Settlers-of-Catan kind of person, and you're more of a head-to-Joshua-Tree-with-nothing-but-a-coffee-can-full-of-peyote kind of person. You have to find your common ground and meet in the middle. It's imperative that you learn how to effectively communicate and figure out the best way to work together.

Last, you share profits. To keep things from getting weird, outline how profits are shared in your partnership agreement. You might be saying to yourself, "I'd never let money get between my business partner and me," or "My business partner would never screw me over," and we hope that's true. But you'd be a fool not to prepare and protect yourself by considering and outlining policies for every possible "what if" scenario. Again, money—or the feeling of a lack thereof—makes humans do strange things.

Limited Partnership (LP)

If you want to bring on partners to help with capital investment, but you don't want all partners to have a say in the running of the business, then a limited partnership might be for you. In a limited partnership, the "general partners" have management authority to run the business and take on full personal liability, while "limited partners" generally have no management authority and are only liable up to the amount of their investment. Profits are shared and should be clearly defined in your partnership agreement. Like a partnership and sole proprietorship, this is a pass-through entity, so each partner files their personal income tax return, without a separate business return. Just like a general partnership (mentioned above), we highly recommend you draw up a partnership agreement! Just do it. If you're unsure which kind of partnership is best for you, as always, we encourage you to consult with your attorney or accountant.

Limited Partnerships are generally handled at the state level.

Pros/Yay! Earn capital without giving up control.

As the general partner, you can join up with investors and make them limited partners, so you maintain control over decision-making in how the business is run.

Cons/Bummer. You're liable.

The general partner is liable for any debts or issues that arise with the business.

Limited Liability Company (LLC)

An LLC is considered a hybrid entity because it is a mix of a corporation and partnership or sole proprietorship. LLC regulations vary from state to state, so be sure to research your state's specifics. Generally, an LLC has pass-through income taxation (like SP and Partnerships), and members are protected from being held personally responsible for debts and liabilities from the business (like a corporation).

LLCs are registered at the state level.

Yay! You have limited liability, and there's more operational flexibility.

In an LLC, you can be personally protected from your business liabilities (meaning, if your business falls into debt, your creditors cannot go after your personal assets to pay for those debts). LLCs have less registration paperwork than an S-Corporation but similar start-up costs. Profit sharing is also less restricted than with other structures. Income from an LLC passes through to the members. This means members need only file their personal income tax returns. Most states don't restrict ownership (meaning individuals, corporations, other LLCs, foreigners, and foreign entities can all be members), and you can structure management however you want. In most states, the lifespan of the company can continue even if a member leaves or dies.

Cons/Bummer. There's a little more involved in forming one, and you need to pay self-employment taxes.

States require you to file Articles of Organization and draft an Operating Agreement to form an LLC. While not as extensive as forming a corporation, it's still more involved than an SP or Partnership. Like a sole proprietor, LLC managing members also have to pay self-employment taxes. There is often an annual state fee for LLCs. You will also need to apply and pay for a federal EIN (Employer Identification Number). Be sure to clarify in an agreement among members how to handle a member leaving or selling their membership.

Corporation (S or C Corp)

A corporation is a more complex business structure with many more ongoing requirements, but it also gives owners the strongest personal liability protection.

Corporations are formed at the state level.

C Corp

The C corporation is the standard corporation, and is a completely separate entity from its owners. Unlike the previously mentioned pass-through entities (SP, GP, LP, LLP, and LLC), C corps require a business income tax return on top of owners filing personal income tax returns. Unfortunately, this can mean that, "In some cases, corporate profits are taxed twice — first, when the company makes a profit, and again when dividends are paid to shareholders on their personal tax returns," according to the SBA (https://www.sba.gov/business-guide/launch-your-business/choose-business-structure). Ownership is much more flexible in a C corp. C-corp owners hold business shares (which are why they're also called shareholders) and can leave the business or sell their shares without major disruption. C corps can sell stock to raise money or offer it as an employee benefit.

S Corp

S corporations are pass-through entities. The business's deductions, losses, income, credits, and profits pass through to shareholders, who report their share of the business's performance on their personal tax returns. The S corp avoids the potential double taxation that comes with a C corp (previously mentioned). Unlike the C corp, an S corp does have ownership limitations: There can be no more than one hundred shareholders/owners, shareholders must be US citizens/residents, and shareholders cannot be C corporations, other S corporations, LLCs, partnerships or certain trusts.

Pros/Yay! You have limited liability and better long-term options.

Both S corps and C corps offer limited liability protection to business owners (or shareholders), and can continue to exist even if ownership or management changes. Unlike sole proprietorships and partnerships, which are dissolved if an owner leaves or dies. Unlike partnerships or SPs, corporations also let you easily transfer your share of ownership in the company. It's as simple as endorsing and signing over your stock certificates representing your share of the company. This attribute can make your company more appealing to investors, to whom you can easily transfer shares. Most experts would agree that corporations are the best structure for companies that intend to eventually be publicly traded or sold.

Bummer. It's more expensive to form, there's more paperwork and obligations, and with C corps, there is potential for more tax burden..

The work involved in incorporating is extensive and best done by a professional, which we highly recommend. It's worth the investment to save you the headache. S and C corps require extensive articles of incorporation to be filed with the state, which a professional can help you prepare. Both also require ongoing corporate obligations like issuing stock, adopting bylaws, holding shareholder meetings, filing annual reports, and paying annual fees. If the rules of incorporation aren't followed, a court could pierce the corporate veil of protection and hold owners personally responsible for the business debts and liabilities. Sometimes, your tax burden will increase when you incorporate. Just as the filing fee for incorporation varies per state, so does the annual fee.

The above are the most common business types for creatives. Other business types that you could research further include:

- Benefit Corporation or B Corp: Similar to a C Corp, a B Corp is usually adopted by businesses that are not just for profit but for a cause.. A good example of this is Patagonia, which donates to and supports environmental causes.
- Nonprofit: If you plan to work solely for charities or educational institutions, this might be right for you. Check out the agency Ideo for an example of this.

Which Business Structure is Right for You?

Corporations and LLCs are more advanced business structures that might not be the best investment of your money at the early stages of your business. You can likely get by as a partnership or sole proprietor while you test the waters of self-employment and prove your business model. Consider incorporating your business when your liabilities and income grow to the point where you would not want to be personally liable. Our CPA gave us a specific income goal to meet before we incorporated. Up till then, our risk was not very high, and the price to incorporate wasn't justified yet. As always, ask your CPA or business lawyer what the best solution is for you individually.

Get your Tax ID, Licenses, and Permits

Obtaining Your Tax Identification Number (TIN)

In the United States, you usually don't need any licenses or permits at the national/federal level. But you may need to apply for a Tax Identification Number. To get your licenses and permits at the state and city level, you'll likely need a Tax Identification Number (TIN), which is a number the Internal Revenue Service (IRS) associates with your business for tax purposes. Your TIN will either be an Employer Identification Number (EIN) that you'll have to apply for through the IRS, or your existing personal Social Security Number (SSN), which is issued by the Social Security Administration.

According to the IRS, you need an EIN if any of the following apply:

- Your business has employees
- You operate your business as a corporation or a partnership structure
- You file any of these tax returns: Employment, Excise, or Alcohol, Tobacco and Firearms
- You withhold taxes on income, other than wages, paid to a non-resident alien
- You have a Keogh plan (a tax-deferred pension plan available to self-employed people or unincorporated businesses for retirement purposes).

If none of the above apply to you, you can use your Social Security Number as your Tax ID when filing. Visit www.IRS.gov for more information and to apply for an EIN.

After you've worked out your Federal Tax Identification Number, check if your state requires a state tax ID number or charter for filing taxes. This can usually be found on your state government's website.

These are some of the common licenses, permits, and other items you might need

- Business License
- Seller's Permit (required in most states if you plan to have a shop, whether online or in person)
- Tax Identification Number (TIN) or Employer Identification Number (EIN)
- Doing Business As or DBA

Obtaining Licenses and Permits

Depending on your city, county, and state, you'll need a number of particular licenses and permits. The requirements vary statewide and even down to the city! So contact your city or county government first. They can tell you about local requirements (like a business license or seller's permit) and hopefully advise on who to contact for state requirements. If you live in another country, contact your local government about requirements. Government has never been known to be the model of efficiency, so expect some frustration and low-quality hold Muzak along the way.

Licenses and permits need to be renewed periodically, depending on the license type and issuing governance. Luckily, much of this can be handled online these days. When you make an online account to file for these permits and licenses, you can sometimes opt in for email reminders when it is time to renew. If not, find out the renewal schedule and set a calendar reminder to avoid fines or issues.

Registering Your Doing Business As (DBA)

If you want to name your business anything other than your personal legal name (if you're a Sole Proprietor) or anything other than the legal name of your partnership/corporation, you'll need to register a "Doing Business As" (DBA) in most states. This paperwork is usually filed with your county clerk (in the USA), and it simply ties your legal business entity's name to any other name you use to do business under. This is a great way to update your name down the road without having to re-form your business entity.

Chapter Checklist:

① Choose your business structure and register the necessary paperwork in your state.

② Find out whether your Tax Identification Number (TIN) should be your Social Security Number or an Employer Identification Number (EIN), and apply through the IRS (or the equivalent in your country).

③ File for any required licenses or permits. If you plan to sell physical goods, you'll likely need a seller's permit, and your city will likely require you to have a business license.

④ File a DBA if you are doing business under a name other than your personal legal name or your business's legal name.

⑤ Talk to your lawyer or accountant about ongoing obligations you might need to meet based on your business structure. And ask about what laws you need to be keen on before you start conducting business. For example, as a corporation, you'll need to file a "Statement of Information" yearly with your Secretary of State.

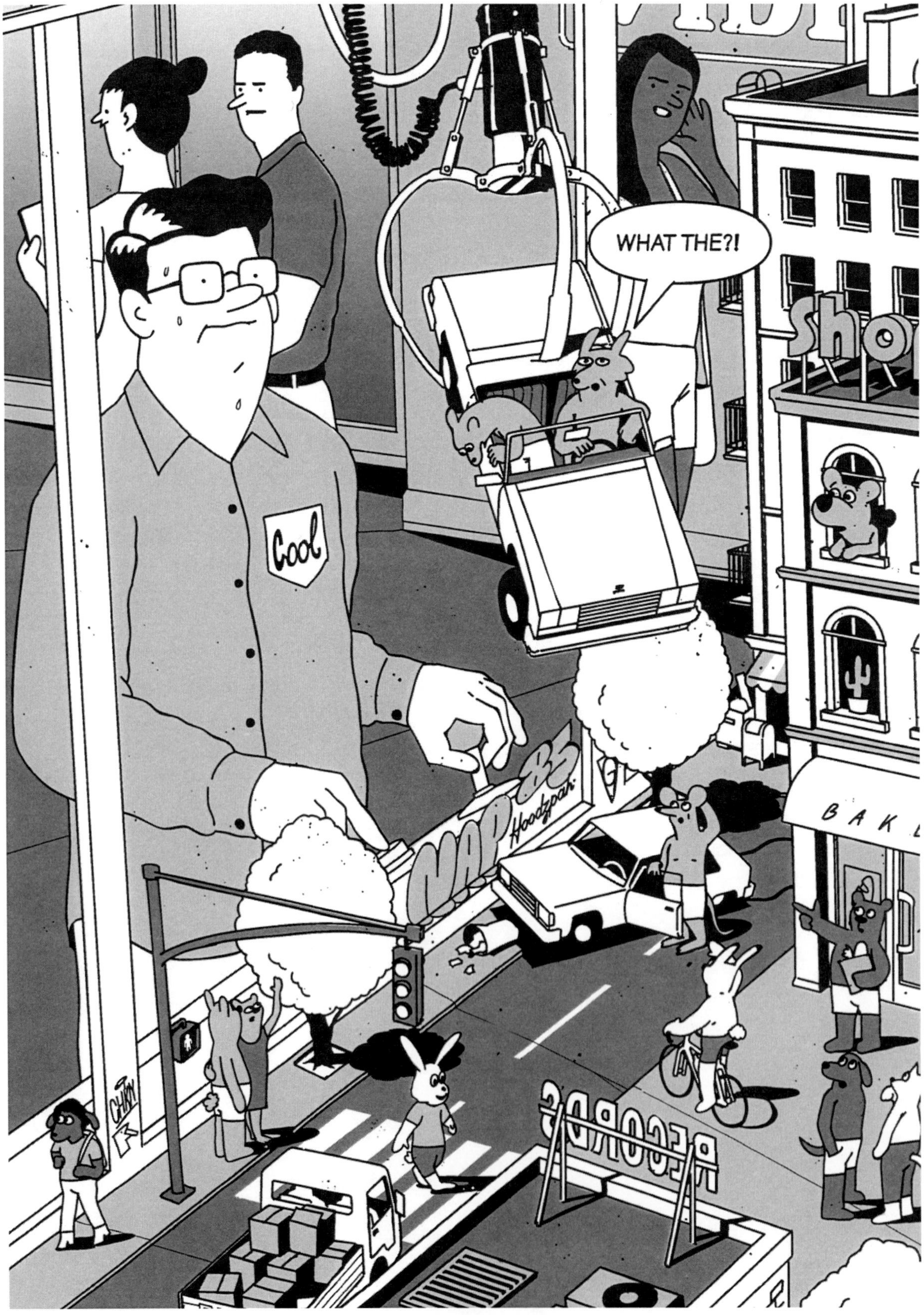

Illustration by: Nap Kawon

9
Getting Clients

What is a business without patrons? Clients pay our bills. Unfortunately, the "build it and they will come" method of marketing is not a reliable one. You have to be proactive and consistent in putting your business out there if you want to start attracting an audience and eventually a client.

The good news? You don't need a ton of money or even a brilliantly clever campaign to start building a client roster. Most of the marketing efforts we make at Hoodzpah are very straightforward and just take time, effort, and a bit of personality. When starting out, don't be too precious. Try a lot of things to see what resonates with your target audience. More about marketing in the next chapter.

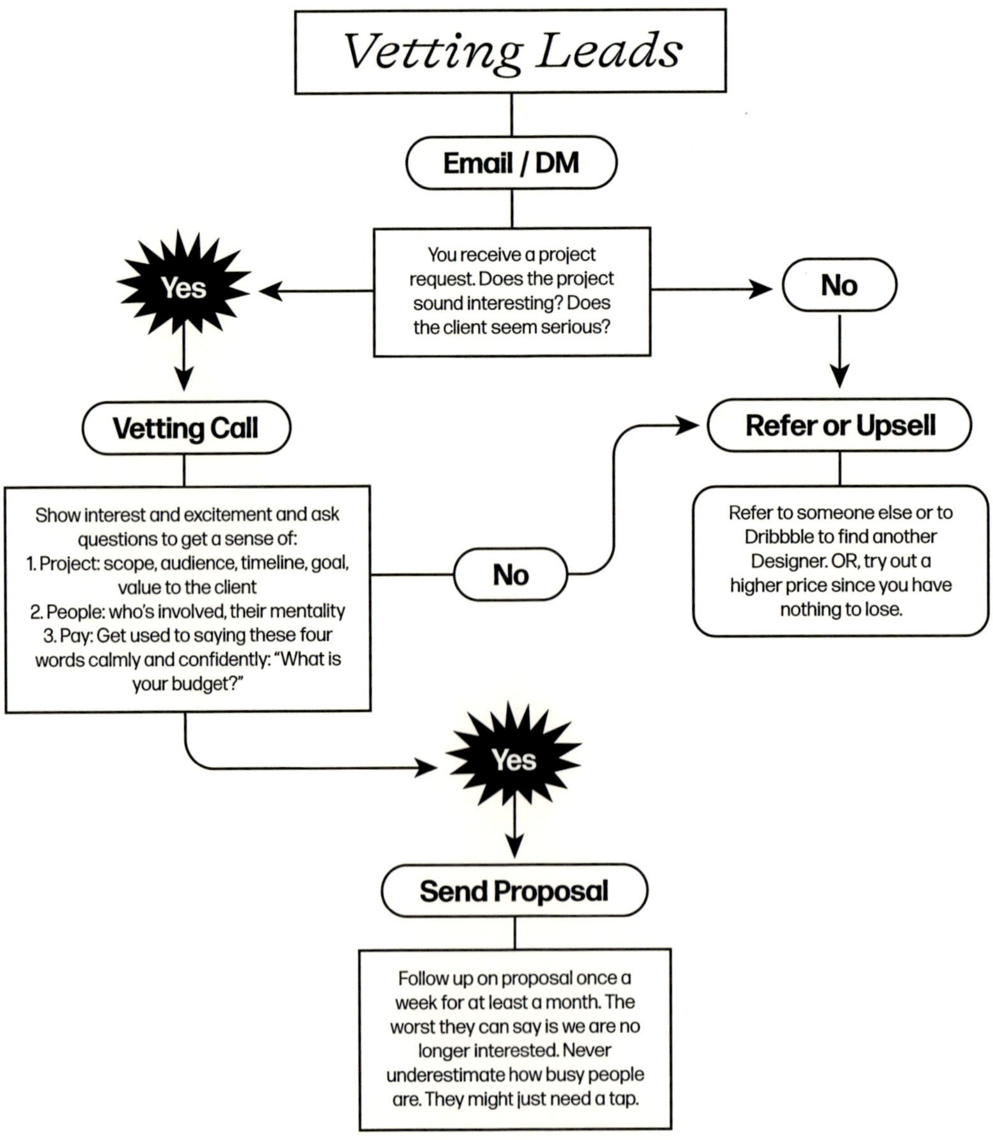

We talked with the founder and Chief Creative Officer of a really successful agency in Los Angeles. They're twenty people in size and probably bring in four to five times the work we do at Hoodzpah. The work they bring in is high-value and high-quality: known brands, well-funded companies, and brands with hefty marketing budgets. We asked what their client acquisition method is. Like Hoodzpah, they don't have a traditional sales team, and they don't spend money on ads. Most of their projects come through genuine connections made by organically building community (online and offline) and from referrals and word of mouth. Their social following is not even massive, with about 7,000 Instagram followers, no TikTok presence, and 10,000 followers on Behance. They're able to land great work for a decent-sized team without being "famous," without a salesperson, and without ads. What do they have? A beautiful website that shows off their skills, quality of work, and warm personality; a consistent online presence across sites like X, Instagram, Behance, and Dribbble; great organic engagement with their social media audience; good involvement in their offline community; and quality service and deliverables that lead to past clients recommending future ones. These are all things you can work on for your own studio, just as we did with ours.

You really can achieve a lot with a small budget, a genuine approach to people, and a good work ethic. Just be sure to give yourself time. Your first few years will be the hardest as you build a reputation and grow your initial audience from scratch. Put in the time and effort to find your rhythm, and you will become more aware of who your target audience is and what they want. At some point, word of mouth will start to work as hard as you do, and your audience will start to grow exponentially.

Where Our Work Comes from at Hoodzpah

In the beginning, all of our jobs at Hoodzpah came to us via a friend or a friend of a friend, and we're forever grateful to them. Our following on social media was minuscule. Our SEO rankings were buried deeper than the Titanic wreckage. Word-of-mouth recommendations and referrals were our bread and butter as we proved our capabilities and slowly built a name. Their recommendations soon led to work from people we didn't know directly.

Even today, we get the majority of our work through personal relationships, word of mouth, referrals, and recurring projects from existing clients. Investing in building our reputation through our website, social media, events (attending, hosting, and speaking at), podcasts, and more has helped us land some amazing work. All of these things build brand awareness and foster a community of connections who might turn into clients.

Here is a chart [Fig. 6] listing the ways we've landed some past work. Some of these projects were years in the making (from when someone met or heard about us to when they actually hired us).

How We Got The Client

Client Name	Key	Found Hoodzpah Via	Scope of Work
Nettie	◉	Dribbble search	Brand identity & packaging
Sonny	◉	Dribbble search	Brand identity & packaging
Edens Garden	❞	Referral via a photographer friend	Strategy, brand, web & packaging work
Industrial Light & Magic	❞	Employee's wife read *this* book and referred us	Strategy & extensive rebrand
20th Century Studios	✶	Art Director found us on Instagram	Repeat title treatment work
Disney & Hulu	❞ ▚	20th Century AD & old friend each referred us	Repeat title treatment work & layout
Remind	❞ ✶	Referred by a mutual on X	Extensive rebrand & website
Pacific Gold	❞ ✺	Referred by a mutual in the local creative scene	Brand identity & packaging
Kiva Confectionaries	❞	Referred by a member on the internal team	Sub-brand identity
Target	❞ ✶	Referred by a mutual on X	Gift card design
Louie's Restaurant	❞	CFO's fiancé was a fan of our work	Brand identity
Los Angeles Lakers	❞	Referred by a friend at The Anaheim Ducks	60th anniversary poster design
Sacramento Kings	◘	Spoke at MLC Conference and met the CD	California Classic brand identity
Fanhood	◘	Founder saw our work featured on *Brand New*	Brand identity
SkinTour	◘	Founder read a local magazine article about us	Website, marketing design, retainer
Prometheus	◘	Founder heard us on a podcast	Brand identity & retainer
RenoRun	◘	Director of Brand heard us on Chris Do's podcast	Extensive strategy & rebrand
SeatGeek	◘ ✺	CD saw us speak at Brand New Conference	Logo, custom typeface & more
Nike	✶ ▚	CD found us on Instagram	Capsule collection & campaign
RedBull	✶	Marketing VP found us on Instagram	Many event brand identities & more
Skip Self-Checkout App	◘	Designer saw our work featured on *Brand New*	Brand identity
Happy Tooth	❞ ▚	Skip designer referred us to work with him again	Brand identity, placemaking
Kansas City Chiefs	✶	Creative Director followed our work on Instagram	Limited edition poster
Noah Kahan	✶	Creative Director followed our work on Instagram	Merch designs
Datalily	✶	Founders followed our work on Instagram	Strategy, rebrand & website
Nicoletto's Pasta Co.	♥	Old friends from the Nashville music scene	Rebrand, packaging, placemaking
Anaheim Ducks	♥ ✺	Friend from the Orange Co. CA creative scene	Limited edition poster
Almond Surfboards	♥ ✺	Friend from the Orange Co. CA creative scene	Merch designs
Known Supply	♥ ✺	Friend from the Orange Co. CA creative scene	Poster designs
Column Five	♥ ✺	Friend from the Orange Co. CA creative scene	Many projects for various clients
Learn & Earn	♥ ✺	Friend from the Orange Co. CA creative scene	Brand identity
Blur	♥ ✺	Spoke at Valiocon and befriended Dir. of Design	Brand identity & retainer
Bench Clearers	♥	Old friend from high school	Brand identity & merch
El Cholo, Il Gatto, Etc.	▚	Repeat client	Brand identity
Helen Diller Foundation	▚	Past client's charitable foundation	Brand identity
Beyond Meat	❞ ✺	Referred by a mutual in the local creative scene	Brand, placemaking, packaging & more

Key & Aggregated Totals

”	Referral	11	▚	Repeat Collaborator	5
✶	Social Media	8	◉	Online Search	2
♥	Friends & Family	8	✤	Outreach	0
✳	Networking/Events	8	◇	Paid Advertising	0
◘	Press/Speaking	7	◒	Other	0

The Conditions for Getting Clients

In order to get clients, you need the following:

1. Skills: the ability to do something.
2. Proof of Skills: a portfolio, capabilities deck, website, or social media profile. The more proof points, the better.
3. Appropriate Brand Positioning: your brand identity and service / product offering appeals to a target audience that wants or needs it and is willing and able to pay for it.
4. Brand Awareness: a pool of potential clients who know about your business.
5. Demand: a level of interest in your skill that justifies paying the price you're asking.
6. Positive Reputation: credibility that comes from outside opinions and perceptions of your business. Think testimonials, press features, referrals, and a solid work history or client roster. These things can influence a potential client to choose you over someone else.
7. Opportunity: that moment when someone needs the thing you do, and you're able to offer your services/product.

How many of these listed items can you confidently say you have? As entrepreneurs, we aren't just artists. We are salespeople—not sellouts, but salespeople. If you're having trouble landing work, your culprit is likely within that list.

Maybe you have a great skill, but the demand for it is just not strong enough to support you full-time. Which means you either need to better prove the benefits of your services, deepen your skill set to attract a broader client base, be more proactive with promotion to remind your audience you're there, or try new marketing tactics to get the right eyes on your business.

If you have incredible work and a beautiful website, but you hardly get any inquiry emails, maybe you need to invest more time into building brand awareness. Try increasing site traffic by posting to social media or sharing work on aggregated portfolio sites. Consider providing valuable and consistent content in a newsletter or attending events to broaden your network. The internet is far too massive a place to hope people will stumble upon your site without any luring or guidance.

If you get lots of inquiries for work from potential clients that don't suit your service offering or price range, you probably need to look at your brand positioning. What is it about how you're presenting your skills, work, and expertise that is attracting the wrong kind of client? Is the portfolio on your site actually showing the kind of work you want to do? Does your brand identity appeal to your target audience? Do your marketing materials and messaging justify the price you're asking for?

If you get a lot of quality leads for work but your quotes aren't getting approved, you might need to look at your pricing or proposal structure. Are you proving the value of your skills in your proposals? Maybe your proposal is too underwhelming and doesn't educate on why the price tag is worth it. Maybe you don't have enough relevant portfolio work to convince a potential client that you are the right fit for the project. Maybe your price is just not on par with your audience's perceived value of the service. Or maybe you are targeting an audience that cannot afford your pricing. We see this a lot with creatives who want to work in the hospitality or non-profit industries where margins are low, and budgets are even lower.

If you used to get a lot of clients, but things have suddenly slowed down, it could be something outside of your control. Economic shifts are scary to navigate as a studio owner. As we're writing this, we're in the middle of an economic slowdown. Many big companies that used to contract a lot of creative work have shed their creative teams and trimmed their budgets. Big-name and no-name creatives alike are feeling the effects. These are times when you have to go back to the basics and be as gritty as you were in those first years as a business owner. You have to pound the pavement, knock on doors, nurture existing relationships more intently, offer new services, and figure out products or services that can be sold at a more accessible price point. We've seen this with the rise of "sprints," which offer a high-ticket-price item at a lower rate by slashing the scope of explorations, revisions, meetings, and in-depth strategy. The idea is that there's a condensed timeline with minimal revisions (if any) and only one proposed concept, but the client still gets a package of core brand assets by the end. They trade off options and control for a lower price. Design sprints, brand sprints . . . you can sprint anything!

Opportunity cannot be directly planned for. But, you can put yourself in the path of opportunity by positioning your brand well, growing your audience and awareness, ensuring your skill has sufficient demand, and building a reputation through good work experiences and consistent self-promotion.

Business Development

Business development is any work to build and maintain relationships with future, existing, and past clients.

As a studio owner, business development will be a big part of your life. Make time for it rather than treating it as an afterthought. Schedule time for it into the work week to stay consistent. You can't wait till you need clients to start because it's something that develops and grows over time. When work is slow, that's the perfect time to invest in your audience or industry to grow brand awareness or to try a new service or personal project to show off a skill that your clients may not know you have. Don't be afraid to evolve and adapt to this ever-changing world. You'll come to know your slow periods, when it's an industry-wide economic shift, or when you personally are uncharacteristically slow, and it's time to mix things up.

Types of Leads

A "lead" is sales-speak for a potential client. A cold lead is someone who has little to no interest in your brand or service for whatever reason. A warm lead is someone who knows a little about you and is interested but might not be ready to use your service immediately. A hot lead is someone who you have already connected with and is very interested in using your services in the near future.

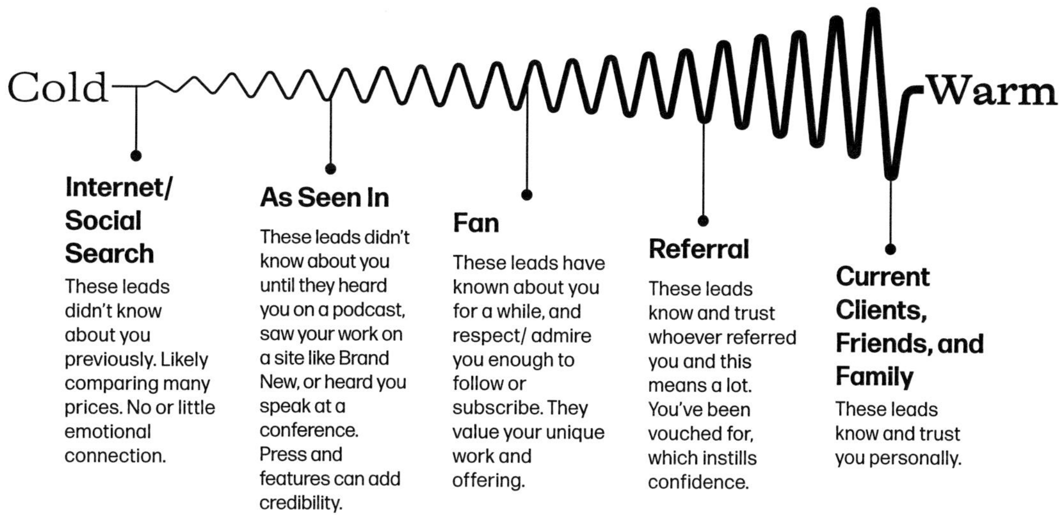

Meet Your First and Easiest Clients: Friends and Family

You likely won't be landing dream gigs straight out the gate as a new business. You might be thinking, "So what do I do in the short term? I need work. And how do I get referred if I haven't even won my first client?"

As a newbie in business, your first clients will be your friends and family, or acquaintances of your friends and family. Many people warn against working with friends and family, but you have to start somewhere. These people will help you get past that awkward hump of your first one hundred followers on social media. These people will hire you even when you have a sparse portfolio (or no website at all). They'll trust you with types of projects you might not have any experience in. So in some ways, these people are doing you a favor as much as you are for them.

Be thankful for these early adopters in your existing friend group and family, even though they can be—how shall we say—cheap? Flaky? Picky? All of the above? Look at these first jobs as your business internship. Your soft launch. These people might not have the glamorous projects or the big budgets, but they're willing to trust you even though you're untested. They're going to get that "new" stink off of you. You can beta test your process with people who love you (hopefully) and are more forgiving (ideally, but we are talking about family). The work you do for this initial group of people will help you fill in your early portfolio, glean some glowing reviews/testimonials, get over the jitters of driving the project, and build some much-needed work history as a new business.

Remember, cheap gigs for friends and family ideally allow you a lot more creative freedom as a trade-off. Just be clear about this up front: "I'll give you a great rate if you trust me with the creative direction." Put as much passion and effort into these first projects as if they were for a name brand paying top dollar. Follow the true process and don't cut corners. If you phone in the work, you'll miss the opportunity to get an amazing portfolio piece out of the deal.

If you can impress this built-in fan club with your professionalism and quality of work, they'll carry your banner to the ends of the earth.

Meet Your Second Easiest Clients: Repeat Clients

Getting repeat work from an existing client is much easier than landing a project with someone you've never worked with. So, as important as building your audience is, it is equally as important to give a high level of service that encourages repeat work from the clients you already have. Delivering quality work on time, through a productive process, at a fair rate will make you into your client's favorite collaborator.

A good experience will turn your existing clients into your business development team. There are tons of creatives out there, but reliable creatives who are enjoyable to work with? Creatives who know how to navigate constraints? Creatives who can help clients find consensus? That narrows the field considerably. It's likely they'll refer you to a friend or colleague somewhere down the road, or even hire you again should they move companies.

Every project you take on is an opportunity to build your reputation and invest in a long-term partnership instead of a one-off job. So show up and give it your all. Being an ally for your clients means less time chasing new work.

Winning High-Value Projects is a Long Game

Most freelancers and studio runners we meet are interested in learning how to land dream projects with name-brand clients.

First, know that it is very possible to land big projects with dream clients, even as a small studio. Think of Jessica Hische, who redesigned logos for Southern Living, Mailchimp, and Eventbrite. Jon Contino's Contino Studio rebranded the Tampa Bay Buccaneers with the help of four trusted subcontractors. Paul Hutchison of Hype Type Studio worked on Sonos's global wireless sound packaging as a studio of two. Daniel and Kate Wadie of Mrs&Mr have worked together on visual identity redesigns for SoulCycle and Tabasco.

At Hoodzpah, as a studio of four (only recently we added our fifth designer), we have worked on a rebrand for Industrial Light & Magic; logo redesign, poster designs, and a proprietary typeface for SeatGeek; title treatments for entertainment studios like Disney, Hulu, and 20th Century Fox.

We are happy to report that many big brands are looking beyond the typical mega-agencies and trusting smaller studios more and more. They know that large agency rates tend to be bloated. They know that much of top talent is going independent. They like the idea of saving money, having a more agile project experience, and working with specialized teams. This is a competitive edge for smaller studios when the economy is weak and companies have to tighten their purse strings to keep shareholders happy. When companies downsize internal creative teams and cut back on big agency retainers, small to medium-sized creative teams with a good reputation can benefit.

Second, it's important to remember that banner projects don't come along every day. The big rebrand, the new website, the packaging redesign, the new product launch campaign. These high-value gigs are rare and competitive to land compared to everyday work. Creative leads at a big brand aren't just Googling to find a random studio to do these kinds of things at the last minute (at least not usually). This is something a brand's in-house team has been thinking about for a long time. The project has been discussed in many meetings and passed up the chain for stakeholder approvals. It's tied to big expectations for the company. The success or failure of this project will affect bottom lines, future budgets, employee bonuses, stock prices, and public perception.

These kinds of projects are managed by a senior creative team member at the company, be it the Creative Director, CCO (Chief Creative Officer), Marketing Director, or a trusted Art Director. Big brands usually have an internal creative team for their day-to-day needs. But they tap outside collaborators when it comes to specialty, high-value projects that their in-house team either doesn't have the time, skills, or expertise to achieve. Creative leaders usually have a list (even if only mentally) of creatives and agencies they might want to work with that they've been curating for years. Those lists contain studios and agencies they've already worked with, ones they've seen or heard about from trusted peers or outlets, or ones they've discovered along the way (met at an event, found on social media, etc.).

The key to landing a high-value project with a high-value client: Your business needs to be on one of those lists before the project is greenlit. Since there's no way to know when that is, build relationships and grow awareness around your studio so you can work your way into the hearts and minds of the creative leads at these companies.

According to *Harvard Business Review*, " . . . buyers already have a list of potential vendors in mind before starting the search process, and 90% of the time end up buying off that day one list" (Sherrard, Dave, and MacGregor, "What B2Bs Need to Know About Their Buyers" September 2022).

Landing high-quality creative projects is a long game that relies on a lot of factors being in place when the opportunity comes along. If your client roster, past work experience, and portfolio do not prove you are able to perform on a high-value project (even for a smaller or lesser-known company), you need to focus on improving those areas. Work on building your brand reputation, deepening your experience, and curating quality case studies through more accessible clients in the meantime. Helping a smaller business make a splash without a hefty marketing budget could be a bigger testament to your creative skills than making something inconsequential for a big-name client who's "too big to fail."

How I Got My Last Four Projects

We asked eleven of our studio runner/freelance friends how they connected with their last four clients and what projects that led to. We asked people at various stages in their careers, in different locations, with various levels of online presence. The results are fascinating.

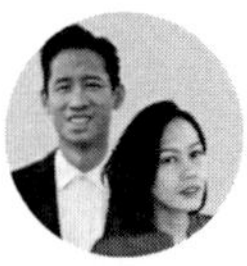 **Larry Nguyen & Wendy Tuan** *Founders, Outfit Branding & Design*	Behance Search → Branding for Fashion Footwear Company
	Behance Search (again) → Rebrand for Contemporary Theatre Company
	Behance Search (third time!) → Rebrand for Real Estate Company
weareoutfit.com	Referral from Current Client → Website Redesign for Celebrity Book Club
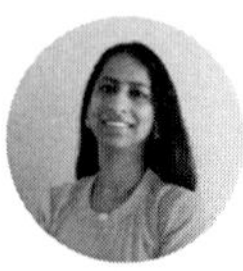 **Aradhana Modi Bejarano** *Co-founder & CD, The Little Labs*	Repeat Client → Design for an Interactive Game on a Streaming Platform
	Word of Mouth → Animations for an Interactive Toy
	Outreach → Animated & Illustrated Assets for an AI Powered Tech Company
thelittlelabs.com	Repeat Client → Design for Multiple AR Interactive Games
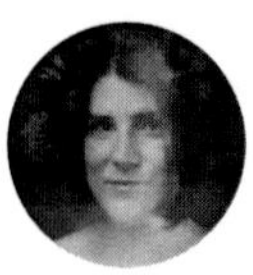 **Lindsey Laseter** *Partner & CD, Lasso Studio*	A Creative Acquaintance → Motion & Brand Project with Apple
	Someone who saw an old project in the Wild → Coffee Shop Branding
	Fellow Studio Owner/Friend → Multiple Custom Animations
lassostud.io	Met Someone at an Art Show → Branding Project
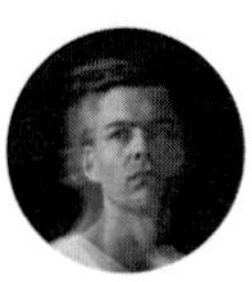 **Alex Rinker** *Founder & CD, Rinker Brand + Design Studio*	Client Referral → Brand Identity/Visual System for Global Video Game
	Longtime Hospitality Client → Brand Refresh & more for Boutique Luxury Hotel
	LinkedIn → Web3/IP Brand Identity
rinker.co	Design Colleague Referral → Tech Startup (Sports) Brand Identity/Visual System
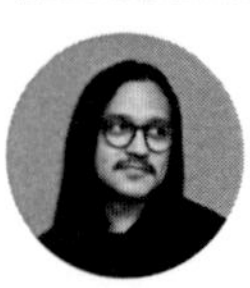 **Ethan Silva** *Co-founder & Motion Designer, Bad Lucky Studio*	Social Media → Boston Symphony Orchestra Brand Animation
	Repeat Client → Tubi Studios Product Video
	Repeat Client → Blast Web/Product Animation
badluckystudio.com	Word of Mouth → Sentury Tire Brand Animation
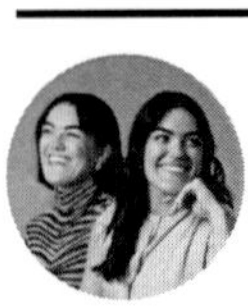 **Jenna & Kelly Freitas** *Founders & Designers, A Good Pear Design Studio*	Former Colleague Referral → Brand ID/Naming for TX Short-term Rental Property
	Instagram → Merch Design
	Existing Client Referral → PR Agency Branding
agoodpear.studio	Wedding Meet Cute → Brand for Wedding Videographer

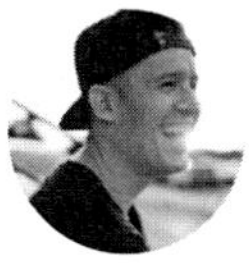 **Jesse Showalter** *Founder & Product Designer, Good Fight Creative* goodfightcreative.com	”	Former Startup Boss Referral → VC Website, mobile app, long-term relationship
	✶	Posting on Dribbble → 2-year contract w/ Apple as Senior Product Designer
	◒	Sent free mockups of a redesigned app (w/process video) → Long retainer for app
	”	Local referral from a friend → 6-figure contract for web app design
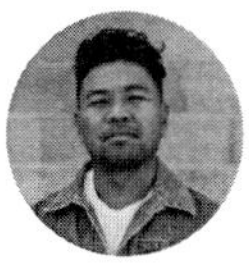 **Steve Cachero** *Founder & Director, Hynt Films* hyntfilms.com	”	Referral from Friend → Long-term retainer producing a video series
	▚	Repeat Client → Video was used in association of a feature film premiere
	”	Word of Mouth → National commercial tv/streaming played during 2024 Olympics
	▚	Repeat Client → Video was used in association of a feature film premiere
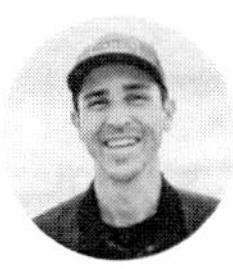 **Scott Snyder** *Photographer, Scott Snyder Photo* scottsnyderphoto.com	✶	Found me on Instagram → 20+ Photography projects (and counting) for Sonos
	”	Existing Friend/Client Referral → eComm & Brand Photography Assets
	✶	Found me on Instagram → Conceptual Stills and Motion for Pharmacy Startup
	♥	Friend → Surf Shop x Car Company Collab Video Production
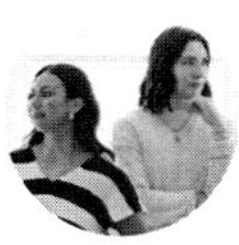 **Arabela Espinoza & Elle Mitchell** *Founders & Photographers, Weekend Creative* weekendcreative.co	✶	Instagram Search → Product Shoot for Rebrand (ongoing)
	✶	Long-Time Fan on Instagram → Product Shoot (ongoing)
	✳	Met at Conference (Adobe Max) → Paid Sponsorship
	♥	Creative Colleague → Product Launch Shoot + Paid Sponsorship
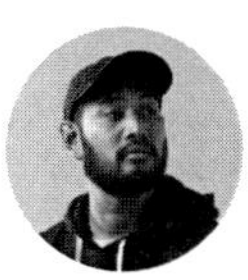 **Christopher Reath** *Founder & Designer, Mononym* mononym.com	▚	Repeat Client → Branding and Web Design for AI Startup
	”	Colleague/Client Referral → Branding and Web Design for Web3 Project
	✶	Twitter DM → Art Direction for Email Startup
	✶	Instagram → Music Collective Branding and Art Direction

Key & Aggregated Totals

”	Referral	13	◒	Other	2
✶	Social Media	13	✤	Outreach	1
▚	Repeat Client	8	◇	Paid Advertising	0
♥	Friends & Family	3	▣	Press/Speaking	0
✳	Networking/Events	3	◉	Online Search Result	0

Now, don't these results restore your faith in human connection? Whether it be a personal relationship or an online one, human connection is not only good for you mentally, it's also the best way to get work. Keep in touch with people, invest in what others are doing, and don't be afraid to talk about your work. It pays off and it makes life much more enjoyable.

Tenacity

Our friend Andrew Hochradel *only* flies Southwest. His phone's camera roll is full of Southwest plane liveries (his goal is to fly on all of them) and he follows them on X. In 2020 the airlines shared photos of old tickets and Andrew responded with, "this would make great merch." Being a graphic designer and a "can do" person, Andrew saw an opportunity, and began a campaign to get this merch made. He designed a full campaign, then rolled it out online and tagged Southwest. No response. He kept going. He looked up the Southwest marketing team on LinkedIn and began tagging them in the social media posts. Then, a DM. Their marketing reached out to him saying they'd love to consider a collab down the line, but not at the moment. Andrew explains, "If you don't give me a flat out no to my face, I'm of the mind that this can happen. I'm just going to keep going till you say, 'absolutely no.' →

Big-name brands tend to hire known and vetted agencies/studios for big projects. *But, there's an easier way to work with dream clients.*

You could be a perfect fit for a big brand's lower-risk, lower-value project. Or you could be a perfect subcontractor for an agency that does book bigger projects with known brands.

At Hoodzpah, it took us three years to land work with a brand-name client. And we didn't book it directly. We were subcontracted through the brand's agency of record to do smaller projects like infographics and spot illustrations for email campaigns. But bless the agency Column Five (and our friend and C5 founder, Josh Ritchie) for trusting us with those tasks and letting us share about it! That portfolio work added much-needed credibility to our website and proposal decks so we could eventually land work directly with a big company.

A few years later, we worked on event branding for Red Bull—this time we booked directly with the client. Event branding projects have a smaller scope, smaller budget, and smaller risk level than branding a new product or the whole company. There are also usually fewer stakeholders involved, less oversight, and more willingness to take a creative chance (because the work is for a limited event rather than a long-term initiative). This can lead to some really fun, creative output! The event usually happens once over the course of a few days, and might only be regionally marketed. The shelf life and limited audience mean the value is not as high as something that will be used worldwide every day for the next decade. We jumped at the chance to work on a small project for a well-known company. That led to more work with Red Bull on more important events and campaigns. It also helped us build our reputation, which led to a gig designing a capsule collection for a marathon with Nike (sadly this never saw the light of day due to Covid). This gave us a great body of work to show in our proposals. Large brands had trusted us on multiple projects, and we had the work (or at least logos on our site) to prove it.

Find your version of event branding. There are plenty of $5K–$20K projects like these that big brands regularly contract out. When their in-house design team is too inundated with daily tasks and the project is too small to take to the premier agencies, this is when creative leads like to try out new talent. Company merch, event branding, micro-campaigns, regional brand activations—these are projects where your studio could shine for these brands. Getting smaller projects with big brands is a bonafide way to build your reputation and rapport so you can eventually be considered for that "big deal" project when it comes around.

Once you've been noticed by a creative lead and added to their list of potential collaborators, the game is still afoot. A large brand will usually court a few different people for any project. For larger projects, they'll likely send out a Request for Proposal (RFP), have meetings to narrow in on a few favorite studios/agencies, and then pick based on a variety of emotional and practical considerations: price, timeline, personality, approach, experience, vibe, and so on.

We have sent out many proposals for projects we felt sure we would get, only to find out we had not won the project, or to never hear back. This is normal. A lot of time and work go into courting big brands and big projects, and the potential for winning them is lower. So our work schedule is filled with small- to medium-sized projects for big brands, big projects for small and medium brands, and retainer work that is deliciously reliable, albeit less sexy. These projects keep healthy cash flow coming in while we work on landing those more elusive, once-in-a-decade banner projects.

Attracting Clients is a Long Game

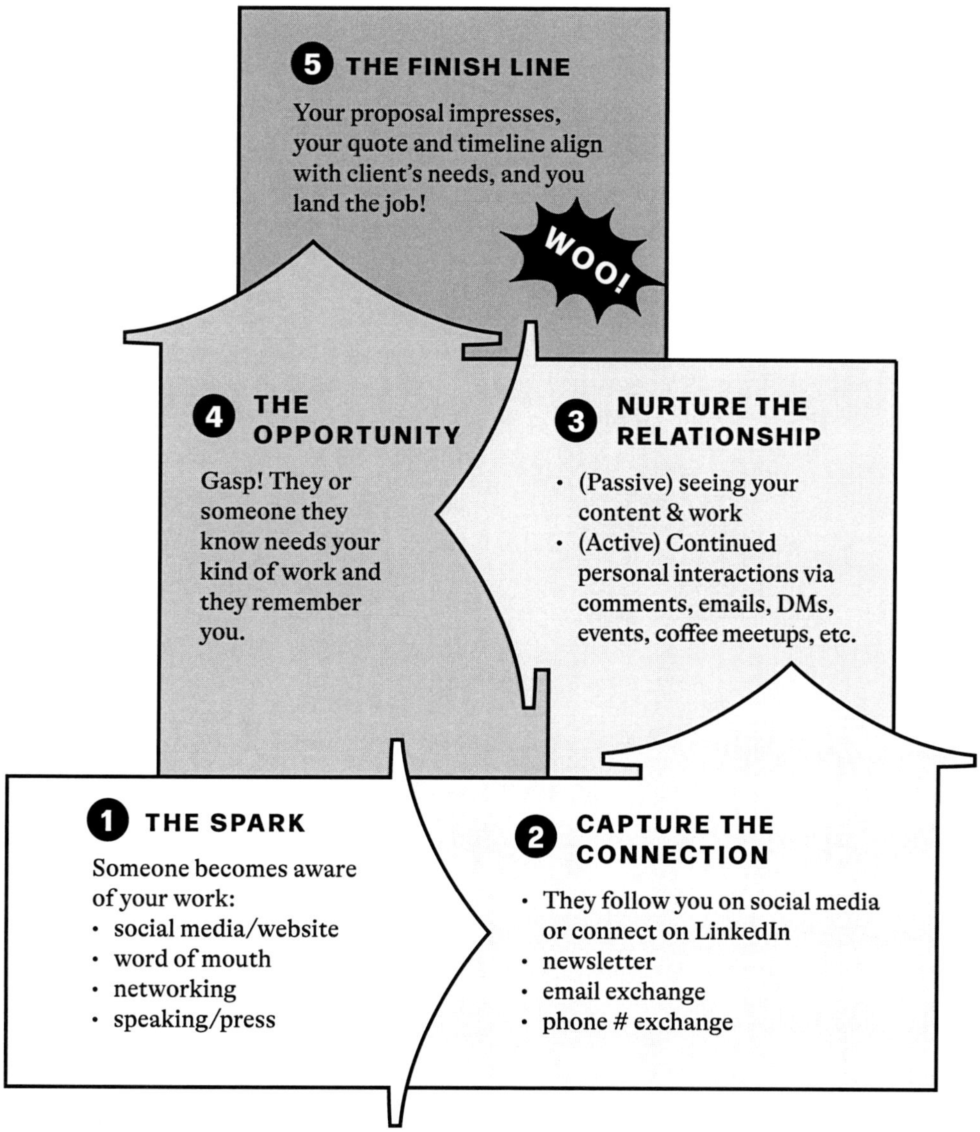

Make the Kind of Work You Want to Get

When you start your business, you're probably desperate for work. We definitely were. You don't have the luxury to be picky about the work you take on. You take on projects that don't reflect your goals to pay the bills, and that's perfectly fine.

→ Because you might be two steps away from saying, 'yes.'" Andrew reached out again months later, this time pitching the merch as a Press Box. It looked promising, but conversations fizzled. Then Andrew reached out again with a last ditch question: "What would be an easy yes?" They linked him up with the Southwest company store and the collab finally became a reality. The merch was made, they did a photoshoot on a plane, AdWeek picked it up, and Andrew got flown to Southwest HQ for a creator day with influencers. What made the difference? Mostly, doggedness. Andrew was passionate about the idea, sincere about it. And it eventually won the Southwest team over. This project has garnered Andrew new clients, similar projects, and speaking opportunities. "I look at it as marketing and PR," says Andrew. "It's the best portfolio piece I have." This story is a true testament to making your own opportunities.

See it at hoch.co

But it's easy to fall into autopilot and let your business happen to you. You quote whatever happens to come into your email inbox without going after what you really want. Thus, a vicious cycle begins: The work you have to show, which you're not very excited about, leads to similar work that you're still not excited about. A related issue is the accidental niche. You did a great project for one gym, which led to more gym projects, and now you're "the gym girl." You want to do something different, but your portfolio is working against you, and people can't see the wood for the gyms. Natural niching like this can easily happen.

So let's be proactive. Think of your dream clients and projects. Now, look at your portfolio and body of work. If you reach out to those dream clients, will they see the connection between your work and their brand? If not, you need to work on positioning yourself and your portfolio for the work you want to get. It's up to you to grab the wheel and steer your business ship. One small change in direction can result in big things over time.

A self-initiated passion project is a great way to show off new skills and begin to position yourself within a certain industry. You pick the project, the theme, the subject, the style. You get to make exactly what you want. Many successful creatives still do passion work. It's not just for beginners.

A passion project is most successful when it shows you can think creatively in a larger system or series. One cool graphic may be a fluke, but three cohesive and cool graphics with a common theme show vision and consistency. A one-off logo might be interesting, but a full brand suite with type, color, and applications shows design thinking. One photo might get you a few likes, but an ongoing, engaging series of photos will capture an audience and show a distinct point of view.

Ask yourself these questions to help define your passion project.

1. What creative skill and style do I want to show off in this project?
2. What is an industry I'd love to work in? How can I tailor this project to that industry?
3. What is a culturally relevant event or topic in this industry that I could use to capture the attention of others? If you want to work in sports, create something relating to the playoffs or a star player. If you want to work in tech, create something for a popular tech event or tool. If you want to work in entertainment, create something to launch during the season finale of a popular show you like.

Whatever you create, share about it as much as you can to get the most out of it. Share behind the scenes. Get feedback on social media. Talk about it to your friends. Post the final work on your website and social profiles. Tag relevant people, add relevant hashtags.

Another way to fill your portfolio with work representative of your goals is to offer a grant or pro bono service to a deserving client or cause. Baby Grand, a brand studio in Memphis, Tennessee, offers what they call "Baby Grants," which include free branding services and a cash investment. Local people apply with a business plan, and Baby Grand awards the grant to a promising business they feel passionate about investing in. You don't have to include a cash investment with your pro bono work. But we love this approach because it is a win-win for you and a deserving cause or person. You invest in your community, and you build a positive reputation.

Find Your Passion Project

Dream Clients

*Example: Lakers

No. 1:________________________________

No. 2:________________________________

No. 3:________________________________

No. 4:________________________________

You Dream Clients' Initiaves

*Example: NBA Finals, NBA Cares, NBA Draft

No. 1:____________________________

No. 2:____________________________

No. 3:____________________________

No. 4:____________________________

Your Skills

*Example: Logo Design, Illustration, Funny Gifs

No. 1:________________________________

No. 2:________________________________

No. 3:______________________________

No. 4:____________________________

Your Project!

*Example: Animations of key Lakers game moments.

No. 1:____________________________________

____

No. 2:____________________________________

____

No. 3:____________________________________

____

No. 4:____________________________________

____

The Power of Passion Projects

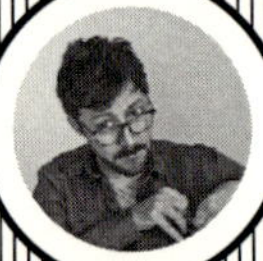

Dan Cassaro

Partner, Young Jerks

youngjerks.com

The Project:

50 and 50: The State Mottos Project was a large scale collaborative project I did in (holy shit!) 2010, not long after I graduated art school. I invited 49 designers to illustrate their home state's motto (I did New York) and shared them online and eventually in an art show at the Ace Hotel in New York.

The impact:

It garnered a lot of attention online and was written about in the Wall Street Journal and The New Yorker. But the biggest thing impact was the instant community I made working on the project. I can track most of my current design industry buds back to that project.

Did you book similar paid work after this project?

Yep, especially for the first few years after it. I think for the first part of my career I was doing a lot of the chunky swashy, lettering I did for this project.

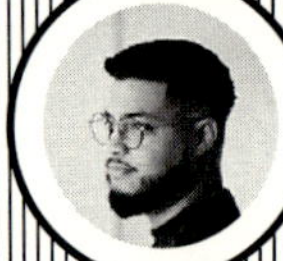

Kevin Rostran

Co-founder & Designer, Rostran Design Co.

rostrandesign.co

The Project:

My favorite passion project was Dunks Sports Bar, a retro 1970s inspired basketball sports bar that combines my love for chicken wings and basketball.

The impact:

...It defined our style and created a standard of aesthetic we wanted to achieve in every project. It clarified our mission of helping restaurants think more creatively about their brand, not just the food they serve. It also gave us goals to reach for, helping us identify the kinds of clients we wanted to attract... [Passion projects] act as both a testing ground and a showcase, giving you the freedom to explore ideas while also shaping how others perceive your work.

Did you book similar paid work after this project?

I secured several bookings as a result of the Dunks Sports Bar project... A pizza place called Humble Oven in San Luis Obispo, California, Pluma Fried Chicken in Miami, Florida, and most recently, a sub shop called Subbin, also in Miami, Florida... that made Dunks such a defining project for us.

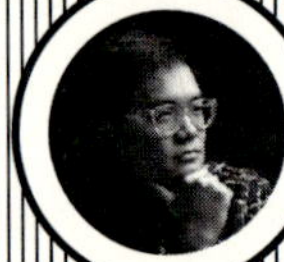

Edward Sun

Designer & Creator at Edward Creates

edwardcreates.com

The Project:

...Just out of pure excitement about the brilliance of designers I admire, I've been making videos highlighting the most inspiring design projects I come across from studios around the world. I share these videos on my social channels, and the response has been totally unexpected.

The impact:

...these videos unexpectedly brought in tons of new work. I thought they'd just drive business to the studios I was highlighting, but potential clients also trusted me because of my ability to recognize and present what made the work great. Not only that, studios actually started reaching out to hire me to cover their work...

Did you book similar paid work after this project?

...I ended up editing 2 seasons of teasers (~20 videos) for Matchstic's podcast A Change of Brand... And Smith & Diction hired me to produce a video in this series covering their incredible work for Living Roots.

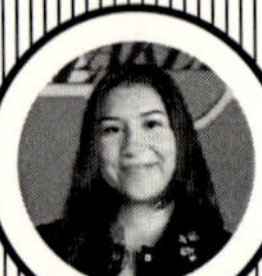

Lisa Orona

Graphic Designer, Illustrator

lisaorona.com

The Project:

When the Lakers won their 2020 chip, I was inspired to illustrate the celebration...creating my own type, and dedicating it to Kobe and Gigi.

The impact:

The project revealed that I love designing and illustrating the most when it's focused on sports and athletes. That pushed me to pursue that in my professional life.

Did you book similar paid work after this project?

In my pursuit of working in professional sports, my entire portfolio held work that was self-initiated. I didn't wait to gain experience in the field and soon enough the self-initiated work landed me a role in women's professional soccer.

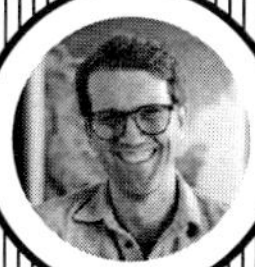

Mike Smith

Co-Founder & Art Director

smith-diction.com

The Project:
The S&D Process Document

The impact:
It completely changed our business. Not only did it help young designers maybe trying to find their footing with their own process, it also propelled us into much bigger conversations because it signaled that we knew what we were doing. It wasn't just some little rinky dink studio that got lucky every once and awhile. We had a process that people could see... No smoke and mirrors.

Did you book similar paid work after this project?
Absolutely. It led to many more serious inquiries from serious people. We'd send it to new clients and they would...be excited about having some clarity of what they were paying for. They weren't throwing their investment into a black box and hoping for the best. It also scared away a lot of those unqualified inquiries because it was so in depth. Those people would just be like,"Oh I don't need all of this."

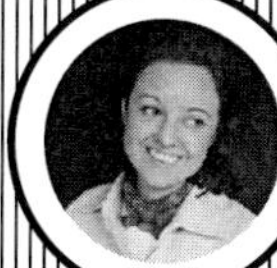

Carra Sykes

Creative

carrasykes.com

The Project:
Mother + Daughter: I photographed my mom and me almost identically in different spaces wearing my clothes. It was an exploration of documenting the connection of generations...

The impact:
For me, personal projects are usually birthed out of a place of feeling burnt out or down...I start personal projects to rekindle the creativity I've felt disconnected from... My Mother + Daughter project went semi-viral and ended up in a ton of publications... It got people to my website and introduced them to my illustration and design work...I will always cherish these photos with my mom and her willingness to get creative with me.

Did you book similar paid work after this project?
While I don't get booked for photo projects often anymore, I've been able to use the project in my portfolio to demonstrate my photography and photo direction skills.

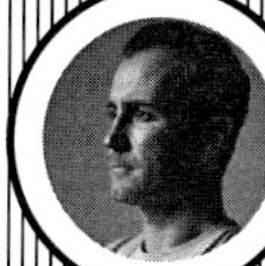

Scott G Toepfer

Photographer & Director

sgtoepfer.com

The Project:
...My favorite project from the past is still "It's Better in the Wind." There are some new ones in the fire, but I still believe the impact of this project lives with me and helps to remind me of what I am capable of when I endure with my passions...

The impact:
First, it showed me what is possible when I finish a large project... It gave me purpose and a way to define my style when left to my own devices. Finding a confident and genuine voice as a creative is as important as any one part of your portfolio... Opened my mind up to my own possibilities in the creative industry.

Did you book similar paid work after this project?
...The film helped me get in the door as a cinematographer and as a commercial director with storytelling capabilities. The self-published book earned me my first project with Harley-Davidson, as well as leading to my involvement with launching Iron & Resin...

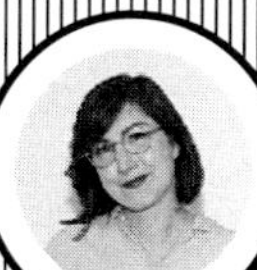

Jessica Hische

Lettering Artist, Author

jessicahische.is

The Project:
Studioworks! Which is a tech startup I recently co-founded creating business software for creative studios (starting with invoicing and payments but with big, big plans).

The impact:
It's really a coming together of previous personal projects and interests from over the years–pulling together my love of tinkering on the web as a creative playground and my background as a creative business owner and passion for sharing business resources... Studioworks has made me excited about working on larger and more ambitious projects that require collaboration.

Did you book similar paid work after this project?
While I can't make a direct correlation, I do think having a presence in the tech and software space while also being an expert in typography and logo design has brought more logo clients to my doorstep. Understanding startup culture has definitely opened doors to clients in that space because I can better speak their language and understand their needs.

However you go about it, don't be afraid to create your own prompt to show off your best skills. We live in the "Show Me" era. If people can't see it, they can't imagine it. So don't wait for the perfect project to come along. Make it!

Some of Your Best Clients Won't be Your "Dream Clients"

As you think about clients, resist the suspicion that great work can only happen with known brands on "dream projects." You can make any project a dream project with a clear vision and a great client. We never would have landed the projects with the "big clients" if we hadn't gone all-out on smaller projects with local or little-known companies. These things build on each other and slowly take shape. They don't appear out of thin air like Jake from State Farm.

On a similar note, some of your best clients—who are easy to work with, pay well, and have steady demand—will not be household name brands and will be in supposedly unglamorous industries.

*"As you become an adult you realize that things around you weren't just always there; people made them happen. But only recently have I started to internalize how much tenacity *everything* requires. That hotel, that park, that railway. The world is a museum of passion projects."*

—John Collison, co-founder of Stripe

Real estate, health care, business services (lawyers, accountants, IT professionals), personal services (dentists, plumbers, cleaners, contractors), education, government, manufacturing industries, and more. These industries still need great creative services. You don't have to show the work in your portfolio if you don't feel like it aligns with your positioning, but it will pay the bills. Routine work or a retainer for these types of clients can alleviate a lot of the stress of booking new clients every month.

Plus, there's greater potential to make a big, creative impact in an industry that isn't known for creativity than in an industry where good design is the bare minimum. Instead of only working with companies already doing it right, why not help the companies who have no clue? Help the companies who have heart but no swagger. These are the fun and unexpected projects that stand out! In our minds, there are no boring projects. Any project can be made into something truly interesting if you and the client have a goal to make it so.

Every project you take on won't make you feel head-over-heels inspired, and that's okay too. It doesn't mean you've sold out. Many creatives refer to this as doing "one for the reel and one for the meal." And honestly, it's nice to have a mix of production-style work and creative strategy work. What do they say? "You can't eat caviar every day." And we can't spin gold from hay every day, either. Sometimes, you just have to bail hay, and that's fine. Sorry, our Kentucky roots are showing.

One of our earliest jobs was redesigning a mop catalog for a local mop supply business. The owner was a really fun guy with a good sense of humor. With his blessing, we made that mop catalog as engaging as possible. There were sidebars with funny how-to comics, and the layout was creative compared to competitors. The client was thrilled with how much his audience loved it. He became a source of many referrals after that.

Later on in our careers, a past client (hi, Dustin Locke!) connected us with a pediatric dentist named Tyler Hanks. Tyler was starting his own practice called Happy Tooth, and Dustin was helping. They wanted to make a completely unique and fun brand for their office that would make kids feel comfortable and excited to go to the dentist (tall order). We worked on epic murals, kid-centric environmental design, a custom basketball half-court design for kids to play in while they waited, and so much more.

Happy Tooth became a banner branding project for us, garnering tons of attention. We had always wanted to design a custom basketball court. We never realized a dental client could be the means to that! We've had close to fifty pediatric dentists reach out to us for quotes after that project, as well as tons of other companies looking to break the mold of their current industry with something more playful. One of our best projects to date is not for a global shoe brand or renowned company but a regional dental office.

Fellow Creatives Make Great Clients

A great way to find work is by getting to know other creatives. Creatives who do a complimentary skill could refer you to their existing clients and subcontract you to offer a broader range of services to their existing clients. These are great allies because they are not a direct competitor, but they probably already have clients who need your services as well as theirs.

For example, we used to know a ton of local photographers in our area. Many were friends. They would pass along our name when asked for design referrals. One such photographer was Matthew Morgan. His referral continues to echo benefits to us more than a decade later! While we had never worked with him directly, he knew us through mutual friends and followed us on social media in our earliest days. He referred us to one of his clients, Edens Garden (who became an amazing, longtime client for us). Edens Garden went on to refer us to their own friends and family, leading to three other projects. And one of those companies referred us again, leading to another great project. Delivering a great experience and quality creative output was part of this referral path, to be sure. But that first chance at a project in our second year of business was huge.

Surprisingly, creatives who do the same thing as you can also be great resources. They can subcontract you when they have too much work or refer you when someone is not a right fit for their studio. We know this because we do it constantly.

We have a whole list of other studios that we love to refer work to. This list is made up of people we've met online and offline. Some got on our radar through cold emailing. Many we met through our *Freelance and Business and Stuff* online course and community.

Think of web developers, writers, photographers, videographers, editors, creative directors, designers, and others you can reach out to. Offer a referral fee if they send you work. Any work you land from their referrals, they get *x*%.

Agencies are another great pool of creatives who need to flex their team to suit projects. Get on their radar and stay in touch. Follow them on social media, congratulate them on awards and projects. Comment on their posts. Email them every so often to see if they need help on any creative work. They will notice after a while.

Referral Fees

A 5-10% referral fee is a great range to consider. The referrer typically only gets the fee on the first project from the referral. So they don't perpetually earn a fee on all projects you work on with the client afterward. Pay out referral fees after you have been paid in full for a project, just in case a project gets canceled early and your total fee changes.

How to Ask for Work on Social Media Without Losing Your Dignity:

"Wrapped up some projects early, and have some availability! Shoot me an email, and let's make some magic."

"Now taking on clients and projects for the next two quarters! If you need X, Y, or Z, we'd love to help."

"Just had some availability open up. If you have a project you want to chat about, DM me."

Growing Your Community is Growing Your Potential Client Base

Your community doesn't just have to be local. Communities can be cross-continental thanks to the internet and the industrial revolution that brought us trains, planes, and automobiles. Make time to attend events in and out of your industry to meet new people and widen your network of friends and acquaintances. If you live in a more remote area, try to save up to go to an event in the closest nearby city or attend online events and courses instead.

Don't go into these events with solely sales on the brain. That's like going on a first date with wedding plans. You'll come off as overeager and too intense. Go in with the genuine goal of learning about people and making real connections. Talk about anything. In fact, sometimes the people we remember most from events are the ones who we talked with about watching Love is Blind or the Lakers, not about design capabilities. Work is a big part of our life. But you're a human with facets. Think about these events as opportunities to make friends, not land deals.

As you meet people, capture those connections by adding one another on social media, exchanging emails, etc. You want to continue nurturing these relationships in direct (email, phone) and general ways (social, newsletter). Only a very small part of your network is "in the market" for your services or product at any given time. If you're only posting about work once a year and not regularly staying in touch with your audience, you're minimizing the chance of being top of mind when they finally need your services.

You don't have to be on social media every day or attend networking events multiple times a week, but make networking and community investment a regular part of your work schedule.

Keep Tabs on Your Network with a CRM Sheet

Use a Client Relationship Management (CRM) spreadsheet or a tool like Trello to track your outreach efforts and stay on top of things. We like a Google Sheet, a Notion document, or a Trello board because they're both free (to an extent) and easy to maintain. Some paid CRM SaaS (Software as a Service) tools are almost too feature-heavy and are more suited for megacorps than small studios.

Your CRM can help you keep tabs on:

- Existing, past, potential, and dream clients. List their contact info, the people you know at the company, and the kind of work they would need from you.
- Status of each client. Track your communications and their level of interest in your work.

A Business Development Challenge for You

If you want to build your network and broaden your audience, invest at least an hour per week in one or all of the following outreach methods: social media, email, and in person. Don't have any clients yet? Spend even more time on this till you get a client.

You'll notice we didn't include phone outreach. You are more than free to use a phone too! It's just that a phone call is a waking nightmare for many people. And with so many robo-spam-calls going around, we prefer social, email, and in-person outreach.

We used to teach the Professional Practices class for senior graphic design majors at Laguna College of Art + Design. Halfway through the semester, we required our students to get an Instagram and X account and follow creatives who worked at companies they admired and/or wanted to work with. They had to interact with at least ten people per week (through written comments or replies, not just likes and reshares). They weren't limited to talking about design or work. They were encouraged to try to connect on any human level. They also had to send at least three cold emails to dream companies per week. The goal: getting them comfy with reaching out, conversing, and making themselves known.

We had them report back throughout the semester. They were always so excited when they got responses from their design heroes or emails back from prospective employers. Not every interaction led to a response, but it got them over the fear of engaging. They learned that if you put yourself out there enough, it will pay off. It's a numbers game. Almost every student got some sort of tangible benefit out of this exercise.

You can do this same challenge. Think of agencies, brands, companies, and bucket-list dream clients, and add them to your CRM sheet. Find people who work at those companies—you can look up employees on LinkedIn using a reverse search. Check where these people are active on social media. Follow their social profiles and start casually interacting with them to build rapport. Find things you have in common. Music, sports, pop culture, causes, television, food, workout habits, lounging habits, etc.

Social Media Outreach

1. Refer to your CRM sheet's Dream Client list. Follow these companies and people who work for them on social media.
2. Reach out to at least ten of these people per week on social media. Aim to actually interact, not just like or repost. Leave a memorable comment. Better yet, ask a good question.

In-Person Outreach

1. Look up the businesses on your local main street(s) or even in nearby bigger cities. Add them to your CRM. Drive to those businesses, and bring something you can leave behind: a business card, postcard, or brochure with your contact details and context about your business. Now, start walking into businesses and talking to the owners or people working there. If you make a connection and get a good response, leave your

A story about literally knocking on doors

"My first couple jobs as an independent designer were sold by literally knocking on doors. It was early 2021, so I masked up and went for a drive.

The agency I had just left did not let me publicize that I was starting my own company till after I left. So on my last day, I hopped in my car and went driving around to local businesses with some brochures/ business cards. I was super lucky and sold projects to the first two companies I talked to, one of which was a branding project priced in the 5 digits, and a client who I still do work for today. All that to say, knocking on doors works!"

- Lyndon Gehman Founder, Lyndo Studio www. Lyndo.design

The power of referrals

According to the Nielsen Trust in Advertising Study from 2021, 89% of consumers surveyed said they trust recommendations from people they know most, up from 83% in 2015. So the easiest way to get more business is to do right by the business you do have.

business materials behind for them. If no one is available, still leave behind materials. If they tell you to get off the premises, well, their loss.

2. Look up businesses in industrial parks in your area (the part of the city filled with warehouses and factories). Same routine as before: add their info to your CRM, visit them, and try to start a conversation. Ask if they ever need design services. Leave your materials behind.
3. Do the same for the business parks in your area. You know the drill.
4. Find local, regional, or destination events you can attend and meet people more casually:
    - → Business-specific networking events are great because everyone is there for the same reason: to grow their business opportunities together.
    - → Industry-specific creative events and conferences can introduce you to peers and collaborators.
    - → Non-business events and clubs can be just as good and much more fun. Intramural sports and beer leagues, walking clubs, book clubs, cooking classes, art classes, you name it. Wherever you can meet new people, you can also meet new clients. Might as well have fun at the same time! Just be sure to bring up your business. You don't have to force the issue. Almost every single person you meet will give you an easy lob to take a swing at when they ask, "What do you do?" or "What have you been up to?" This is where you talk passionately about your latest projects and clients.
5. Follow the places you visit on social media, and regularly interact with them to keep in touch

Email Outreach

Now it's time to email the people you've been researching or meeting online and offline. And no, it won't kill you. Keep your message short and sweet. We hate to say it, but there's nothing more daunting than seeing a four-paragraph email from someone you don't know. Anything more than two paragraphs will cause someone's eyes to glaze over and their heart to fail. This world is too congested to be adding that noise. Be punchy and poignant. One paragraph or five to seven sentences is a perfect length.

The following is what we like to see in a cold email:

- Let the receiver know why you enjoy what they're doing. Try to be specific and show genuine interest. We can always tell when someone is just listing the latest portfolio project on our site to act interested. The recipient should feel you are honestly interested in what they're doing, and the email is more about them than you. Also, beware internet sourced email templates. We get hundreds of cold emails a week and can spot a template a mile away. Use them as a guide, but make an email your own to get the best return on your effort.
- Tell the recipient what services you offer that could help them. Be succinct. A list of common services or broad fields is fine.
- Link to your website, so they can see your portfolio. We repeat: *link to your website.* Ain't nobody got time to email you back to ask for it after the fact.
- Show your personality in the email. The emails that stand out the most are the ones where we can hear the distinct voice of the person writing them. They feel like a message from a human, not a generic, formulaic sales email.

- Make the subject line original and unique to you. Keep tabs on subject lines that grab your attention in your own inbox. Humor goes a long way, but if you're not innately funny, try something interesting or unexpected instead.

You stand to lose nothing by reaching out, but you stand to miss out on a great client by doing nothing. After you email, if you don't hear back, don't worry. It's almost assuredly not personal. They're probably too busy to respond and don't need what you're offering at that very moment. But they might need your help soon. If you reach out to ten people, one in ten are likely to respond. If they don't respond via email, continue to keep up with them and comment on their social media to casually stay on their radar.

Check back in a few months. Persist without being a pest. On the second reach out, vary your email and keep things light and airy. Don't use passive-aggressive language like, "I never heard back from you . . . ," or "Since you didn't reply . . . ," or "Did you get my last email?," or "Like I said in my last email. . . . " Just remind them of who you are and mention something timely or relevant to them—maybe they released a new project, received an award, etc. By making your follow-up emails about them and not you, it doesn't feel like you're pestering them. More like you're just interested and invested in them.

We have a friend who does custom music, which is a rarer need than custom design work. But he is always busy and gets a good amount of work from cold emailing. His name is Johnny Knittle, and he did some amazing "surf country" to accompany our Freelance, and Business, and Stuff online course promos. He uses a schedule for reach outs. After cold emailing, he reaches out a month later, then again in another month, then in six months, then in a year. Sometimes, a project comes a year from his original reach out. People who never responded before will suddenly say, "I am so glad you reached out, we do actually need this!"

Be careful not to circumnavigate the proper channel for reaching out when it comes to cold emailing. Don't use a personal email if it wasn't given to you or shared online for public use. The person could see it as an invasion of privacy. For us, it's a big pet peeve when people sneak around our contact form and contact page and somehow find our personal email addresses (they're not publicly listed) to contact us directly. This is spam, even if it's a nice email from someone who likes what we're doing. Reach out via the means offered on our company website. Most people probably feel the same. An inbox is already a chaotic place. Unadmitted crashers aren't a welcome addition.

The Secret Sauce: People

If you take anything away from this chapter, take the following: the "secret" to getting work, which is truly no secret at all, is it's all about making a positive connection with people. If you can capture their interest, relate to them, and show how you can help them achieve their goals, they will want to work with you. If you can deliver and make the process easy and painless, they'll return to work with you again and again.

How people perceive your studio and their experience working with you will make or break your business. It only takes a few happy customers to keep you booked with referrals. If you

When someone asks, "What do you do?" how you answer matters!

Tired:
"I have a small graphic design business."

Interesting:
"I run a graphic design studio. We just kicked off an amazing project with [your customer here] that we're super excited about! We'll be [describe the project a little and how you plan to make it special]"

Ways to make your intro memorable:

Mention a well-known local client in your community

Mention one of your interesting or niche services that might spark conversation. At Hoodzpah, we work on movie title treatments (aka movie logos). This is an instant conversation starter!

Mention a unique project you've been working on. We once had a client who turned people's cremains into diamonds for loved ones. It was an amazing conversation starter.

get more than that, great! Now, you have the luxury of choice and can scale your business. The size of your audience is not the only answer to getting good quality jobs. This has never been more evident than in the social media age we live in. Growing organically and genuinely through personal conversations and unique interactions is way more effective than blasting your business to millions of people through paid ads that fail to rise above the noise. We know plenty of social media "famous" creatives who struggle to make ends meet.

So don't worry about getting 100,000 followers on social media or working with huge brands when you first start out. Think about making a handful of genuine connections in your day-to-day life and community.

Undercover future clients are all around you. When people ask how you are and what you're up to, that's your opportunity to fill them in on your business and the projects you're excited about! Your business is not some embarrassing secret. If you're excited about it, that passion is infectious! You're just one conversation away from someone needing your service or having a connection with someone who does. The most mundane conversations can turn into an amazing project. So when you're out and about in the world, be an ambassador for your business, show respect for people's time and effort, and be a positive influence on the room instead of an emotional vampire.

Chapter Checklist:

① Think of a great passion or pro bono project to fill in the gaps of your portfolio

② Research local meetups (both creative and non-creative) you could attend to build your network

③ Create a CRM Sheet and add to it:

- → Past and existing clients
- → Dream clients
- → Local creative agencies and studios who could subcontract you
- → Friends and family with businesses who could be future clients

④ Do the Business Development Challenge

⑤ Regularly check in with contacts on your CRM to warm up relationships and build rapport (whether through social media, email, hangouts, phone calls, or otherwise).

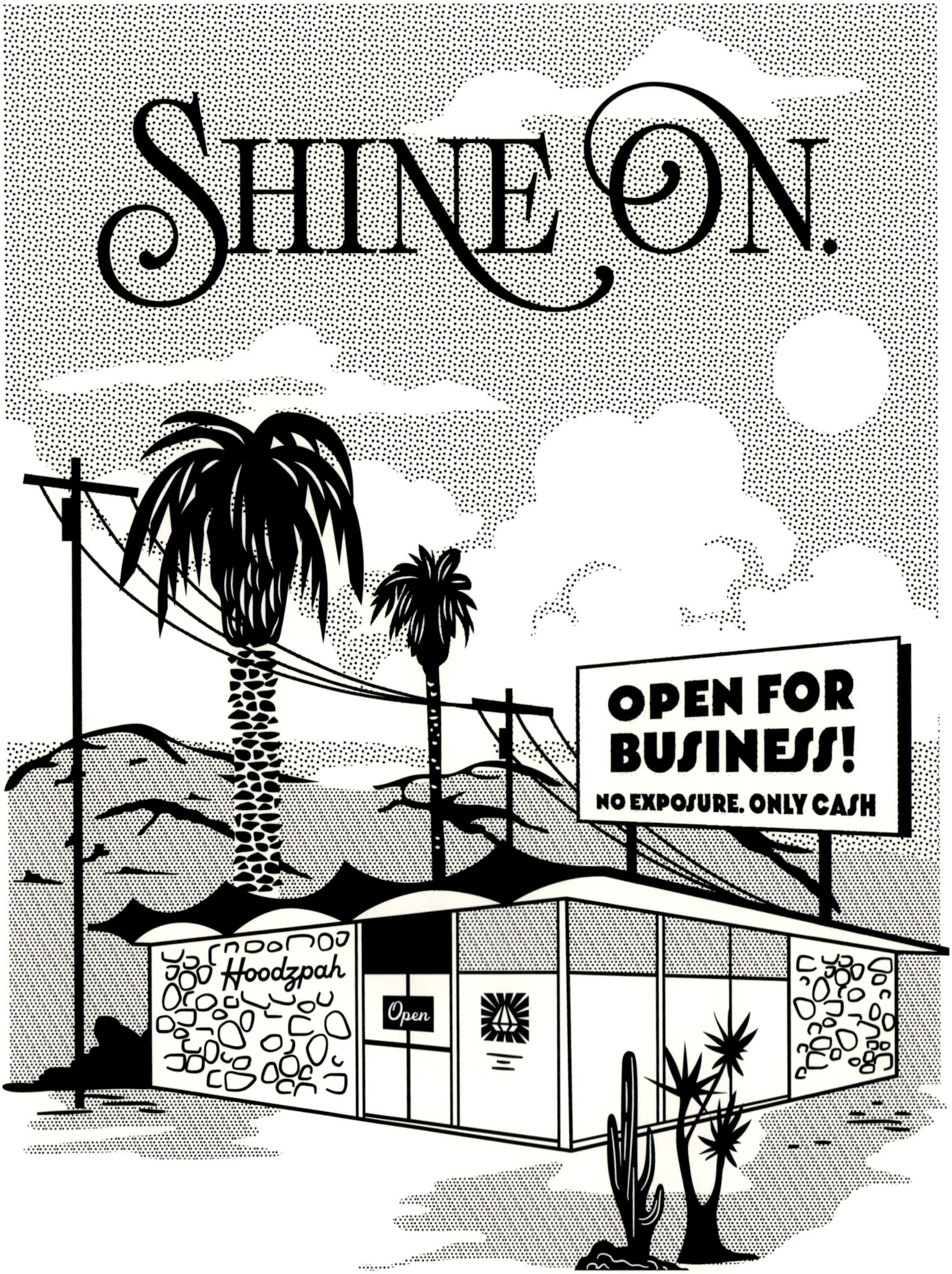

Illustration by: Jennifer & Amy Hood

10

Marketing, Brand Awareness, and Reputation Building

The word *marketing* can feel like a tease. There's always this suspicion that it actually means something more than what it does. Like there's some angle to it that only a savvy NYC consultant would understand. Don't feel daunted. Marketing is merely the act of promoting your brand and business.

The "how" of marketing changes as technology and culture shift. But, the "why" of marketing is always the same: Marketing is how we engage with an audience to increase brand awareness, show differentiation, encourage interaction (transactions being a big one), and maintain brand loyalty.

In order to do marketing well, you need a good grip on the following:

1. Your Target Audience. The ideal customer for your brand offering. This potential buyer should have a need/want for your type of service and the ability to pay for it.
2. Your Brand Positioning. How you present your brand and service/product offering to set a perception and expectation among your target audience. Ideally, you have an angle of differentiation that can help you appeal to this audience in a unique way. Your differentiator could be your creative style, your reputation, your quality of work, a unique skill, or even just your tone of voice or approach to your work.

As you start working on your marketing strategy, research creative agencies and studios you admire that are working with your dream clients. Look at brand heroes who you think resonate with a similar client to yours. Analyze their website, messaging, social media, service offering, products, customer journeys, and user experience. Take note of what they do that works really well, and consider how you could apply similar tactics in your own unique way. How are they staying in the public discourse through their content strategy? What tips can you apply to your own plan? Take note of what they are missing. Is there a gap for a fresh perspective or tactic?

Now that you know what others are doing well, or missing out on, think about completely new ways to promote yourself and connect with your audience. Research is great, but we're creatives. We can also invent. And inventing your own campaigns is how you really stand out from the crowd and even blaze a trail.

Looking at the current marketing output is to look at ideas developed maybe a year ago or more. You're seeing a delayed result of ideas already aging. And by the time you make something similar, even more time has passed. You might wind up on the tail end of a trend instead of finding a unique voice and angle. Instead of mimicking what's out there, reinterpret it. Use your research to inform new ideas rather than just riffs on old ones.

Building Reputation and Brand Awareness

When thinking of marketing goals, think beyond just booking client work. Marketing isn't only about promoting sales. Building your brand's reputation and increasing brand awareness among your target audience is an equally important goal. This will lay a critical foundation for booking work later on.

Author, teacher, and design system advocate, Dan Mall, recently shared an interesting photo in his newsletter (which we highly recommend). It was a picture of a billboard for Buc-ee's, a beloved country store/gas station/convenience store/eatery with locations mostly in the Southern United States. But the billboard was located on the New Jersey Turnpike. The billboard simply said:

"↰ 581 miles. Buc-ee's."

This is such a classic example of marketing for the goal of brand awareness. As this billboard was 581 miles away from a Buc-ee's, the goal wasn't transactional. It was to continue to spread the lore of Buc-ee's into far-off places!

Lets cover some of the best tools to get your marketing campaign out to your audience. By the way, if you find you consistently don't have time to keep your website and social media updated, hire someone to help you. If you're that busy, you can justify a junior designer or paid intern to help you.

Creating an Objectively Good Website

Your website is the hub of most of your marketing efforts (online or offline). Whether someone saw you on social media, read about you online, or heard about you from a friend, they go to your site to verify you before they hire you. Especially in the post-catfish/AI/deep-fake world we live in. Likely all of your online campaigns will lead back to your website.

Like it or not, we live in a very digital world. If you're serious about running a successful studio, you need a professional, dedicated website. Social media and portfolio sites like Dribbble and Behance are a good starting point to get your name out there and start building an audience, but on their own they can give the air of "small time" more than "professional studio." If you have visions of grandeur and want to eventually grow your team, land creative direction or art direction work, and court bigger projects and big-name clients, a website is a must. Especially when you think about the fact that social media platforms and portfolio platforms are borrowed land you're being permitted to post on. It's good to build equity around a site where you have control over your work, your posts, your connection to your audience, and your data.

Your studio website is a dedicated space to show off your brand positioning exactly as you want. You can set the perfect tone and appeal to your target audience more effectively than through Behance, Dribbble, LinkedIn, X, Working Not Working, or Instagram. Most medium to large clients expect a website. They might find you on Behance or Dribbble first, but they will look for your website when it comes to vetting you to pitch your services to their boss.

There are talented freelancers and studios without websites. But they are usually people with decades of experience and a deep network of past clients and collaborators to lean on for ongoing work. This is the exception to the rule. Most of us mere mortals are under the rule, not the exception.

When we want to subcontract a creative and they don't have a website, we think twice about how serious they are about their business. Is this a side gig for them? Will they disappear into the night if they lose interest or get busy with other things? Can we trust them to follow through?

If you had to hire someone for work that costs tens of thousands of dollars, would you want to go with someone who just has a profile on Yelp? Or someone with a Yelp profile and a website that really shows off their differentiating qualifications? When it comes to landing quality work, you need to show you are reliable, professional, and investing in your own business as much as you will for your clients. A website helps you do this.

Making a website can be one of the largest hurdles for a new studio owner or freelancer. We've all shed tears in our beers about the design of our site. We want it to be amazing, but we don't know where to start. We want to show our skills, but we're afraid of coming off as braggy. We want to articulate our process and expertise, but we don't know what's relevant and what's too in the weeds for clients to care about. So let's break this down simply.

A successful website will help you with the following:

1. Explain what you do in relation to the value it can bring your customer/audience.
    a. Your capabilities
    b. Your process
    c. Your team
    d. Your purpose (value proposition/positioning)
2. Prove your expertise.
    a. Case studies
    b. Testimonials
    c. Awards, honors, features, etc.
    d. Current and previous clients list
    e. Blogs or resources
3. 3. Capture your audience (not as creepy as it sounds).
    a. Social media
    b. Newsletter
    c. Contact form

Let's dig into these.

Explain Your Studio

Why do so many freelance/studio websites barely explain themselves at all? We show stunning pictures of work with no explanation of the problem solved, the services rendered, or the process used. We think all will be made clear through osmosis of the eyeballs. And sure, a lot can be inferred by visuals. But have you ever sent a proof to a client with no context or explanation? No. It would be a cardinal sin. Because non-creatives don't understand creativity in a vacuum. They need a spirit guide to interpret the vision. Don't make the same mistake on your website.

Your Purpose. Think about what you do from the perspective of your target audience. What are their needs, and how do your capabilities solve those needs? The answer should be reflected in your copywriting. The formula goes something like this: You help [target audience] do [goal] by [your service]. Then, spin this formulaic sentence to be original and interesting.

Your Capabilities. Listing your skills and services will reinforce your brand positioning. It shows what you specialize in and will eliminate pointless emails from people wanting things outside your wheelhouse. This is such a simple but powerful data point on your site. If you say you make websites, what kind? What platforms? Be specific to help people understand.

Your Process. This is where you tell your audience a little about how you approach work. While you might think it's non-essential, this is a great area to prove your expertise or focus on differentiators. It's also a place to preemptively answer frequent questions from customer inquiries.

Your Team. Part of building trust with a future client is showing you are a real human. Just seeing a picture of you or your team will humanize you and alleviate common fears people have when hiring strangers. This is also a place to tout personal or team awards and honors and reveal brand personality. In your team bios, you can talk about your hobbies, interests, and inspirations. Sometimes, small commonalities like this can really help bridge a gap.

Prove Your Expertise

Once someone knows who you are and what you do, they want to be sold on you. They want to know why you're better than the other studio. You may be thinking, "My work should speak for itself. I shouldn't need to sell it." As universal as this sentiment feels to us as artists, we would never advise our clients to take such a passive role in marketing their business. When it comes to working for yourself, the age-old adage of "do unto thyself as thou wouldst do for a client" remains a North Star to realign your perspective.

People in buying mode look for points of verification to justify their spending. It's true for us when we hire someone, and it's true for our clients when they consider hiring us. That's where the oft-eschewed brag comes in. Here's how to do it without hating yourself:

Case Studies.

- Include the "who, what, how, and why." It doesn't have to be a novel, but concise blurbs explaining who the client is (everyone might not know the company), what the client needed help with (problem), why the project was important (goals), and how you achieved those goals through your creative work (solution). If you have data to prove a successful project, show it. Even a positive testimonial from the client can serve as anecdotal proof of success. One to two paragraphs is plenty.
- A scope list of the services you performed on the project.
- Credit anyone who worked on the project outside of your team.
- Show off the project with compelling visuals that celebrate all the details and strategic thinking. Photography of your project is amazing, but mock-ups can be just as good if you get the right ones. Motion graphics are another great tool to show off the solution in an exciting way that keeps your viewer engaged.

Testimonials and Reviews. A great testimonial is like when Dominic Toretto (Vin Diesel) shifts beyond the mere five gears into sixth, seventh, and twentieth gear in *Fast and Furious*. They're magical extra boosts not to be underestimated.

- According to The 2023 Local Consumer Review Survey, 84 percent of people said reviews played an important/very important role in whether or not they use a service-based professional.
- WikiJob conducted a split test in which they added three testimonials to a landing page and saw a 34 percent increase in conversions (Marie Dean, "Testimonials: How and Why to Get Them," CXL.com, February 4, 2020). If you're completely new to freelancing, you can still gather testimonials from previous bosses and coworkers. The goal here is to show validation for your skills from a third party. Former coworkers can do this just as well as clients.

Accolades, Awards, and Other Proof of Expertise. While we have mixed feelings about design awards, there's no question that the words "award-winning" look damn good to a client. When you see a movie trailer and the little Sundance or Cannes wreath icons appear, you automatically think, "This film must be good." Potential clients are looking for the same markers when making their decisions. Awards aren't the only way to do this. Consider other accolades or honors you and your studio might have. If you start to feel slimy, don't. A potential client is on your site because they want to learn more about you. They want to be convinced that you are the right creative partner. Now's not the time to be coy.

- Have you judged any creative competitions?
- Have you been featured in any blogs or design annuals?
- Have you ever been covered by Under Consideration's Brand New or something similar?
- Have you ever spoken to an industry group, at a conference, or at a design school?

Clients List. By including the logos of real clients you have worked with, you're telling potential clients, "Look, they trusted me, and you can too!" It's subliminal, but it works. Even if the company isn't a name brand, it works. Clients want to know this isn't your first rodeo. They want to know you've been around the proverbial block.

Resources, Articles, and Blogs. Creating valuable content or tools regarding your industry and skills can be a time investment, to be sure. But it can really pay off when it comes to further proving your expertise, building your reputation, and driving traffic. By explaining creative principles, offering insight, or just explaining processes, you create transparency that customers trust and peers crave. Proving your expertise like this could lead to speaking gigs, teaching gigs, or an opportunity to create products for your industry peers in addition to your client work. Win-win.

The most important thing when creating content is adding value, whether it's informative or funny. Don't just half-ass a blog because people say you should be blogging. Doing something just for the sake of it misses the mark.

Capture Your Audience

It's great when someone visits your website, but how do you capture their information and attention for the long haul?

1. **Contact Page.** Make it easy to capture the information of people who are ready to inquire about your services. Visitors should be able to easily find your contact info without having to dig. Make a dedicated page and link to it from your site's main menu.

2. **Newsletter Sign-Up Form.** Contact pages are great for visitors who are ready to start a project. But that's just a fraction of your audience. Consider the visitors who are interested but don't need your services *right now*. Consider creative peers who might not need your services themselves but admire your process and insight. A newsletter is a great way to stay in touch with "sooners" and fans. Put a newsletter subscription form in a prominent area on key pages of your site.

   Your subscriber list will be made up of your most loyal followers. This is more than a passive like or follow on social media. These subscribers are giving you access to their personal inbox! That's one of the highest commitments you could hope for from a person, short of contacting you about a project or giving you a profile on their Netflix account.

   Even if you don't know at this minute what you would write or send to an email list, start building one. This is an engaged part of your audience you want to nurture and grow. They're already primed to engage you for services, buy products you release, or refer you.

   Want inspiration for your email newsletter design? Check out: www.reallygoodemails.com

3. **Social Media Links.** Encouraging visitors to follow you on social media is another great way to capture an audience that likes what you do but maybe doesn't need your services now. Put your social media icons linked to your profiles prominently on your website's navigation, sidebar, or footer so they show up on every page of your site.

A website on its own is like a beautiful restaurant in a remote forest. Now you need to find a way to bring people to your doors. Keep reading for some ideas.

Getting Discovered and Driving Traffic

You can use portfolio profiles on sites like Dribbble, Behance, Medium, and Working Not Working as springboards to your own website and social profiles. These sites are well indexed and highly trafficked. If you don't have a network or a reputation yet, people are much more likely to find your work on these websites than on your own website. Use these portfolio profiles as a launchpad. Post regularly to these profiles and link to your website. Backlinks from high-ranking websites like these will help boost your SEO rankings and drive traffic.

Art directors and creative leads at companies often search these sites to put together mood boards and find potential collaborators. These sites can also lead to a lot of junk leads. But the few quality projects that come through are worth wading through the riffraff.

We built a lot of our network through portfolio sites. A post on Dribbble would gain traction, and people would share it on their social media, and we'd get social media followers as a result. Or people would find our work on Behance, go to our site, and follow us on Instagram to keep tabs on our studio for future projects. Someone we connected with on Dribbble (yo, Nick Slater!) referred us for our first speaking gig at Creative South, which put us on the speaking circuit for years after, lending credibility and building awareness around our brand.

You can use the same photo, video, and content assets you use on your own website. Make it a habit to update your portfolio sites at the same time you update your own website.

And Then There Was Social Media

Facebook, X (Twitter, to those of you still digging your heels in), Instagram, TikTok, Pinterest, LinkedIn, YouTube—as a creative, all of these social media platforms are great tools to share your work, vision, and brand. They're especially magical places because they create opportunities for you to connect with peers, mentors, and potential clients from all over the world. You're not constrained to your regional acquaintances and cousins. You're goin' global, baby. Or at least there's the potential. Each site allows you to link to your website, driving traffic to your portfolio, newsletter sign-up, and contact page.

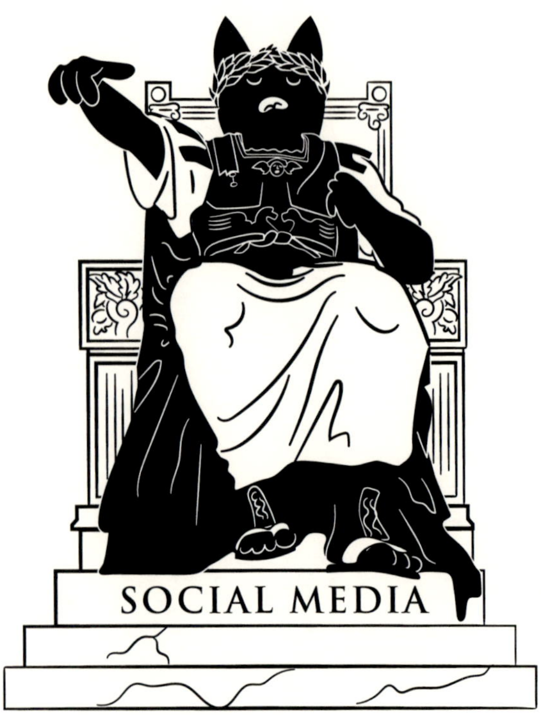

Social media profiles are a great way to capture an audience and keep them updated on what you're doing. As a new brand, it might feel overwhelming to think of all the possible channels. Focus on two or three that you feel have the best potential to show off your brand voice and skills while putting you in the path of your ideal client.

Believe us when we say you don't have to post every day to get benefits from social media. Yes, channels like TikTok seem to reward consistency, but Instagram can yield amazing results even if you just post once a month. You don't have to go viral or rack up thousands of followers to see returns on your time investment. The goal is to make genuine connections with people who could one day refer you or hire you for a project themselves. Beyond traditional client work, your content and perspective could lead to speaking gigs at conferences, sponsorships, or collabs.

When it comes to social media, try not to think about your return on investment solely through the lens of monetary gain. Building brand awareness and investing in brand storytelling in itself is an important and ongoing part of marketing.

Social media can quickly become a time-sucking distraction if you let it. If you find your day disappearing with not much to show for it, try isolating your social media activity to certain days and times so you can focus on the actual work of the business.

You probably already have personal accounts on some of these platforms. But do you need a separate business account? It's up to you. We recommend studios and freelancers get dedicated social accounts for their businesses if they are serious about doing it full-time at a high level. Here are some pros and cons to consider:

Dedicated Social Media Accounts for Your Company

Pros:

- A business account silos your work from your personal life, so you can have more privacy. There are things you might want to post for friends and family that wouldn't be appropriate or even interesting to your clients and business followers.
- You can build an audience that's specifically following your creative work, and curate content for your target audience and brand.
- If you have any plans to grow your business in the future, you'll eventually need a separate business profile more representative of your team. Having a separate account readies you for growth.

Cons:

- Having a separate account means more work. But that's business, isn't it?
- Gaining a new following can be rough at first. But hang in there. Plus, you can use your personal accounts to reshare posts from your business accounts to gain followers from your existing network.

Personal Social Media Accounts that Double as Work Accounts

Pros:

- You already have a following built up.
- Some of your existing audience, who wouldn't normally follow a new work account, might be won over by seeing your work on your existing account.
- If you're freelancing and doing business as your personal name, then using your personal account may make sense. This can be a good solution for artists taking more of an influencer approach. They are selling themselves as a brand as much as their product or service. So the glimpse into their life is part of how they market their brand.

Cons:

- Your followers might be thrown off or annoyed by work content when they follow you for personal updates.
- You have to be more cautious about what you post. What you may be cool with your friends seeing, you may not be cool with your client seeing.
- A personal account with occasional posts about creative work will not be as effective at

Lock Down Your Social Media Username/ Handle

positioning your brand, targeting an audience, and attracting clients on a professional level. Most clients who are used to working with studios and agencies will be underwhelmed by a dual-purpose personal/work social account. They will question your professionalism and level of expertise.

When choosing your username on various platforms, try to get the same username across all platforms. If you Google "social media handle checker," a myriad of online tools will pop up like namecheckr.com and namechk.com. With more and more businesses forming every day, this becomes harder and harder to do, but a consistent handle makes it easier for your audience to find you and trust that it's your real account and not a phony.

Tidy Up Your Social Media

We've all Google-stalked someone. Don't pretend you haven't. You meet someone, you get curious, you hop on your computer and awake from a trance two hours later with 147 browser windows open. Your clients do it too.

You should assume that any potential client will do a deep dive before hiring you. Maybe they're just looking you up to see your work. But when they search your name, your social media profiles are likely to pop up too. What will they find if they click on your Instagram or TikTok account? The world has access to so much personal information about all of us, thanks (or curses) in large part to social media.

Consider whether or not you want to make your personal social media accounts private so only followers can see them. If you keep any of your personal accounts public, you'll want to review them through the eyes of a potential client. We're not suggesting you pretend to be someone you're not to get a job. But we all know there's often a side we show at work, a side we show with family, and a side we show with friends. We're faceted humans.

Here's how to review and tidy up your online presence:

Google yourself. You might be surprised what accounts are still active that you don't even use anymore. That old Blogspot where you posted outfits of the day, or that Tumblr account with a dangerous amount of Dashboard Confessional content. Unless you're saving it for posterity, delete dormant accounts you no longer update.

1. Update bios and avatars. Remember the branding chapter? It's all about repetition and consistency. Use the same avatar image (whether a photo or logo) on all of your business accounts, so people can easily find you. Keep bios consistent too. The ideal bio includes your business name, a short blurb about your service and offering, and something fun or memorable. The tone of voice should match your brand identity positioning. Don't forget to link your website, dadgummit! If you're keeping public personal accounts aside from your work accounts, mention and link your work profiles on those for even more traction.
2. Remove content you no longer want to be public. There's no need to scrub your entire history. It's not like you're running for president. But just be considerate of what could be seen as inappropriate, offensive, or off-putting:
    - → Content about abusing drugs or alcohol
    - → Bad-mouthing of employers, employees, or clients
    - → Discriminatory comments about race, gender, religion, sexual orientation, etc.
    - → Provocative photos
    - → Content that discredits you (if you've said one thing on your website and then your social media says another, that's not a good look)

Tailor Content per Social Network

Different social media platforms have different benefits and angles. Here's a cheat sheet of the top social networks for creatives and what content tends to work best (but as always, test your own angles and outlets).

X (formerly Twitter), Threads, and Bluesky
These networks are for voicing thoughts and opinions about your industry, your life, and the world. These spaces can be great for connecting with peers and pillars in your creative world. Most creatives are managing their own accounts here, which means no gatekeepers (secretaries, managers, PR agents, etc.). We've found it's easier to communicate with creative heroes on these sites compared to Instagram. Why? Many X/Threads/Bluesky users are passive (just scrolling, liking, and retweeting), so it's much easier to stand out if you're an active participant in the conversation (i.e., commenting and creating your own posts).

On Instagram, well-known creatives get thousands of likes and comments per post. But on X/Threads/Bluesky, that same creative might only get 140 likes on a post and even fewer comments. Cutting through the noise is so much easier. If you have a unique voice and respond in a clever way, they will probably respond to you or at least see your comment. It's a magical place in that sense.

We do have a work account for Hoodzpah on these sites, but we tend to get the most benefit out of using our personal accounts to keep in touch with peers and fellow creatives more casually. Even though it's a "personal account", we treat it like a networking account, and are considerate in what we post while not being joyless or soulless. These sites are a fun place to let your personality show. People who enjoy these platforms like to read and share personal insights that aren't so brand curated. Everything doesn't have to be work-related. The best accounts are smart, silly, sometimes vulnerable, genuine, off-topic, and work-related all at once.

Instagram
This is perhaps the easiest network for visual creatives. You can post progress shots, finished projects, pics of your team, before-and-after photos, studio shots, etc. If you use the right hashtags on your content, you become more easily discoverable to new followers and clients. Once you hit a certain number of followers, the numbers almost seem to perpetuate themselves. It's that herd mentality. Instagram Stories let you be more spontaneous without worrying about the video living on your feed forever. This is the most unguarded way to connect with your audience and make a human connection; thus, it can be the most compelling. Instagram Live is a great way to do quick tutorials or AMA-style interviews with your followers. Videos you want to keep on your feed for longer can live on Reels. We have gotten so much value out of our Instagram. Art directors find us here. Clients find us here. We meet friends here. We meet peers here.

LinkedIn
Don't sleep on LinkedIn! We know many peers who get great work inquiries through LinkedIn. People and companies use LinkedIn to find and vet contractors. For years, LinkedIn was hardly the go-to social media network. It was a useful tool to fact-check resumes and job hunt. But lately there has been a LinkedIn revival! Potentially, because

The Internet is Forever

According to a 2022 Job Insights survey conducted by The Harris Poll on behalf of Express Employment Professionals, 70% of companies use social media to research job candidates. The same study revealed that a little over 50% of hiring managers who research candidates via social media found information that caused them not to hire a candidate.

John Luu, Creative Director and former AIGA National Board Member, makes a case for LinkedIn this way: "If you have a fairly unique name and a LinkedIn profile, chances are your LinkedIn profile shows up in the number one spot when someone searches for you on Google. This is a pretty powerful personal brand management tool when you think about it."

of how much the vibes on X and engagement on Instagram have changed over the last few years. Many people who used to love X left the platform when they perceived the tone shifted to more negativity and aggression. Those people are now using LinkedIn like they used to use X. Because the platform is professional-focused, there is a level of "play nice, the boss is watching." While this weeds out a lot of trolls, LinkedIn boasts a special breed of "well, actually" types who like to correct or one-up you regardless of what you post.

LinkedIn is great for keeping up with professional acquaintances, clients, and collaborators. Building your network will come in handy down the road when you're looking for an introduction or a common network with a certain person or company. Also, the platform makes it easy to ask for recommendations from connections and clients. A recommendation is basically a testimonial about you from someone who confirms they have worked with you. You can repurpose them on your website.

Pinterest
If you upload your own work to Pinterest with proper attribution (your name and website), Pinterest can be a very powerful tool. By pinning your work alongside similar work in curated boards, you teach the Pinterest algorithm to surface your work when people search for that kind of content. This helps people discover your work when they're looking for inspiration or searching for creatives.

Use this platform to amplify the visibility of your work, your name, and push traffic to your site. Plus, if you can create pins for your work first, you can avoid someone else pinning it without proper attribution. Most people repin: they rarely create new pins. Nothing worse than seeing your work all over the internet with no attribution. Pin it first and pin it right. It's also a good idea to post your products here if you have them.

Behance
Behance is a platform where you can post your creative work. Lots of people, agencies, and companies cruise Behance to find talent for their projects. The way you post on Behance will likely mirror your portfolio posts on your site.

Behance features their favorite projects daily. It's a great way to get some notoriety and clout without having to apply to an awards competition. Behance is now owned by Adobe. Attend Adobe Live events on Behance or YouTube, get to know the hosts and moderators and actively participate in the chats. Attendees to these virtual events have turned into paid Adobe Live event guests. Being featured on a vlog like Adobe Live will build awareness around your brand and add to your perceived expertise.

Medium
This is a blogging platform where creatives can write think pieces on their industry, go in depth on the process behind a certain project, analyze the success of a recent project, or discuss current events. If you're looking to establish yourself as a thought leader in your industry, here's a great place to clarify your unique positions and ideas. If you want to speak at a conference one day and you enjoy writing, start writing your thoughts down in places like this.

Substack
This might be better categorized as a publisher platform than a social media platform, but

for lack of a better place to put it, we'll include it here. Substack is like a blog and newsletter with a community aspect. You can build a subscriber list, charge for your content, and promote your content across the platform to readers interested in your topics. It's a great way to build an audience around a newsletter. Many influencers and writers are beginning to monetize their content on Substack in a way that was harder to do on platforms like TikTok and Instagram.

TikTok
TikTok is less a place for a hard sell and more a place to show off your brand personality through low-stakes, low-pressure content that is less curated (or seemingly so) than Instagram or Behance. You'll need to approach TikTok with a different tactic than Instagram or YouTube. Beautiful shots of your portfolio or well-edited process videos often just don't hit the same there. What seems to work is snappy, unpolished, and more off-the-wall content. You need to have a distinct perspective that quickly catches attention. TikTok is less about who you follow and more about discovery and instant gratification. The potential to "go viral" here is more democratized and less tied to your following size.

Many creatives succeed on TikTok with content about industry culture, creative trends, industry jokes or bits, and entertaining how-to or process videos. Amber Asay of Nice People (@womendesignerspod) has done a great job at making design-focused content that is smart and entertaining. Neil Shankar (@tallneil) shares his opinions on brand campaigns and releases in a casual but super interesting way that proves his expertise. Jack Harrison (@mrjackio) shares his process for making motion graphics and has landed clients like Kings of Leon along the way. Ilana Griffo (@ilanagriffo) of GoodType shares short but helpful tips on lettering and licensing your artwork. Eugene Healey (@eugbrandstrat) posts insightful takes on post-millennial brand and marketing trends. Max Kolo (@cool_lookin_bug) redesigns ugly flyers he finds on walls and street posts in NYC. Find your unique angle. You might not land your next enterprise client on TikTok, but you could build brand awareness, establish your perspective as an industry leader (conferences are looking for unique voices), and attract brand partnerships.

Be careful about how you share stories about clients. Remember your NDAs. If you share a client story that taught you a great lesson, keep it vague. If you're sharing multiple stories about horror clients, people will start seeing you as the common denominator. Even if your experience with a company was bad, blasting it on TikTok for likes might make other companies wary of working with you.

YouTube
When you're looking for a tutorial or a how-to video, where is the first place you go? YouTube. This is great for longer format and more in-depth content, as opposed to the short, quippy, and humorous content you might do for TikTok. You can do live streams, how-to videos, interviews, or just keep a vlog here.

After doing a few live streams with Adobe Live, we got an amazing boost in visibility, and our YouTube audience grew significantly. Our audience was so vocal about wanting more of this type of content that we began doing live streams on our own YouTube channel when we had time.

Marketing Advice from a Commercial Artist

Our friend Josh Ariza, commercial artist & CEO of Chomp Brand has been a business owner for nearly two decades. Here's some of his tips to longevity:

- Learn marketing. It's the only way you'll feed yourself long-term.
- Marketing sells good design. Good design cannot sell itself.
- You are a salesperson. Every product needs a face. You're it.
- You're building a personal brand whether it's intentional or not. Make it interesting.
- Happy customers become the best marketers.
- Trolls aren't constructive. Take feedback from customers, not haters.
- Market across a few channels. Don't get monopolized by one.
- Success is only experienced in moments, not forever.

joshuaariza.com

Our YouTube monetization doesn't bring in a ton because we're not very active (one to four videos a year), but we are able to promote our products within the streams. A lot of the people who subscribe to our YouTube are our prime audience for our shop products (decks, fonts, templates, courses, etc.). So it's worth it to us to nurture this audience.

Facebook
Facebook mainly feels like an over-fifty AOL chat room these days. But if you have a great network there, you'll find value in it. While personal Facebook profiles are mainly for family/friend interactions, a business page is where you can keep people apprised of projects you're working on, announce new products, and share behind-the-scenes processes. We rarely use Facebook these days, but we keep the page and just push Instagram posts there via our social media management software (Later). We rarely get work from our Facebook page, so we don't focus too much effort there.

Tips for Using Social Media to Your Best Advantage

1. Be you. Create work and posts authentic to your brand, not parroting someone else. You're more likely to get clients you'll vibe with if you're honest about your style, approach, and brand culture. If you're not funny, don't try to be. If you're not the world's leading expert on branding, don't pretend to be. Play to your strengths and find an angle that celebrates your own journey. Rick Steves vs. Anthony Bourdain vs. Cunk vs. Richard Ayoade. They're all talking about travel but in completely unique voices.
2. Balance quality and quantity. Quality, when it comes to social media, is very relative. There are tons of quality content with low production value. Quality comes down to content that is valuable or entertaining. Feed clogging with crap posts will do nothing for your brand. And yet, you do want to post regularly enough to build brand awareness. If your heart's not in it, posting every day just to please the algorithm lords could annoy or bore your existing audience. The internet is full of clickbait slop made to feed a bot and earn false traffic. AI is doing plenty of that. Don't add to the meaningless pile. Make work and share content that is interesting and valuable. It doesn't always have to be high-quality productions to interest your audience. Denzel Washington did an interview with Jamie Foxx for the Grey Goose OFF SCRIPT series, and his advice to his actor sons was, "You want people to go, 'I can't wait to see him.' Not, 'I see him everywhere . . . you wanna keep some mystery.'"
    - → Jot down ideas for interesting and funny content so you have a backlog.
    - → You do not need to post every day—or even every other day. Once a week is great, and more is even better if the content is quality and you have the time.
    - → If you don't have anything to say, you can still post about your work and process. You don't need words for that. Play to your strengths.
    - → If you're not an expert, you can still curate valuable content you are learning from others or share work from others (with credit). Again, not in a bot way, but to build community and support other artists. Be careful to share in a way that makes it clear the work is not your own.
    - → Stop saying, "I'm sorry for not posting."
    - → Stop saying, "I have to post today."

3. You can be social and also maintain privacy and boundaries. If you give all of yourself all the time, you will eventually feel used and dried up. It can be emotionally draining and leave you feeling empty. At the end of the day, as much as you appreciate and feel you know your audience, it is a parasocial relationship. You only know what they share, and they only know what you share. They might be over you tomorrow and onto something else. So save bits of you just for yourself, your friends, and your family.
4. Give as much as you ask. Remember, when it comes down to it, social media is meant to be fun. If users see you're constantly hard selling, they might stop listening and following. It's give and take, like any relationship. Be focused and even-handed, mixing business with fun, interesting info that provides value to your audience. Invest in them, not just yourself.
5. Post about self-initiated projects to fill in the gaps of your portfolio. Want to get logo work? Do a personal project and create a logo for it. Share it and tag/hashtag accordingly. There's a reason so many successful creatives recommend doing this. It works.
6. Support your friends the way you want to be supported. This is not a tit-for-tat kind of equation. It's more of an implied system. If your friend just opened the brewery they've been building for the past year and you share a post about it to all your followers, you're supporting their dreams and goals. When you launch a new endeavor, they might feel moved to support you in kind. You have talented and connected friends doing very cool things (hopefully?), and they're your allies as much as your avenue to potential clients. Support them, and they will support you. Maybe not all the time, but sometimes. The by-product of this is brand alignment. The people and businesses you support and align yourself with become a means that others can use as a character reference for your brand.
7. Consider how future clients will discover you. Use hashtags and keywords so that people can find you. TikTok, Instagram, and YouTube are not just social media platforms; they are search engines. People use them as a means to find inspiration, answers, community, and collaborators. Hashtag and keyword your posts to grow your audience beyond the people already following you. Don't go crazy; just use a handful of hashtags that best apply to the content piece. Try to come up with a catchy, short, easy-to-remember hashtag for your company. We use #Hoodzpah on every piece of content we post. And we created the hashtag #FABAS for this very book (soft sell to tag us, yo).
8. Embrace two-way conversation. If someone responds to your post, write them back! Even if it's just an emoji of recognition. Followers love to know you've heard them and appreciate them. Comment on other people's posts. Engage with peers and brands you want to work with. Staying on their radar in a supportive way will come back in spades.
9. Consider your tone, timing, and risk. You're allowed to have opinions. You're human, and there are many important conversations that happen online. Just remember that without the context of your in-person face and mannerisms, things can easily be misunderstood. What you think is a harmless joke or sarcastic remark could be taken as a blatant insult by someone else. Social media can turn into the Thunderdome in milliseconds. Proceed with caution, and consider the result of careless remarks. Sometimes, just the timing of a remark can be in poor taste.
10. Remember that your brand's social goal is to connect with your audience. Going viral with mass society for acting a fool doesn't exactly serve your goal of building a perception of brand expertise and winning clients. Sure, it's cool for a moment. But people laughing at you doesn't necessarily translate to people trusting or hiring you.

It's a balancing act. Ideally people laugh with you and feel a connection with your perspective or personality.

11. Say it directly and say it indirectly. You can talk about the theory and broad process behind your industry and skill set, but you can also show it by doing in-depth posts on real projects, paid or personal. Show what the client asked for and how you made it happen for them. It's easier to brag on our clients and the work we made together than to hard sell your services like Billy Mays hocking OxiClean.

Social Media Content Planning

Plan out your content calendar. If your strategy is a mix of social media, long-form content like newsletters and articles, and portfolio posts, put together a spreadsheet or calendar listing when you'll post what. Then, create draft posts with your content and images so you're ready to roll. Social media can be fun to do off the cuff at times, but having the majority of your content prepared ahead of time helps you stay active online even when your work week gets swamped. Choose a slow time in your month to plan this out. There are great apps out there that can help you plan social posts (we use Later app).

If you're choosing two to three platforms to invest in, we recommend at least one of the portfolio sites (Behance or Dribbble) and then two of the others. If those gain good results after a few months, you might test other platforms, especially if it's easy to tailor and reuse content (e.g., whatever you post to TikTok can be easily shared on Instagram Reels).

Measuring Success on Social Media

Analyze the in-platform analytics (TikTok, Instagram, Twitter, YouTube, and Facebook all have in-depth analytics) to see what content your viewers are connecting with best. Pivot your approach based on what works.

Besides these data sources, install Google Analytics (www.Google.com/analytics) on your website to see your referral traffic from social media all in one place. With Google Analytics you can see all your traffic sources and learn about your audience, their habits, and behavior on your site. Learn the basics of reading data, then use it to your advantage in content planning. We've often been very surprised at what content hits with our audience and what doesn't. The thing you work hours and hours on inevitably falls flat while the thing that took one minute pops off. And sometimes your most viral content may not convert as well as posts with seemingly less traction. It's often the quality of the engagement, not the quantity, and analytics can help measure that.

Often, the benefits of social media aren't quantitative (services booked, products sold, dollars earned) but rather qualitative (a growth in audience, an investment in your industry, something that reinforces or grows brand awareness, something that positions you as a pillar in your industry, a way to test content that you could later turn into a book or course).

That said, you can't pay rent with likes and clout. Don't get too caught up in the popularity contest. If it's leading to work, helping find your community, or fulfilling you in some other way—great! Keep doing it. But if it becomes a burden, scale your efforts back to focus on the platforms you feel will be the best investment of time. Social media is just one tool among many. When you see how fast a social media platform can rise and fall (like MySpace or, more recently, Facebook), it's good to remember not to put all your eggs into that basket. Invest in reaching out to your audience with other tools you can control: your newsletter, meetups, your blog, good old-fashioned coffee dates, and lunches.

These general guidelines are just the beginning. It'll take some trial and error to figure out what works for you and what kind of unique content your audience wants. With some helpful feedback from your followers, you'll soon figure out the perfect equation. No one has time to use all of these platforms. If you did, you'd have to change your title from Designer/Photographer/Illustrator/Whatever to Social Media Manager. Pick the two or three social platforms you enjoy the most and get the best traction from, and focus your energy there. If you let it, social media can become a huge time suck.

When Your Work Gets Ripped on Social Media

The internet can be a wily place. One way or another, your work is likely to get dispersed. Should your work get posted on social media without credit on an aggregate account, or you just see it ripped off by another creative, don't lose your cool yet. First, try dealing with the party sharing/using/ripping the work via DM or email. Be calm, firm, and concise in your initial email. Often, they will reply with the intent to take the post down, add attribution, or remove the offending rip-off. If only every creative degree program required a section on copyright infringement and inspiration vs. stealing. It seems unthinkable, but sometimes the offenders are unaware that their work is a rip-off. We've dealt with numerous cases like this. One person told us, "I only used your work as inspiration." She had live-traced a logo mark we designed and placed her own client's name into it—and she was genuinely shocked that this was copyright infringement. We had to explain to her that our client owns the trademark to that logo mark, and if she gave it to her client, it could put them in legal danger, which is a lose-lose for everyone.

If they ignore your message or respond with something salty or surly, then it's time to let them know you are prepared to take legal action. Download a boilerplate cease and desist document. Customize the key points as they relate to your circumstance, and send that to the person. If they still do not respond, reach out to your legal adviser for next steps. If it also affects your client and the work they have the copyright to, inform them so they can have their legal team send a similar cease and desist. The goal here is to get this settled with a little pressure so it doesn't have to go to court.

A thought on social media as a forum for public shaming: More and more we're seeing people bypassing legal methods for a good ole fashioned trial in the court of public opinion. AKA a trial by social media. Mainly, this is in response to plagiarism or misuse of uncredited work. Calling out a creative thief publicly on social media can result in enough pressure and bad press from your network of friends and peers (and their friends and peers) to force the offender to take the ripped work down. Just be careful and think hard before using this tactic. It's great for pressuring Goliath companies with more money and legal power than you, the way Tuesday Bassen did with Zara. However, if the public shaming is pointed at a young and/or green creative who thinks they've just used your work as inspiration, this could ruin them and have permanent lasting consequences. Once it's on the internet, it's nearly impossible to undo. Yes, it was 100% wrong of them to steal/use your work without your consent. But we always recommend trying to handle this in private before summoning the mob. Public shaming has very real and very lasting consequences and can easily turn into cruel and unusual punishment. So just consider all possible scenarios and try all other avenues before you resort to this, if at all.

Building Reputation Through Content Marketing

Half the battle is convincing a potential client that you know what you're doing and that this isn't your first rodeo. Try to demystify your process so the client can understand what to expect. They may see the pretty portfolio photos and love the outcome, but showing how you got there is as much of a sales tool as the final product. If you have to get a surgery, you don't want a doctor coming in and just whisking you away to the operating room. Wall of framed diplomas be damned, you want to know what's going to happen, any potential complications and how they can troubleshoot for that, how long you'll be out, and how much it's going to cost you. You may not understand half of the doctor lingo—that's why the doctor's doing the surgery after all—but hearing the doctor clearly go through the process puts your mind at ease. This is what you're aiming to do for your clients.

The right content can position you as an expert or curator in the industry. In this case, the content doesn't focus solely on your own work and process, but rather industry trends, insights and takeaways.

There are many ways to share your process or thoughts. Some are more casual and some are more time intensive. Pick the one that lends to your specific voice and strengths. Here are some ideas:

- **Vlogs.** Longer-form video content is a great way to share your thoughts and insights. It's internet searchable, and platforms like YouTube will continue to serve the content to new audiences through their suggested content features.
- **Short-Form Video Content.** These short clips are more forgiving and low effort. The audience expectation is much lower as far as production quality. Short-form videos can be a great way to test out different styles, tones, and approaches as you build your audience and find your voice. Some short-form videos are temporary (i.e., Instagram stories that disappear after a certain period of time). So you can be more casual and off the cuff.
- **Blogs.** Blogs help garner traffic to your site while also showing off your expertise and tone of voice. The content can be more evergreen and encourage internet search ranking. With platforms like Substack or LinkedIn, you can grow a newsletter while also releasing blog content (and even charge a subscription). These platforms become searchable and discoverable, so other users could discover your blogs in a way they might not if the content was only on your website. Medium works similarly. These platforms make your written content go farther.
- **Guest Blogs and Articles.** Reach out to popular blogs and reputable sites in your

industry to offer a guest post. You create valuable content for their audience, either in return for a fee or in return for your promotion to their network.

- **Monthly Newsletter.** A newsletter captures your audience and delivers exclusive content right to their inbox. Typically, your newsletter subscribers are your warmest audience members. These are people very interested in what you do. They tend to have a higher conversion rate than social media followers.
- **Original Research and Reports.** Well-researched reports and surveys on your industry can be an amazing way to capture attention and grow your audience. You can require a reader to subscribe to your newsletter to get access to the report, which grows your network. And then you can submit insights from the report to press outlets for media coverage. Articles that use stats from your report then credit you and even link to your report as a source, leading to more brand awareness and traffic back to your own site. Report content can be spun out into a lot of micro-content for your social, as well.
- **Podcast.** With podcasts, you can share your industry perspective in a way that lets people experience your voice and personality firsthand. It's much more personal than the written article. Podcasts are a great excuse to meet heroes, too. Invite people you admire to be guests. You get the benefit of learning from them, and the benefit of their audience tuning in to the final product. Ideally, they also share about the experience, broadening your reach even farther. A podcast can gather like-minded peers around you, and position you as a voice in your industry. **Caveat:** everyone thinks they can be a podcaster, but it truly is a specific talent. You may be interesting in person, but that may not translate in audio. Podcasts are a lot of work, and everyone seems to be starting one these days. Consider this one seriously before you go all in.

Stellar Research & Reports

Great examples of original research and reports are Paul Worthington's "Off Kilter" newsletter on all things brand, Jones Knowles Ritchie's "Be Distinctive" Report, Elizabeth Goodspeed's reporting for *It's Nice That*, and Neil Shankar's @tallneil TikTok account full of interesting consumer brand thoughts and comparisons. There are a myriad of great ones out there. But these are some of our favorites to look at.

Submit Your Work for Press and Awards

Every industry has its trade publications and designated awards. The creative arts are no different. Creative leads often keep tabs on industry press and awards sites to identify potential collaborators. If you feel like your organic reach has plateaued, this is a good next step.

Awards

We've never much subscribed to the importance of industry awards, but we have friends with agencies that set aside a certain sum of money every year to cover awards submissions. No doubt awards lend credibility in the eyes of your colleagues and potential clients, and they're definitely nice to have conspicuously perched on the studio bookshelf in your Zoom background. But award competitions can get very expensive to enter (not to mention you often have to pay for the awarded statue even if you win). So perhaps set aside a small budget, and pick a few categories to enter if you have projects you're really proud of. It seems everyone is an "award-winning design agency" these days, but it might be just the thing that helps a client feel comfortable entrusting their project to you over the next studio. You'll likely notice that certain awards favor certain styles, so do your research and find the best option for you.

- D&AD Awards
- Communication Arts Awards
- The Dieline Awards

- AIGA Awards
- Logo Lounge Awards

Industry Media Outlets
We've found more benefit to getting placements and features in design outlets like Communication Arts, The Dieline, or Brand New. Earned press trumps awards submitted for, in our opinion. Usually, media sites also attract a broader audience of regular readers. These kinds of sites contextualize your work, sometimes along with a critique, and there's an internet trail that lives on where new people can discover the article as long as the site is alive and well. Plus, this press is free! Here are some outlets to look into:

- It's Nice That
- Brand New by Under Consideration
- The Dieline
- AIGA Eye on Design
- Communication Arts
- The Brand Identity
- Fast Company
- Creative Boom

Marketing Through Live Events

Live and in person is back, baby (in an Al Pacino voice)! After years of socializing online, the pendulum is swinging the other way, and people are eager to make real-life connections again. In an age of scams, deepfakes, catfishing, and people taking "fake it till you make it" to whole other levels, people are looking for more authentic ways to connect. We tend to remember people we've met face to face (in person or on a video call) so much more than online-only friends we've chatted with asynchronously via social chats, messages, and threads. Maybe it's the audio and visual combination? Regardless, here are some ways you can tap into live events online and in-person to build your network or market your business:

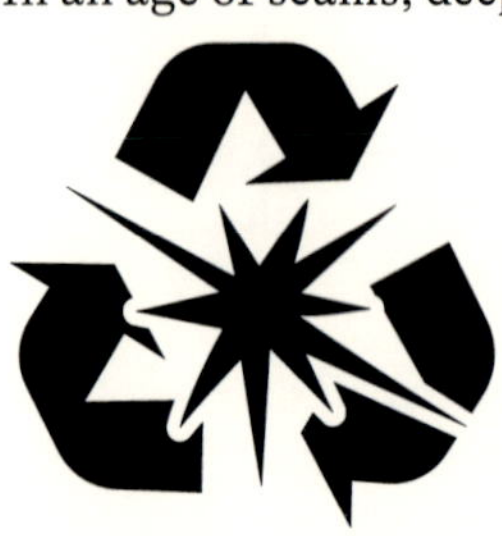

- **Participate in event series (online or offline).** Creative meetups, chamber of commerce events, portfolio reviews for local colleges or universities, brand-hosted speaker series, etc.
- **Sponsor an event in the creative space or in an industry where you want to gain brand traction.** For example, a studio that wants to work in the restaurant space might sponsor or donate design services for a restaurant week in exchange for brand presence on marketing assets.
- **Set up an event booth.** This could be at your local street fair, selling products, or at an industry conference where you just show off your service/offering.
- **Hold a live workshop (online or offline).** Find local education institutions or community

groups looking for creative programming, or host a workshop through online education communities that allow you to host live events with video conferencing.

- **Live stream your process or hold an "office hours" session.** This is a great way to gather like-minded folks to work and hang out together with their cameras and mics on.

The Goodyear Blimp of it All

Everything we've covered in this chapter is pretty common knowledge. These are turnkey blueprints almost anyone in any industry can use. But there's another tier of marketing out there available to the brave (and maybe foolhardy). We're talking about the brand activations and campaigns that have no prior blueprint. The kind you make up completely from imagination for your unique audience. This is where being a creative is a distinct advantage.

We live in Southern California and have the joy, every once in a while, of stepping outside to see the Goodyear Blimp just moseying along the 5 freeway to the 405 all the way to Long Beach airport where it's moored. This is one of our favorite brand activations because—why? Like, why does a tire company need a blimp? Perhaps not for reasons tied to click-through rates on ads, but as far as brand awareness is concerned, this thing is iconic. Its randomness is its strength because no other tire brand—or any major brand really—has a blimp. So it's uniquely associated with Goodyear.

So what is your Goodyear Blimp? What is a roadside attraction of sorts that you could make that would be memorable and newsworthy for your brand? To quote a TikTok recap of a conference talk, "To break into a creative field is like breaking out of prison. Once someone has done it one way, it's almost impossible to do it that same way again."

Try not to fall back on things you've already seen done. Think of your ideal client. Now think of original, memorable ways to capture their attention and imagination. It might be hard to track quantitative responses and results, but when done right, it will result in a huge qualitative response. These kinds of brand exercises can really deepen interest in your brand and have knock-on effects long after. For example, many years ago we made a seasonal Halloween campaign called the Washed Up Dead. We made a custom page on our studio website with an Advent-style calendar that revealed a new washed-up celebrity's career obituary each day leading up to Halloween. It had nothing to do with our studio as far as the content goes. But the campaign was funny, gave us thirty-one days of content that encouraged people to come to our site to see the latest reveal, and showed off our skills in web design, illustration, writing, and overall creative direction. We have never had so many people respond to our studio newsletters than during this period.

Another great example: Max Kolo is a graphic designer in New York City who finds DIY-style flyers hanging around the city and redesigns them. It's such a clever and charming idea. He'll grab a flyer for someone looking to rent a room (the kind with the little tear-off phone numbers at the bottom) or for a local restaurant. He chronicles his creative process as he adds all the good vibes, style, and sauce to a newly designed flyer, and then he hangs the new work of art in place of the old. It shows off his amazing community, his skills, his personality, and it's a very original idea. It is his Goodyear Blimp.

While the blimp is effective, Goodyear has some comically bad merch—namely, a T-shirt that says in huge letters across the front: "Blimps are cool. Buy tires." We don't know why, but distilling the blimp's charm and brand effectiveness down to this unvarnished phrase just removes the majestic wonder. If we were to create a campaign about the blimp to sell tires, we would show a pit crew putting Goodyear tires on the blimp (it's weird to think, but the blimp does have landing tires). The blimp would take off and then an F1 car would pull in for the pit crew to put Goodyear tires on. The F1 would speed off and then a common, old sedan would pull in for Goodyear tires to be put on. Then the sedan would peel out and take flight too. End with tagline: "Fly like the wind on Goodyears."

Examples of Promotion Done Well

Following are some other fun examples from brands that might get the juices flowing.

RedBull's action sports stunts like the record-breaking Stratos high-altitude skydive with Austrian skydiver Felix Baumgartner associate the energy drink with extreme feats. On the less dangerous edge of the spectrum, RedBull's annual soapbox derby competitions invite competitors to create and race ridiculously extravagant, handmade, themed box cars. The experience and content are hilarious, reflecting that Red Bull is all in for a good time.

In 2019, Amazon celebrated *The Marvelous Mrs. Maisel*'s twenty Emmy nominations by offering 1950s and '60s prices at a variety of locations across downtown LA, including gas stations, movie theaters, and The Hollywood Roosevelt hotel. The snaking line for thirty-cent gas made big headlines.

Ahead of its season two premiere, *Severance* had their cast show up to Grand Central Terminal in NYC to work a couple hours in a recreated Lumen Technologies set.

Spotify launched the "Wrapped" brand activation in 2016, and it has been a viral sensation year on year. Wrapped shows listeners their top artists, songs, genres, and more through an interactive online experience with shareable graphics that encourage users to post to social. The narcissism in all of us loves to be seen and to feel wholly unique, doesn't it? Any activation that can tap into that aspect of the human condition is smart.

Drumeo, an online school for drummers, hosts a video series called "For the First Time". In the series, famous drummers are invited to listen to a song they've never heard before with the drum track removed, then create their own drum part in real time. Metal drummers get Taylor Swift songs, jazz drummers get prog rock songs ... It makes for amazing content that appeals to Drumeo's target audience but also music fans at large.

Kelli Anderson, a graphic artist and paper engineer, has undertaken three tactile book projects that have all gone viral: *This Book is a Camera*, *This Book is a Planetarium*, and *The Letterform Book*. *This Book is a Camera*, as the name promises, is literally a usable camera! Her ingenuity is put on the most incredible display in these interactive and dimensional books. They are clear labors of love.

Patagonia's "Get Outside" Black Friday campaign encourages buyers to ditch the most lucrative retail sales day of the year, Black Friday, to get outside and enjoy nature. It's a bold move that appeals to their audience of nature-loving, conscientious buyers.

Pizza Hut's BOOK-IT! program rewarded kids reading milestones by awarding them pizza. This promotes community education while creating positive associations between younger generations and a pizza brand. They're making fans for life (or at least it worked on us)!

Anyone remember Marlboro Miles? This 1990s marketing initiative allowed people to trade in barcodes from Marlboro cigarette packs for branded gear that appealed to their audience. Our step-dad was fully kitted out thanks to the program, with bright red, Marlboro-branded tents, jackets, coolers, you name it. Talk about turning your audience into walking billboards.

When Luka Doncic was traded from the Dallas Mavericks to the Los Angeles Lakers in 2025, within his first 2 weeks in Los Angeles, he donated $500,000 to California wildfire relief efforts. Luka and the Jordan Brand (by whom he's sponsored) prepaid for local parking around Crypto.com Arena for fans attending his debut Lakers game. They also released an amazing teaser video showing Luka changing his Texas plates to California plates while George Strait's "All My Exes Live in Texas" played. Round it out with gifted bumper sticker packs to local fans attending the game that read "Can't spell Luka without LA", "Honk if you love Slovenia" (Luka's home country), and "How's my driving (to the hoop)?" This was such a thoughtful and fun way to embed Luka into the hearts and minds of Angelinos.

Grilli Type creates a gorgeous microsite with every font they release. The sites are interactive, illustrated, and beautiful. It gets you high on creative fumes and ready to impulse buy a $600 typeface family.

Petre Spassov of Reform Studio creates an elaborate end-of-year gift to send to clients and peers. The gift always shows off their design chops in a new and fun way. One year it was a coffee bag with custom packaging and a satisfying unboxing. One year it was a beautiful wood block game. Every year it's different, and every year it makes you thankful you're on Petre's gift list. Is this what it feels like to be on Tom Cruise's infamous coconut cake list?

Sae Design Group, a boutique design studio based in Wailuku and Kaka'ako, Hawaii, made an online Snake-style Game (Millennials will remember playing this on their Nokia 3310s) to celebrate Lunar New Year and the upcoming Year of the Snake 2025.

Every Christmas our bank, Farmers & Merchants, sends us a basket of pears, cheese, and chocolates. Even though we could buy our own pears from the market, when December rolls around we eagerly await the arrival of our free bank fruit. Because when your bank foots the bill, it's notable. It's a gesture that really aligns with their brand's focus on genuine customer service and commitment to their clients. Chase Bank, we've not seen one pear from you. Your move.

It doesn't have to be blimp-level big to be effective. What's your thing?

Chapter Checklist:

① Lock down your social media handles.

② If using a personal social media account for work, do a social media tidy up.

③ Choose which social networks to focus on (two or three).

④ Research brands you admire to get cues on how they're using social media effectively. Think of ways you can riff on these ideas for your own brand content.

⑤ Plan out your content calendar.

⑥ Dream up your Goodyear Blimp idea.

How to Get Big Name Work in a Secondary Market

Now more than ever, location isn't a deterant to getting big name work. Sure, there is something to be said about being in a cultural hub where lots of business goes down—Los Angeles, San Francisco, New York City, etc. But these nine creatives show you can do big business from a smaller market city. Here's how they make it happen.

	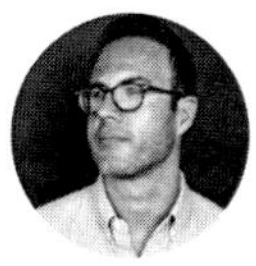 **Tad Carpenter** *Co-Owner/Designer Carpenter Collective* carpentercollective.com	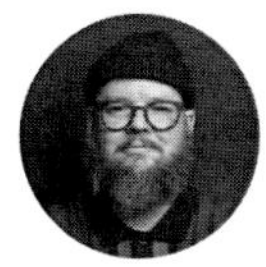 **Clark Orr** *Freelance Designer/ Illustrator, Co-Founder Hellcats USA* hellcatsusa.com	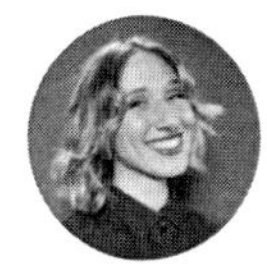 **Audrey Havey** *Art Director, Graphic & Motion Designer, Illustrator* audreyhavey.com
You've worked with house-hold name clients. You don't live in LA, NYC, or SF. How did you land your bigger clients?	Almost all of our clients are by word of mouth. We try very hard to listen, be kind and build lasting relationships with our clients. More often than not, they then share our name, process and the work we built together with other businesses or friends in the industry. We are very grateful for clients who pass our name forward.	Clients usually tend to have familiarity with past work which they've seen featured in my portfolio or other promotions of my body of work. Think group art shows I've participated in or graphics work that was showcased in a public medium.	Honestly, by keeping an eye out and commenting on job posts (specifically LinkedIn) from Art & Creative Directors within companies I would love to do work for! It always seems like a daunting thing to throw your hat in the ring among 100+ other candidates at times, but if the AD's/CD's out there are serious about finding the right talent, they'll look into everyone. It was partial luck, timing, and having my portfolio site in a great condition. Outside of that, having friends in the industry who love to vouch for you...never hurts. Make friends in all crafts, learn from each other, be humble, and it'll take you all sorts of places.
What's your advice for people living in secondary markets who have aspirations to work with big brand names?	Location is not really a hindrance in our eyes anymore. We live in Kansas City, MO and love the central location...We travel to meet clients and direct on-site photoshoots but often much of that can be done in our studio remotely. We'd always encourage designers to not be afraid to keep sharing your work and never be too proud to reach out directly to a client or person you want to work with...	Create a solid body of work and get to know people from various regions. Community is often global now and you never know who has eyes on your work. Your work can be recognized on a massive scale, but you also want to back that up with genuine relationships with peers, and potential clients. It comes a little easier though, when there isn't ulterior motives.	Be vocal about the work you do, and the work you want to do more of. The more your work & process is out there in the world, the more top of mind you're likely to be... If you're not doing the work you aspire to be doing, pour yourself into personal projects that best showcase your interests, passions, and of course talent - and it will definitely shine through to those potential clients.
Location	Kansas City, MO	Orlando, FL	Boise, ID

Continued

	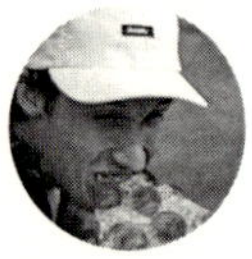 **Max Hofert** *Founder at Max Hofert Design* powerbomb.io	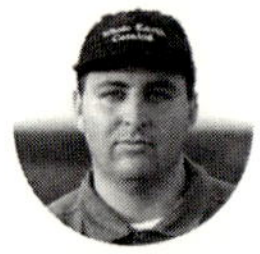 **J.D. Reeves** *Independent Brand Designer* jdreeves.com	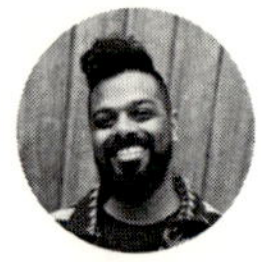 **Ashwin Chacko** *Founder, Author & Illustrator* whackochacko.com
You've worked with house-hold name clients. You don't live in LA, NYC, or SF. How did you land your bigger clients?	Like everything else in life, the community and relationships you create will dictate the trajectory of your career. Relationships are everything, and when you put yourself out there in hopes of making genuine connections instead of selling s***, things naturally happen... You also have to have insane dedication to your craft...and constantly be sharing it with the world. I post daily on LinkedIn, and on Instagram as much as I can, which makes our studio top of mind for all of the cool buds I've met along the way. Social media gives you access to the world...	Initially I reached out to agencies to offer my services as a contractor if they were too busy. Once I was in that network...my name started getting passed around. This was how I first started to work on projects for larger tech clients. Once I had those projects in my portfolio, I was able to go in-house at Retool as a brand designer. Collaborating with the talented team there, we created work that gained recognition across the tech industry I've also spent many years networking and making connections with people in the industry. When I was considering going full-time freelance, I tapped that network and they began to send some amazing work and referrals my way.	Most of my clients come through three channels. The first and the biggest is word of mouth from friends, family and subcontracts from larger Agencies. The second is my website and social media. Instagram and LinkedIn have been great platform to share and connect with potential clients. The third is a mix of what I call social currency, secondary websites Illustrators Guild, podcasts, media features etc. The combination of all three working in tandem creates a flow of opportunities.
What's your advice for people living in secondary markets who have aspirations to work with big brand names?	Put yourself out there. Be vulnerable. Have a unique point of view and just be yourself. I've met some really rad people by doing crazy shit to get their attention, and making them laugh. Practically zero by email. One involved sending a big ol' styrofoam gravestone to the business, with a fake obituary saying that I gave my life to be able to work with them. It worked. Be creative - it's your job!	Just keep chipping away. Keep posting work, keep reaching out to people, keep getting on Zoom calls with people, etc etc. People can't hire who they can't see so you need to make yourself visible. The larger your network, the more likely you are to get connected to the right people. Just keep going. Also, never feel like you're "less than" just because you don't live in LA, NYC, or SF. Be proud of where you're from, own it...	Know who you are and what value you bring to the table. The better you are able to articulate the value your skills bring to a brand the lower the barrier for conversion. Secondly, show don't tell... How can you show the problem you can solve with a smaller brand that is just as relevant to the big brand you are pursuing. Lastly share your work everywhere, the more visible you are the harder you are to ignore.
Location	Boulder, CO	Tulsa, OK	Northern Ireland, UK

	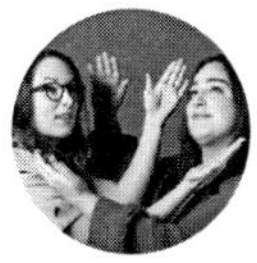 **Allie Mounce and Clare Freeman** *Founders and Designers at Pretty Useful Co.* studio.pretty-useful.co	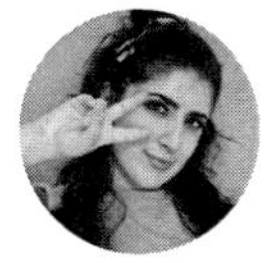 **Nina Tsur** *Multidisciplinary Artist* ninatsur.com	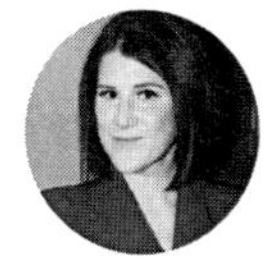 **Lindsey Laseter** *Partner & Co-Creative Director, Lasso Studio* lassostud.io
You've worked with household name clients. You don't live in LA, NYC, or SF. How did you land your bigger clients?	Friends in the design world and social media mostly! Our biggest breaks have always come from our peers that know our work would be a good fit for a project and recommend us.	A combination of word of mouth, me reaching out to brands, and stumbling across posts on social media where people are looking for creatives. A good mix of luck and putting myself out there.	Relationships and friendships have always been how we've connected to clients big and small. Even if clients felt like a surprise connection, we'd often discover that a friend or former colleague recommended us, either from working within the company or simply as a friend-of-friend connection.
What's your advice for people living in secondary markets who have aspirations to work with big brand names?	Attend smaller conferences to meet people and make friends - it doesn't have to be sweaty networking, try to make genuine connections. Pitch yourself to speak at events locally and then use that experience to speak in larger markets. Make content that appeals not just to potential clients, but also to the larger creative community. It doesn't have to be just showing work, share what you're really interested in and excited about.	I think now more than ever it's easier to work with big clients because we're remote!	Location no longer acts as a hinderance to landing large clients. Your superpower is creating work with a powerful POV and fostering relationships within the creative community. Other creatives are just as important as leadership at the companies you want to work with. With every project, show you're great to work with...The work matters of course, but the way you communicate and guide the people is gold. Those good people will tell more good people.
Location	Memphis, TN	New Milford, NJ	Nashville, TN

Group Poll

How did your most well known client find you?

Subcontracted by Another Agency

Referral

Social Media

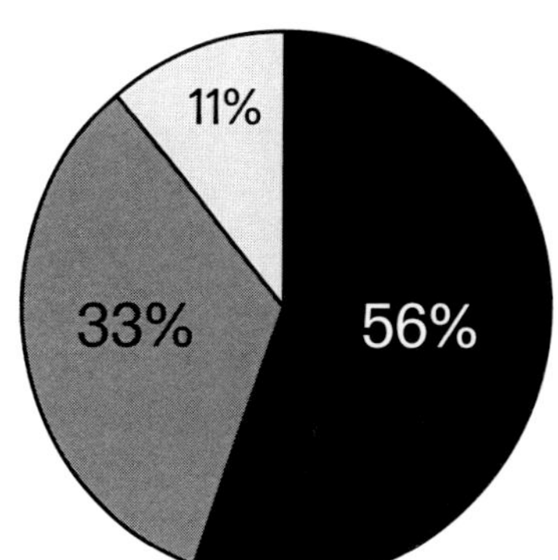

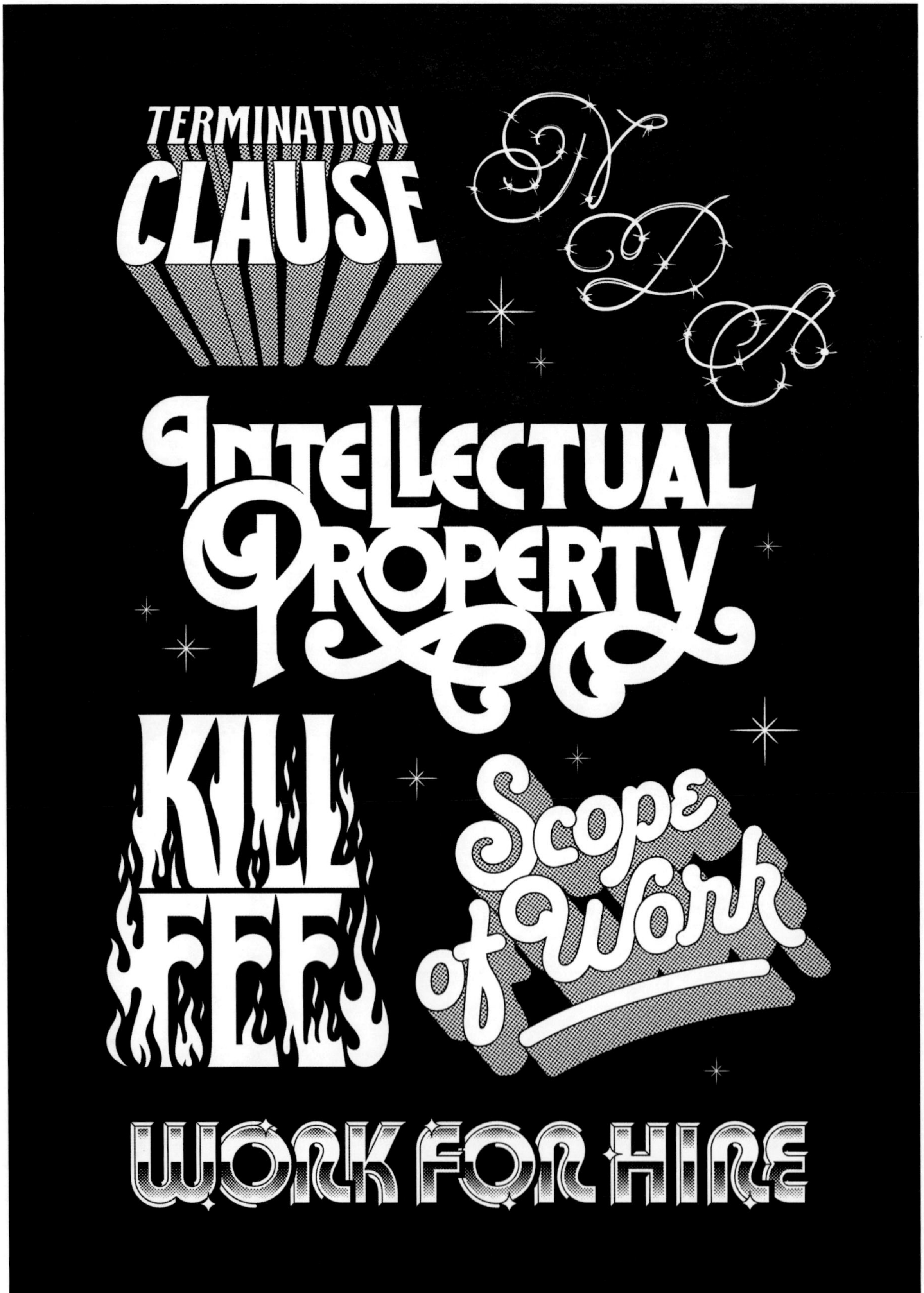

Lettering by: Rob Alba

11
Contracts

Disclaimer: We are not lawyers. Nor have we played one on TV. The information we're sharing with you is not legal advice. It's research we've done on these topics for our own business. These are our thoughts on the subject from our own experience and "aww shoot" moments. Consult with your own legal adviser to decide what is right for you personally, especially concerning how you write and execute your contracts.

Contract Templates

Some places offering contract templates for creatives are Creative Contracts, Bonsai, Honey Books, and Not Your Father's Lawyer.

Rule number one with contracts: always, always, always sign one before starting a project. Even an as-played-on-TV lawyer would agree with that. If a potential client is trying to avoid signing a contract, this is a giant red flag.

For centuries, cultures have been using agreements and contracts to conduct business. This is no novel thing. It's a part of commerce, and we do it every day. When you sign a credit card receipt, you're signing a contract. When you click "I agree" as you install your latest iOS update, you're signing a contract. In order to get a driver's license, rent an apartment, buy a home, or open a bank account, you have to sign a contract. If someone you're working with is trying to skirt it, beware. And herein lies the power of the contract: It can weed out unserious or unscrupulous players.

A good contract protects both the creative and the client. It shouldn't be scary but rather reassuring for both parties. It means both sides will get what they want, provided they do what they agreed to do. Anyone trying to avoid this is either a little naive, a little nefarious, or worse. It may feel awkward to ask your early clients (i.e., friends and family) to sign a contract, but it doesn't have to be if you keep it short and clear. It might be the step that takes you out of the daughter/nephew/cousin/etc. role in their mind and puts you into the qualified graphic designer role.

We have contract templates for our most commonly performed services and a general subcontractor agreement. You can customize them for each unique client or collaborator as needed for the scope of work, timeline, price, payment terms, and intellectual property rights.

Our master service agreement (MSA) is based on a free template from the AIGA (bless them, truly). Thankfully, there are many contract templates made especially for creatives available for free or for purchase online. If you do use a template, you'll want to be sure it is created by a reputable lawyer for your specific industry and with your own country's laws in mind. If you can't find a good template online, look up small business lawyers in your area to get one custom-made. It is worth the investment.

At Hoodzpah, the contracts we use the most are:

1. Project Service Agreement. This is a project-specific agreement outlining all the terms and scope for a single engagement of work. We usually use this for first-time clients.
2. Master Service Agreement (MSA). This is a high-level agreement defining the terms of our relationship with clients for ongoing work. This is great for clients we'll be working with regularly, as it sets the overarching ground rules for working together in the future. This agreement is not project specific, so in addition to this MSA, you'll need to sign or agree to a Statement of Work per project.
3. Statement of Work (SOW). This is a project-specific agreement that leans on an existing MSA as a parent agreement. The MSA defines overarching terms, while the SOW defines the project-specific details. SOWs are usually much simpler because they only need to cover the unique aspects of the project, not the other terms already covered in the MSA.

4. Contractor Agreement. If you subcontract other creatives to help you on a project, use this agreement to define the terms of their work. We use a contractor agreement when hiring motion designers, photographers, developers, and so on. It's a service agreement where you are the client as opposed to the provider.

Templated contracts will save you tons of time. Like, enough time to have a *Simpsons* marathon with a *Law & Order* marathon chaser. After you quote a project and the client says "yes," you don't want their ardor to grow cold while you try to create your agreement from scratch. Would you propose to your dreamboat on the Jumbotron at Yankee Stadium without having the ring? Nay.

As much as possible, we like to use our own contracts rather than signing a client's. We know how to define creative terms and parameters, and we know our contract has an even-handed consideration for both parties. Larger companies will usually insist on using their standard agreements. These documents can be long, convoluted, and more one-sided in their approach. You'll be tempted to skip to the signature page, glossing over words like "liable" and "severally." You don't want to sign anything blindly. Get used to reading agreements. Research terms you don't know.

Don't be afraid to push back on clauses or provisions that are predatory or have no bearing on the work you will be doing. We once had an agreement sent to us that stated if the client didn't like our work at the end of our services, they were not required to pay us. You don't want any agreement hinging on the client's subjective view. Another large client sent us a contract template made for sponsored athletes. It was way too far off the mark to be edited. So we suggested that we use our own agreement tailored for the kind of work we would be doing.

Negotiating contract terms is a very normal part of business. If a client gets weird or defensive when you ask for revisions, they are either very naive or very controlling. Most clients are open to making the terms work for both parties. Even Fortune 500 companies have been cool about revising things we weren't comfortable with. It's rare to get everything you ask for when it comes to agreements, but it cannot hurt to ask.

Early on in your business, making and reviewing contracts might feel stressful and daunting. But the more you review, the better you'll get at understanding the tenor and terms.

Key Things Contracts Should Include

You and your client's legal business names. Get it right because you can't enforce a contract against someone who doesn't legally exist. Make sure everything is spelled right.

Definitions. This clarifies the meaning of key terms in the agreement: deliverables, initial concepts, working files, working art, final art, etc.

Fees and Payment Schedule. Include the amount the client will pay you for the specific services provided. Outline how the payments will be broken down and whether they are due based on time or milestones. For simpler projects, we'll usually charge half up front and half upon completion. If the project is more involved, we prefer to tie payments to milestones so our work doesn't get ahead of payments or vice versa.

Payment Terms. Outline how long the client has to make a payment on an invoice. Net 30 days is more than fair and industry standard in most circles. On our initial deposit invoice, we require it to be paid before we begin work, so most clients will pay more promptly than the thirty days. Larger companies often won't pay anything up front and usually request net 60 or even 90 in their standard contracts. We find this absurd, but such is the wild, wild business world. Try to negotiate this window down to at least net 45. If the client won't budge, consider whether the work and eventual payout are worth the delay in payment. If you have a good amount of savings and cash flow, maybe this isn't an issue for you.

This section of the agreement could also include information about:

- Late fees apply to unpaid invoices. While we rarely enforce these, it's a very handy clause to have if a client is continuously stalling to the point of wreaking havoc in your scheduling.
- You have the right to stop work if payments are past due.

Schedule. This isn't required, but if you and your client have agreed to a specific delivery date or certain milestone goals, include a detailed schedule in the agreement. To keep yourself protected from delays caused by the client, include verbiage explaining that deadlines are a two-way street. If the client doesn't meet their deadlines or supply necessary feedback, information, or assets in a timely manner (be specific on the time window), then your deadlines will be delayed proportionately to the client's delay.

Scope of Work (or Proposal). If you already sent your client a detailed scope in your proposal, you can attach it for this section. Be specific about how many concepts or initial creative assets are being supplied, how many rounds of revisions are included, and what final deliverables the project will include. Will the client receive working files for artwork or only final assets? If you don't create black-and-white boundaries, the limits of what you're expected to do are left to speculation. You can even include a list of what is "not included" in the scope.

Termination. Think of this section as your prenuptial agreement with your client. This section outlines how or when a party can end the contract before the project is completed. When a relationship needs to come to an early end, the last thing you want is to haggle about money, especially if things have turned sour between you and the client. Leave no room for interpretation here.

Note whether or not the intellectual property transfers in the event of early termination and what, if any, files will be delivered. In our scope/proposal section, we typically put a line-item value next to every single step of the scope (even if we quoted the project as a bulk sum). That way, in the termination section, we can say something simple like, "In the event of early termination, final files and intellectual rights will transfer from Designer to Client for only the work that has been completed and fully paid for in relation to the value outlined in the scope/proposal section."

Governing Law. This defines which region's laws will govern the agreement. In the USA, different states have different laws. Having your home state oversee any litigation about your contract is desirable for convenience and familiarity with laws. For international contracts, definitely have a lawyer advise on special precautions, as laws vary from country to country. Something enforceable in the United States may not be enforceable in another country.

Force Majeure. This section protects you from unforeseen catastrophic events and "Acts of God" that inhibit you from performing your work as promised, by no fault of your own. For example, if your home is hit by a tornado and your computer is destroyed, you don't want to be held liable for missing a contractual deadline. There was no way for you to avoid the incident, and so you are cleared of liability.

Indemnity and Liability. "Liability" pretty much means responsibility. Liability outlines who is financially responsible for what in the event of legal actions relating to the work or services done. To indemnify someone means to compensate them for any loss or harm caused by your failure to fulfill your service agreement. An indemnity clause says that if you fail to fulfill your side of the agreement, the other party can seek restitution for the resulting damages. It should go the same for your client. Beware of agreements from large corporations where you bear all the liability and indemnity, but the client has none.

For example, if the client provided website content that infringed on someone else's trademark, you don't want to be held responsible for any resulting damages. The client provided the content and warranted it was safe to use, so the fault lies with them.

If a client neglects to get their logo mark legally reviewed for trademark clearance, you don't want to be held liable if a similar logo is already out there. Many lawsuits happen because of unintentional similarities of work despite a creative's best efforts to make something unique. Two people invented calculus completely independently of one another: Isaac Newton and Gottfried Leibniz. The same can and has happened in creative circles.

For this reason, try to limit your liability as much as is reasonable. That's what a limited liability clause is for. According to most states' laws, this must be in bold or all caps so both parties can clearly see it before signing. Here's where you can clarify that you can't be held liable for more than the price of the project.

It's also a good idea to purchase liability insurance to help cover your business in case any legal action is raised against you. Some contracts will require you to carry certain levels of commercial liability insurance for these kinds of situations. Look into Professional Liability (also called Errors and Omissions) insurance as well as General Liability Insurance.

Severability. This section establishes that if one part of your contract is deemed unenforceable or void by a court, the rest of the contract remains in effect regardless. One misstep shouldn't nullify the rest.

Copyright and Licensing Terms. This might also be called the Intellectual Property Assignment section. In the United States, you are automatically considered the author and copyright owner for anything you create unless you state otherwise in a contract. This section outlines what rights do and don't transfer to the client. For something like brand identity work, the client will need full copyright of the final works to use everywhere (some agreements literally and funnily put "throughout the universe"), forever (in perpetuity).

For creative work like fonts, illustration, or even photography, you might agree with the client to only license rights to your work in a limited way. In your agreement it's important to be specific about what the license covers.

- **Media limitations.** This limits usage to a certain kind of media, i.e., print and online, only print, only on the client's website, only on soft goods/apparel, only on hats, etc.
- **Numbers limitations.** You can limit how many times your work is printed, seen, or used within those media rights. For example, the client can use your illustration on T-shirts only, and can only print and sell up to 50,000 units. After that, they have to seek a new licensing agreement with you for further use.
- **Time limitations.** You can restrict the usage of your artwork to a length of time, like a year or two years. This is often easier to enforce than keeping track of numbers limitations (which rely on your client to track and update you on).
- **Location limitations.** You can restrict a license by country or region. Why? Well, if a regional Italian T-shirt company wants to license your design for their fall line, you might not want this to limit your ability to also sell the design to a company in the USA. It helps the client keep their costs down because they're only purchasing limited rights instead of full copyrights, and it allows you to license the artwork to others in noncompeting locations. It's a win-win for you and the client!
- **Exclusivity.** If someone wants full, exclusive rights to a work for, say, three years, it significantly increases the licensing fee because it means you can't license the work to anyone else for that time.
- **Ownership of original art.** There is a difference between reproduction rights and ownership of the original work. If you've made an original illustration using charcoal, you may want to retain rights to sell the original artwork while also licensing the digital version of the art to clients to reproduce.
- **When the rights transfer.** At Hoodzpah, we stipulate that rights only go into effect once full payment is received. This way, if the client doesn't pay their invoice, we have leverage.

Reservation of Rights. This clause goes below your copyright and licensing terms and states that any rights not explicitly granted remain with you, the creator. This is assumed by law, but it's good to state it emphatically. For example, you might state here that working files, unchosen concepts, or preliminary works remain in your ownership and are not included with the final artwork rights as outlined in previous sections.

Moral Rights. This is a big one. This is where you stipulate whether or not you can share the work you make with a client for self-promotion purposes, among other things. According to the Graphic Artists Guild contract glossary, the four rights covered by this clause are "1) the right to protect the work from modifications that would harm the reputation of the artist; 2) the right of attribution, so that authorship is acknowledged; 3) the right of disclosure, to control presentation of artwork to the public; 4) the right of recall, to withdraw or disavow a work if it is changed."

At Hoodzpah, we don't care if clients modify our work after we've delivered final files, or whether the client credits us every time they use the work. These would be very unlikely requirements in the world of creative services. As branding designers, we expect our clients will need to modify and build on our work after we deliver it. And we can hardly expect them to credit us every time they use their own logo. These terms apply more to creatives who are original artists and want to preserve how their artwork is used or displayed.

For creatives, the most important part of this section is the right to show and promote the work you create for the client in your portfolio and through other promotional means. This is very important to retain as a professional. Imagine: You finish the creative project. It's magnificent. All that stands between you and glory is the case study. But wait—the client says you're not allowed to share the work! There is a clause in their agreement prohibiting you from posting it to your site. Don't let this tragedy befall you.

If the client hesitates to agree to let you share the work, you can clarify that nothing will be shared until the project is publicly launched. Agree that both parties will only share things that have been made public, which are no longer under confidentiality. You can even give them the right to approve your case study copy before publishing, although we really try to get approval up front. Some clients are inexplicably squirrely about this clause. Agencies that subcontract you can also withhold this right because they might not want their client to know they used subcontractors on the project.

If clients are adamant that we cannot share, we usually tell them we'll have to charge extra. Why? Because showing our past work is one of the most significant ways we land projects. This is our core form of marketing. Removing this right will cost extra. This is a good thing to mention up front so you can quote accordingly, instead of waiting until the contract is almost signed and having to start from scratch.

Client Content. This section states that any content provided by the client (photos, fonts, layouts, logos, copy, trademarks) remains the client's property.

Responsibilities and Warranties. Here, the client and the contractor make promises about the integrity of their content and deliverables. You want the client to warrant that they have the legal right to use the content they provide and that it is accurate to the best of their knowledge. You also want them to warrant that they will adhere to usage terms for third-party materials like fonts, etc. As the contractor, you warrant to your client that you will not knowingly provide them with any work that infringes on other people's rights to trademark, intellectual property, copyright, etc., and the services will be performed to reasonable professional standards. There could be other warranties, but these are big ones.

Signer Details and Signature. Be sure to have the appropriate person sign the agreement on behalf of your client. Note their title and contact information in the agreement below the signature field. And most important of all, make sure they sign and date the agreement! If there are attachments to the agreement (like a proposal), you can also have them initial those pages. Somewhere in your agreement, you can put a Signatory Clause, which states that the person who has agreed to sign does, in fact, have the authority to act on behalf of the company.

Consider E-Sign Technology

E-signing through online platforms like AdobeSign (included with Adobe Creative Cloud subscriptions) or Docusign will save you and your client the hassle of printing, signing, scanning, and mailing physical copies (what is this, 1998?). You might need to include a provision in your agreement that deems e-signatures binding and legal.

The E-SIGN Act of 2000 made e-signatures legally binding and enforceable in all fifty states in the US.

Keep Contracts Safe and Sound

Contracts are your leverage when sh–, things go sideways. Make sure you keep them stored somewhere safe. All our contracts are e-Signed and saved to a secure Dropbox folder that is backed up on the cloud. Even if our office burns down or all our computers implode, we can access a virtual copy.

What Happens When Someone Breaks a Contract?

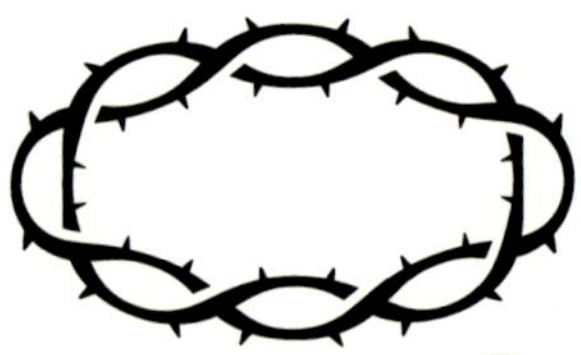

About 95 percent of the time, you will sign a contract and never think about it again. But when things go wrong, you might be unsure how to right the wayward ship.

If your client has done something not contract-kosher, start by giving them the benefit of the doubt (barring a gross and flagrant overstep). In many cases, agreement missteps are merely a misunderstanding on your client's side about the scope and limitations that you agreed to. We like to try to get on a phone call with the client to talk calmly and casually first. Talking on the phone can help avoid passive-aggressive email escalation while confronting the issue head-on. It could be the client simply misunderstood or forgot the terms of the agreement. Even high-ups at big corporations are guilty of blindly signing a contract without reading a word. They might be clueless that they're even breaking your agreement terms until you explain it to them.

If the client gets hostile when you approach them about the issue, or if they refuse to respond to your calls or emails, you might have to take more aggressive action to get their attention.

Remember, we are not lawyers. If you find yourself in a contract dispute, reach out to a small business attorney for a consultation regarding your specific situation. They can give you an idea of your recourse options and possible costs. Sometimes, the cost to enforce an agreement is way more than the amount of money you're chasing from a client. And that sucks. But sometimes, you cut your losses and walk away.

The following are some common contract issues and ideas on how we approach them.

Situation #1: You finished the work and delivered the final files to your client, but now they won't pay your final invoice.

Ideas:

- Your agreement hopefully states that copyright to work only transfers from you, the creator, to your client once all payments are made. If a client never paid the final invoice, you technically still own copyright to the work. So, their use infringes on your copyright until they pay. You can send a Cease and Desist letter on these grounds.
- If the client has fallen on hard times, see if you can arrange a payment plan to ease the burden of payments while ensuring you eventually get paid. Better to get it in drips than not at all.
- Collections agencies can be hired to chase payments for you, but they usually charge a percentage of the invoice (anywhere from 10–50 percent). Some offer tiered percentages based on the amount collected (higher percentage fees for smaller amounts, lower fees for larger amounts).
- You could take to social media to try to shame the client into paying you. Even a public picket could work in front of their physical office. This could be a last resort for clients who have stolen your work and refuse to respond. We have seen freelancers call out big brands for stealing work or not paying, and wow, the brand could not hide from the public outcry.
- Your last option could be to take the client to small claims court or regular court if the project is big enough. Keep in mind that the cost of lawyers and the stress and time of a court battle can be very taxing. But if the outstanding amount is significant, it may be worth the time and cost (which is the advice for all these options).
- This kind of situation should also motivate you to revise your agreement to state that final files will only be delivered once final payment is received. Then, hold steady and do not waver.

Situation #2: You never signed an agreement with a client. You completed and delivered work, but the client won't pay you.

Ideas:

- As with the previous situation, copyrights usually remain with the creator unless signed away. So you can send a Cease and Desist letter for copyright infringement.
- Some courts will count an email as a sufficiently binding agreement if both parties clearly agreed to terms in those emails. This might be enough to act as an agreement even without a signed document.

Situation #3: Your client doesn't want to pay you for your work because they don't like it, even though you have an agreement.

Ideas:

- Unfortunately, sometimes clients turn wishy-washy or just plain nasty. They came to you loving your work and wanting you to "do you." Then you "do you," and they hate it for some reason that they cannot clarify. They turn aggressive and demand their money back. At this point, you can lean on your agreement and try to calmly point out how the work you did fit the brief. Explain that you did professional work based on what the client asked for, but you cannot account for subjective feedback. If they don't like it, that's within their rights. But you did the work in a professional manner and need to be compensated for your work regardless.

- At this point, having invoices tied to benchmarks hopefully means you've already been paid commensurate to where you've landed in the project and won't have to chase them for money.

Situation #4: A company has stolen your work and used it without an agreement with you.

Ideas:

- Reach out to them privately via email or phone call. You could direct message the brand on social media, but depending on the size of the brand, this message might get lost in the shuffle. Try to use official channels where you can talk directly to someone. You would be shocked at how many young or untrained designers have traced our work and repackaged it for their clients, not realizing this was theft. We reached out to them privately and explained that we needed them to take it down as it infringed on work we made for our clients. We let them know our client could sue them for infringement. Luckily, most times it's just a case of someone not understanding copyright law and the fine line between imitation and infringement. Even with larger brands, you can get the same problem with creative staff who are ignorant about the laws around copyright. They get used to grabbing things blindly off the internet and then making works that are much, much too closely inspired. Creative education institutions need to cover this better!
- If a private approach to an infringer goes unheeded or ignored, try taking to social media to draw attention to the issue. Be sure the work is truly a rip-off, and not just someone else doing work in a similar style. Many people can do a certain style of creative work without copying one another. We have seen some creatives get overly sensitive, thinking they created a particular design genre. They try to take down anyone who does work remotely similar to theirs, and it's a bad look. But if they truly have stolen your work, drawing mass attention can help give you leverage to force their hand to do the right thing.
- Seek legal help from an attorney. You may have grounds for a lawsuit.

Chapter Checklist:

① Look up template contracts for creatives from reputable lawyers and creative associations. If you're in the US, look up AIGA's free master agreement template. You can also have one custom-made by a small business lawyer.

② Pick your e-sign technology solution (Adobe, Docusign, etc.).

③ Consider how you might offer licensing options to clients for services where it makes sense. Outline common license usage scenarios for your work so you have a template to start from when a prospective client reaches out.

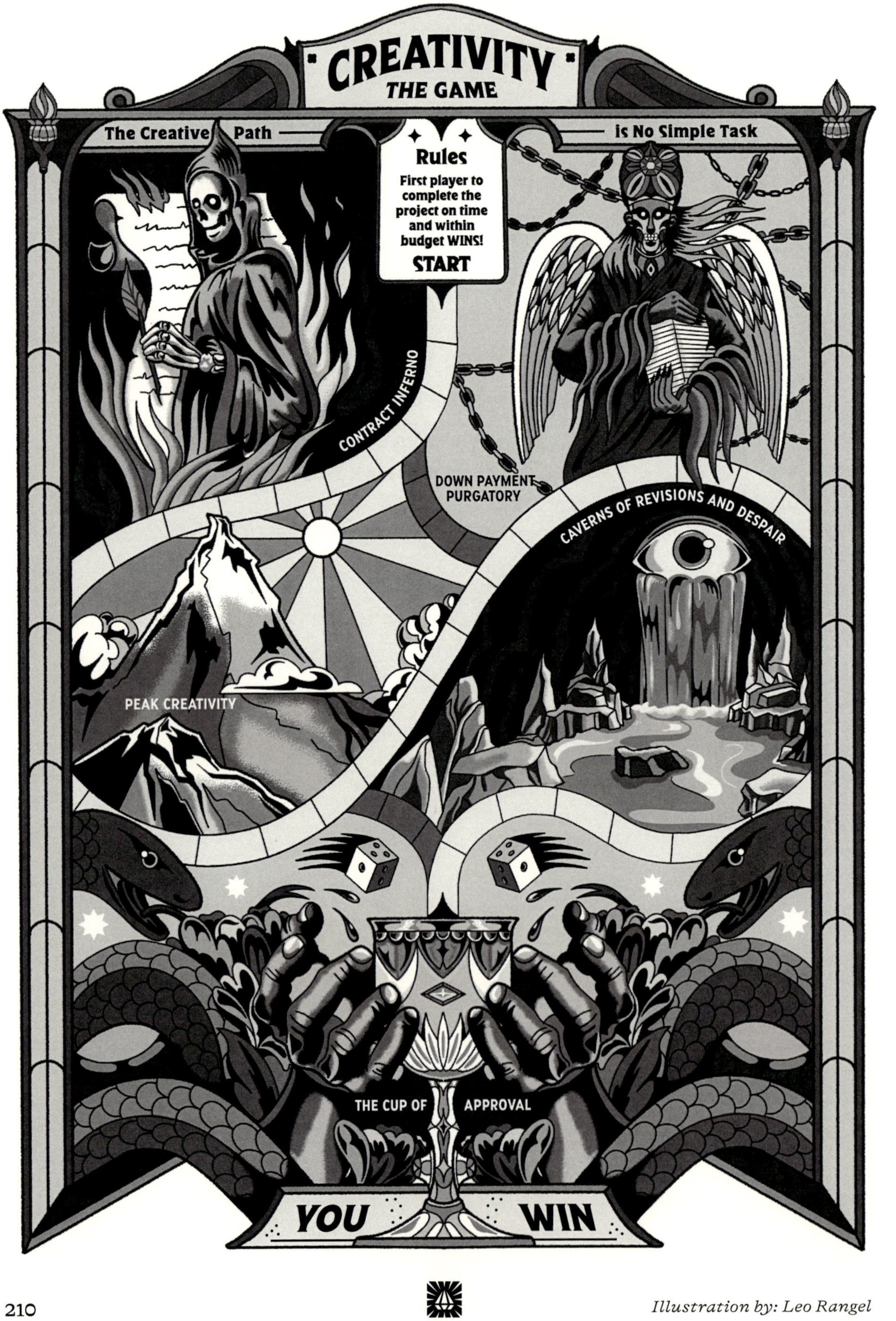

Illustration by: Leo Rangel

12
Workflow Mojo

Most great creatives practice their art and plan their masterpieces—they don't stumble upon them out of the blue. It's why they call it a creative process or practice. Creativity and organization aren't in rival gangs; they're star-crossed lovers. Creativity thrives within consistency and structure.

Having efficient business systems and project workflows will give you a framework to rely on with every future client engagement and save you a lot of time and stress, better spent on billable creative output. Without a baked-in process, you'll work on the fly, make mistakes, forget steps, and become frustrated and overwhelmed.

Here is a broad overview of the systems and procedures to make your business hum along smoothly:

- **Financial Systems**
  These are your ways and means of managing and tracking money coming in and going out.
  - → Bookkeeping
  - → Taxes
  - → Payroll
  - → Vendor and Contractor Payments
  - → Financial Check-ins (running financial reports, reviewing bank accounts, etc.)
- **Business Systems**
  - → File Management
  - → Time Management
  - → Project Management
    This is not about one project, but about how you keep track of all of the plates you have spinning. You need one place to see all current projects, upcoming projects, important benchmarks and dates, and responsible project leads.
  - → Business Filings (annual reports for corporations, Beneficial Ownership Information Reports, etc.)
  - → Insurance
  - → Business Reviews. Monthly and quarterly check-ins to review overall workload, project progress, financial reports, sales pipeline, and marketing efforts.
- **Marketing Systems**
  These are your tools and processes for how you promote yourself, build brand awareness, grow your network, and maintain client relationships—even after projects end.
  - → Content Plan (website, social media, newsletter, etc.)
  - → Client Relationship Management
  - → Website
  - → Advertising
  - → Web Analytics

- **Project Workflow**
  From quote to portfolio post, these are the steps to take to court, land, and onboard the client; manage the project; and market the final work on your portfolio and elsewhere.
    - → Quote and Proposal
    - → Contract
    - → Client Communication
    - → Creative Process
    - → Proof Reviews
    - → File Sharing
    - → Invoicing
    - → Final File Handoff
    - → End-of-Project Debrief
    - → Portfolio Post and Marketing
- **Personnel Management.**
    - → Onboarding new employees or contractors
      This includes signing a contract, setting up benefits, reviewing the Employee Handbook, and training employees on systems and procedures.
    - → Internal communication
      This could include Slack for quick, day-to-day communications and email for more important reviews like initial briefs, proofs, and key updates.
    - → Sick time and vacation
    - → Employee Benefits
    - → Employee, contractor, and team check-ins
    - → Roles and responsibilities

The Job Board and Project Management

More projects mean more money. It also means more expectations to meet. In the rush of new jobs, you might accidentally forget existing responsibilities on older projects. We still have nightmares from our time waiting tables, as all former servers do. Remember when you would get so busy with tables inside that you would completely forget about your table on the patio? Suddenly, you would feel the intensity of four people staring daggers through the patio window—their eyes saying, "Where are our iced teas?!" Don't let a client turn into your lonely, hungry, verging-on-complaining-to-the-manager table on the patio. Stay on top of all your clients, projects, and internal tasks with a job board.

Your job board is where you track all of your current client projects and internal projects. We used to do this on a dry-erase board or chalkboard because it was handy having it on the wall, plain as day. When our team began working remotely, we started using Google Sheets before switching to Trello. There are tons of feature-rich SaaS tools dedicated to project and job management: Basecamp, Asana, Notion, Monday, etc. In most of these programs you can make job boards, to-do lists, time track, schedule, collaborate with team members or contractors, attach files to projects, and so on. If you don't feel like paying for software or learning a new software, you can use trusty old spreadsheets. We like Trello because it's visual, collaborative, free, to a point (as of writing this), and is not so feature-heavy that it's clunky.

Whatever the app or tool you use, you want a big-picture overview of all your projects, with the ability to attach tasks and info to each project, so you can make sure every detail is delegated and taken care of on time and under budget.

This is what you want to track for each project:

- Project Name
- Client
- Status of the Job
  We use these status breakdowns:
  - → In progress
  - → Waiting on client
  - → Proof out
  - → Approved
  - → Invoiced
  - → Done (this means all invoices are paid and all final files are delivered)
- Project scope (a quick reference for what you need to complete and ensure there is no scope creep)
- Schedule for each item to meet the goal deadline
- Goal time investment (if you're working flat rate this helps ensure each project is profitable)
- Billing schedule (if working hourly, you might invoice weekly. If working flat rate you might invoice by project milestones)
- Time tracking
- Team roles (Who's leading the project, and who's responsible for what?)
- Links or attachments with relevant assets and information

At our studio, we use our job board to track all internal initiatives and projects, like, course development, for-fun projects, marketing, and product development. We always treat these projects like we would a client project; we track time, set goal deadlines, and assign roles to make sure internal projects get done instead of collecting dust on our hard drives.

Do you want to know how to keep your client happy and confident across the span of your project together? Stay ahead of their questions and worries with weekly updates on your progress. You don't have to deliver creative work every week. It would be awesome but isn't always possible. What you can deliver every week is an update on how things are progressing and when they can expect to see the next thing.

Project management is not just about tracking the tasks you need to finish to complete the scope. It's about maintaining good communication with your client, so they understand the progress, the timeline, and what's required from them to keep things moving forward. We've been running a creative studio for over a decade, and one thing we know for sure is when you don't regularly communicate with clients, they will panic. They'll start thinking about all the what-ifs and worst-case scenarios; they'll start to doubt you and your abilities and worry about the outcome of the project. Then they try to take over the project.

So instead of leaving them to doom spiral, keep your client updated. Like a doctor talking a patient through a visit or a procedure. This communication changes nothing about the procedure, but it does put the patient at ease. Clients are trusting you with something very important to them, and they can feel very out of control. Good communication will calm their fears and instill trust.

Pick a specific day of the week (Fridays are great as an endcap to the week), and send your clients a quick bulleted update on the status of their project tasks, what you still need from them, etc. Your clients will love you for this.

Along with the weekly updates, we set a standing meeting with the client stakeholders for updates and progress reviews for most of our larger projects. We prefer to meet every two weeks, as weekly meetings can be pretty taxing on a small team. By having a standing meeting on our calendars every two weeks at the same time, we avoid the nightmare of finding a meeting time that fits everyone's schedule every time we need to review something. It keeps us creatives working toward a regular check-in, and it keeps the client clear about when they can expect updates, removing the "when can we see . . . " or "where are we at with . . . " emails.

Scheduling and Time Management

A crucial part of good project management is keeping a calendar. Within your job board software, you can usually set dates for when each project will start and finish (if all goes to plan, which it never does, so always add some buffer time). This allows you to track your studio's workload and see how much room you have available for new clients or projects.

Besides the broader studio calendar, you and your studio teammates should have calendars to schedule internal meetings, client meetings, key deadlines, and internal creative reviews. We make personal reminders on our calendars for when we need to finish proofs or send a check-in to clients. And we make shared events with clients so they know when our next proof review or standing meeting is. We're at the point where, if it's not in our calendar, it doesn't exist. Every time we tell a client when they can expect their proof, we add an event for the due date in our calendar and invite them as well as any associated team members (if we don't already have standing meetings scheduled).

You can also set up calendar events for internal things like your newsletters, preparing quarterly taxes, when federal taxes will be taken out of your bank account, preparing 1099s, and even a schedule for preparing holiday gifts or cards for clients.

Besides broader studio scheduling and planning, be diligent about tracking your time for tasks and projects. It really is a great way to get better at quoting, scheduling, and project management. Even if you're not charging by the hour, track time on your projects to analyze the accuracy of your flat-rate quotes. Dividing the flat-rate price by the actual hours worked will quickly tell you if you need to up your rates or find more efficient ways of doing things. We even track our time on non-billable hours. You might be surprised at how much time you're spending outside of client work to run your business. Knowing where you're allocating time can help you decide when to hire or outsource and help you better plan your work weeks. There are tons of free apps that can help you with time tracking.

Time tracking has become addictive for our team. At the end of each project, we can see how our time breaks down by phases. In our year-end recap emails and marketing content we like to recap how we spent time across a few key projects. We've found that to be human is to be nosy because these kinds of posts are always a big hit. Who doesn't love a behind-the-scenes look?

Your job board and calendar are great for a high-level view of your business workload and project timelines. But motivating yourself on a micro-level helps you get through a day. Look at your job board and calendar and isolate the things you need to do today by writing them in a notebook or on a sticky note. Why write it? So you can cross it off and get that wave of euphoria at your accomplishment! And also so we can keep the art of handwriting alive. It is dying, people. Like the lazy pandas, too busy eating bamboo to bother procreating, handwriting is a dying breed. On your to-do list, write down all the things you need to tackle for today in order of importance. If you're honest with yourself, you can probably only accomplish one big thing and maybe two or three smaller things. Include client tasks and studio tasks. The great thing about a written notebook is you can write your tasks, then click "go" on your task timer, and close your web browser until you're done. Project management software can be an addictive place to linger and worry over instead of doing work. So we like to close these tabs once we have our mindset prepared for the day, so we can focus on the actual creative work.

If you run a small studio or practice where you manage the business and make the creative, this next piece of advice is very important.

You probably know yourself well enough to know when your creative energy thrives during the day. Sometimes, it's early in the day, sometimes late. Many of us prefer to run our own studio so we can have this flexibility to work when we want and when we're most energized. Once you know your ideal window for being creative, do everything in your power to protect that creative window. If you can carve out three hours in a day for uninterrupted, quality creative time, you will thrive. During your three-hour window, close any browser windows or apps that will try to thwart your act of art. Close social media, Slack, Discord, even email, and of course social media. Turn off your phone (or at least the ringer). Unless you're on standby for a time-sensitive deadline or a life-saving surgery, you should be able to step away from communication for two to three hours without everything devolving into chaos. Making this a daily habit will help you get the most out of your time.

Apps and tools are addictive. Not just social ones, work ones. *Especially* work ones. Slack and email, Trello and Notion can make you think you're working when you're actually just addicted to checking on your lists, teammates, and clients. When we're overwhelmed, this is a classic way our stressed brains deflect from what we should be doing. Train your mind to step away from planning and coordination for pure, uninterrupted creative time.

Along the same lines, we try to keep all our meetings and client calls to two or three days in the week. Meetings can take a heavy toll on your energy. Every time you have to switch into a new task, you expend mental energy, especially getting ready for and reflecting on what happened in a meeting. Even one meeting can break up your day and add subtle but looming stress. Having full days without meetings is so helpful to get into a state of flow. It's just another trick to protect your creative windows.

Your Go-to Project Workflow

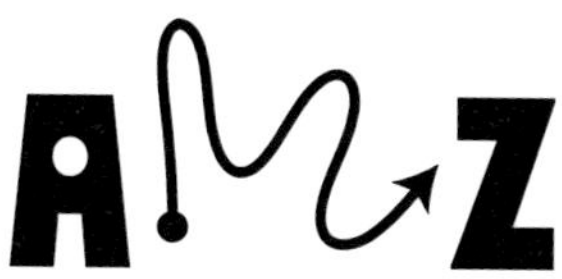

Every job you work on will have a unique scope and set of parameters, but the project workflow should generally be the same. We learned so much about organization and project workflow from our first creative job at a local magazine and print house. Between three designers we designed forty to fifty ads and laid out two magazines a month. We had to be organized to make the print deadline. We adopted the system we learned at the magazine for our own studio, Hoodzpah. In our early years as a business, we often wondered, "Is this how the big agencies are doing it?" Having compared our systems to hundreds of peers, collaborators, and clients over the years, the answer is, yes. The apps might differ, but generally, most successful and organized teams do something very similar to what we're about to teach you. The following process is geared more toward designers, but can easily be adapted for writers, photographers, videographers, and other creative fields.

Project Workflow

1. Receive a quote request from a potential client.

2. Respond to the request in a timely manner. If the project looks promising, set up a vetting call. If you can tell the project is not a good fit, recommend other creatives who you think is a better fit, or let the client know you're not able to take the work on at this time.

3. Get on a vetting call. All you need is fifteen minutes to get to know the client, hear about their project, and gather needed information to see if the project seems like a good fit for your studio. Do you have the time? Can they afford your rates? Is the project in line with the kind of work you do? If the project looks promising, prepare a proposal. If the project is with an existing client, or it's something small or straightforward, you may skip the call and gather information via email. For emails, we aim to respond within one to two business days.

4. Prepare a proposal. We have proposal deck templates pre-built for our most common jobs, which saves us a ton of time, while still wowing the potential client. Read the Proposals chapter for more info.

What's the difference between a quote and a proposal? A quote is the bare-bones scope and price. A proposal is a presentation that provides context for your process, qualifications, and the value of the project, culminating in a quote.

5. Negotiate the scope and terms of the proposal if needed. Did the client agree to your proposal? Yay! Proceed to the next step. Did the client decline due to their budget? You might

How Long Does It Take?

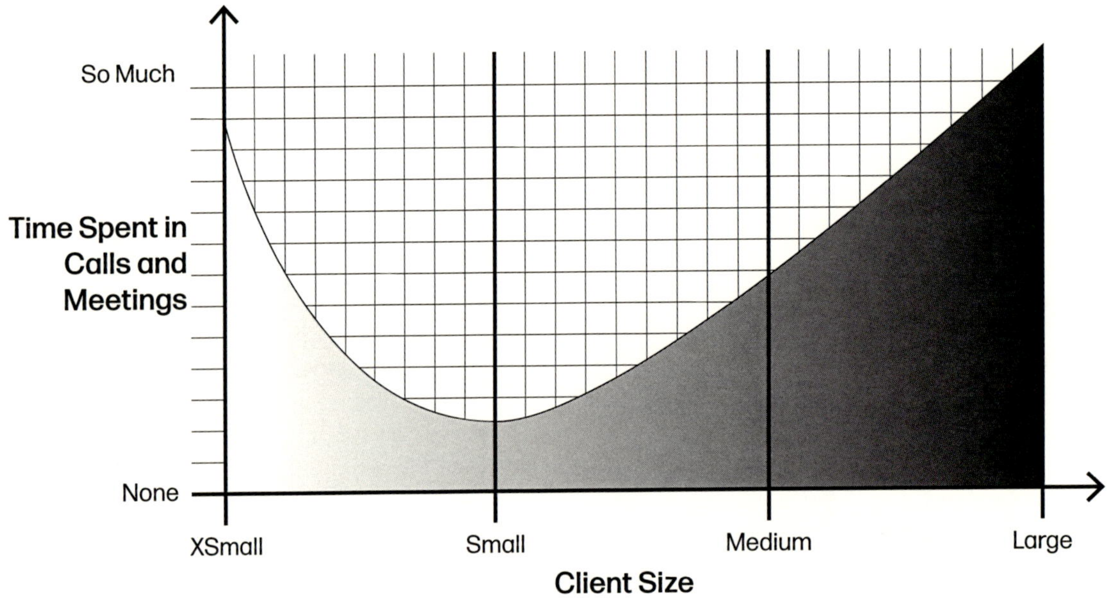

Big Company

Lots of stakeholders and extensive deliverables

* Decks, stationary set, website style guide and a few key pages, flyers, merch, and more

** Motion subcontracted. Time not tracked.

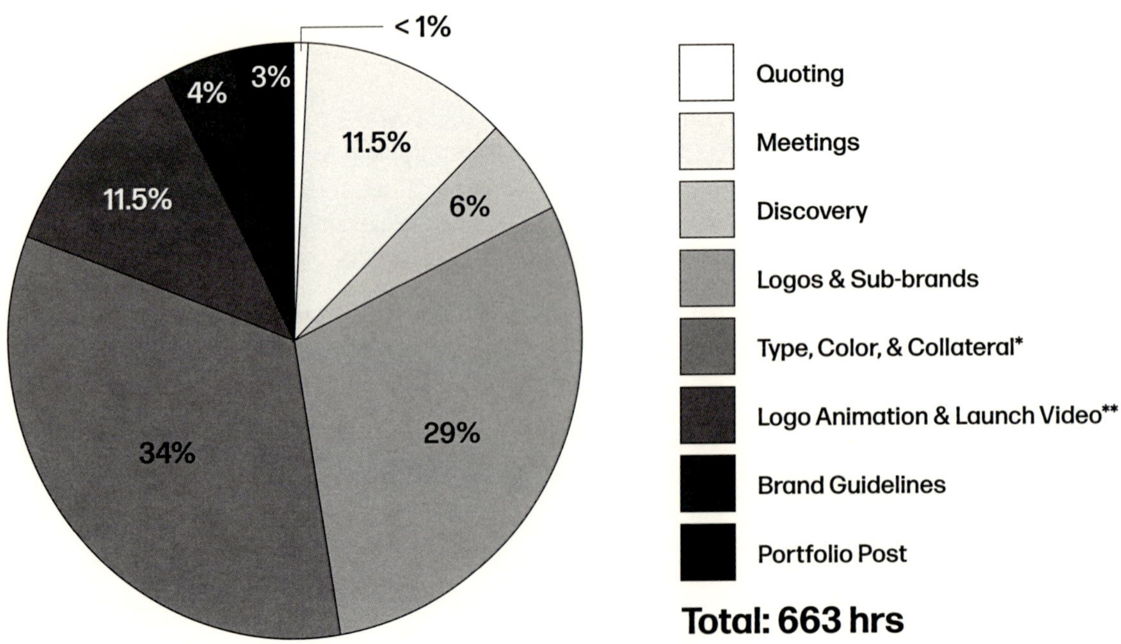

Total: 663 hrs

Small Start-up

Few stakeholders and fewer deliverables

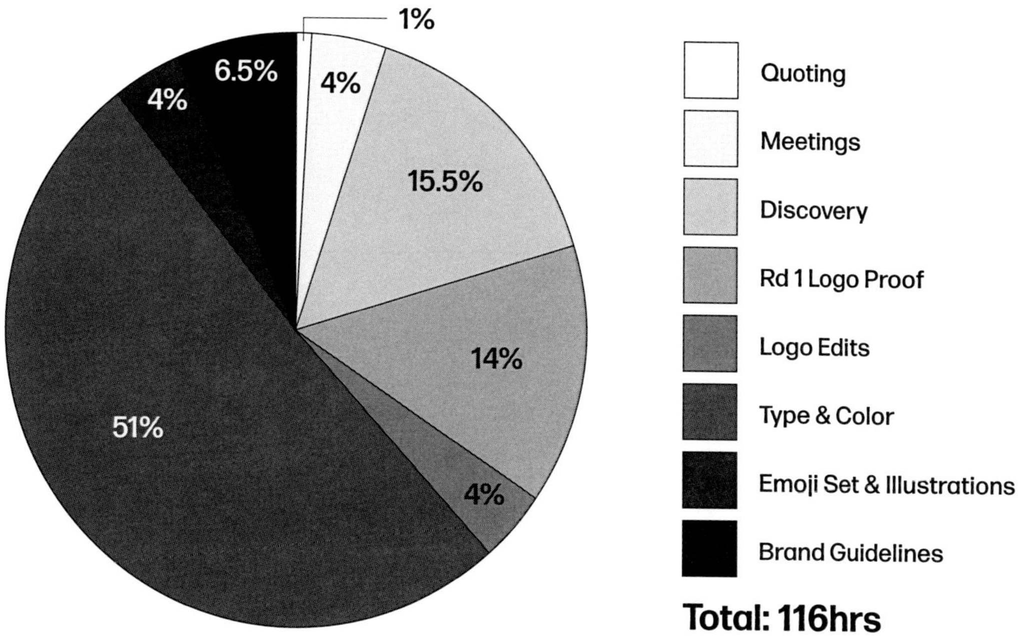

Total: 116hrs

Small Business

Few stakeholders and deliverables, high trust

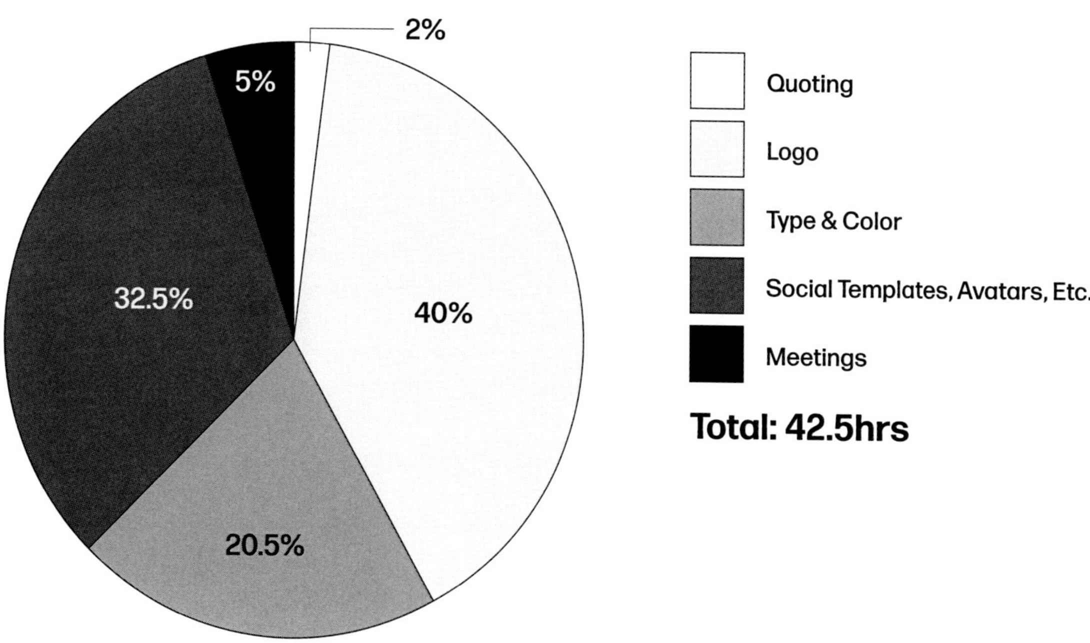

Total: 42.5hrs

Project Process

Landing the Client

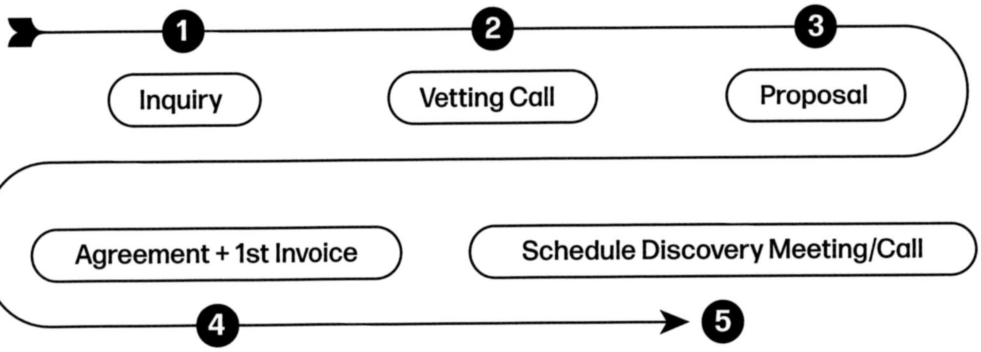

Creative Process

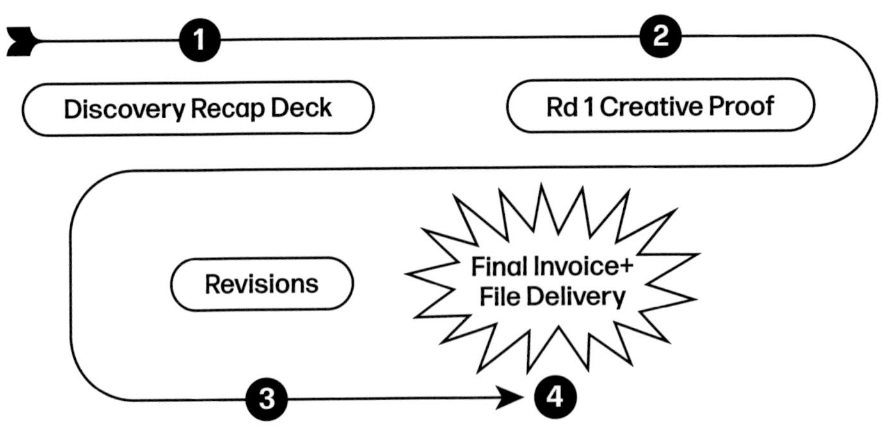

suggest a lower rate for a smaller scope if you still want the job. Did the client go with another studio or freelancer? Don't stress out. It wasn't meant to be, and it just leaves you time and space for clients who are a right fit. Plus, you'd be surprised how many people decline our quote—thinking we're overpriced or under-experienced—only to return in a year later after a bad experience with someone cheaper, or after shelling out for a big-name agency, only to get disappointing results.

Wish the potential client well on their project, and end things positively if they gave you a courtesy email letting you know you did not get the job. It's rare that anyone takes the time to send those kinds of emails anymore, and it's so appreciated when they do. If a good chunk of your proposals are turned down in a row, take a look at your price and proposal presentation, and see where you can better prove your value. Or consider why you're attracting clients who aren't a good fit for your pricing and services? Maybe there's an opportunity to adjust your website, messaging, marketing, and brand to better appeal to your target audience. Lastly, consider that you might have a higher perception of your service's value than the market can support.

6. Sign a contract with the client. Always get a signed agreement before you start any work. Save the signed contract in a safe place within your client folder so you can easily refer back to it if—nay—when the client starts to creep on the scope.

7. Send your first invoice. Don't start any creative work until you get your down payment, if at all possible. Outline your payment plan in your contract. The client might pressure you to start, saying, "The check is in the mail." Don't cave till you have it in hand. If they're in a hurry, tell them they can send an ACH (Automated Clearing House) digital payment. The exception is if you're working with a large company that has net 30 or net 60 payment terms (meaning: they pay you thirty or sixty days after the work is approved). Some of the big corporations out there just will not budge on this.

8. Send your W-9 to the new client for their tax records (if you're in the USA). If you live elsewhere, check with your accountant or lawyer about what documentation is helpful to send to clients for tax purposes. These documents give clients the info they need from your business for year-end tax documents. Sending them at the beginning of the job saves your client the hassle of having to chase you down for it when tax season arrives. Make your client's life as easy as possible.

9. Do a discovery phase to align on a creative strategy. This is arguably the most important part of any creative project. This is the phase where you learn as much as you can about the client, the project, the stakeholders, and the goals. Even if the client provided you a written project brief, set up a phone call or meeting with the key people involved in the project to review the following in more depth:

- Core problem to solve through the project
- Target audience for the project
- Brand values that should be reflected through the project
- Brand traits that would influence the style and voice of the creative work
- Competitor solutions for the same creative to identify ways to differentiate.
- Criteria for success
- Project considerations and constraints
- Mood board to align on aesthetic goals

These are things you briefly talked with the client about when you first vetted them to prepare a quote. You want to dig into these things even deeper before you kick off any creative work.

It's important that any decision makers on the client side attend this call. If the CEO will have a choice on the final creative, they should attend this meeting and the initial creative proof review. Even if their time is limited, you want to build rapport, get a sense for their motivations, and win buy-in before they see any creative work. That way, you can refer to

Everyone Wants to Feel Heard

Mirroring: Being able to use clients' own words to show how your creative solution meets the agreed-upon goals is like using a cheat code. It's a communication tactic called mirroring, where you repeat what someone said back to them to make them feel heard.

statements they made in this meeting when you present the creative back to them. Waiting to involve the CEO till the creative is finished will always end in tears. If you went in direction "*x*," the CEO will inevitably want to have seen something in direction "*y*" or "*z*." So always involve stakeholders early, so you can account for all voices.

For discovery sessions, a live meeting (whether in person or via video call) will give you a lot more insight into the personalities, motivations, and expectations of your client. You'll be able to hear perspectives from all the parties involved, ask follow-up questions, read body language and attitude, and take the temperature of the group—by bringing up your ideas for the project. Keep this session really collaborative and casual. This should be a discussion. Bring ready-made questions to spur conversation around important points, but let the conversation evolve naturally. You'll be surprised how much your understanding of the project shifts after having a discovery call or meeting. Things you assumed from the brief will be turned on their head.

Take notes or record the discovery session, and do your own follow-up research based on what you and the client talked about. Synthesize your insights and discovery call findings into a concise and clear deck: the Discovery and Strategy Deck. The goal of this presentation deck is to mirror back the goals, vision, and context of their project with an added level of creative insight for how you plan to achieve their goal.

Discovery Deck Template

Want more help with putting together a Discovery Deck and running the Discovery session? We sell our template along with our session starter questions on our Hoodzpah website. We also sell our proof deck and proposal templates. You can get them all for a bundle deal.

In our opinion, the Discovery phase is the most important part of the whole project. It sets the tone for everything that follows. You'll be shocked how pleased and excited your client gets when you review this deck with them on a follow-up conference call. When they see that you understand the value, purpose, and potential for their project, they'll breathe a sigh of relief and feel confident you can rise to the creative challenge. This step is invaluable for creating trust and goodwill with a client, leading into the creative process.

Have your client approve this deck. Getting approval early on in the project, before any creative has been made, generates amazing creative momentum. Tell them that the findings in this deck will act as your North Star to guide all future creative decisions. This will make getting feedback and approvals much easier because it keeps the core goal in mind. Once you've agreed on "what," "why," and "how," all proofs can be critiqued objectively based on how the work supports or detracts from achieving those goals. This simple test helps you and the client quickly separate valid feedback from subjective opinions. It also helps define what is successful and what isn't, so you can easily prove when your work is a right answer—nay—*the* right answer.

The client may provide their own creative brief and strategic direction, but this discovery phase is still important as it gives you the time to review what they've sent, ask questions, and provide any additional insight. This research phase could be short and sweet or more in depth, depending on the type of project and the budget.

You might not even need to send a discovery deck if your project is for production work (meaning you're making changes to existing creative or creating derivative work from existing brand guidelines, templates, and assets). A simple phone call to talk through the client's needs is more than sufficient with production work.

10. Create the work!

11. Create a proof deck to contextualize the work. Key creative proofs deserve a proper proof deck for context. In your proof deck, restate the goal and creative vision you agreed on in the discovery phase. Label options clearly, if presenting more than one (e.g., "Round 1 Option A," or "Option 1A"); show the work on its own; contextualize the work in key application examples (if applicable); write brief bulleted notes about why the work meets your strategy goals; compare various options in a recap page (if applicable); and lastly, give the client a reminder of where you're at in the overall project scope and what you need from them to continue progress. This last one is a game changer for protecting scope boundaries.

12. Present the proof deck to the client. As much as possible, present key proofs in person or live over a video call. This is especially true for the first proof of creative (like round one of a logo). Don't send the client the proof in advance, walk them through it live to pace it and tell the story. Show excitement about the options and explain why the work meets the brief. If you can't do a meeting, at least record a video walkthrough to give your creative the best shot of being understood and getting approved, especially if you're presenting an idea that's more cutting edge or risky.

When preparing for your presentation, anticipate possible negative reactions, and have your responses ready. Know which elements you're willing to negotiate on and which are crucial to the success of the project. Be prepared to make the case or to negotiate.

Walk the client through the proof with passion and conviction. Don't downplay the work, couch your decisions in self-deprecation, or come off as bored. Show confidence; it's contagious. Why should they care if you don't? Avoid saying things like, "I dunno, we can change it if you don't like it," or, "I wasn't sure this worked but wanted to show you anyway."

After you've presented the proof, open the meeting for discussion and guide feedback. Frame your questions positively and call on people directly. "Pete, which option was your favorite from what we showed?" This encourages them to focus on wins, not on what they didn't like. Avoid broad questions like, "What do you think?" People tend to go to negative critique when given the chance.

When discussing the work, try not to get defensive about your client's feedback. Non-creatives will often fall back on visual association as a first way of processing the new information. They'll say things like, "It reminds me of this." Try not to get too hung up on this, unless they feel the work is much too close to something else, from an infringement perspective. If they're too overwhelmed to have a concrete favorite, try guiding their feedback into certain aspects of the work.

If they are being really vague and seem unsure about the work, there is usually a simple and easy answer that they are just unable to identify. They aren't creatives, so help guide them in finding what it is that's not working for them. Take them item by item through the different elements of the work. Do you feel this font suits our goals? Does the style of this photography align with what we were aiming for? These kinds of questions will usually reveal that a very simple change can change their perspective. We have found color to be a very stealthy villain in this category.

Sometimes, if it's clear the group is getting hung up on a small thing, we might screenshare our creative file during the call to quickly adjust little things based on feedback. Suddenly, everyone is in love with the concept with a few simple tweaks.

The Power of Mockups

Mock-ups are a great way to show how the creative work would look in the context of key applications. Many clients have a hard time imagining creative in a vacuum. Mock-ups can quickly prove a concept's suitability. Earn extra points by making your own mock-ups using the client's own assets and photography. For example, take a photo of your client's store using your phone, then mock-up your proposed new logo and signage on their building.

While a live call to review a proof might seem scary, if you've not presented work like this before, it's a very productive way to review work. It gives you the opportunity, on the spot, to address misunderstandings, calm fears, and remind the client that you have rounds of revisions to continue to refine this work into exactly what they need.

For proofs that are low stakes (the client is already all in on the concept, you're just making tweaks and adjustments), you can send a proof over email with a brief explanation of your updates. We also use Loom for these kinds of proofs. Loom lets us record a video while we screen share the deck, so we can give context in our own words without having to schedule a meeting.

13. Send invoices as needed. Keep track of any milestone payments scheduled between your down payment and your final payment. If the client becomes delinquent in their payments, pause work and don't deliver any files until they catch up. Be strict about your payment rules to engender a healthy respect for boundaries.

Once final approval is given on the project's creative or your scope limit is reached, send the final invoice. If at all possible, do not deliver final files until you receive final payment. This should be written into your contract and agreement. Most large clients will not agree to this. But make it a policy for small and medium clients as much as you can. The best way to avoid chasing payment from clients is to hold files until final payment is made. If you've broken down payments to coincide with when individual phases for the project are done, then you can deliver files as the client pays for the completed phases, rather than all at the end. This can be helpful to a client on large projects that span many months or even years.

14. Send final deliverables to the client. Gather the final files in a well-organized and labeled folder, and send to the client. Dropbox, Google Drive, Box, and WeTransfer are all great options for sending large bulks of files like this. If the scope limit is reached and the client requests further changes or creative work, agree to a new flat rate or an hourly rate before continuing work.

15. Clean house. At the end of the job, clean up the project folder and back up files. Our post-job cleanup looks like this:

- Delete unnecessary assets (photos or files we didn't use at all).
- Archive unchosen options. Gotta save that stuff for the career retrospective coffee table book.
- Keep the final files in a clearly marked main folder.
- Back up the files: If we know we won't work with the client any time soon, we will back up the files to an external hard drive, as well as to the cloud.

16. Check in on the client after the project launches. They'll be glad to know you're invested in their success. If you see the work posted somewhere, reshare, comment, like, and generally celebrate the successful end result with them! If they're really happy with the outcome, ask them for a testimonial to include in your case study for the work.

17. Post a case study about the work on your portfolio, and bask in your accomplishments. Well-earned gloating is fairly self explanatory, right? Share it to social media and relevant industry media outlets.

File Organization

Can you imagine what it'd be like trying to drive through a place that didn't have regulated road markings, street signs, and traffic codes? Anyone who's driven in Boston knows the feeling.

Having a structured way of navigating your files is just as important. Save your sanity and figure out a system for file organization before things get out of hand.

Here's how we do it at Hoodzpah. We use Dropbox, which allows us to work and save files to our hard drive locally and also sync files to the cloud, where we can share with clients and collaborators. The cloud also provides a virtual backup of our files if our hard drive and hard backups ever fail. Each folder on Dropbox has tailored team access, whether it's for everyone, just the founders, or for outside collaborators.

This is how we organize our company drive on Dropbox:

1. Hoodzpah Internal.
    a. Logos and Branding. All of our studio's branding assets.
    b. Assets. A repository of creative assets we have purchased—fonts, mock-ups, textures, templates, stock photography, etc.
    c. Hoodzpah Products. The products we develop ourselves like typefaces, deck templates, and art files for apparel, posters, and otherwise.
    d. Internal Projects. Passion projects, experiments, and other such stuff.
2. Clients.
   All of our client content. Within this main "Clients" folder, are five subfolders with clients grouped alphabetically in chunks. (A-D, E-K, L-P, Q-T, U-Z), so we can navigate faster than scrolling through a bulk list. Each client has its own labeled folder with subfolders per project. The individual project folder is broken down further into subfolders for provided assets, archives (unchosen options and working proofs no longer relevant), and the individual phases of the project.
3. Marketing
    a. Ads
    b. Website
    c. Social Media
    d. Newsletter
    e. Streaming
4. Business.
   Financial and business information, including taxes, filings, contracts, proposals, employee and vendor documentation, etc.
5. Courses and Talks.
   Assets for any speaking engagements we do, as well as our education initiatives, like our *Freelance and Business and Stuff* course.

We've organized our files based on what we need to access quickly, as well as the main buckets of our business.

Organize your files based on what works best for you, but be sure the system is consistent and intuitive. Your file system should be user-friendly for your own sake, but also for when you grow your team or bring on subcontractors. Everyone should be able to easily jump into the system and find their way.

Tips for Organizing Files

Use clear and consistent file naming. A computer's search function is thorough, but not telepathic. The file name should contain the client name (or a common acronym for it), the project name (or a consolidated moniker for it), and the proof round or version number, e.g., "Nicolettos_logo_v1.ai"

Avoid file structures that won't scale or be easily adoptable by a future team. We have heard rumors of studios who organize project folders by year, not by client. This might seem manageable as a team of one for a few years. But once you're six-people strong and twenty years in, tying projects to years is a tall order. Also, if you have a client with multiple projects, it's much easier to group within a main client folder, so you can toggle easily between projects.

Use number prefixes to control the order of your subfolders. We like our project folders to have subfolders for phases in order of our progress, so we just use number prefixes to force this.

Get in the habit of making new versions of files for each new proof. Meaning, instead of having one Illustrator file that you overwrite as you make changes, save the file as a copy and rename it "Version2" or "v2" to keep a record of progress, just in case a client changes their mind and wants to return to an old proof. Even after a project is finished, we're pack rats who are afraid to throw anything out. So we just move workups and unchosen options into an archived folder.

Keep records of your client's feedback and approvals. Save emails with important approvals and feedback. This paper trail might save your butt if a client tries to blame you for something

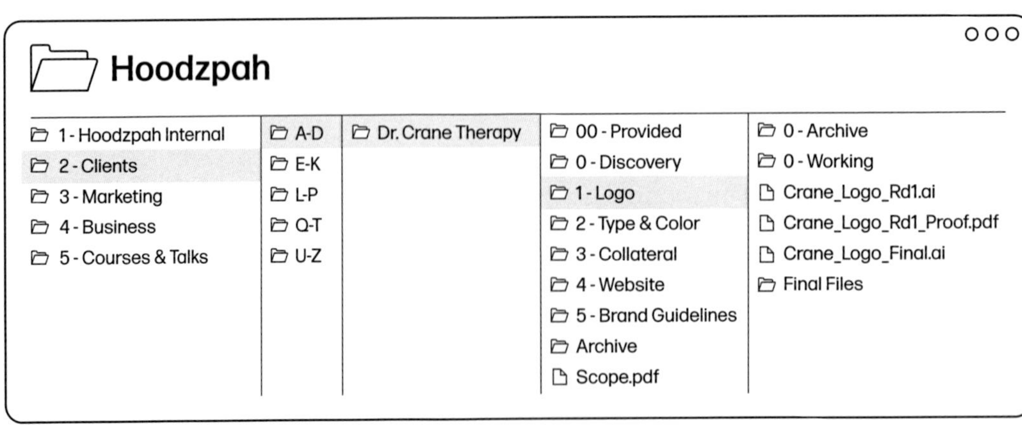

down the road. Having timestamped logs of their requests and approvals will protect you if you ever get into a legal battle over a project.

"Working" folders are great catchalls for assets and odds and ends within a project folder. You can fill the working folder with fonts, stock photos, screenshots of feedback, inspiration, and any other assets that don't have a clear place in a subfolder. Just like a house, every project needs a junk drawer.

Save received assets and downloads in proper places the minute you get them. Otherwise, you will lose it in the void that is your "Downloads" folder. Be diligent for future-you's sake.

Chapter Checklist:

① Create a job board with any current and upcoming client projects and internal projects in the pipeline.

② Create your job calendar.

③ Get a to-do list planner.

④ Choose a solution for time tracking.

⑤ Choose your days for meetings versus creative work.

⑥ Choose and protect your creative window.

⑦ Create a file management structure to organize your business and client files.

⑧ Extra credit for creating a backup system or choosing a cloud-sync storage service to back up your files.

⑨ Talk to your business lawyer, accountant, or CPA about your other systems: financial management and payroll, your insurance systems, business filings setup, contracts, and any other relevant business systems.

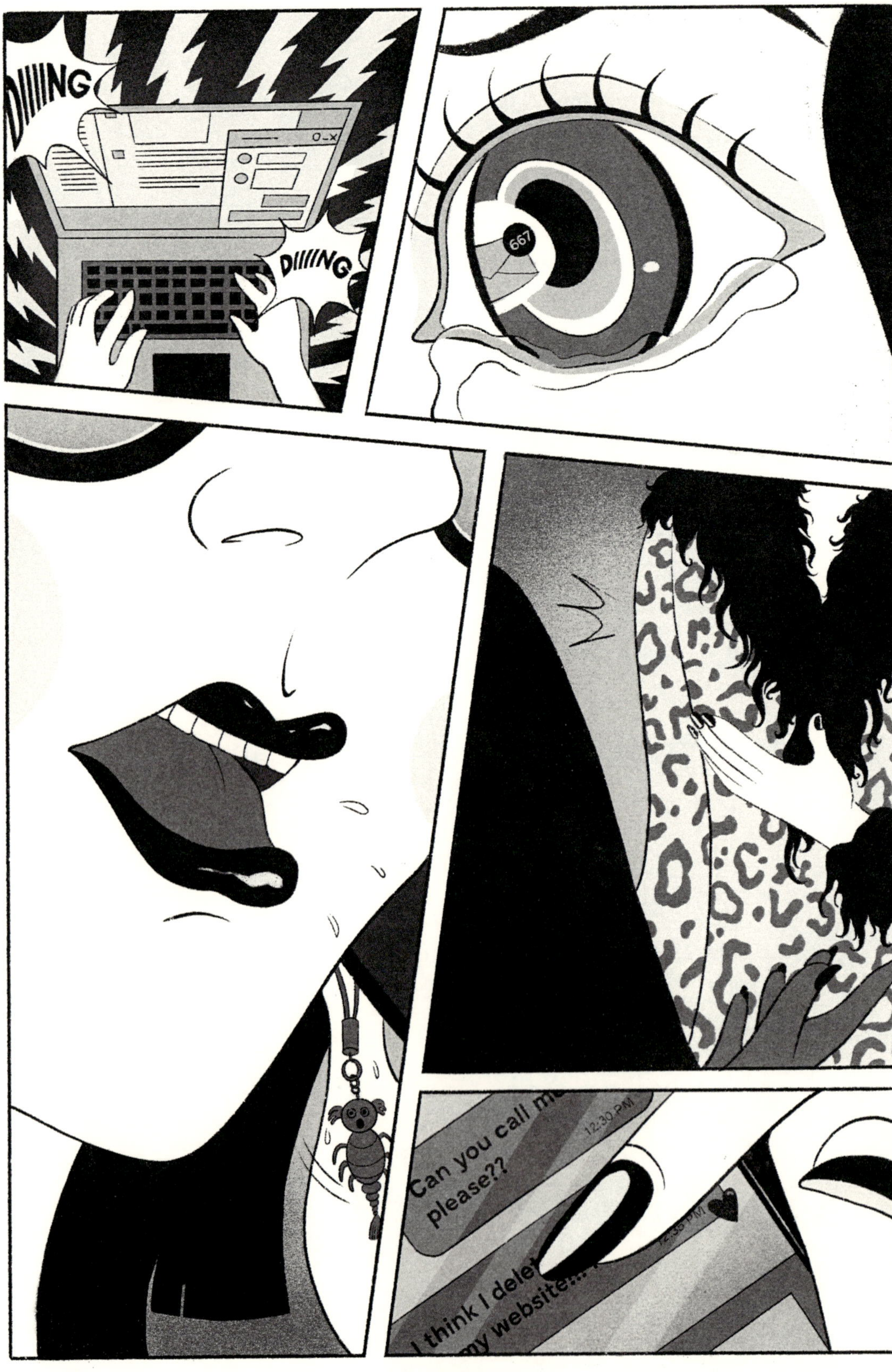

Illustration by: Chau Luong

13
Communication and Collaboration

The Secret Sauce: Soft Skills

What so many creatives take for granted when running their own business is the human experience of it all. As new entrepreneurs, we're usually fixated on things like:

Is my work good enough?

How do I make more money?

What should I charge for x, y, or z?

How do I get more clients?

Here are some questions that are equally as important but tend to be less top of mind.

How do I make a potential client feel joy, trust, and excitement when they experience my brand through my website or social media?

How do I speak to my potential client's hopes and needs through my marketing outreach?

How do I make my clients feel understood in the early stages of my process so they trust me when I present creative work?

How do I communicate my work in terms the client can understand?

How do I help my client navigate tough decisions during the process?

How do I make my client feel appreciated during the process?

How do I make my client's life easier?

The first set of questions is centered on your own perspective and goals. The second set is centered on your client's. It's impossible to create a great customer experience without learning to identify with your client's needs, wants, and motivations. Your customers have hired you to deliver a creative end result, yes. But what they also want and expect is a seamless, reliable, positive experience while getting to that end result. It's the journey. A great customer experience makes for loyal clients who shout your name from the rooftops like a teenager in love. It's what woos and wins over your clients from the first meeting to the final approval.

Good work is the baseline for running a creative business. By "good" work, we mean performing a service or skill at a professional level to solve a specific customer need. We're not talking about genius work. Not even great work. Just good work. Work that is not lazy or careless.

We know plenty of people doing *just good* work who make a great living at it. And we know plenty of people doing incredible work who struggle to make ends meet as independent creatives. That's because your work output is rarely the key factor. A customer's perception of you before they work with you, as well as their experience during and after they work with you, is what makes the difference. Customers prefer a positive, reliable work relationship that results in just good creative output over a miserable and flaky working relationship that results in genius work, hands down.

There are no big secrets to uncover regarding how to run a business, but if there were ever a cheat code, it would be good soft skills.

There's what you do: your hard skills as a designer, filmmaker, developer, marketer, photographer, etc. And there's how you do it: determined by soft skills like critical thinking, flexibility, responsibility, collaboration, appreciation, communication, understanding, honesty, leadership, and negotiation.

Soft skills are social, emotional, and analytical tools you can use to put yourself ahead of the pack when it comes to landing a job, getting an approval, or saving a project from a cliff when a client gets worried, panicked, or upset. Soft skills deal with the human side of your relationship with your audience and clients. They help you build a positive reputation, making for easy repeat clients, glowing referrals, and a strong connection with your audience. Without these soft skills, you'll likely be up against unhappy clients, a shrinking audience, and a reputation in free fall. Again, despite what your work looks like.

Have you ever been to Denny's? The American diner restaurant chain? Grand Slam breakfasts on Sundays were the jam with our grandma. The food wasn't five-star cuisine, but it was tasty, affordable, ready in ten minutes, and the servers treated us like family, telling us all the best gossip "from town" while they topped up our coffee. It easily became our every-Sunday staple while growing up in Bowling Green, Kentucky. This is the power of a reliable and enjoyable human experience. You don't have to expect *the best* from a brand or business to be an extremely satisfied repeat customer.

Think about your favorite stores, brands, and services. What makes you choose them again and again? Why go to the same bar or coffee shop instead of trying something new? Usually, it's down to friendly service, value for money, and a reliable experience—same thing with a babysitter, hairdresser, developer, or mechanic. You want to work with people you trust and ideally even like. Design is no different. Go beyond good work output into great soft skills, and you will have better client retention, better working relationships during your process, and more word-of-mouth referrals.

You were born with some soft skills baked in. Your horoscope or Myers-Briggs personality classification has probably made you aware of which ones come easily for you. Consult any one of your exes to see which traits you lack. It's worth it to seriously reflect on what you need to work on when it comes to social or communicative weaknesses.

Do you have trouble communicating ideas? Practice by recording yourself talking through a creative proof or pitch deck, then watch it and take notes on how to improve. During the pandemic, we started using Loom for proof deck and proposal walk-throughs. Loom is a screen recording platform that makes it easy to record yourself and your screen so you can keep the human element of meetings without being in a meeting. We use it all the time at Hoodzpah. But when we first recorded ourselves presenting proof decks, we were shocked at how unclear and unconvincing we sounded when we rewatched the videos. Despite what we thought, it came across that we lacked conviction about the work. Not to mention, we talked a mile a minute. So we worked on talking slower, with more confidence, and with more positive energy.

Loom claims it has saved us hundreds of hours that we would have otherwise spent in meetings, which would be true if not for the fact that we usually have to rerecord our Looms about three times to get the good energy across. Still, we thank them for inadvertently helping us work on our communication and presentation skills.

Do you tend to clam up in social settings? Try to attend meetups and local events with a friend as a safety net. Ideally, a friend who is better at socializing than you are. They can help grease the wheels. Plus, being a duo will instantly make you easier to approach. But don't wait for people to come to you. Try to meet three new people by the end of the event.

Have people in your life told you that you come off rude? This is probably code for a few things: you tend to focus only on yourself and your own point of view, you don't listen to what other people say, you're insensitive to how your words and actions affect other people, or you give unwelcome critique. In short, you might be operating in stream-of-consciousness mode rather than learning to listen and consider others as well as yourself. You don't have to completely mute your own thoughts and perspective to be a considerate person who people like to work with. That would be self-censoring and fake. Leave room for everyone in the group, whether in a conversation or on a project. Give as much as you take.

The easiest way to practice being more giving and socially considerate? Ask people a question about themselves, and listen carefully enough to ask a good follow-up question. This will sharpen your ability to listen and teach you to look for points of interest and commonality that can help you and another person get on the same page. Avoid the urge to critique, correct, or weigh in on everything another person says. Even if it's just to make a funny joke. Humor can solve almost anything. But applied too loosely and liberally, it can come off as rude and sarcastic, making natural conversation almost impossible.

When it comes to offering critique, try asking if you can offer a suggestion before you give it. This might sound odd, but asking permission makes people feel curious to know what you have to say and puts them in a mindset of being ready to receive a differing view. Remember, as with any relationship, you can't fight every battle. Learn when to negotiate and when you're willing to make a stand. Learn what is preference and what is dogmatically true.

Do you tend to be defensive or passive-aggressive when responding to feedback? Defensiveness about our creative work is natural. We've invested a lot of time making what we think is the perfect solution for a problem. And now, after days and nights of toiling, a client or collaborator looks at our work and has a differing opinion to ours. There's no easy way to deal with this except to learn to expect it. You will never have a client or collaborator respond to your proof without any feedback at all. So stop going into review meetings looking for all-in praise, and learn to expect a negotiation.

A lot of the feedback process is just someone getting familiar with your work in real time. They're processing something they have never seen before. The first, most common way people process new creative input is to provide "This reminds me of ____" feedback. This is annoying but very natural. They are trying to find ways to digest and understand the work. For the most part, you can usually ignore this feedback and just smile (unless the resemblance is much too close and infringes on copyright).

The truth is, most people are not trained in how to critique creative work, so their feedback tends to seem vague or even harsh. This is not intentional. They tend to think subjectively at first. They consider things from their personal perspective. It's your job to help them put words to their feelings and remember to judge the creative through the lens of the brief and the target audience. This is why a great proof process is so important (not just showing a creative end result but contextualizing it). Your proof should make a strong case for why you made the decisions you did. It should prove how your creative decisions directly tie back to your agreed-upon project brief and goals. If you can do that, most of your feedback will be minor nuances, not massive overhauls. Unless you totally missed the brief, but won't admit it, or your client is trying to abandon the brief and won't admit it.

If you and your client aren't seeing eye to eye, listen to them closely and ask specific follow-up questions. If they say, "I just don't like it," or "It doesn't feel luxury," ask them about unique elements of the creative work to see which part in particular is the offending object. You might be surprised how a small tweak can change their perspective.

You know your skills and services. And the client knows their industry and business. They are seeking your expertise, but don't discount or overlook the insight they can bring to the table. This doesn't mean there isn't room for you to challenge their thinking. But at least listen and consider their perspective.

In a perfect world, we would all agree and know innately the one right answer. The answer to rule them all! But in the real world, there is often more than one right answer to any creative problem. That means we have to reason together, building consensus through respectful collaboration until we land on *our right answer*.

Beware a life in stasis. You might be thinking to yourself, "Well, I am who I am; people can take it or leave it." But come on, human existence isn't a level plane. It should be an upward trajectory of growth. There's room for evolution in all of us. And bettering ourselves doesn't mean losing our personality or being untrue to our convictions. The soft skills we're talking about here aren't about pleasing people at the cost of quality or integrity. They're about getting the best out of people and projects in a world where there are no absolute victories, only well-negotiated compromises. Soft skills can be learned and developed and are worth the effort. These skills are what will propel you farther, faster.

Appreciation and Open-mindedness Help Win Collective Buy-in

The reason we get to do what we do is that clients trust us with their money, reputation, and projects. Whether it's a photo shoot or a logo, a client's project will affect how their own boss, customer, or audience sees them. They think this project is important, and they trust us to help them. They want to know we care about it going well as much as they do and are actively going to work toward the best outcome we can achieve. If the situation were reversed and you hired someone to do something very important, wouldn't you want to feel like the studio you hired values your project and is excited to work on it with you? People crave affirmation. And we can give it to them.

This is an easy but surprisingly overlooked way to show your client you care: verbalize your interest and appreciation. You don't have to spew a bunch of hot air or flatter them. Just let your guard down and show your interest.

When we do an initial call with a potential client, we try to convey our excitement and thank them for considering us as a partner. Then, when we send the proposal, one of the first pages always says something like: "Thank you so much for considering us for your project to do *x*, *y*, or *z*." We're showing we care. We listened. We understand they can go elsewhere. Then, if we land the work, we make it clear in the discovery meetings that we're excited and confident about the outcome. Throughout the process, when the client gives feedback or sends assets, we like to acknowledge their efforts, even if the feedback is negative. Something like: "Thank you for sharing your thoughts, it really helped us understand your perspective."

Besides clients, there are likely tons of people who will contribute to the success of your business over the years. Great print vendors are a true gift. Say thank you, and celebrate their great work when you get it in hand. A good accountant is the rarest of gems, so make sure they know you appreciate their long hours during tax season. A friend or mentor listening to you complain about a rough day or giving advice when you're stuck on something can be a lifeline on darker days. Make sure they know you appreciate their ears and feedback.

This approach to people helps diffuse tension, encourages progress when decisions get hard, and lifts morale. People often mirror the experience they receive. When you show gratitude and care, people are more apt to return it.

When working with Industrial Light & Magic on their rebrand (truly a dream project for us!), we were so impressed by their company's work culture. Everyone was so considerate of each other's thoughts, and anyone in a meeting could speak their honest opinion without being shot down or sidelined. Leadership intentionally created this work environment and took pains to accommodate. In our calls, they would discuss their opinions together, weigh those thoughts against the project goal, and then the leader on the project would make a decision about which position best served the desired outcome. Team leaders and team members alike would often openly thank one another for their work to keep the project going. This regular practice of gratitude created a dynamic where everyone felt appreciated, even if their ideas were not always used or chosen.

This kind of considerate environment might seem simple, but it's not the easy way to deal with people. The easy way is for a leader to dictate how things will go, what should be done, and to keep input to the bare minimum. This saves a lot of time and effort. It cuts down meetings. But while this approach might feel simpler in the short run, it doesn't gather consensus and can lead to more division down the road. Winning buy-in and trust along the way means it's more likely that clients will feel confident in the final creative solution.

When it comes to showing appreciation, words go a long way. But gifts don't hurt either. Referral fees, gift cards, coffee, swag from your studio. Tokens like this let people know you value them and their interest or involvement in your business. And when people feel valued, you get the best out of them.

Caring is Cool

As a service provider, part of a job well done is solving a client's problem. Beyond the big problem your project is addressing, there will be any number of smaller issues that your client faces. Anticipate what might confuse or frustrate or hinder your client, and try to account for those things in your process. Most people think about how to make their own lives easier, usually to the detriment of their clients. If you can figure out how to make your client's life easier in ways they didn't even think to ask for, you'll become a highly valued asset.

Showing care and consideration can be achieved in pretty simple ways. Example: A client is asking if you can also coordinate printing for a project, but you don't provide this service. Instead of just saying "I don't manage printing", you could go the extra mile to help them get started with something they know nothing about. Point them in the right direction. Refer them to printers you know, or give them a hint on what to Google to find some vendors.

Another example: When we work with clients on branding, by the end of the scope, we have a lot of files to hand over. The logo assets folder alone has a lot of options for RGB or CMYK with various file types in between. To the client, we might as well have handed over plans to build a rocket ship. We don't just label the folders by design terms; we give clues in the folder names that help the customer navigate the options: "CMYK for Printing" instead of just "CMYK" and "RGB for Digital" instead of just "RGB". These considerations make your client's life way easier.

We like to quote projects with this in mind. When we quote, we land on a price that gives us the time and resources we need to not just barely do the work, but to do the work above and beyond what the client expected.

Honesty is the Policy

Some of us conflict-avoiders struggle with having honest conversations with clients and collaborators. But honesty is important when pushing back on client feedback that could derail the project's goals, addressing instances where a client is disregarding respectful boundaries, managing expectations of what a client thinks a project's outcomes will be, and presenting an opposing viewpoint to your client's.

This is where soft skills can really come to your rescue. Something that could come off rude, aggressive, or defensive can be presented in a calm and considerate way. It does you and your client no favors when you fear to tell them the truth. In fact, when we learned to constructively and respectfully challenge a client's view or feedback, we found most clients appreciated our insights and perspective. Most clients don't want yes-men (beware those who do); they want specialists who can help them do what they don't have the skills and expertise to do themselves. At the beginning of your projects, it can be helpful to share a deck explaining how to get the most out of the collaborative project. Explain that you will give your best advice throughout the project and do your best to find ways to harmonize their input with what will be best for their project and target audience.

We get a lot of inquiries about visual identity rebrands. And sometimes we can tell that the potential client thinks a new look will solve problems that go much deeper. A nicer logo cannot solve an inherently bad business model. A better design system cannot make up for a terrible product. In these cases, the company needs to overhaul their internal values, product, and experience along with a redesigned visual identity in order to truly change how their customers perceive their brand. This is an instance where an honest conversation is in order to make sure the client's expectations of our work are realistic. The client needs to understand their role in a rebrand as much as our role.

For example, the client wants you to change the black text in your layout to a light blue, but it will decrease legibility and will just plain look awful. Instead of saying "No, that won't work" or "That color looks ugly" or just cowing down when you know it's the wrong decision, try to present an alternate solution and explain why. Clients do their best to prescribe feedback, but they look to you as the expert to help guide their decisions. Don't be afraid to interpret the feedback and read between the lines. You might respond to them with: "That blue color is cool! Unfortunately, when that color is used on text, it fails the accessibility test for visually impaired users. So what if we do this other blue here, which is still in the same tonal family but more legible?"

If a client gives you feedback on a proof that is subjective to their own preferences but works against the project goal, you need to be able to show them that their own tastes don't necessarily represent the tastes of the project's target audience. Try to bring them back to the objective goals of the project, not subjective feelings.

Sometimes, a client refuses to be swayed by reason, research, or your professional expertise. Once you've made your strongest case and spoken your piece, you've done all you can do. At this point, the paying client is the final decider, for better or worse. They will have to live with their own consequences. You can't force their hand.

It's rare, but sometimes you might decide to terminate the project if you feel that the client's attitude and feedback would be too damaging and compromising to the end result.

Being Solution-oriented and Flexible While Protecting your Boundaries

We business owners are often terrible at protecting our boundaries. We let clients go beyond scope, we take on too many projects at once, we undercharge, and the list goes on. However, we can also easily fall into the opposite predicament and get to the point where we have so many boundaries that we become a stubborn and unhelpful partner.

In real life, things never go to plan. A client's brief might change, a vendor might ghost you or mess up an order, a schedule might unavoidably change. In these times, you can really shine if you learn how to ideate on new solutions rather than fixating on what's going wrong.

Example: Your client's company gets new guidelines from their legal team about language in their marketing, which means they need another round of revisions to the design you sent. But there are no revisions left in the budgeted scope. Instead of saying, "Sorry, we don't have any revision rounds left," which leaves the client in a predicament, you can say, "We'd be happy to make these revisions for you at our hourly rate of $XXX since we've already reached the end of our scope." Or, you could offer to swap another part of the scope with this added revision. You helped your client, and you also protected your boundaries. Win-win! Beware of adding on freebies and gimmes without consequence. It will make protecting your boundaries in the future more difficult.

Mastering Communication Styles

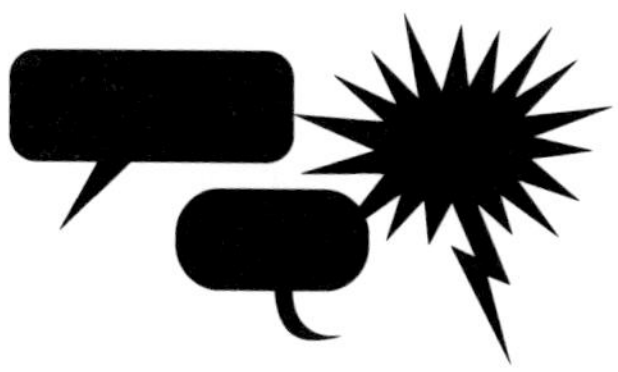

As you run your business, you'll deal with all kinds of people with all kinds of different communication styles. If you listen carefully and pay attention, it's easy to learn someone's communication style so you can meet them where they are. Think: "love languages" for business.

At Hoodzpah, if our client prefers short, to-the-point emails with no small talk, we cater to that. If our client always inquires about our weekends and likes small talk, we mix in some fun conversation too. If our client uses lots of emojis and GIFs, we're ready and very able to go there!

If our clients have a really hard time getting back to us via email, we call them. With a live conversation, we can guide them through feedback and help them align on decisions. Then, we follow up with an email to confirm the feedback in writing (always keep a paper trail!).

Certain clients want us to be more available to them via Slack throughout a project. This can be amazing if it's a large project with a lot of moving parts. You can connect with the client's team easily throughout the day rather than just for official proof review meetings. But being that available can also really break up the day and hinder you from getting into the creative zone. Try to still protect windows of focused creative time.

There are caveats to accommodating your client's manner of communication and collaboration. Sometimes, clients have unreasonable expectations about availability and turnarounds, like expecting responses within moments of any communication, even after work hours or on the weekend. We tell our clients that we'll respond to communications within a business day, unless we have all agreed to be available to each other for important launches or tight deadlines.

The one thing we don't accommodate is collaboration via text message or social media direct message. It's just too easy for things to get lost in that never-ending thread. If someone texts or DMs us about a project, we'll usually say, "Can you send me this in an email? Things so easily get lost or forgotten on text/DM, and I don't want to forget this." Big days like website launches, press checks, video shoots, etc., are the only exception. We'll use texts to get a hold of people quickly because everything is time sensitive. But we always agree to this beforehand.

Most of our projects are flat-rate scoped with specific deliverables and timelines. We know what deadlines need to be met; we set up check-in meetings and send regular update emails in between. So there's usually no need for constant back and forth throughout the day. If a client is getting panicked and calling or emailing you multiple times a day, perhaps you need to be clearer with them about the timeline and when they can expect a new proof. Give them a friendly call to explain that everything is going well. Send them a calendar invite for when they can expect the next proof or update. If they continue to hound you, tell them you need them to trust the process. You need focus and uninterrupted windows of creative time to do your best work.

Email, Meeting, or Call?

The more important moments of your client relationship are better handled through live meetings, whether in person or virtual: presenting pivotal proofs, reviewing a project proposal, or talking about project problems. In those moments, being able to see the client's face and talk to them live will help you communicate the most effectively.

Be very cautious of letting a client claim too much of your time through unnecessary meetings. Phone calls, emails, and meetings are a necessary part of any project. But every round of changes doesn't require an in-person meeting that lasts an hour.

A phone call is an unsung tool in business these days. Everything seems to be either virtual meetings or emails. But if you get an email from an unhappy client who's panicking about the project, the best thing you can do is hop on a quick phone call as soon as possible. Neither party has to worry about being camera-ready, but you can still talk live. In situations like these, a client needs reassurance, a considerate ear. Remind them of the project goals, calm their fears, address their concerns, and explain how you can improve the situation. Many a project has been saved by a simple phone call.

Used properly, emails can be an invaluable tool. Used improperly, emails are like a hydra. Write one bad one, and ten spawn in its place. Join us in making a stand for efficient, comprehensive emails! They should be short, sweet, and well organized. None of us have enough hours in the day, but we can claim some of them back if we can get this email beast under control.

Email Like a Champ

Use subject lines correctly. Include the project name at the very least, so it's easy to search for. Besides that, you can include the project round or a small teaser of what you'll be talking about. "Louie's Branding Round 1 Proof." "Cora Website: Assets Needed to Start."

Reread emails for specificity, succinctness, and clarity. Many email tools now have features that help you rewrite emails to be more concise and clear. Sending one rushed and confusing email means more emails in its wake to make sense of it all, and lost project momentum as a result. Even worse than a confusing email is a *long*, confusing email. To most people, an email longer than one paragraph is an affront to all that is decent and good. They'll push it aside to be dealt with later and intentionally or unintentionally move it to the bottom of their priorities. Edit your email to be short and powerful. If it's impossible to make it concise, maybe you need a meeting instead.

Use formatting to make the email easy to skim. Bulleted or numbered lists are a great way to quickly communicate updates or feedback. Highlight your key, actionable request. If there are multiple points to the email, bold sections so the user can scan to the relevant information.

Include your email signature with contact information at the bottom of every email. Make it easy for clients to contact you by phone or find your work online.

Verbal and Non-verbal Communication

We all know that sometimes it's not what you're saying but how you're saying it that matters. Your body language and non-verbal cues can really make a difference when presenting work or meeting a client for the first time.

Look engaged and interested! This might seem like a duh, but we can't tell you how many interviews we've held over the years at Hoodzpah with candidates who look bored to death. When you're in a conversation, make an effort to show you're engaged by using non-verbal cues. Nod when a good point is made. Laugh when a joke is made. Try to avoid fidgeting. Consider your listening face. You don't have to hold a perma-grin, but you definitely don't want to have a "WTF are you talking about" face on. Only Abercrombie & Fitch models from the 2000s can win sales from Resting Fitch Face.

Make eye contact. You don't have to stare the other person down, but if you don't make eye contact, you'll come off as shifty, insincere, or uninterested. Most of all, don't look at your phone while others are talking.

Sit up straight: Lean in. Don't lean back in your chair or slouch.

Walk tall and with purpose. Don't scoot, scurry, or shlump. Convey confidence through your composure, not just your work.

Smile. It's good for you and good for your clients and peers. British researchers found that one smile can stimulate the brain as much as up to 2,000 chocolate bars and can be as stimulating as receiving up to $22,000. Smiles are linked to reward centers in our brains, which release "happy hormones." And smiles are contagious. So when you smile, it triggers your client to smile, and soon, you're both on your way down a happy hormone spiral that's good for everyone.

Give a firm handshake. A floppy, flabby handshake is a downer.

Speak with passion and conviction. Show excitement through voice modulation. You are not a robot. Let your enthusiasm out of the cage. The time for uncertainty is when you're developing your creative work. But once it's time to present, stand behind the work proudly. If you don't believe in it your client never will.

Speak clearly. Ar-tic-u-late. If you find you get panicked and frazzled in conversations, bring a notebook and write down your thoughts so you have a cheat sheet when you start talking.

Don't try to use big words to sound smart. Big words don't make you smart—clear, well-thought-out ideas do. Speak in a way that is natural to you and that the client can understand. It's not helpful to your client if you're speaking over their head with industry jargon they're not familiar with.

Don't interrupt.

Don't pretend to understand if you don't. Ask questions to clarify if you need to. This is not a weakness.

Present Creative Work Like A Pro

Words are some of our main means of communication, but words can unintentionally deceive. Inadvertently, one word can mean many different things depending on who is saying it. Personal preference and experience fill that word with a unique definition for each person. Generally, we all know what "modern" means, but what does it mean specifically when your client says they want a modern website or a modern logo? Listening is the first step. Let the client explain to you what they mean by further describing and giving examples. Then interpret. A picture is worth a thousand words. Create a mood board with your client with visual examples of "modern." Now, you are visually and verbally on the same page. You and your client are building a shared and mutually understood terminology.

When presenting proofs to clients, show that your solution meets your mutual goals for the project. Use the client's own words in your presentation.

"You explained to me that *X* was a goal for this logo. This logo meets that goal because of *Y* and *Z*."

Then, contextualize the work visually to further prove the success of your solution. Show and tell as much as possible when reviewing creative.

Treat your proof presentation analytically. Go into it knowing what you're willing to compromise on. What are non-crucial elements of the work that are open to change or could be removed? Be flexible with the client on those things. But be prepared to make a solid case for non-negotiables. Doctors don't let patients choose how they set a broken bone, but they do let them choose the color of the cast.

Our friend Bayan Joonam (formerly of SoulPancake) once shared a helpful exercise with us. Before each client proposal or proof review, he personally anticipates any questions or reasons the client might have for saying "no" to his idea/proof. Then he writes down his best answers to those sticking points. Poking holes in your own plan may seem strange, but by considering all the possible problems, you can shore up your argument. You'll be able to answer their questions before they even have a chance to ask them. This extra prep will also help you identify your own biases. Things you don't have a good reason for, but you just prefer. If your client can make a good case against your preferences, be ready to "kill your darlings," as they say.

Communication Pitfalls

Now for some hindsight wisdom. After more than fourteen years running our own studio, we've made many a misstep. The facepalm moments were many. We've also seen talented creatives sideline themselves through bad habits like public whining or oversharing about private client interactions. Avoid these communication pitfalls.

Gossiping. If you talk trash on your clients, people will assume you do the same about them to others. A gossipy conversation tells a client you don't respect people's privacy and reflects poorly on your trustworthiness. Let's be real; we all need a good gossip session. But that's what friends, sisters, bartenders, and hairdressers are for. Not clients.

Whining. We all know those people in our social media feeds. They relish in a good whine. But it's draining to hear about it. Would you feel comfortable hiring someone who's constantly complaining about everyone and everything publicly? You could be their next topic of woe. Have you ever met someone who seems to have a falling out with everyone they've ever worked with? You start to wonder if they are the common denominator. Remember that your clients (current and future) are busy people with their own issues and worries. They don't need to be burdened with wondering if they'll hurt your feelings by saying the wrong thing. This isn't to say you aren't allowed to share your feelings. But living permanently in "life isn't fair" mode is just not a positive vibe for a work collaboration. Clients want collaborators who can meet a problem head-on, workshop issues, pivot, and find a way to overcome odds.

Cussing. You can be professional without being a tool, and you can be "real" without sounding like a Tarantino character. It's not that cussing isn't allowed. Just proceed with caution and know your audience. After all, sometimes a well-placed cuss really seals the deal. Other times, it shows you the f*%$ing door.

Inappropriate and hateful conversation. Don't be racist, sexist, homophobic, hateful, elitist, or otherwise disrespectful to collaborators or clients. Avoid all things not safe for work. No dirty or tasteless jokes.

Oversharing to the point of compromising trust or respect. Clients don't need to know how horrible your last Tinder date went, how you can barely make rent, or how you woke up hungover in a gutter this morning. It's healthy to keep some distance between you and your clients when it comes to really personal details. They are hiring you for professional service, not friendship. You can be casual and conversational without oversharing inappropriate details.

We Just Disagree

Sometimes, despite best efforts, you cannot get on the same page with a client. You and your client seem to agree on overall project goals and aesthetic direction, but when you show them progress proofs, they are unhappy or unsure about the results. You show how your work aligns with original mood boards and goals, but they can't be convinced.

"I just don't like it" is not a valid response to a proof that meets the requirement you and your client have agreed on for success. This requires an honest conversation with the client about their expectations. Some lines to try on wishy-washy clients:

> "The work I have done meets the project goals that we outlined and approved together at the very beginning. We outlined goals to have a means to measure success. Based on our original criteria, this is successful. See how my proof is in line with our mood board . . . "

"This work might not be your personal preference, but we know your audience wants *X*, *Y*, and *Z*. This proof delivers on those needs in the following ways . . . "

"If you have unlimited time and money, then we can continue to revise and rework to see if we can make exactly what you 'envision'. But neither of us has that luxury, so let's finalize what we've come up with, which we know meets our goals, even if it's not your 'perfect' ideal. Perfect is the enemy of good. This is a good solution."

"Let's take our personal opinions out of it and launch this iteration to a test group of your users/audience. If the proof does well with the test group, then we'll have our answer from the voices that matter most: our end user."

"Based on your feedback, it sounds like our original project goal has changed. Our scope of work was based on a specific goal and style that you signed off on in the research/discovery phase. If you want to change the direction, that's okay, but I'll need to re-quote you for a new phase of creative exploration."

If this kind of sound reasoning doesn't work on your client, you might have to terminate the project. You cannot help someone who cannot articulate helpful feedback, changes their mind on a whim, or is seeking validation from their "gut" rather than from objective waymarks agreed to in the discovery phase.

End the relationship as professionally as possible and according to your contract terms. Get paid for what you are owed, and then give the client any work you owe them. Don't ghost your client or ignore them. This is why a termination clause is crucial in your agreement terms.

Terminating Projects

Client indecision isn't the only reason to terminate a client contract.

Harassment. Drama is great on TV, but not in your work relationships. If clients are verbally or physically harassing you, cannot respect professional boundaries, or are consistently disrespectful, you need to end the relationship.

Financial delinquency. If a client's payment is late, give them a chance to make it right. But if they are chronically avoiding your requests for settlement, then stop all work. If they refuse to pay what is owed for the work you've done, do not give them any project files until they pay what is owed. If they already have possession of your work, consider a cease-and-desist letter. Hopefully, your agreement on copyright or licensing terms stipulates that the client is only allowed to use your work if they have paid for the services in full. This means the client is infringing on your copyright if they have not paid for the work that they are using.

Tragedy. When something unexpected comes up in your or your client's life, and you/they are physically or emotionally no longer able to fulfill responsibilities, you might need to cancel the project. Be sure your contract allows for this kind of termination, in case you need it. Tragedy can strike without warning, and you don't want a lawsuit looming over your head just because you need to take a step back from your business. Be very careful about how you bow out. Try to replace your position if you can. Refer them to a trusted colleague who can continue the work. At the very least, alert your client to your situation as soon as possible, so they have enough time to find someone to pick up the work.

Saying Goodbye to a Client

Sometimes you outgrow a client relationship. A client that was a great fit for you early on might no longer make sense for your studio three years later. This can definitely be the case with hourly retainer work. Hourly work on a retainer is great at first because it's reliable, and you always get paid for your work. But it can be a huge time and energy suck, preventing you from working on higher-value projects. When demand for your time and services grows, you get the benefit of choice as to what work you take on. This might mean offboarding clients who are no longer in line with the kind of work you want to do or cannot afford the rates you can now charge.

Before you end a client relationship, see if you can move them to your new rates. Then consider hiring/contracting a junior designer to help you do the client's work while still freeing up your time for new, more lucrative work. This means you'll make income on top of what you pay your junior designer while growing your business into more lucrative services.

If you don't have the bandwidth to manage a junior designer and maintain your client's ongoing work, kindly tell the client you'll no longer be able to handle their projects. Give the client enough heads-up so they can make arrangements to find a new designer. Better yet, refer your client to designers who you know and trust. You don't want to leave a partner in the lurch. Make the transition easy for them to maintain a good relationship.

Chapter Checklist:

① Reflect on your strengths and weaknesses when it comes to soft skills.

② Identify what soft skills you want to work on, and make a plan to practice them by putting yourself in social settings regularly.

③ Practice verbal and nonverbal communication skills in your meetings

What Makes an Invaluable Subcontractor?

	What is the main trait (other than talent) you look for in a creative subcontractor?	*Are there any "toxic traits" or common mistakes that make a subcontractor hard to work with? Things that make your life harder as a CD?*
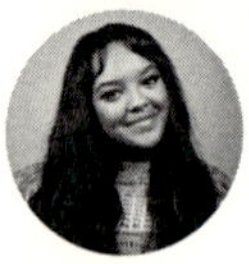 **Banna Tesfay** *Creative, Global / Consumer Products, Netflix* bannatesfay.com	Thoughtfulness. My best creative partners don't just care about the design work, they care about the IP it exists with, and the fans who consume what we make for them. When I work with creatives who can bring a holistic approach to design, we're all eating cake.	As someone who used to be a contractor, let me just say I know how hard it is. I commend anyone who has to navigate this market and promoting themselves. That being said, I think unreliableness is where I tend to part ways the most. Meeting deadlines, clearly executing a brief, and asking for clarity timely is invaluable to me. And listen- we're human. Life can be unpredictable. But unresponsiveness or poor communication can cause much larger ripples and compresses other teams schedule.
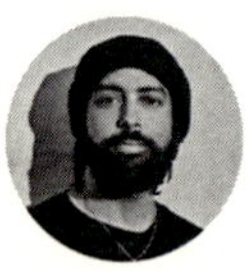 **Marcus McDougald** *Freelance Creative Director, formerly LAFC* marcusmcdougald.com	I'm most interested in someone's level of creative investment, not just in the project, but in themselves. I regularly return to collaborators who take initiative, not only in meeting a projects deadlines and deliverables, but also in how they own their impact within the creative ecosystem. That impact is amplified when they see and treat each project as an opportunity for personal growth. Ultimately, I'm drawn to people who treat the work like it matters, because in our world, it absolutely does. Most of us have chosen creative livelihoods not just to put food on the table, but because this work illuminates our values and feeds us at our very core. It should never be just about aesthetics or deliverables; it's about transformation and growth for everyone involved. When someone gets that, and builds from that place, I'll bring them in time and time again.	For sure, there are a few significant "toxic traits" that I tend to keep an eye out for during a "chemistry test" phase: 1. Energetic flakiness: Dependability is key. I need to trust that a creator will show up on time and communicate early, clearly, and often. If not, our collective creative potential is limited out of the gate. 2. Over-promising, under-listening: When someone is inclined to being agreeable or having all of the "right answers" more-so than deep listening and thoughtful questioning, it's a red flag and a major limiting factor. I want to grow too, and in order for that to happen, we need to be introspective, vulnerable, and willing to challenge assumptions together. These growing pains usually feel awkward at first, but once trust is earned, this dynamic becomes a source of limitless creative inertia. 3. Unchecked ego: Collaboration is an energetic exchange. When someone brings defensiveness or unexamined pride into the process, it constrains our creative capacity. I fully expect, and even embrace, a certain level of ego (it often comes with talent), but it must be met with self-awareness. That's what allows us to navigate the friction points that lead to real breakthroughs. I value humility, adaptability, and creative introspection because those are the qualities that consistently invite brilliance to the table.
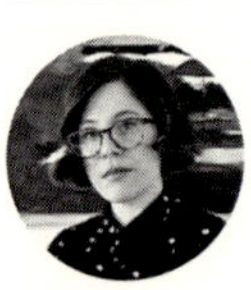 **Aisha Hakim** *Freelance Creative Director* aishamadeit.com	People who are enthusiastic and take the job as seriously as a full timer would.	I think many contractors phone it in, lots of double dipping and split attentions. Double dipping is fine, but you need to be careful your work doesn't slip because of it.

What is the main trait (other than talent) that Creative Directors and Art Directors look for in a creative subcontractor? The trait that makes them want to work with a subcontractor again and again? We asked six creative leads to weigh in.

	What is the main trait (other than talent) you look for in a creative subcontractor?	*Are there any "toxic traits" or common mistakes that make a subcontractor hard to work with? Things that make your life harder as a CD?*
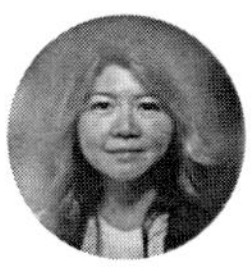 **Alana Louise Lyons** *Creative Director, Kimmelot, formerly AWS* alana-louise.com	Overall attitude on what we are building together. It makes a huge difference when we are both genuinely excited about the project.	Being reactive rather than receptive. I was once a freelancer myself so I am thoughtful about how I deliver feedback. Don't take things personally. After all, it's literally just graphic design! It's not that serious.
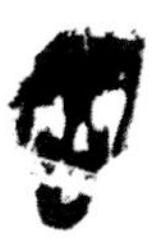 **Neri "El Skeleto" Rivas** *Executive CD, WC+A, Formerly Disney* ordineri.com	Easy to get along with. Really being involved in the project(s)	A toxic trait would be wasting time and not asking enough questions. If the direction given wasn't clear don't try and solve it yourself.
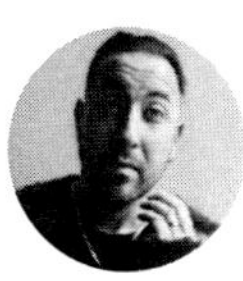 **Alex Center** *Creative Director, Center, formerly Coca-Cola* center.design	Positive Attitude.	More focused on the "work" than the process or the people they are doing the work with. AKA lack of collaboration.

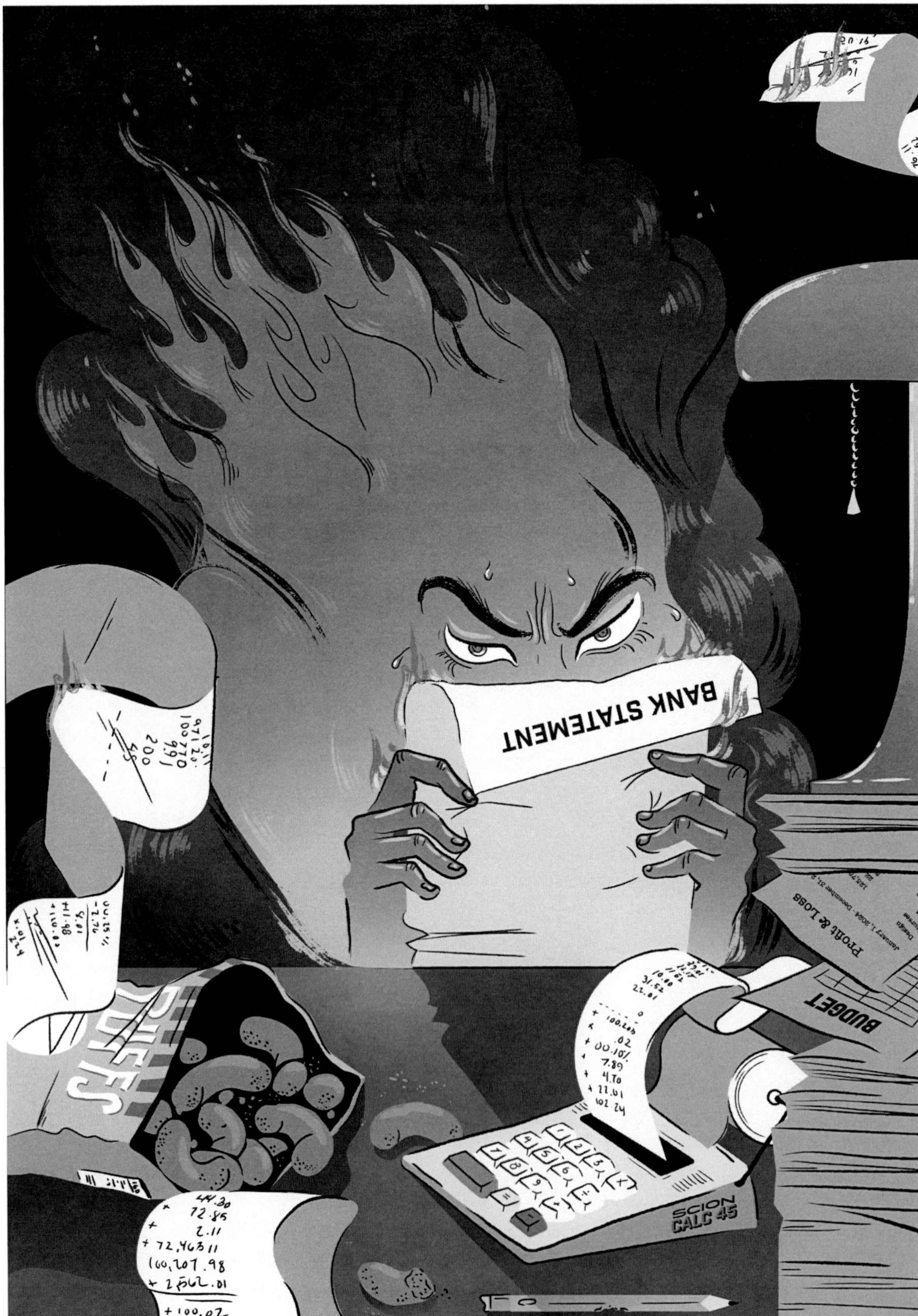

Illustration by: Jennifer Hood

14

Taxes, Accounting, and Measuring Financial Health

Let's zoom out and take a macro look at managing your overall business finances and health. In short, keeping the invoices sent, the taxes paid, and the bank accounts in the green and growing. Some of these things will be specific to readers living in the United States (the tax portions), but there's also good general advice for measuring and analyzing your business's financial success. Run these things by your CPA or accountant to be sure they are right for your unique location and situation.

Bookkeeping and Accounting

What's the Difference Between Accounting and Bookkeeping?

Bookkeeping: A bookkeeper records the day-to-day financial transactions coming in and out of your business bank accounts for things like invoices, vendor payments, business expenses, and payroll.

Accounting: An accountant analyzes bookkeeping data to prepare financial statements, income tax returns, and offers financial guidance to business owners.

Some accountants also offer bookkeeping services. Ours does, and it makes things even easier come tax season.

Get Started with Accounting and Bookkeeping Software

Doing your own bookkeeping is an easy way to save some cash when starting your business. Especially if you're only freelancing part-time here and there. Plus, the dopamine hit of reconciling a payment to an invoice is unmatched. But we always recommend asking a professional accountant or bookkeeper to help you set up the software so it's done properly.

You can handle your own bookkeeping with the help of accounting software that is fairly intuitive to learn. While these are labeled "accounting software," they almost always include bookkeeping features. Do some internet research on "accounting software for small business," and you'll find a lot of affordable options.

With accounting software, you can create customized and branded invoices, receive payments online, track profit and loss with the click of a button, record expenses and income, and more. Most accounting software is cloud-based, meaning you can do it on your laptop or even from your phone as long as you have an internet connection.

Most leading accounting software options have extensive support forums and customer service options to help you get started. We have used two of the leading options (QuickBooks and Xero), and the onboarding and interfaces are very user-friendly. You can ask your CPA or bookkeeper which accounting software they recommend if you're feeling overwhelmed.

Modern accounting software links to your business bank accounts to automatically sync all your income and expense transactions from your account. This takes a lot of manual entry out of the equation. Once the bank transactions are automatically synced with your accounting software, you just have to match the transactions to contacts, invoices, and expenses you create in your books. This matching and recording is called "reconciling" in bookkeeping terms.

While you reconcile your bank transactions, you can also attribute the income and expenses to different categories. For example, you can log some income to a "branding" category, others to a "digital design" category, others to a "physical goods" category. You can tag some expenses as "transportation", some as "utilities" (office internet, electricity), some as the cost of goods sold (paying print vendors to make merchandise). This helps track how your income breaks down by your services and how much you're spending in different areas.

Reconcile your expenses and income regularly. Seriously. Just set a standing calendar event for bookkeeping every two weeks or at least monthly. This makes it much easier to remember what transactions were for. While you're doing your bookkeeping, check on your invoices and customer payments. Stay on top of late payments before things get too out of hand, and while you still have leverage. The longer you let a client's unpaid invoice go, the more work you're doing for free while they hold out. Better to try to keep invoice payments ahead of milestones and final file delivery. Don't deliver final project files to clients until your final invoice is paid until your final invoice is paid (be aware that some larger companies may not comply with this).

If you try your own bookkeeping and end up making costly errors or just don't have the time to stay on top of it, it's probably time to delegate this task to a paid professional. Saving money by doing it yourself only saves you money if you do it properly. There's no shame in delegating!

Anticipate Taxes

When it comes to filing year-end taxes and planning for quarterly estimated tax payments, that's when it's time to find an accountant. While you might have been able to DIY personal taxes when you were a W-2 employee, it's more complex to do your taxes as a freelancer and especially as a small business owner with more than one employee. It's worth the cost to get your taxes done right, believe us. It might seem expensive, but it will save you a ton of time and stress. Once you find a great CPA or accountant, hold on for dear life. They are hard to find. Having one who is with you for the long haul and understands your financial history is invaluable.

Plan for Quarterly Taxes

Please. Don't. Overlook. This. Planning for quarterly taxes will save you shock and horror at the end of the year. What many freelancers and studio-owners don't realize in their first year of business is that they are usually required to pay quarterly estimated taxes in advance and in addition to year-end taxes. There is a penalty fee if you don't. Talk to your accountant to set up estimated quarterly tax payments. This is where you estimate what your business income will be (usually by analyzing what you made last year) and pay taxes based on that estimate, divided into four payments. Often, you can set up an automatic withdrawal from your bank account to make it easy breezy. Set a calendar reminder so you can be sure you have the funds available in that account.

Once you've set up your estimated quarterly taxes, make sure to update your accountant if anything big changes for you financially during the year. About our third year of running Hoodzpah, we had an unexpectedly great financial year. We got some huge projects that we weren't expecting, and it was amazing! Except, we didn't remember to tell our accountant about the big change in income that would affect our quarterly estimated tax payments. We had a real "oh sh*t" moment at the end of the year when we realized we owed *way* more in taxes. So remember to update your accountant if anything big changes and you're making more or less than you estimated. These kinds of changes are easy to keep track of if you are doing your own bookkeeping or at least reviewing your books regularly.

Plan for Annual Taxes

Every time you work with a new US client, you should have a current W-9 form filled out and ready to send them. The W-9 form provides your client with your official business name, tax ID, and other information needed for annual tax purposes. At the time of writing this, if you make more than $600 from a client in a tax year, they have to report this to the IRS through a 1099 form. A 1099 is the contractor's equivalent to a W-2 that employees get from employers. You should receive a copy of these forms from clients by the end of January, maybe later if they're procrastinators (and haven't we all been there). If you have contracted a freelancer for over $600 of work in the year, you or your accountant will also have to prepare a 1099 to send to the contractor by the end of January.

At the end of the year, it's time to look over your bookkeeping and export reports for your accountant to file your taxes. When the taxes are filed, be sure to save a copy of the final tax filing forms in your own system. You might need these records in the future.

Tax systems, seasons, and rules will vary for readers outside of the USA. Ask your bookkeeper or accountant for guidance on what they need and when they need it to file your taxes in your region. And see what forms you need to send to new customers to help them file their own taxes.

Analyze the Profitability of Your Business

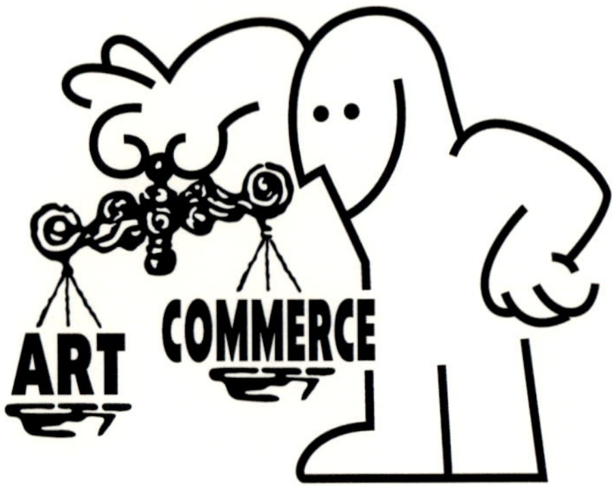

Don't leave your business baby to be raised by wolves. Like any new child, it deserves regular checkups and parental supervision. That means financial health checkups.

Without a healthy cash flow and a good financial standing, your small business can turn into a money pit fast. Stay on top of it. If you see your expenses starting to get too high, it's time to make a change. Remember, rule number one of good finances is profit, profit, profit. It will be tempting to take loans out to buy equipment or rent office space you can't afford. But always ask yourself: Do I really, *really* need this right now? Until your income can justify the expenses, find ways to stay lean.

Instead of renting an office, make an at-home workspace. You've just saved yourself thousands of dollars a month. Instead of taking out a loan or using credit cards to buy expensive cameras or lighting equipment, rent them until you can save enough to buy your own. Credit cards will be a very tempting option when you cannot afford things. But these can lead to cumulative interest that can bite you later when you miss a payment. Start your business with good financial habits. Only pay for things you can afford. If you do use a credit card, pay it off immediately so you don't accrue a ton of interest.

As in your personal life, the goal with your business life is to earn more than you spend. That's how you grow a profitable business that has the savings to weather the unexpected rough patches like an economic recession or health issues that limit your working ability. Check on your business books regularly by running a profit and loss report and a cash summary report. These are key tools for a business financial checkup.

Profit and Loss Statement

Your profit and loss statement (P&L) shows how much income you're bringing in versus how much you're spending within a specific period of time. P&L statements count invoices for future income even if they haven't been paid by a customer yet. So this anticipates your total profit, including future payments owed. But it could also be a little misleading if a customer ends up ghosting you on an invoice (unfortunate, but a reality).

When you run this report, you can compare a time period in your business with previous periods. You could compare your company's profit and loss this quarter versus last quarter.

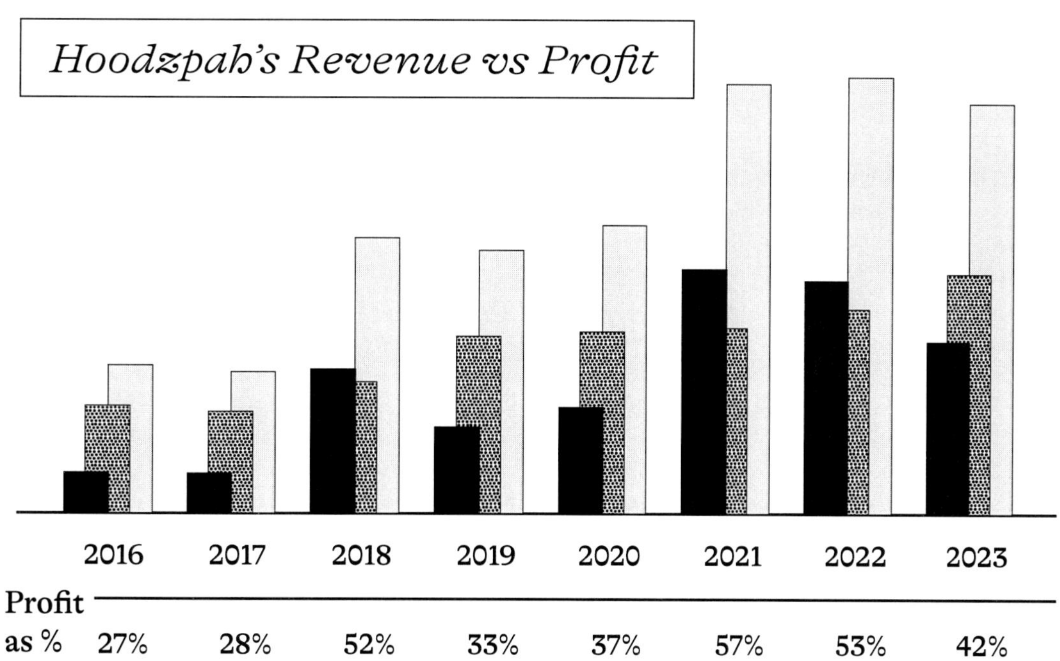

Better yet, this year's first quarter (January through March, or Q1) with last year's Q1 for a more accurate view of seasonal spending. We have found Q1to be very busy with new year work slated. But Q3s (July through September) can be a little slower because many people are taking summer vacations or are starting to save the remainder of their marketing budgets for year-end sales and promotions. So comparing Q3s year by year is a more accurate comparison of our business health than comparing Q3 with Q2 (April through June) since we know our Q2s tend to be better as a rule.

Cash Summary

A cash summary shows the actual amount of cash spent versus cash in your business bank account. Unlike P&L, which anticipates money coming in from invoices, even if they're not paid yet, a cash summary is an exact snapshot of how much you paid out versus earned in a specific window of time. At Hoodzpah, we run this statement weekly.

Review Income and Expenses

As you run these statements, look at the categories of income and expenses. At Hoodzpah, we have expense categories for payroll, subcontracting, software and tools, cost of goods sold, and more. When we run the cash summary or P&L report, we can see how much we spent in these categories and identify areas that are getting out of control. Even more exciting is seeing the categories of income where you're making the most money.

- Are there areas of expenses cutting into your profits too much? See if you can cancel any subscriptions or cut back on anything that is more of a want than a need.
- Which of your services are the most popular? Consider testing slightly higher prices here or marketing this service to a broader audience.
- Which services are the least popular? Why is this do you think? Are you not clearly communicating the purpose and value of this service in your website messaging? Or do you need to get in front of clients who need this service more?
- Is there a new type of service you could offer that complements or dovetails into your most popular services? For example, a web developer could offer an ongoing maintenance retainer to website customers once their site is done.

Your goal is to always make a profit by the end of the month. If you have two or three consecutive months where your expenses outweigh your income, it's time to re-examine and make some changes.

Are you not getting enough leads? It may be time to do some cold emailing, marketing outreach, and networking events. Are you working a lot but not making enough? Then you have plenty of demand, and you can probably increase your rates. Are you not converting enough leads (meaning you quote a lot of things, but hardly anyone approves the cost)? Maybe you need to look at your website and proposal to better prove the value of your services to justify the cost. Or perhaps your pricing is just too high for your current client base, and it's time to venture into other industries.

Are the services you offer too niche? You could broaden your services/product offering to diversify your income. Or adjust your messaging to no longer limit your services to specific industries (meaning, offer branding for anyone, not just restaurants, for example).

Trimming expenses is the easiest thing you can do to make a quick and positive change in your financial standing. But there's a point at which you've trimmed as much excess as possible. That's when you have to get scrappy. Try slimmed-down services for more budget-friendly prices. Try introductory offers to encourage new business. Just don't sit there and wish for the best. Be proactive.

It's no fun barely making ends meet between client invoice payments. Especially when most customer invoice terms are net 30 (they have thirty days to pay). And even worse, when bigger clients require net 60 to pay your invoices (it should be criminal). This is why it's so important to build up your business savings when your business is flush with cash—you'll have more cushion to ride out leaner months while trying to pivot and find new income leads.

Something else to consider: If you only work in one type of industry, you could be hit harder by industry-specific lulls. Same thing if the majority of your work comes from one or two clients. This puts you at higher risk because everything rests on two clients rather than a variety of clients in different industries. This is why it can pay off to have a diverse client pool.

Track Project Profitability

Regularly compare your flat-rate project fees to the actual hours you spent on those projects. This is another case for time tracking, even if you're not billing by the hour. A $15,000 project sounds great on the surface, but if you're spending 500 hours on that project, you're only making $30 per hour. As you track time spent versus income made, you can see if you're quoting appropriately or spending way more time than you thought you were.

Watch your Close Rates

Your close rate is the number of proposals and quotes you get approved compared to rejected. At Hoodzpah, we have all our proposals for each year in one file (shout out to Figma). It's so easy to go in and see what we've sent out and quickly see what was approved, ghosted, or rejected. You can also track this through your CRM (customer relationship management) system, be it a spreadsheet, Trello, Notion, or otherwise. If you're getting a lot of accepted quotes and proposals, and you feel completely overworked, it's time to raise your rates! You are in demand. If your proposals are mainly getting rejected, you might need to lower your rates to match the expectations of your target audience. Maybe you don't have the reputation in the industry to land those rates yet (emphasis on yet), or you have the capability, but you're just not proving it through your website or proposals. If you're in this boat, fret not! Refer back to chapter 10 for marketing tips and chapter 5 to get your proposal dialed in.

Review Your Marketing Efforts

There are two ways to gauge how your marketing is doing: qualitative and quantitative. Qualitative looks for meaningful engagement—the quality stuff you can't measure with numbers. Quantitative is based on hard data. Both are important. Modern marketing is obsessed with ROI (return on investment). But some marketing is for the sake of brand awareness and brand salience rather than a specific transaction or measurable click. Other marketing can be tracked to a specific action, usually at the end of the client journey: buying something from you, clicking from your social media to your website, clicking the "contact us" button on your website, or following you on Instagram.

Attending meetups and networking events is very much a qualitative marketing initiative. You can measure the qualitative results by analyzing the meaningful relationships you've developed through these events—not by a click-through rate. The focus is on making your brand name and services known and building a good reputation in your community. Even if you aren't closing sales yet, this groundwork is key. Don't give up on it.

For quantitative marketing like ads with a call to action, or A/B testing two versions of a landing page, these efforts provide data points you can analyze to see your return on investment. We have never found digital ads to work for our services. High-quality services are usually booked based on referrals, word of mouth, reputation, and brand awareness through press, events or social media. But for our products like this book or our Proposal Deck Pro Bundle, digital ads have been a great way to increase sales. With ads, we can easily track ROI and efficacy.

Let's say we spend $50 on Ad #1, and the ad results in 5,000 referrals to our site, but we don't land any purchases from the traffic. It seems like a good deal since we're spending a low sum to get such high traffic. But despite all the traffic, there were no sales. Maybe because the visitor isn't interested in our product or is unable to pay the price.

We then spend $400 on Ad #2, which results in 500 visits to our site and 50 customers who spend on average $30 each. Although the expense on Ad #2 is higher, it's justified because it delivers more return on investment, a quantitative win.

Another example: You hire a social media consultant to help manage your accounts. While they only increase your following slightly, they succeed in changing the audience perception of your brand. Their posts engage your audience better and create more positive buzz about your business. This is a qualitative result that might not be reflected in the hard stats. So consider all the angles before you double down on a marketing effort or cancel a campaign.

Your web traffic can tell you a lot about your audience, how people are finding you, and what marketing efforts are working. Install Google Analytics (it's free as of the publication of this book) on your website to start gathering data. What content is most popular on your site? Consider posting more of that kind of content. Where on your site are visitors dropping off (leaving your site)? What could you change about those pages to encourage engagement? What sites are referring the most traffic to you?

Big-Picture Check-ins

It's easy to lose the plotline in the minutiae of the day-to-day slog. Clock in, check email, send proof, go to meetings, try to get in one hour of uninterrupted creative work, clock out, and repeat. One project bleeds into the next, and before you know it, the year is over, and you never got to any of your big plans for your business. Make time to remember the big-picture goals and to celebrate the wins. Set an actual date each month to check on everything and work on your business plans.

At Hoodzpah, we have a standing weekly meeting to plan and review the week's tasks and progress, while also keeping track of our bigger internal projects and goals. This is our opportunity to talk about lingering stresses or friction points in our business. Usually, a recurring annoyance can be righted with a change in process or the admission that this is something we need to delegate since we clearly don't have the bandwidth or ability.

We also try to meet with industry peers and mentors regularly to talk shop, commiserate, maybe brainstorm a problem, and just encourage one another. Every time we leave one of these meetups or calls, we have inevitably learned something new, and we have a fresh sense of excitement. You know some things, but you don't know everything. Surround yourself with people in different locations, age ranges, levels of experience, creative niches, and industries, and you'll never stop learning.

At Hoodzpah, we have one big review meeting at the end of every year. We run all our financial rcports to see how much revenue we brought in, how much profit we made, what services performed best, what clients booked the most work, and to look for any trends. We take this time to set financial goals for the following year and to see if we met the financial goals we set for ourselves the year prior. We review our budget and estimate our income for the coming year. We list dream clients we'd like to get and industries we'd like to break into. We think of new marketing initiatives we could execute in the coming year. We also think about what products we'd like to launch across the year in our own shop. We note everything down in a shared document so we can see what worked and what didn't at the end of the year. You'll be shocked how much it helps to verbalize and document these goals, rather than just keeping them in your fuzzy mind palace to rot and fade away.

Take this a step further and start telling your friends and family members about your goals. Tell your followers and industry peers. You'll be surprised at what results. Your friends, family, and followers want to go to bat for you, but how can they do that if they don't know what you want? Start being more open. Next time you're at a meetup or hanging with friends, and someone asks you how things are going with your business, tell them what you're trying to accomplish. Let them in on your top goal. So many dream projects have come about for us at Hoodzpah just by telling people what we want and what we're working toward. Sometimes, the answer for how to get to your big-picture goal is through an alternate path you didn't know about till someone in your community said, "Have you thought about this angle?" The other great part about involving your community in your goals is they become your accountability partners. They will follow up and they will check in on your progress because they're invested. This is peer pressure at work for good! Sometimes, that's all you need to help you start taking action.

Surviving a Recession

Sometimes, slow financial periods are not specific to you or your industry; they're widespread across the economy. If you stay in business long enough, you'll go through your share of economic slowdowns and recessions. Listen to industry peers and keep an eye on industry and

How one small studio navigates a down economy where creative budgets are often the first thing to get slashed:

"We've navigated budget constraints by staying flexible. Offering one and two-week identity sprints, blue sky explorative projects and building services like Tagteam to support fellow creatives with case studies and marketing. Any downtime is spent building tools, plugins, mockups or creating passive income streams. Adopting new technologies and embracing AI for development, strategy and copy has been a huge benefit for our small team, allowing us to offer more while getting curious about what's possible."

—Evan Place and Jordan Jenkins, Co-founders Outland Studio enteroutland.com

economic news. If you notice a lot of layoffs and a lot of fellow business owners bemoaning how "slow" business is, take note. Where you previously may have had the luxury of cherry-picking projects, you might have to take on less glamorous or smaller-paying projects to keep your cash flow healthy. In hard economic times, even companies once flush with cash start to tighten their budgets.

Look back at US history over the last two hundred years, and you'll see recessions about every five to twenty years. According to the National Bureau of Economic Research, a non-profit organization that identifies American recessions, the US has gone through thirty-four recessions since 1857. Every nation experiences them. In these times, people often reduce spending, and that includes your clients. Proposals you easily landed in an economic boom will become fewer and farther between. In these times, you'll be thankful for your savings cushion, and—if you're smart—you'll find ways to get creative in offering new or limited services at a smaller price point. If you're at the top of your industry, you may not feel a recession as much as newer businesses or generalist agencies, but you will feel it.

During a recession, you might see lots of layoffs, bloated or less-established businesses closing, and client budgets shrinking. But you'll also notice new businesses and scrappy competitors popping up. All those talented folks getting laid off can now use this time to finally make that thing they've been thinking about. To finally start that start-up. All that to say, work never dries up completely; you might just find it in a different place than you're used to. People who can pivot and adjust in these times will survive.

Even if you have to pick up some side work that has nothing to do with your industry, it's better than digging a hole of debt because you just waited and hoped for the best. There's no shame in supplementing your business income with an hourly wage service job. Do what you can to make money and make ends meet during the tough times. The slowdowns won't last forever. And then when the economy is good and money is flowing in—SAVE, SAVE, SAVE. Curse the button that offers you to buy now and pay later for things you cannot afford. That rainy day *will* return.

Keep Records

Lastly, some housekeeping advice for financial and business recordkeeping. Signed contracts, receipts for company expenses, copies of government forms filed—keep copies of all of it. You may need these for tax filing purposes, proof of legal compliance, future audits, lawsuits, or for your own business planning purposes. Here's a general guide to what records to keep and for how long (from a US perspective). The requirements can vary by your geographic region or industry, so check with your accountant and attorney if you're unsure what applies to you.

Record to keep	For how long
Invoices and receivables	5 years
Checks and payables	5 years
Auditors reports	Always
Annual statements	Always
Payroll	6 years
Personnel contracts	4-5 years
Personnel files	3 years
Insurance records	5 years
Client contracts and copyright information	Always
Licenses and permits	As required
Tax returns	Always
Employee withholding	7 years
Tax bills and statements	Always
1099s	Always

Chapter Checklist:

① Set up your accounting and bookkeeping software if you haven't already.

② Ask your accountant about estimated taxes and tax planning if you haven't already.

③ Review your marketing initiatives for effectiveness.

④ Make a savings plan so you start building a cushion in case of a recession.

⑤ Write down your business goals for the year.

⑥ Make a regular schedule (weekly or monthly) to review:

- → Business goal progress
- → Profit and loss and cash summary reports
- → Expenses
- → Acceptance-to-rejection rate on proposals
- → Time spent versus rate earned for any projects you've time tracked

⑦ Reach out to your industry friends or mentor and just say "hi," or make a plan to hang out. Be curious about their goals and don't be afraid to tell them about yours.

⑧ Create a safe place to store your records (your computer hard drive plus a backup solution).

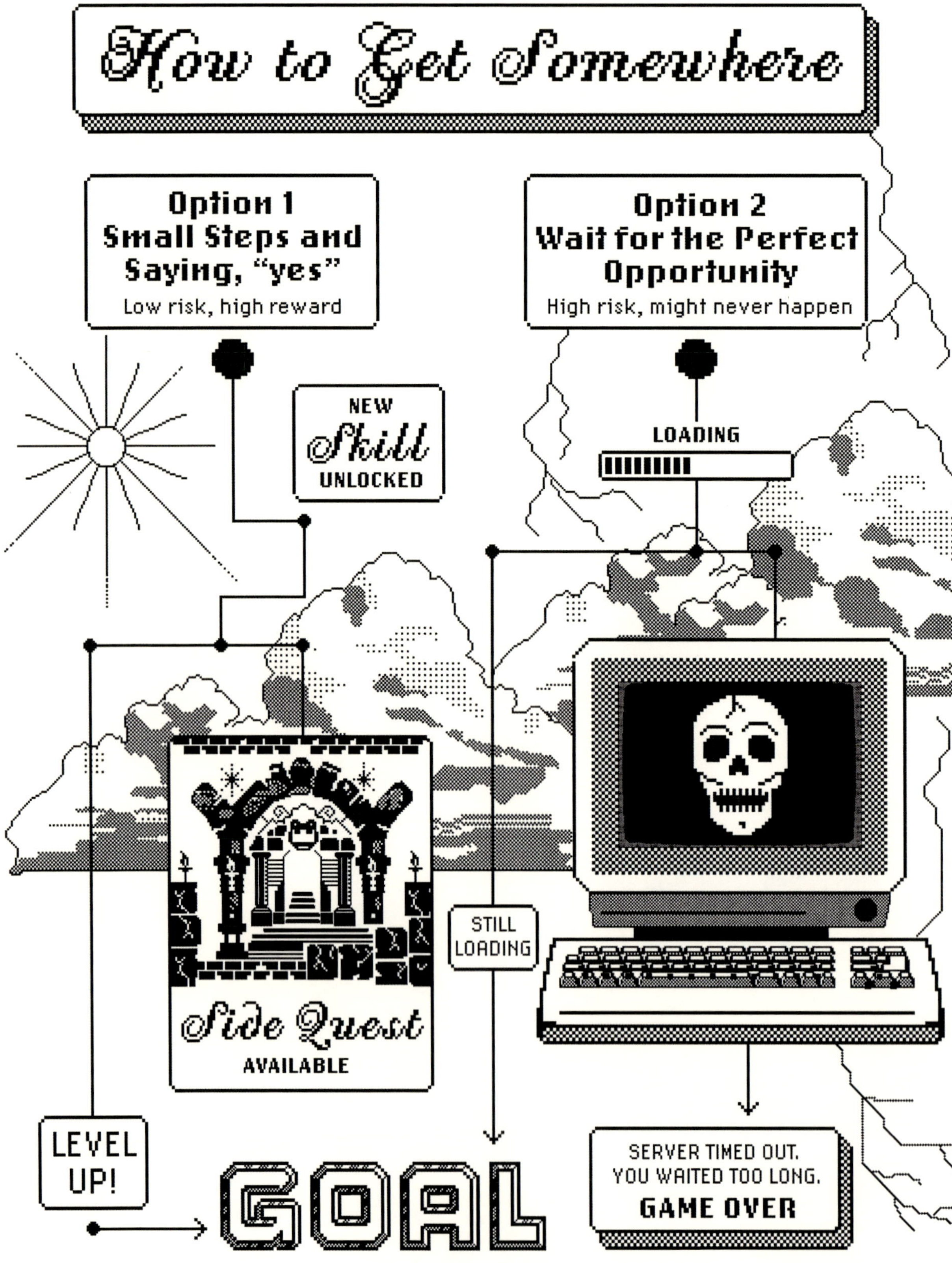

Illustration by: Bea Morgan

15
Staying Competitive and Adaptive

The creative world has always been a competitive and demanding one. Even before internet trolls. Even before your clients started using AI to critique your work.

Just ask Horatio Greenough.

This amazing anecdote is from a fascinating and funny article by Ronald G. Shafer in The Washington Post: "The First Statue Removed from the Capitol: George Washington in a Toga" published January 25, 2023.

Horatio Greenough was commissioned by Congress in 1832 to carve a commemorative statue of President George Washington. He was surely told by the client, "We want you to 'do you,'" but when he unveiled the statue in 1841, it garnered widespread criticism and mockery. Horatio's piece enshrined America's first president like a Greek god: twelve-feet tall, brawny and bare-chested, with a loosely draped toga over his lap. The harsh, yet hilarious, response from critics at the time rivaled the best of today's Brand New comments.

"The man does not live, and never lived, who saw Washington without his shirt," said Congressman Henry Wise.

"I fear this statue will only give the idea of entering or leaving a bath," former Capitol architect Charles Bulfinch commented. He continued, it ought "to be placed in the Parthenon with other naked great men."

Former New York mayor Philip Hone said, " . . . like a great Herculean warrior . . . with a huge napkin lying on his lap," said.

But perhaps the most cutting feedback is from Sen. William Preston: "The most horrid phantasmagoria I have ever beheld."

The next time your client responds to your work with an "Mmm, it's just not there yet," you can be grateful that at least they didn't call it a "horrid phantasmagoria."

You are a member of a very large collective of people struggling every day to make things and make money. And most of the ones who seem to succeed have no proprietary secret. They just find ways to pivot and press on. Surviving as a creative business owner is the same as surviving in life: try, iterate, adapt, endure, recharge, and repeat. As with anything, if you try to do this alone, it'll take a lot more time, effort, and resources. But if you plug into a community to gain meaningful tips, support, and feedback, you'll go farther, faster. We cannot overstate how valuable it is to find a group of peers and mentors. Whether online or offline, make this a top priority: Find your support crew (who you will support in return, too).

Losing touch with your creative community, the mentality of your consumer, the sentiments of the world, or the methods of your industry is how your business slowly loses traction, loses relevance, and slides into decline. Find new ways to engage your audience and your own interests. Keep learning in your field. Keep challenging yourself and your skills. Your passion and approach are infectious to those working with you.

You're going to go through phases in your career where you feel like you've lost your edge or lost interest; like you're washed up, like the industry and trends are unrecognizable or inhospitable; like you've seen it all before, and you wonder if you'll ever get another novel idea. When that day comes, do anything but stand still. Try something new. Change your tack. Get out there and dig into new methods, movements, and technologies. Attend a conference to broaden your sphere of peers and influences. Find a new hobby completely outside your profession to give you a new source of inspiration and satisfaction. And if you've tried everything else, there's always improv classes.

No job is without peaks and valleys.

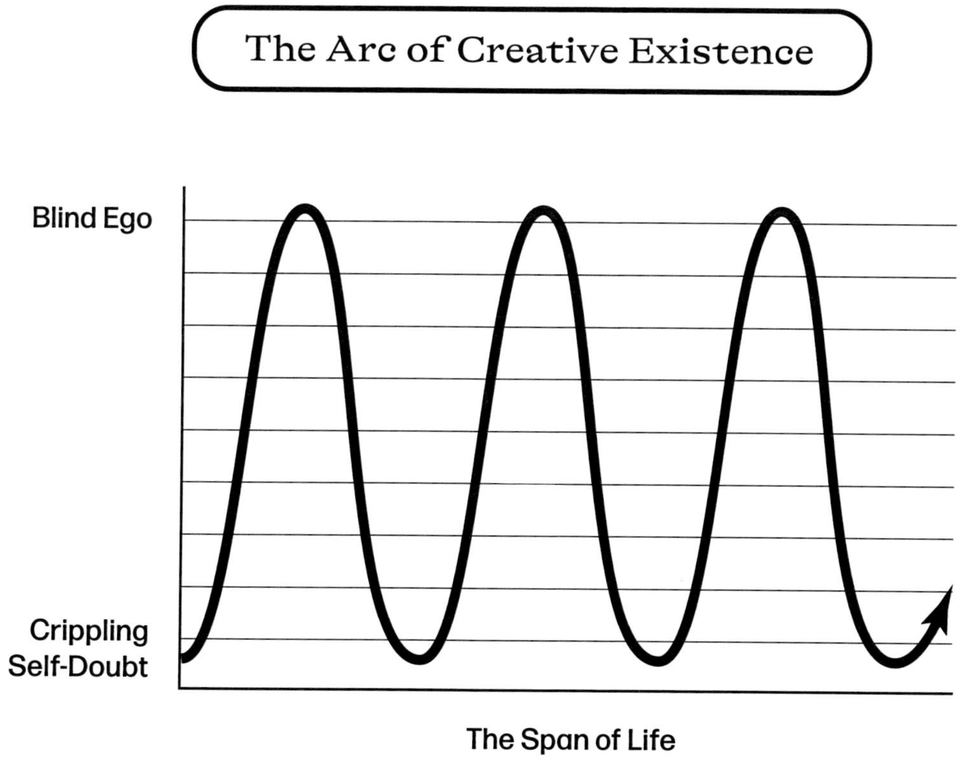

Let's Start an Intellectual Movement

The Renaissance, between the fourteenth and seventeenth centuries, was an explosion of creativity, discovery, and understanding. This boom was spurred thanks to the invention of printing, which allowed people to share their studies and works on a broad scale. It was spurred on by an intellectual movement called Humanism that encouraged the sharing of wisdom, free inquiry, and criticism. Inspire a revival of creativity in your own life and community by promoting shared knowledge and critique.

Stay Adaptive

According to research studies, when you are found to be right in a situation or are given validation in your opinion, the reward center of your brain lights up, similar to the way it would if you were high on drugs. And like any drug, the feeling can be addictive. This can lead to confirmation bias—the tendency to interpret new evidence as confirmation of one's existing beliefs or theories—which can impair your judgment as you seek that feeling again and again.

As we continue to hone our craft and elevate our skill, we are confirmed and rewarded for a job well done. This confirmation triggers those addictive reward responses in our brain. We continue to chase that high of being right. No one wants to be wrong or to be embarrassed by a mistake.

It's natural to want to win rather than lose. As we get further into our professional careers, especially as self-employed creatives, we encounter fewer healthy ego checks and critiques. As children and teens, we are regularly corrected and critiqued by teachers and parents as we learn and grow. Once we graduate from schools and move away from family, that accountability dwindles as we start embracing our independence. But if we're not still welcoming feedback and critique in our evolving lives, it's easy to start thinking that we're above it all. That we're untouchable. We know the answers. Our clients are dumb. Our boss doesn't understand our art. The world is stupid. Therefore, they don't deserve our respect or our ear. We can get addicted to the idea that we're always right, and anything wrong that happens is always someone else's fault.

Left unchecked, this addiction to confirming one's own opinions can lead to seemingly capable people becoming a total drag to be around. To the point that they alienate clients and peers and slowly kill their own business. As William Preston would say: what a horrid phantasmagoria. We've all worked with that pompous, self-centered, unaware person.

The need to always be right (or for some, the fear of being wrong) can lead us to surround ourselves only with people who are just like us. Detractors and critics are avoided. This is how dictators rule. They cut their country off from the free flow of information, avoiding any contradiction to their own way of life. The result is a suffocating bubble. Instead of forward progress because of an influx of fresh, new ideas, they end up getting left behind: a society stuck in time. It's just a matter of time before the revolution. Why impose this same kind of mentality on your own life and creative work?

Seek Inspiration in the Unfamiliar

This sounds easy, but it's not. We're not talking about scrolling through Pinterest for an hour a day. We're talking about eyes-on, hands-on, out-of-the-box, creative challenges. Get a hobby outside of what you do every day for a living. Something where you can unwind from pointing and clicking. Something new that challenges you to grow your creativity in uncharted ways. Take breaks. Take vacations. Go on adventures. This doesn't mean you have to hop on a plane to Stockholm (although that's cool!). There's adventure all around us. Instead of going to the same coffee shop you always go to try a new one in a different part of town. Take a new detour home. You'll be amazed at all the things you didn't even know existed. Look up hikes and trails in your area.

Beauty and inspiration are all around you. Sometimes the simplest deviations from your routine can expose you to something magical and new, leading to a new way of thinking, possibly resulting in a revelation about how to solve a problem. You don't want to spend so much time working that you have no time for absorbing the new and unexpected (they said to themselves in the mirror). Without this inlet of fresh water, you'll get stagnant. Stagnation breeds frustration, and frustration breeds resentment. Resentful people see the world as the enemy instead of the proverbial oyster.

What Really Matters: People and Community

It can be really hard to cope when change happens that's outside your control. But change is inevitable. A client letting us go, a project failing, a new technology replacing our skill set, and so on. If you were a marketing creative working pre-internet, much of your life's knowledge and gut instinct became irrelevant when the internet hit. It will likely be the same for many professionals with AI. What's right today could be wrong tomorrow. Keep your eyes open, and never assume that life as we know it now is the way it will continue to be. Try to find anchors in your life that provide value and meaning outside of your work. You are more than your work. You need purpose beyond your work.

Industries rise and then fall. Businesses succeed and fail. One day, our own business will close its doors. But the one thing that endures is the people we impacted and the communities we made. That's what matters. And it's the one thing we can take with us. Isn't it the whole lesson of *It's a Wonderful Life*? People didn't rally around the Savings & Loan at the end of the movie; they rallied around George Bailey and his family because he had invested in them.

Get hooked into your local creative scene. Contribute to your local community. If you're in a small or remote area with no creative hub, look online for a community or start your own group. There are so many ways to meet people. The hard part is playing an active role. Wherever you go, commit to engage.

Look for ways to lend your talent and time to making your non-creative community better, too, locally or globally. This will lead to positive ties between your business and the community. Whatever you do, don't fall into the habit of hermiting away in your home or office with only your backlog of podcasts and your cases of LaCroix to keep you warm. Get out in the world. Go out and have fun. Invest in relationships. Make a conscious effort to pursue new relationships with people from different industries, life stages, and neighborhoods. It will genuinely make for a more enriched existence, and that will translate to a more productive and gratifying work life in turn.

Advice from Seasoned Pros

	What was a big change in the industry/economy/your business that required a big pivot to keep afloat?	What's your biggest tip for maintaining longevity as a studio runner or solopreneur?
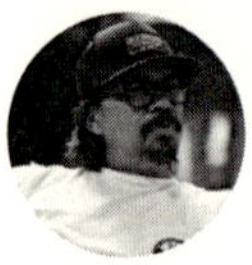 **Luke Takahashi** *Founder & Creative Director, Related Grey* *18 Years* relatedgrey.com	Covid was a difficult time. Meeting clients in person used to be standard and incredibly helpful. We still haven't fully returned to that format, and we believe it's a huge loss for the creative community.	Visibility in as many areas of the industry as possible. It's easy to get comfortable and cruise. There will always be somebody more hungry out there. Get chatty.
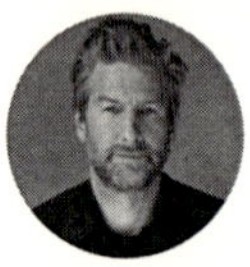 **Paul Hutchison** *Founder & Creative Director, Hype Type Studio* *25 Years* hypetype.studio	Our biggest pivot came during the pandemic when budgets tightened and client work slowed. We leaned harder into our type foundry. We'd always made custom type for client projects, and expanding into retail fonts created additional revenue that balanced out the client work and gave us more independence during that time.	Longevity comes down to consistency and relationships. Do great work, deliver on time and on budget, and be nice to people. Word of mouth and referrals have done more for us than any marketing. Stay adaptable, involve clients in the process, and keep pushing the work to always be better.
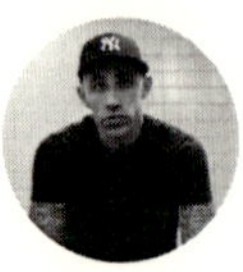 **Jon Contino** *Founder, Contino Studios* *28 Years total in freelance and as a studio/agency.* continonewyork.com	So many things! Technology (mp3 players), recessions, social media algorithms, influencer status. I'm in my early 40s, so there's probably been more changes to the world during the time I've been a working professional than any sort of stable ground to build my business.	Always look forward, never behind. If you want to stay relevant, you need to be ahead of trends or just not care about them at all. Make sure people understand you have a perspective that is unique. We all have that, but sometimes we forget that people are interested in things other than current trends. Creativity always has a seat at the table and consistent creativity and perspective gets noticed 100% of the time.
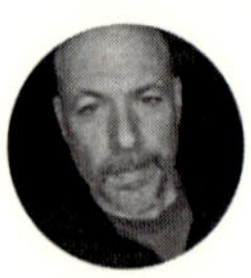 **Jamie Stark** *Design & Branding Consultant* *30 Years* jamiestark.com	The subprime mortgage crisis derailed much of my business, but it turned into a big opportunity with one client, leading to some of my best financial years. I worked with the marketing department of a mid-sized manufacturing company. They relied on a big agency for most work, and I had a small shop, always fighting for scraps. When the recession hit, that big agency's $30K retainer–which included no actual creative work–was cut, and I was next in line. Business boomed for a while. Being a lower-cost, low-overhead, nimble provider is a real advantage when the broader economy tightens and companies need to trim bloated budgets.	Be easy to work with. Longevity in business comes from building relationships and trust. If people trust you to produce high-quality, professional work and deliver it on time, they'll give you more work. I've had clients change jobs multiple times and hire me at each new company, and I've worked with some companies for over 20 years.

If you've been freelancing or running your own studio for more than ten or fifteen years, you've gone through your share of ebbs and flows in business growth, the economy, and tech/software changes. We asked nine of our studio runner/freelance peers how they've weathered these storms.

	What was a big change in the industry/economy/your business that required a big pivot to keep afloat?	**What's your biggest tip for maintaining longevity as a studio runner or solopreneur?**
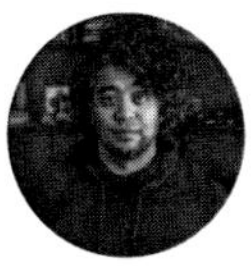 **Dan Mall** *Founder, Make More Money* *11 Years running Super Friendly* makemoremoney.design	The more "full service" we became, the tougher business got. Once we doubled down on a niche–design system practices for enterprise organizations–that's when everything started to click.	Create systems that keep you top of mind for your ideal customer that require as little of your time as possible.
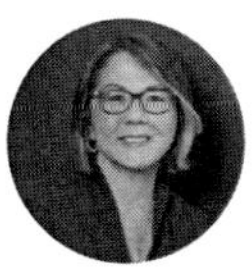 **Saedene Ota** *Founder & Brand Strategist, Sae Design Group* *29 Years* saedesigngroup.com	The still evolving transition from print to digital. Fortunately we have a solid reputation in packaging. So that experience made up for the drop in print. Leaning into an area that is a staple helped keep us relevant as we built up our digital team. That being said we completely lost our largest industry of clients during COVID19. With government support, layoffs, and cuts in pay, we were able to survive. Tourism (hotels and resorts) represented a third of our portfolio. But because Hawaii is a small market, we have always had to work with a variety of businesses. Non-profit, finance, restaurants, education, health, CPGs, are amongst the other types of industries that we were fortunate to have worked within, making our portfolio diverse yet not fully reliant on one type.	Find team members that are more talented than you are.
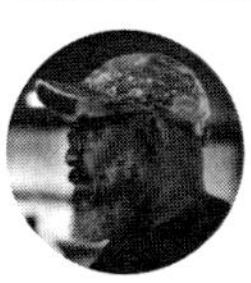 **Rob Zilla III** *Professional Sports Doodler* *10+ Years* @rob_zilla_iii	Covid– the industry pressed pause and people in key places migrated to other places.	Combo moves are better than single punches. Basically, find creative ways to not be a one hit wonder with clients.
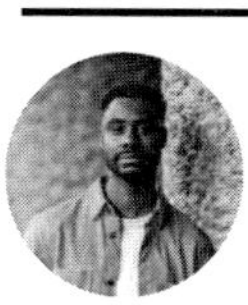 **Kieron Lewis** *Freelance Designer and Host for Adobe & D&AD* kieronlewis.com	My type of work is focused on print (editorial). With a few of my client wanting to focus on more digital-led projects, I found myself having to adapt my skillset in order to meet their demands.	Understanding your skills and capabilities. We can always push ourselves to try new things and experiment more, however Its essential to know what you can deliver for the client. If you don't deliver to the standard they're looking for, this can not only break trust between yourself and your clients but it can also tarnish your reputation as a freelancer.

Farewell for Now. . . .

You did it! You finished this book. It was a lot of work, and you've hopefully come away with a heap of applicable knowledge and actionable next steps. But none of that knowledge counts for anything if you're not applying it. Trying it. Just start. Today. We can hear the cogs of your mind whirring, thinking of a million reasons why you're not ready. Why now isn't a good time for you. Why you can't. The truth is: It's never the "right time." You're never ready enough. It's never without risk. And in that sense, what better time than now?

Shine on,

Amy Hood and Jen Hood

PS: Do you have more questions? We'd love to hear from you! What you loved, hated. What we got wrong. Tag us on social with your feedback

Instagram, X, TikTok: @HoodzpahDesign

YouTube: /Hoodzpah

Linkedin: Hoodzpah